Anaïs Nin is of Spanish, Cuban, French and Danish descent. She spent her childhood in various parts of Europe until, at the age of eleven, she left Paris to live in the United States. Later she returned to Paris, where she studied psychology under Otto Rank and became acquainted with many well-known writers and artists.

Her first book was published in the 1930s. The quality and originality of her work were evident at an early stage, but as is often the case for *avant-garde* writers, it has taken time for her to achieve wide recognition. The publication, internationally, of her *Journals* has won her new admirers in many parts of the world, particularly among young people and students. Countries in which her books have been published with great acclaim include France, Germany, Italy, Holland, Japan and the United States.

Anaïs Nin, who now lives in the United States, is presently engaged in editing further volumes of her *Journals*, which she started writing in her childhood. Even before publication – when read in manuscript by a number of leading writers and critics – these *Journals* had assumed a legendary reputation, as a major literary work of the twentieth century.

THE JOURNALS OF ANAIS NIN
1934–1939

EDITED WITH A PREFACE
BY GUNTHER STUHLMANN

QUARTET BOOKS   LONDON

Published by Quartet Books Limited 1974
27 Goodge Street, London W1P 1FD
Reprinted 1974

First published in the British Commonwealth
by Peter Owen Limited 1966

Copyright © 1967 Anaïs Nin

Preface copyright © 1967 by Gunther Stuhlmann

ISBN 0 704 31089 9

Printed in Great Britain by
Hunt Barnard Printing Ltd, Aylesbury, Bucks.

THE JOURNALS OF ANAIS NIN 1934–1939

PREFACE

When Anaïs Nin's *Diary*: *1931–1934* appeared in the spring of 1966, Karl Shapiro, the Pulitzer Prize-winning poet, wrote in *Book Week*: 'For a generation the literary world on both sides of the Atlantic has lived with the rumour of an extraordinary diary. Earlier readers of the manuscript discussed it in breathtaking superlatives as a work that would take its place with the great revelations of literature. A significant section of this diary is at last in print and it appears that the great claims made for it are justified.'

Indeed, the reception of the first volume showed that Miss Nin's enormous lifework, which for various reasons may defy publication in its entirety, did not lose its impact and uniqueness in the inevitable fragmentation of partial presentation. For even the sizable segment of this first volume, covering a little over three years in Miss Nin's life, encompassed merely some 600 pages of the 15,000-page transcript of the original diary volumes, which today fill two four-drawer filing cabinets in a Brooklyn bank vault.

To choose from a cohesive, organically developing text like that of the diary, with its weaving and reweaving of time and incident, its natural gaps and duplications, its gradual maturing, is always a precarious undertaking. The author's own initial selectivity in writing her diary is re-enacted, for the second time, in the editorial process. And the original diary itself, in all its fullness, after all is merely a *reflection*, a re-fraction, of the totality of the author. It is not the full, round-ed, day-to-day Anaïs Nin portrayed in place and time with an eye toward presenting herself to the world. In her unabashed, sometimes unflattering exposure of the inner person, of her spontaneous reaction to people, events and ideas, Miss Nin takes us into a confidence undisguised by the art of the writer. But it is her very gift and skill as a writer, even in her early years, that breathes vibrant life into the pages of the diary, that gives even to the fragment the sweep and impact of a unified whole. Wherever we pick up the diary we are caught, as it were, in the novel of her life, a novel that moves in-stinctively, logically, like a dream, with its own rhythms, tensions, actions and counter-actions.

The first volume opened at the time Miss Nin was about to make her literary debut with a brief, passionate study of D. H. Lawrence. She was then living, with her family, in an ancient, shuttered house in the sleepy village of Louveciennes, on the outskirts of Paris. But the surface calm of this rural setting – after the glamorous turmoil of Miss Nin's Catholic childhood in Europe and the trying years of her exiled youth in the United States – was soon shattered by her growing, intense involvement with a host of artists and intellectuals, foremost among them the then unknown 'gangster-author', Henry Miller, his remarkable wife, June, and the fevered surrealist poet, Antonin Artaud. Pressed into many self-imposed, multilateral roles as artist, wife, sister, daughter, caretaker, muse, confidante and glamour-girl, she found herself trapped between the polished vacuity of 'society' and the abrasive freedom of 'Bohemia'. Pursued by an often excruciatingly painful self-awareness, and haunted by the elegant, egotistical shadow of her father, the Spanish composer–pianist Joaquin Nin, who had deserted the family in her childhood, she tried to understand and untangle through analysis the many strands of her personality. But neither Dr René Allendy, the founder of the French Psychoanalytical Society, nor Sigmund Freud's banished pupil, Dr Otto Rank, with whom she explored both the role and the creative possibilities of woman in the modern world, could provide her with more than partial answers. In her refuge, the diary, which she carried with her like a magic

2

amulet, she analysed the analysts. In November 1934, at the end of Volume I, two months after Henry Miller, with her steadfast support, had published his first book, *Tropic of Cancer*, she was about to leave Paris. Dr. Rank, driven by the Depression to shift his practice to New York, had urgently called her to join him for a time in his work in the United States.

The present volume continues the diary directly with Miss Nin's arrival in New York. Like the first, it is a self-contained unit, bounded by events which, both externally and internally, mark significant changes in Miss Nin's life and provide a natural framework within the over-all flow of the diary.

The text of this volume represents about half of the original diary manuscripts – volumes 40 to 60 – covering the period from 1934 to 1939. Certain people, including Miss Nin's husband and members of her family, again had to be eliminated. The names of some of her analytical patients had to be changed or omitted, and the dates provided by the editor merely summarize the specific and – due to Miss Nin's later reflection on a previous event – sometimes confusing dates in the originals.

If there is a difference, a slow shift in emphasis, between this and the previous volume, it is, perhaps, a move away from introspection, a strengthening of Miss Nin's stance vis-à-vis the outside world. To be sure, Miss Nin's critical lens still focuses sharply and candidly upon herself: 'What I like best about myself,' she writes, 'is my audacity, my courage. The ways I have found to be true to myself without causing too much pain or damage . . . What I hate so much is my vanity, my need to shine, my need of applause and my sentimentality. I would like to be harder. I cannot make a joke, make fun of anyone, without feeling regrets.' But her need, the confessional function of the diary, is changing. She has slain the ghost of her father, though she still seems to be instinctively looking for a 'leader', a father figure. Her attitude toward Henry Miller and his Bohemian friends is undergoing a change. She is less tolerant of people's eccentricities, of the waste of talent. Her involvements with her own work, with Gonzalo, the wild Indian revolutionary, and his wilting wife, Helba, with the young Lawrence Durrell, acquire a new dimension, a new solidity. She still 'cannot stay quietly rooted anywhere because of the many sides of myself constantly sprouting, the layers of latent mysteries, the things I am not yet'. She still is caught in the web of her different personae, but the world, somehow, is becoming more real, more tangible, the choices clearer.

'The diary,' she writes in the late 1930s, 'was once a disease. I do not take it up now for the same reasons. Before it was because I was lonely, or because I did not know how to communicate with others. I needed the communion. Now it is to write, not for solace but for the pleasure of describing others "out of abundance".

Her inborn technique, the selective eye of the earlier diary, which gave such urgent immediacy to the previous volume, is becoming more and more a conscious artistic principle: the captured moment of intense emotional reality. Her 'portraits', she explains, were done only 'at the moment when a person was important to me. The person rises and sinks, appears and vanishes only in relation to me.' The external narrative, the merely descriptive, remains fragmentary. 'It's like a statue without arm or hand, unearthed, and having to be deciphered, divined.' Thus, when she arrives in New York, the characters who so intensely peopled her Paris life fade before the onrush of new situations, new entanglements. Her diary bulges with the stories of her analytical patients. When she returns to France, having been forced to choose between the analytical profession and her need to create as a writer, the same process involves her New York friends. They flash on to the diary screen only at the heightened moments of concern, of actual, emotional contact.

The shift in emphasis in this volume, the change in the purpose and function of the diary, perhaps also reflects the growth of Miss Nin's instinctive awareness of the inevitable choice facing the individual, and especially the artist, in the modern world. Confronted with the gathering political storms in Europe, with the Spanish Civil War, that bloody dress rehearsal of the horrors to come, she confesses: 'I have not been unaware of the political drama going on, but I have not taken any sides because politics to me, all of them, seemed rotten to the core and all based on economics, not humanitarianism.

The suffering of the world seemed to me without remedy, except by what we could give individually. I did not trust any movement or system.' And even as she actively engages her sympathies, while she attends rallies and types out letters for the Loyalist cause, she cannot shed her basic political pessimism that 'nothing changes the nature of man. I know too well that man can only change himself psychologically, and that fear and greed make him inhuman, and it is only a change of roles we attain with each revolution, just a change of men in power, that is all. The evil remains.'

As a woman, as an artist, she has made a choice that reaches back perhaps to the solitude of her childhood: 'I have built a private world, but I fear I cannot help build the world outside.' Yet her choice is not a mere retreat from the uncontrollable. It is an act of defiance, an optimistic staking out of a corner that is 'livable' in her own terms. As a friend, a listener, a supporter of what she deems worthy of support, she has engaged herself in a private struggle against the evils of man's fear and destructiveness. Louveciennes, the tear-stained hotel room in New York, the houseboat on the Seine, touched by her personal magic, become exemplary islands in a troubled sea. Living fully, richly, and concerned about others within the means of her own capabilities, Miss Nin provides her own answer to the dilemma of human existence. Following her reflection in the intricate labyrinth of the diary may provide others with a key to the vast chambers of the self that await exploration. For, as Miss Nin so aptly writes: 'The personal life deeply lived always expands into truths beyond itself.'

New York
November 1966   GUNTHER STUHLMANN

[NOVEMBER, 1934]

My ship quite fittingly broke all speed records sailing towards New York. It was night when I arrived. The band was playing, and the skyscrapers were twinkling with a million eyes. I was looking for Dr Otto Rank on the wharf, staring at the Babylonian city, the tense people, New York a dream wrapped in fog and sea smells.

Rank was there. Through the influence of a powerful patient of his, the formalities were quickly disposed of and I was whisked away, baggage and all, into a taxi and to a room reserved for me at what I immediately called the 'Hotel Chaotica'.

We sat at the bar. His pockets were filled with theatre tickets, his arms with books for me. He had plans for every evening in the week. He had made an appointment for me with George Balanchine because I had spoken once wistfully of wishing to take up dancing again.

From where we sat I could see all of New York pointing upward, into ascension, into the future, to exultation, New York with its soft-oiled hinges, plastic brilliance, hard metal surfaces, glare and noise, New York gritty, sharp and windy, and the opposite of Paris in every possible way.

For Rank it is a new life. His days are already overfull.

The very next morning I was at the Adams, where he has his office, both to learn and to help him. Famous people came there, sat in his waiting room. Presents came from grateful patients, tickets to opening nights, the opera, invitations to new restaurants, new schools. He displayed these with pride, as if he had gained control of the life of the city, and I felt immediately at the centre and inside of all activities, where I love to be.

In the evening he took me to see the magic doors at Pennsylvania Station, which opened as one approached them, as if they could read our thoughts, and then the Empire State terrace, which seemed to sway in the wind, so that I could see the panorama. It was beautiful and strong, the whole design a thrust into space, arrogant sharp pointed arrows piercing the sky as if seeking to escape from the earth into other planets.

In New York the acoustics are good for laughter, for life is all external, all action, no thought, no meditation, no dreaming, no reflection, only the exuberance of action. No memory of the past, no looking back, no doubts, no questions.

The plays were one-dimensional and prosaic. Rank and I played at an imaginary rewriting of them as they should have been. In between he talked a great deal about his love of Mark Twain, of *Huckleberry Finn* in particular, on the theme of freeing of the Negro with emphasis on the adventurous spirit. Rank admired Mark Twain's parody of literature, Huck's search for complications, additions, circuitous ways. 'No, that would be too simple, it's not the way it's done in books.'

Rank's office is a three-room apartment on the East Side, near the Park. I became familiar with each patient who came, studied their charts with Rank, and he taught me how to handle each case. He explained his method of dynamic attack, his seizing of the present conflict, immediacy, a quick-moving progression from present conflict. He demonstrated every step, every pattern. Every talk was full of suspense. He believed the neurotic was like a paralytic, emotionally, and that he should not be allowed to stand still dwelling on his impotence.

Perhaps because the life of New York was so intensely active, events seemed accelerated and the atmosphere changed from day to day, but the temperament of Rank's dynamic analysis also seemed to accelerate his patients.

Suddenly I was in the heart of political intrigues, at the core of the life of the opera, the theatre, the millionaires, the movie stars, the Foundations and Fellowships. I could not reveal their names (it would have been unethical) but their stories fascinated me as a novelist.

Curtains rise on plays far deeper and more terrifying than any play or film. Behind the great powers, tragedy, frustration, fears, bitterness. Death by suicide, death by psychological murder. All day I hear them whispering in the closed office. I sit in the smaller room, studying and making notes. A symphony. I open the door to a man who holds in his hands the destiny of the opera, another who is building a chain of hotels, another who can influence Wall Street stocks. A thousand stories.

Rank is beginning to love his life here, but more, as he said, when I look upon his work as a novelist, when I respond to the dramas and surprises. His delving reveals new plots and new aspects of character.

The deeper I enter, through him, into the lives of these characters, the more like a synthetic symphony they seem outside, in the streets, in the restaurants.

The transparent brilliance over all things, from shop windows, to cars, to lights. A texture which is not real, and not human. Days all bright and glossy. One feels new every day. The poetry of smooth motion, of quick service, a dancing action, at counters, changing money for the subway. Rhythm, rhythm, rhythm. After knowing what seethes within them, I do not dare to look at the people too closely, for they seem a bit artificial, like robots, parts of concrete and electric wiring. A million windows, high voltage, pressure, vitamin-charged, the city of tomorrow, and the people of tomorrow who cannot be human beings, and who, perhaps knowing it, come to Dr Rank to weep and complain for the last time, for they too may be a vanishing race. Just as the aristocrats are a vanishing race in Europe, perhaps here the human being who thought this was to be his world, is also being sacrificed to something else. Here in Dr Rank's office I hear protests, revolts, sorrow, but outside they seem a part of the white-enamelled, sterile buildings.

*

I gave up the idea of dancing with Balanchine's class, to concentrate on this new art, the art of exploring human beings at a deeper level, archaeology of the soul.

Anaïs, the assistant secretary, is not very efficient. But Rank is tolerant because I make up for it by understanding his ideas. In fact, I understand them so well that now he wants me to work on the translations made of his books, to work on elucidations, because in some of these rough, direct translations from the German there is a ponderous quality which makes his ideas obscure.

My small desk is weighed down with huge books with German titles. Work for a lifetime. Every day the translator brings what he has done and I rewrite it in a clearer way.

At six o'clock all work ends. We go to a restaurant. We talk about the patients. Rank cannot help teaching all the time, for his interpretative mind is constantly at work. I tire of abstractions after a while, so I suggest Harlem.

Harlem. The Savoy. Music which makes the floor tremble, a vast place, with creamy drinks, dusky lights, and genuine gaiety, with the Negroes dancing like people possessed. The rhythm unleashes everyone as you step on the floor.

Rank said he could not dance. 'A new world, a new world,' he murmured, astonished and bewildered. I never imagined that he could not dance, that he had led such a serious life that he could not dance. I said: 'Dance with me.' At first he was stiff, he tripped, he was confused and dizzy. But at the end of the first dance he began to forget himself and dance. It gave him joy. All around us the Negroes danced wildly and gracefully. And Rank sauntered as if he were learning to walk. I danced, and he danced along with me. I would have liked to dance with the Negroes, who dance so spontaneously and elegantly, but I felt I should give Rank the pleasure of discovering freedom of physical motion when he had given me emotional freedom. Give back pleasure, music, self-forgetting for all that he gave me.

Driving home the radio in the taxi continues the jazz mood. New York seems conducted by jazz, animated by it. It is essentially a city of rhythm.

Rank could not forget Harlem. He was eager to return to it. He could hardly wait to come to the end of his hard day's work. He said: 'I am tempted to prescribe it to my patients. Go to Harlem! But they would have to go with you.'

My room at the 'Hotel Chaotica' is as wide as the bed is long, with a tiny desk, a bureau, all in russet brown. Rank had selected it because it advertised a 'Continental' breakfast. The 'Continental' breakfast was slipped through a slot in the door with the sound of a revolver shot, at seven in the morning. It was a carton which contained a thermos full of watery, luke-warm coffee, a quarter of an inch butter patty in silver paper and a tough roll a day old. But there was a radio at the head of the bed.

When Rank has a formal dinner or other invitations, I either stay in my room and write in my diary or go out with my own friends.

Rank told me that women practised deception very badly, that many of the women he had analysed, when involved in any kind of intrigue, love or politics, always left a 'clue', wanted to be discovered, mastered, wanted to lose. It was almost as if they continued to re-enact the old primitive forms of love-making, in which woman was overpowered by the strength of the man. To feel themselves conquered, in a more abstract situation, they enjoyed losing.

In Gilbert and Sullivan's musical the soldier gets a cramp trying to play the role of the poet. Rank says everyone gets a cramp, physical or mental, when playing roles. Cramps of the soul, cramps of the body, arthritis of the emotions.

The radio plays blues. Paris, New York, the two magnetic poles of the world. Paris a sensual city which seduced the body, enlivened the senses, New York unnatural, synthetic; Paris–New York, the two high tension magnetic poles between life, life of the senses of the spirit in Paris, and life in action in New York.

Rank working magic all day, magic with pain, words which heal like the hands of the old religious healers, and in the evenings entering into my realm in which I rule, life and the present.

We sat in a restaurant and I began to ask him questions about his childhood. He suddenly launched into endless stories. Then he stopped suddenly and his eyes filled with tears.

'Nobody ever asked me about myself and my life before. I have to listen to others all the time. Nobody ever asked me what I was like as a child.'

I now understood why he loved Huckleberry Finn so deeply. He must have been like him as a boy, freckled, homely, tattered, rough-hewn, mischievous, adventurous, inventive. He liked to remember catching fish with his bare hands in a shallow river, proud to have been swifter than the fish. He must have been spirited and humorous.

The next day I caught him staring at the children skating in Central Park. They wore bright-red wool caps, red, white or blue coats. They screamed and laughed against the white snow. 'I would like to be out there with them, laughing.'

But he was locked up with the desperate and distressed, with people trapped in tragedies, and peculiar tragedies for which the rest of the world had very little compassion. Rank, that morning, the bowed, heavy way he stood by the window, looked like a prisoner of his work, his profession and his vocation. The sick came endlessly, each one who was cured brought father, mother, sister, brother, friend. They multiplied in an alarming degree. Was this a new illness, born of our own times? No time for love, no time for friendship, no time for confidences.

Rank touches all things with the magic of meaning. Those who come to him are like the blind, the dumb, the deaf. When he discovers the 'plot' of their life, they become interested. This interest saves them. This plot created by the unconscious slowly reveals itself to be more interesting than any detective story. Rank uncovers the links, webs, patterns. It is endlessly interesting, full of surprises.

He writes his lectures on the train, on his way to Philadelphia or Hartford.

He insists psychologists know little about woman. 'Because she has not created enough, she is not articulate, she imitates man.' So he insists that when he is dictating a lecture I should make my own comments on the margin, in red ink. 'That way we will hear both sides of the story.'

Every other phrase uttered by Rank begins with: 'I have an idea.' The discovery of significance is what deepens and embellishes experience. No object, no gesture, no action which is not illumined with meaning.

We were standing in front of the brownstone house, 158 West Seventy-fifth Street, where I lived several years of my childhood, where I had known the greatest difficulties, humiliations, poverty.

There was always some member of our huge Cuban family staying there. When none came, my mother rented the top floor and the second floor to artists we knew. The daughter of Teresa Carreño, the great pianist, lived in the basement. We lived on the first floor, in what was once a parlour and dining room. Enrique Madriguera (the violinist who later became a famous conductor but was then a sixteen-year-old prodigy) lived on the top floor. The house was full of gaiety, music, distinguished visitors. José Mardones came to sing, Miguel Jovet played the guitar, my mother sang, my brother Joaquin studied his piano, Enrique practised his violin.

Whenever there was a revolution in Cuba (and there were many) some uncle would be exiled and would come to stay with us. While the relatives stayed with us they took us on automobile rides, to the theatre, and we had a taste of luxury. And when they were gone we went back to housework, and public school. An eventful, picturesque, dramatic and comic life for us, but we were always in debt.

The house, at that time, was only in the second cycle of its history. Its first owners had lived sumptuously, with a kitchen in the basement, a pantry for the butler, maids' rooms on the top floor, a formal dining room overlooking a garden, a parlour full of mirrors, bedrooms with dressing rooms and luxurious bathrooms on the second floor. Past bourgeois comfort was still visible in the elaborate lamps, rugs, and mirrors. But when they sold it, it was partitioned into separate rooms with a bathroom to each floor. My mother and my two brothers and I all slept in what was once the dining room. We washed our faces in what was once the pantry, and used what was once the servants' shower next to the kitchen in the basement. We had two folding beds which became sedate bureaus by day, when we turned the room back into a dining room. The big bay window overlooked a backyard which I promptly turned into a garden. The desk was in front of this window. The heavy woodwork, the scallops, the friezes, made the house seem like the home of a family who had once been wealthy and had fallen into poverty with distinction.

It was there I first invented the theatre of improvisation. Though a writer, I insisted that we act out of our imagination, without script, premeditation or plan. I would merely give a theme. We would get into costumes in one of the unrented rooms, and then I would wait for my brothers or my cousins to start acting. But none of them would collaborate. They would stand paralysed on the improvised stage in their improvised costumes of mosquito netting, Christmas ornaments, curtains and shawls, look at me and say: 'Tell us what to do, what to say.'

I had more success with my storytelling. We would turn off the lights, and I told stories until we terrified ourselves (Grand Guignol stories, horror stories, ghost stories). When we were all frightened enough to turn on the lights I knew I had achieved a good theatrical performance.

Rank knew about this period of my life, and he wanted to see where it had taken place. But after a while he began to talk about himself.

He was rebelling against his profession. He talked about his own imprisonment.

'I have always been a prisoner of people's need to confess. I do not want to receive confessions any more. I am tired of giving myself, of being used by others. I want to begin to live for myself. I am rebelling against sitting all day in an armchair listening to people's confessions. I want to be free, Anaïs. I am never permitted to be a human being, except with you. When people do not deify, idealize me, they make me a demon, or a father, a mother, or a grandmother! Whatever they need to love or revenge themselves against. I am tired of sitting in an armchair when I feel so full of unused life, and I have so much to give in life.'

I had awakened in Rank a hunger for life and freedom, as Henry [Miller] and his wife June had awakened it in me! What ironies!

He had become aware that he had not lived enough. He was rebelling against the pattern of his life, against all the giving, the annihilation, the immolation of a doctor's life. Even at night, he tells me, when he is asleep, they call him up. Cries of distress, threats of suicide, runaways.

That was why he had wanted me to become a dancer rather than an analyst.

I helped him through this crisis. I suggested merely a better balance between his work and pleasure, between work and leisure. He began to control the flow of his patients, to give more time to the theatre, to book-collecting, to his own writing.

To unburden himself, he also sent me my first patients.

Meanwhile, in Paris, Henry met Blaise Cendrars and writes me about their encounter.* Blaise Cendrars wanted to be the first man to fly to the moon, and if he had, how magnificently he would have described it.

Henry heard about his daughter, that she was studying music.

He came to New York, arrived late, delayed by fog. He took a room in the district where he once worked in his father's tailor shop.

*See Henry Miller, *Letters to Anaïs Nin* (Peter Owen, London, 1966). – Ed.

[JANUARY, 1935]

I went to visit Theodore Dreiser at the Hotel Ansonia. It was an impersonal place, with a big window overlooking Broadway. There were many books about, and a desk covered with papers.

Dreiser was pink-skinned, tall, like a farmer. He had a slow voice, and a chuckling laughter, faded blue eyes and freckled hands.

Dinner was served by hotel waiters. We talked about many things, writers, books. He told me that so many people write to him as to a confessor, to tell him all their troubles, and ask for advice, believing that a novelist should know how to direct their destiny. He received so many letters that he had to have a secretary.

'And you, you have nothing to ask of me, you mean you just came to see me, not to ask anything of me?'

'I have nothing to ask of you. I respect you as a writer and I wanted to know you, that is all.'

He seemed enormously relieved. He chuckled with pleasure. He told me a story: 'There was a legend about a king who could turn anything he touched into gold. More and more people came bringing objects for him to turn into gold. More and more people heard about his power and they came from everywhere, crowded into his palace, crowded around him, pressed around him, begging, pleading, pushing, and finally

16

by their massive pressure, suffocating him. That is how I feel sometimes, about all these letters of confused and begging people writing me: "What shall I do?" Why should they think a writer can guide their life?'

Dreiser does not believe in the soul. He is a materialist.

The lights of Broadway danced up and down while we talked. Even in a hotel room he managed to create the same down-to-earth atmosphere of his books.

He asked me how I managed to have an individuality and yet retain my femininity and be unobtrusive.

After dinner he sat in his rocking chair, as if he were in his country house, and he admired my hands which he compared to celery stalks.

I almost laughed at this barnyard poetry but then I thought it was a very Dreiserian phrase. He looked so comfortable in his rocking chair.

When it was time to go, he did not get up, he kept rocking back and forth, smiling. I slipped my coat on and stood by the door.

'You mean you're not spending the night with me?'

'No,' I said politely, as if he were offering me a glass of wine. 'Thank you.'

'Too bad, too bad,' he murmured, chuckling, and then got up and accompanied me to the door, laughing merrily.

At a studio party I met some of Henry's friends: Conason, a doctor, Sylvia Salmi, a photographer, and Emil Schnellock, a painter. In Paris, Henry was always writing letters to Emil.

Rank is leaving for a three-week lecture tour of California. He will also lecture in New Orleans, on his way back.

Rank is just as preoccupied with evil as Henry is. After a day with his patients he made the following note:

Woke up with a full realization that I had never been human in all my life. By that I mean I never reacted naturally according to my emotions. Of course, it was self-protection, which I rationalized as human: not to hurt others. Cruelty, cheapness, meanness, that is human. Human is evil. Being jealous, indiscreet, possessive, lazy and dependent, exploiting others, that is human. Having compassion and understanding, patience and helping others, all of

17

which is considered human, is ideological goodness. Faithfulness in love is unnatural. Not only god and religion, immortality and morality, is man-made ideology, but love too. The man who acts in reality like a woman – who is a woman following her instincts, he alone is human. It is not because he is evil that the woman likes the 'bad man' but because he is natural. It would be more human to throw away all therapy and to be free, not to be bad but to be human, natural. The self-denial which is necessary in order to be good, human, is denial of the bad natural self and is therefore not a sacrifice at all but self-protection, and it is the most selfish thing of all. On the other hand the seeming sacrifice for others is really domination, protection against being too human, and is still giving in to badness by still pretending one is good.

Went with Henry to see 'the street of early sorrows', where he played as a boy. A snowy night in Brooklyn. Small red brick houses as in small towns in Germany. Henry's school. The window of his room, so bare, with an old window shade. The tin factory he described in *Black Spring*. The street which led to the ferry, the one he walked through with his mother. His mother was wearing a fur muff and he never forgot the pleasure of slipping his cold hands into the warm fur. From his talk I would guess that was the only kind of warmth his mother could give him, against snow and cold, animal fur and no human warmth. It was so strange to see now the places and memories which had come to life in Louveciennes in the warmth of my interest, and which became the poetry of *Black Spring*.

Then we walked to the Brooklyn cellar-apartment where Henry had lived with June and Jean. It was now a chop suey restaurant. It was barren and sterile, and without beauty or charm, but no worse than some of the streets and houses where my artist friends lived in Paris, dark dank places without heat or light.

For a long time I have sought the justification for Henry's angers, hostilities and revenges. I believed it was a reaction to unusual suffering. So many American writers show this bitterness and hatred.

But when I compare their lives and suffering with the lives of European writers (Dostoevsky, or Kafka) I find that Europeans suffered far more, and all knew greater poverty, greater misery, yet they never turned into angry, hostile men like Edward Dahlberg, or Henry. Suffering became transmuted into works of literature, and into compassion. The asthma of Proust, the Siberia of Dostoevsky, contributed to their compassion for humanity. In some American writers any deprivation, any suffering, turns into mutiny, criminal anger and revenge upon others. There is an almost total absence of emotion. They hold society responsible and writing becomes an act of vengeance.

It seems to me that the answer lay in the attitude towards suffering. To some American writers anything but paradise was inacceptable. To the European it was part of the human condition, and something shared with other human beings.

It is interesting to read D. H. Lawrence's preface to Edward Dahlberg's *Bottom Dogs*.

The real pioneer in America fought like hell and suffered till the soul was ground out of him . . . The spirit and will survived; but something in the soul perished: the softness, the flowering, the natural tenderness . . . you get an inward individual retraction, and isolation, an amorphous separateness like grains of sand, each grain isolated upon its own will . . . man is so nervously repulsive to man, so screamingly, nerve-rackingly repulsive! This novel goes one further. Man just *smells*, offensively and unbearably, not to be borne. Nothing I have ever read has astonished me more than the Orphanage chapters of this book. There I realized with amazement how rapidly the human psyche can strip itself of its awareness and its emotional contacts, and reduce itself to a sub-brutal condition of simple gross persistence. It is not animality – far from it. These boys are much less than animals. They are cold wills functioning with a minimum of consciousness. They have a strange, stony will to persist, that is all. I don't want to read any more books like this one. Just to know what is the last word in repulsive consciousness, consciousness in a state of repulsion. It helps one to understand the world, and saves one the necessity of having to follow out the phenomenon of physical repulsion any further, for the time being.

For the soul to have been ground out of existence so easily, it cannot have been very powerful in the first place. For the snarling animal to be called out of his lair so easily, he must have been inclined to snarl at the slightest provocation.

Why didn't D. H. Lawrence's ordeals make him hate other

human beings? A human writer realizes that other human beings may be victims like himself and he should unite with them against the aggressor, not become one.

Rank had the same conflict I had, wanting to be good, and becoming unnaturally good, not human. I was not natural with Henry, I played the role of the ideal confidante he needed for his writing.

When Rank saved people they were his creation. He had to continue to be the figure which saved them, the ideal wise man. He was not permitted to be human, or even to love them. The life of an analyst is tragic. A country doctor, a physical doctor, can be human, fallible. He can be loved for what he is outside of his profession. An analyst does not exist in the mind of his patient except as a figure in his own drama.

I think about him while I answer his telephone and sort his mail. 'Dr Rank will be back at the end of February. This is Dr Rank's assistant speaking. Yes, he is on a lecture tour.'

Rank's writing does not do justice to his ideas. He translates mentally from German. He is only concerned with meaning. When I read him what I write he extracts the meaning, he does not notice the form or expression.

He wants me to rewrite all his books with my 'French conciseness'. He is a philosopher, not an artist. The poet is in love, a lover. The philosopher is a commentator.

Just before he left he talked again about his childhood, his great love of the theatre. He went hungry to see a play. He needed to talk about himself. He said: 'I have never met anybody with such an interest in human beings as you have, Anaïs.' I unleashed a flow of confidences. He had written poetry, and plays, he had wanted to be a writer before he came into contact with Dr Freud. I resuscitated a submerged part of Rank's personality. 'I have not talked about myself for thirty years, or even before that.'

What will happen to this writer who lived mute and concealed behind the mask of the doctor?

I had told Rank the story of Richard Osborn [see *Diary*, *1931–1934*] and his dual life in Paris. He became interested in his conflict between being a lawyer for an American bank by day and leading a Bohemian life at night, and his breakdown. From all I told Rank he felt that Osborn should not have been placed in an asylum. 'In the first place, he shows definite symptoms of guilt, and where there is guilt there is a possibility of curing him, and in the second place his symptoms are not the kind which develop into violence.'

I asked Rank if he would help him. Rank offered to visit Osborn and to talk to the people who had committed him.

He rented a car and we drove to the asylum in Connecticut. I expected this visit from Rank to be very effective, because Richard Osborn had read his books and had heard Henry talk about him. I waited in the car. Rank disappeared behind huge doors. He returned sooner than I expected.

As we drove back he told me what had happened. 'I asked to see Osborn. They consented, and they brought Osborn to the waiting room, and left us alone. I said: "I am Doctor Otto Rank." He stared at me, then smiled ironically, and said: "So you say," and he turned his back on me and left the room. That was the end of our talk.'

In spite of the fact that this meant Osborn had just lost a chance to be freed, I could not help laughing.

Henry is writing a story about murder in the Paris suburbs. After that he flew into one of his best lyrical moods, reeling off feverish pages for *Black Spring*, pages on dreams, pouring out images.

[FEBRUARY, 1935]

One of the patients Rank sent me was a violinist in an orchestra. I will call her 'Emily'.

Lying on the day-couch, and I sitting where I cannot be seen, everyone looks vulnerable. Looking first at the hair, then at the brow, down the line of the nose, the mouth, in the pose of sleep, without the defensive masks, every human being looks helpless.

She came in walking like a young man, it is true, wearing flat shoes and a soiled raincoat, her hair tousled and short, walking with a masculine thrust of the shoulder. But when she took off her shoes and I saw the delicate shape of her feet, and noticed the sensitivity of her hands as she pushed her hair away from her frightened face, I knew she was a girl pretending to be boyish, or a girl who did not dare to be a woman. Her experience of man consisted in having once used a toothbrush as a substitute lover and deciding she did not like it.

She was the first one who had dared to come, for in doing so she had eluded the absolute tyranny of the conductor, a woman I will call 'Marcia'.

Emily played her wistful and plaintive melody for me – life in a small town in the South before coming to New York, fears, frustrations. Everything was sinful: laughter, dancing, dressing up, charm, and the plant that was Emily was stunted by so many prohibitions. When she first began to play in Marcia's orchestra, Marcia's total freedom of action and thought liberated her, but at the cost of utter dependence on Marcia.

She talked endlessly about her many 'crimes'. They were small and harmless but they weighed on her. Analysis at times resembles a Catholic confession: I have done this and that, I need absolution, I cannot sleep at night remembering I once wished my sister dead, and she became ill and she died. When she plays the violin she feels she is wooing people, and wishing to charm them so they will love her, and that is wrong.

Emily was not only concerned with her own paralysis, but also about the destructive effect of Marcia's domineeringness on the other musicians.

She felt stronger after a few talks, she felt she was beginning to escape the power of Marcia. Could she bring her friends to me? She was beginning not to feel helpless and hypnotized.

Before Rank left for the West, our last conversation was about my assertion that woman's notorious inadequacy in grasping ideas was only relative. She could not grasp abstract ideas, but she was able to transpose them by humanizing or rather personifying them. But once they were embodied, concretized in a person, then she grasped them perhaps more profoundly, because she grasped and experienced them emotionally, and they could affect and transform her. But they are the same ideas which move men through their minds.

Now analysis is revealing how little objectivity there is in man's thinking. Even in the most rational man, there is a fund of irrational motivations which are personal, and belong to his personal past, to his emotional traumas. So in the end, pure thought rarely exists in its abstract form, it is part of the experience and of the emotions. A synthesis. Invention, discovery, creation, history and philosophy are composed of all these elements. Man generalizes from experience, and denies the source of his generalizations. Woman individualizes and personalizes, but ultimately analysis will reveal that the rationalizations of man are a disguise to his personal bias, and that woman's intuition was nothing more than a recognition of the influence of the personal in all thought.

Rank, who partakes of the two activities, could admit this. He spends his days exposing the fallacies of rationalizations.

My patients multiplied at a frightening rate. I have barely time to pick up my Continental breakfast, to dress, and already the telephone is ringing, and patients are at the door. There is an entrance hall about two yards long between the door and the day-couch on which they lie. Before they lie down I can tell how they feel. I am sitting against the light in a deep armchair. There is only one small window high above Central Park. The smoke of cigarettes fills the small room. And even when the radio is turned off I can hear the faint sounds of music from other rooms. It is the background music of New York. The voices of patients, sad, shrill, loud, whispering, tired, animated, colourful, weary, hoarse, strong, thin, lisping, foreign. The faces of patients, with eyelids down, as if their eyes were now watching an interior drama; the young man who cannot love anyone; the sister who can only love her brother; the writer who cannot write; the man obsessed with politics who cannot take sides; tears, laughter, rages, sullen silences: they fill the small room.

One day I saw so many tears fall that when I found a puddle of water near my door I first thought it was all the weeping, and then I saw the umbrella that had been forgotten weeping on the rug. On other clear, sharp, cold days of snow, of frost on the window, patients came thankful for warmth, for a rest, for a moment of intimacy with themselves. Strange, the loss of the self is a greater sickness than the self's impostor, the ego. The ego is the caricature people mistake for the self, the ego is the fraud, the actor, the transvestite of the self.

Lost selves, confused selves, blind selves. When the real self is born the ego vanishes.

Here lies the remedy against anger, the counter poison which the world has chosen to denigrate and overlook. How many hard, non-human people I have seen melt before my eyes and become human again. How many angers were dissolved, how many false attitudes abandoned, how many hatreds cured.

I have seen twisted and impotent people become constructive, creative, human. Above all, I have seen that the most frequent source of anger is impotence. Hostility is jealousy. Destructiveness is a sign of impotence.

[MARCH, 1935]

When Rank came back I was at the station. He had fallen in love with the West. He was enthusiastic about its climate, its relaxed life.

Then he sat down and read my reports on the patients. He approved them all. He said: 'You have a gift for this.'

Some think analysis is an artificial process because it is a hot-house process, a forced feeding, a hastening of growth. Biologically life continues to evolve by its own rhythms, by its own errors. Analysis becomes necessary only when growth is stunted, when the flaws strangulate growth.

At times analysis creates another form of idealization. Too much is demanded of it. While analysing so many people I realized the constant need of a mother, or a father, or a god (the same thing) is really immaturity. It is a childish need, a human need, but so universal that I can see how it gave birth to all religions. Will we ever be able to look for this strength in ourselves? Some men have. They have also gone mad with loneliness. Woman will be the last one on earth to learn independence, to find strength in herself. My patients turn away from those they love or are loved by when this need is unfulfilled. The feminine young man who came, obviously incomplete, obviously half-woman, was looking for a man who would add to his feeble manhood, a completion.

They demand of love also the fulfilment of a need, a need for growth, and it is in terms of this need that they often sacrifice the love; or are guilty of injustice. I was guilty of the same injustice when I looked for a strength in any man whom I called 'the father'.

Analysis gives vision into the potential self. At times it also gives false hopes, because the potential self cannot always develop. We have loyalties to the past, commitments, promises made, human responsibilities.

The pale winter sun is shining on what I write. I write while I wait for patients. I write after they leave, I write while eating my dinner, at times instead of dinner. I write lying down on a rust-coloured bedspread, with the radio humming over my head. On my dressing table there is a Japanese garden in a bowl. Messages from my patients, and books they bring me.

Rank divides his time between New York and Philadelphia.

I made a strange discovery. I was glad to return to a life not constantly analysed by Rank.

The diary written at odd moments, between patients.

As always my life continues like a musical score, always on several lines at once. By day I am self-effacing, I am confessor and doctor, but in the evenings I lead my own life. Invited to the Wagner's Fifth Avenue palace, butlers with white gloves, eighteenth-century furniture, white walls, gold-rimmed mirrors, and always at the end the lovely quiet drive back in a big car, with a fur rug on the knees. Spent one Saturday afternoon at their Long Island estate, watching a polo game, and when I admired the best horse with the same intuition about horses that I have of wines, Mr Wagner said: 'You're the finest bred woman I have ever known, fine breed.' This amused me, and I was laughing in the foyer, on my way upstairs to dress formally, when Mrs Wagner leaned over the banister on the first floor and from the tone in which she said: 'What are you laughing at so merrily?' I understood immediately the whole tone of their marriage, her paleness, her over-seriousness, over-dignity, and his red-flushed, round face and joyousness.

I am getting so I can guess a tragedy from the flicker of an eyelid. Too much. Too much.

It is what Proust called his X-ray, and mine works overtime, at fancy dinners, at movies, at cocktails, walking through the city.

Patients come and go, they come from all levels of society, rich, poor, ignorant or cultured. The rich are insulated but this only increases the split from reality. If there is no noise from the outside, there is also no weeping, no laughter, no intense living either. A few cannot pay. Emily says: 'I am well, but don't send me away. This is the most wonderful thing which ever happened to me.'

She has a religious attitude towards analysis.

Analysis accelerates growth, maturity, but changes come more slowly than insight. The patterns have deep roots and take time to change.

I avoid all clinical language because as a writer I believe language has power. I also take much trouble to describe each character, each motivation as unique, not to give the patients the feeling of being classified.

Science may heal, but it is the poetic illumination of life which makes my patients fall in love with life, which makes them recover their appetite for it. I avoid labels and the hospital atmosphere.

Rank was at first uncertain about this emphasis on language. I wanted to avoid the algebra of emotion, mathematical human equations, to bring it all back into the realm of a living drama.

Finally he said: 'Yes, you are right. Words are magical. Freud did much in his analysis of the patient's language as a key to his problems, but you are, as a writer, studying the power of the analyst's use of words to affect the patient.'

Then he returned to his obsession that I should rewrite his books, condense and clarify them. He would have a rough translation made of *A Study of Incest in Literature*. It was a six-hundred-page book. It would be a lifetime task. I would have to abdicate my own writing. Already I was shying of too much analysis. Intellectual banquets. Orgies of ideas. The force of a man's ideological creation, and the human tragedy of it. His wisdom attracts people to him. 'I am like a rich man who fears to be loved only for his money.' He is lonely in his world of ideas.

*

Henry, meanwhile, is writing, but also trying to get published. He was asked to expurgate *Tropic of Cancer*. He rebelled against compromises, against pragmatism, commercialism. He felt defeated and frustrated. Life in New York seems mechanical and drab to him.

One night Rank was taken to the opera by an enormously wealthy man he had cured. At midnight he telephoned me from downstairs. Could he come up for five minutes? When I opened the door he was hidden by a giant basket of flowers he had been given and wanted to bring to me. He also wanted to display Dr Otto Rank the Viennese, all dressed up in his new tailored evening suit with cape, top hat, and patent-leather shoes. He came in, and like an actor, he leaped on the couch, took off his hat like a famous singer receiving an ovation, bowed and said: 'The ovation should have been for me, because I made the singer sing his best, I made the rich man back the opera.' He bowed to an imaginary, applauding public. He sang a fragment of a Viennese opera, leaped down, and vanished.

Henry said: 'In New York I fear to be swallowed back into drabness, limited surroundings, slavery.' His childhood. He cannot bear to live as he lived before.

I feel the need to swing away from constant explanations. I want to run away from too much consciousness, too much awareness. At night, I seek dancing, friendships, nature, forgetfulness, music, or sleep.

Just as I wrote this, a woman threw herself out of her window on the seventeenth floor. So one we did not take care of decided to die, not too far from help. I cannot help all the sick. I feel like the king in Dreiser's parable. I have no more free time. They call at night and haunt my dreams.

Henry has written more lyrical passages, as good as the first pages of *Black Spring* he wrote in Clichy. My faith in Henry as a writer absolute.

*

Rank thinks my diary invaluable as a study of a woman's point of view. He says it is a document by a woman who thinks as a woman, not like a man.

When I heard the orchestra tuning up I was reminded of all that Henry includes in his books which I once called the 'tuning up', and which I felt should not be there, should be removed later like a scaffolding. But Henry likes those moments when the instruments are not yet in tune.

'If I am an artist, as you say I am,' said Henry, 'then everything I do is right.'

'But the artist has to include a critic.'

Is this the way Henry keeps his writing alive, by letting it follow the casual, accidental patterns of life itself?

Rank gave a lecture on the psychology of woman. He says I have added to his knowledge of woman. He always wanted to write poetically and dramatically and what I am writing he feels is the poetry and drama of neurosis. So the man who took the diary away from me as neurosis gives it back to me as a unique work by his enthusiasm for it.

When I write in the first person, I feel I am more honest than when a man generalizes.

In analysis I am quite willing to discuss with A. the guilt tragedies in Dostoevsky, knowing all the time he is speaking of his own guilts which he is unwilling to recognize or to name. I am quite willing to talk with B. about the hunger of China or India by which he expresses his own personal starvations. Man's language is that displacement from the personal to the impersonal, but this is another form of self-deception. The self in them is disguised, it is not absent as they believe.

Visited the Planetarium. It restored to me a sense of space and I could detach myself from the haunting patients. To walk in the snow with muffled steps, and into a replica of the sky.

I saw, instead of stars, relationships moving like constellations, moving away and towards each other, small, large, pale or vivid, warm or cold, diffuse or clear, and at times exploding. Trailing smoke and plumes, raining sparks, turning, moving, according to an invisible design, according to influences we have not yet been able to measure, analyse, contain.

Coming out again on the white carpet of snow. Silence as the snow falls. I took a long journey away from human tangles. I breathed space and order.

Rank wrote me a letter from Philadelphia where he spends most of his time.

You are great in life as I am in creation. You lived my creations. And in that sense you are greater, and your philosophy of living is true. It is the one I arrived at – on paper! And because you are rare in living, your writing is not only rare, a unique document, but it is great. If no one else does I will publish *House of Incest*.

The more I explore neurosis the more I become aware that it is a modern form of romanticism. It stems from the same source, a hunger for perfection, an obsession with living out what one has imagined, and if it is found to be illusory, a rejection of reality, the power to imagine and not to sustain one's endurance, and then the creative force turned into destruction.

Many of the romantics destroyed themselves because they could not attain the absolute, in love or creation. They could not attain it because it was invented. It was a myth. The neurotic acts in the same way. He sets himself impossible goals, imaginary goals. He will win the respect and admiration of a parent who is not even alive any more (appealing to his substitutes). He will gain the love of the world by giving the world something it may not want. He will seek union with opposites, perverse contrary relationships with those who turn away. He will seek to conquer the unconquerable. Like the romantic, he is creative, and may apply his power of invention to art, science, history.

Patients weep when they discover they are their own victimizers and not the victim of others. They weep when they discover they are responsible for their own suffering. As I expose an imaginative, subjective interpretation, their world changes according to their concept of it, their own vision.

Rank, in life, can be dark and heavy. He has no *joie de vivre*. His pleasures are of the mind.

He admits that in creation the doctor or the artist can achieve the absolute, but not in life. In life one has to accept limitations. In creation there is autocracy. In life, compromises. The more yielding, the more easily contented. Henry yields, accepts. Rank seeks to change, control. Henry is happier. Wisdom gained from ideas, the effort to control life intellectually is disastrous. This is the *will* D. H. Lawrence railed against.

Limitations of life. Doors closing as one walks forward. Curtains of silence. Inertia. Obstacles like walls. Then to discover that the limitation is within oneself. A malformation wanting the impossible. In all of them the imagination is the trap. Evasion is possible by renunciation of life and creation in art. Or by accepting limitations. I was walking along Broadway thinking: in my books I can ordain, rule, walk, laugh, shout, accuse, act in any way I please. I am creator and king. The same will applied to life may destroy me. Many creators, romantics, neurotics, are tragic figures in life. They are absolutists. They tire of struggling against the limitations of life. In art there are none.

Joy only in the little things along the way. Henry never looks at his life as a whole, but accepts each day, not caring about past or future.

My patients suffer from loneliness. Their illness isolates them. But when they are cured they suffer a different loneliness, because there are more neurotics than ex-neurotics. And the ex-neurotics have a special insight and a special language.

No matter how well constructed, how impressive a rationalization is (a publisher explaining why he cannot publish a certain book, a woman explaining why she cannot marry a certain man, a scientist telling me why he had to abandon a certain discovery, a man in politics giving a reasonable explanation of his betrayal of a friend), I can see the real motivation behind it, the one they do not want to see. It is a terrifying knowledge, like carrying an X-ray machine about and seeing the bone structure.

I can see Rank differently now, the cause for his tragic personal life. If Henry has no will at all, Rank has too much.

The caricature aspect of life appears whenever the drunkenness of illusion wears off. Some Americans have lost the faculty for illusion, they are so pragmatically sober, that may be why they have to drink so much. They have not the power of levitation or escape of the poet or the artist who can make another world within this world.

Henry is finishing the rewriting of *Black Spring*. He wrote the marvellous 'City Man' section, and the pages on burlesque.

I am restless and impatient in my analyst's chair.

Once more I reach the same conclusion. You cannot help others to live. They live on their own power for a while, and then soon start looking for another leader, support, crutch.

Henry's obsession that he is writing in a void, that he is like a rat caught in a trap, even while *Tropic of Cancer* is circulating and *Black Spring* not yet shown to a publisher.

I said to him: 'What would you say then if your books had been burned like the books of D. H. Lawrence, or if you had really been persecuted and put in jail as De Sade was?'

He cannot bear rejections, the silence of conventional publishers, formal rejection slips from magazines, obtuse comments of people.

[APRIL, 1935]

Eleven years ago I received a copy of *Rahab* by Waldo Frank. It was given to me by Hélène Boussinesq, his French translator. I loved the book and Hélène gave me a letter of introduction to him.

He took me out to dinner. He looked like a Spaniard, dark hair, not tall, dark eyes. He called me *La Campanilla*. He is alert but seems a little bitter. 'I am more loved in South America than I am in my own country.' He also talked about his theory that woman is given too high an importance in America because she was so rare in the early days, there were so few of them and men prized them. They retained their privileged position ever since.

When he assumed I would spend the night with him I was annoyed, because there had been no gradual courting, no effort made to sense how I felt, no subtle interplay. It was as plain and simple as ordering a dinner. I laughed. He said: 'I can see you are not filled with me, not deeply interested in me.'

We walked down Broadway, we watched a spectacle which fascinated me: Saturday night on Broadway. The word MAGIC winked from store windows hung with masks, tricks, jokes, fake cigars, false teeth at the bottom of a glass, false money, false eyelashes, boxes of magician's supplies. Prescriptions for delusions. Third eyes, paper snakes with darting tongues, distorting mirrors, mechanical divers who never tired of touching bottom and then ascending, who never stayed to explore the depths. Coloured powders for increased potency, harem beauties of rubber offering rippling hips and breasts, dancing bears, dancing dervishes, books on magic, opium pipes, voodoo fetishes, directions for hexing an enemy, an eye rotating at the bottom of a glass as if your own eye had fallen into it as you drank, a marriage ring which could never be removed, a chain which could not be broken, a lock which could not be unlocked.

There was an auction going on in a jewellery store. The man who was performing wore no magician's clothes. He was dressed like a salesman. He invited you to gamble one dollar on a gold watch. He passed it around for everyone to see. He gathered a small crowd. He talked so swiftly it was a strain to follow his words. His eyes leaped from the watch to the crowd, and when he had the crowd's eyes following his he gave his attention to other objects, as if forgetting about the watch, starting to auction off a doll, a pocket knife. The watch was left on the counter. He diverted people's attention to statuettes, glass bowls, book ends. The crowd waiting and those who had given him a dollar kept their eyes on the watch. The crowd stood. Children were waiting at home, hungry husbands, tired wives, invalids. Time passed. Some grew impatient. The salesman had an interminable flow of words. 'In a minute we will auction off the watch.' They had given one dollar, they could not relinquish the game, the gamble, the expectancy, the suspense . . . 'But first of all I want you to notice the statue of this burlesque queen, it is made of hard candy, it is eatable.' He talked so fast it was impossible to interrupt him. Some people in the crowd had engagements, some had aching feet. I could see them standing first on one foot, and then on the other, or slipping off their shoes and rubbing their feet, and some looked exhausted, but they stayed, they felt engaged with fate. It was not a watch, it was their personal luck which was at stake. It was 'Am I lucky, or am I not lucky?' Will a gift come I have not earned, not worked for, a miracle? I have thrown the dice, I cannot turn my back, the minute I turn my back I will be called and the gold watch will be given to another. The watch is there. It grows more golden. The salesman plays for time. He prolongs the moment of faith, of expectancy.

In the brilliant lights one is dazed. One forgets what one wanted. If one abandons the place, someone else steps into one's place. Trick boxes.

Waldo Frank could not understand why this spectacle fascinated me.

I tried to explain but could not do so successfully. 'It is something about the truth you cannot bear to see so you look at other things. The truth about a relationship appears sometimes in the first words that are uttered, but one does not want to hear them. I was thinking of my patients, and how the worst moment for them was when they discovered they were masters of their own fate. It was not a matter of bad or good luck. When they could no longer blame fate, they were in despair. Illusions. Delusions. That salesman is selling illusions.'

Waldo Frank laughed. He took me to the burlesque show on Fourteenth Street. Only men in the audience. We sat in a red plush box. The art of teasing, and not revealing. The woman who took off everything but kept her long white gloves on.

It is spring and my patients are doing well. But I cannot leave yet.

Rank believes that to create it is necessary to destroy. Woman cannot destroy. He believes that may be why she has rarely been a great artist. In order to create without destroying, I nearly destroyed myself.

Henry is painting water colours with Emil.

Rank made me finish *House of Incest*. He helped me to discover the meaning and then I was able to make a synthesis. It was he who said: 'Why, it ends here, of course, with the dancer. And this page on drugs [when I say to Sabina: 'I'll write for you – that will be our drug'] can't be thrown out. It's important. It says just what I felt when I read the manuscript on the train. It is like a drug. I woke up when I got to the end as if I had been dreaming. If people accept your language, then they will be drugged.'

*

I have had, during analysis, plenty of time to study the effect of artistic language as opposed to scientific language.

Henry finished *Black Spring,* and met William Carlos Williams.

Lunch with Rebecca West. We enjoyed talking about our first meeting in 1932. She had written to me about my book on D. H. Lawrence, praising it and inviting me to visit her. She had written a favourable review. I did go to London, with the manuscript of *Tropic of Cancer*. I liked her immediately, her warmth, her brilliant dark eyes, her wit. She visited me in Louveciennes. We talked so much together we lost our way in the forest and had to telephone to a friend to come and pick us up in a car. In Louveciennes she commented that she had never seen a house where deep talks could be treated so lightly. We made a trip together with her husband and mine, with much gaiety and affection.

She had not finished her book because of her operation. She thought she was not going to live. 'I won't see the spring again!'

But she was here, in New York, lively, keen, and I reminded her of the wonderful scene in Louveciennes when after reading *Winter of Artifice,* she had tears in her eyes and she said: 'Wasn't *our* father a terrible man!'

She introduces me to Norman Bel Geddes and Raymond Massey as the 'woman who wrote the best book on D. H. Lawrence'. We all went to an ice-hockey game. Madison Square Garden. Violence, speed, physical power, strong lights, strong smells, loud music, hoarse voices shouting, broken noses, intensity. Drinks at Reuben's while Eddie Cantor gives a stag party and Director Max Reinhardt shares his supper with two actresses and a stage designer. John Huston joins us, and talks to me intently. Mrs Bel Geddes has mocking eyes. Then to Harlem, first to a nightclub, to hear some singing, and then to a private apartment. Everyone was dancing and drinking. Half white people, half black, beautiful women, well-dressed men, and jazz, it was intoxicating and magnificent, the laughter, the dancing, but I miss the intimacy which grows out of such parties in Paris. Here it is all jokes, banter, evasion. Norman Bel Geddes tells me I look like the women in Persian miniatures, but ten minutes later he no longer recognizes anyone, forgets who he came with. John Huston is rough and vital, cynical, colourful. Raymond Massey is elusive, mysterious, with his slow speech and heavy glance from heavy-lidded eyes.

More drinks. More talks later, at some private club. When cynicism reaches its height I begin to withdraw. When people begin to mock and destroy each other, I feel closer to my troubled patients. I feel closer to people who are suffering than to those who joke, mock, hate.

Frivolous evenings always start very well. I enter the game with vivacity and elation, with curiosity and love of adventure. But gradually my pleasure and exhilaration wane. Irony, mockery, ridicule freeze my blood. As if I witnessed a scene of sadism.

I look for the exit, an excuse to escape. My malaise grows. My throat contracts and I can neither enjoy eating nor drinking. I want to leave. If everybody is drunk and venomous, the need to leave becomes imperative. I give inadequate excuses. Every minute I stay becomes a torment. I come home, angry at myself. I cut off the evening. I am not sure why. Good-bye, good-bye.

I went to visit Waldo Frank. I noticed how bright and clairvoyant his eyes were. He was gentle and human, mellow, and he talked about writing with sensitivity. He received me with such a look of faith and wonder that it made him seem very young. Here I could talk freely. There was a core to him, something rich and true, insight too. He read to me out of *Virgin Spain,* his description of a Catalonian woman. We drank Port. His room was simple, orderly. He said: 'You are one who knows neither death nor finished things. Your discontent is creative restlessness, and not a grouch, it is curiosity. You still expect miracles.'

He gave me a feeling of youth, of wholeness, sweetness. He told me he did not admit everyone into the seclusion he needs for his work. He is a warm, human man who did not harden, or die, as so many American writers harden and die.

He is a poet riveted to reality as poets in America are, but a poet full of talk of God and simplicity. 'God sent you, *La Campanilla*, so that I might finish my book.'

He did not want to go out. He wanted that peaceful, protected feeling in which he finds strength.

Mr Wagner was waiting for me in the lobby, just back from hunting quail in Georgia; his photograph appeared in the Sunday paper. He was leaping over a fence on a famous horse. With him I walked gaily to the Plaza bar.

He pretended to be crystal-gazing into the water bottle and said: 'I see no hope of a love affair in the future.'

What a face he would make if I said to him: I am afraid of becoming a saint. This is what working at analysis has done to me. Living so much for others gives me a fear of becoming a saint, of being lured back into the whitest corner of the dream, nun's wings like small ship's sails. My love for my patients, for that moment of absolute sincerity which takes place, makes me want to stay in the world.

I love the world so much, it moves me deeply, even the ordinary world, the daily world, even the bar table, the tinkling ice in the glasses, the waiter, the dog tied in the coat room.

Mr Wagner has not said I am a saint. Nobody has said it. The watching of the miracle of man being born over and over again, this makes me fear to wake up too far away from the earth.

All day people coming, people asking for strength.

I can see that analysis could create a new kind of dangerous idealism. At times I feel Rank puts too great an emphasis on what *ought to be* rather than what *is*; he never accepts experience as a substitute for wisdom. At times I feel the process of accelerated wisdom may become a dangerous short-cut. It eliminates terror and pain. I feel it should only be used in extreme cases, when the neurotic is paralysed, cannot live, cannot love, cannot work. At times Rank portrays an idyllic state, an expectation of life without pain. Rank is saying that man was born to be happy, that pain is illness.

Levels and levels. It is as if I were in an elevator, shooting up and down, hundreds of floors, hundreds of lives. Up to heaven, terraces and planetariums, gardens, fountains, clouds, the sun. The wind whistles down the shafts. On the next to the last floor, dance halls and restaurants, and music. In the rooms, bars of shadows on the walls from the casement windows. A bower. A confessional. A couch to lie on. Something to lie on, to rest on, to cling to. Faith. Red lights! Down! Down! The telephone operator announces: a man who limps, a man whose hand is paralysed, a man in love with his mother, a man who cannot write the book he wants to write, a woman deserted, a woman blocked by guilt, a woman crying with shame for her love of another woman, a girl trembling with fear of man. Free the slaves of incubi, of ghosts and anguish. Listen to their crying. A tough political partisan says: 'I feel soft and iridescent.' Another one says: 'It is a weakness to listen to the complaints of the child in us.' I say: 'It will never cease lamenting until it is consoled, answered, understood. Only then will it lie still in us, like our fears. It will die in peace and leave us what the child leaves to the man – the sense of wonder.' The telephone announces: 'A cable for you, shall I send it up?' 'Yes, yes.' 'Happy birthday, happy birthday, love.' Red lights! Down! White lights! Going up! Playing at being God, but a god not tired of listening, all the while wondering how the other god can watch people suffer. Music, the solace. Through music we rise in swift noiseless elevators to the heavens, breaking through the roof. Red lights! Down! At the drug store I buy stamps, mail letters, ask for a coffee. Physically I am cracking. It is not the change of floors, the sudden rise and descents which make me dizzy, but the giving. Parts of my life, parts of my energy are passing into others. I feel what they feel. I identify with them. Their anguish tightens my throat. My tongue feels heavy. I wonder whether I can go on. I have no objectivity, no indifference. I pass into them to illumine, to reveal, but I cannot remain apart from them, be indifferent to their bad nights, or their hopes, or their cries, or even their happiness. I look out of my window as Rank looked out of his window. People are skating in the Park. The band is playing. It is Sunday. I could be walking through the streets of Paris, joyous, lively streets where people are in love with life and even with their tragedies. I could be walking along the human and beautiful Seine. I did not recognize my happiness then. I yearned for adventure. The children's laughter rises to the twenty-fifth floor, to the window at which I stand. Red lights! Down! All the way down I am thinking of the problem of emotional symmetry. People's need of retaliation, revenge, need to balance anger against anger, humiliation against humiliation, indifference against indifference.

In the mail box there are many letters. A message from Waldo Frank: 'Why don't you telephone me?' Invitations to cocktail parties, a book from Emily, the week's bill.

One of my patients asked me to pose for her. I had to go to the same building, the Arcade on Broadway and Sixty-fifth Street, where I used to go as a girl of sixteen when I was an artist's model. And just as if I were as poor as I was then, I could only eat a sandwich for lunch because one of my cripples waited for me, to bring me only his illness.

White lights! Going up! When I open the door of my room I sit on the doorstep, so tired out I have the feeling I will not be able to take the last three steps. The telephone is ringing. I let it ring.

James Boyd took me to the theatre. He told me a fascinating story about Hemingway, who is a very close friend of his. He described Hemingway pacing up and down in his den, saying: 'There is another dimension. I am fully aware of it, but I can't get to it.' So he was trapped in his reporting of externals, his faithfulness to the surface, to words actually said.

For all my patients sensuality is a giving in to 'the low side of their nature'. Puritanism is powerful and distorts their life with a total anaesthesia of the senses. If you atrophy one sense you also atrophy all the others, a sensuous and physical connection with nature, with art, with food, with other human beings.

On the mezzanine floor there are concerts I never have time to hear. In the basement there are my empty trunks waiting for sailing time. Where the elevators strike bottom there is darkness and hysteria. On the main floor there is a perfumed Anaïs who meets celebrities, social workers, teachers, very poor people, society people, entertainers, actors, dancers, writers, timid people, slick people, bankers' wives, the flower of Southern aristocracy, snobs, benefactors, newspaper men.

Thirty-six floors, maids cleaning, men carpet-sweeping,

letters falling down the chute. Thirty-six floors to my activities, thirty-six cells, from six to eight patients a day.

The body is an instrument which only gives off music when it is used as a body. Always an orchestra, and just as music traverses walls, so sensuality traverses the body and reaches up to ecstasy.

I rebuilt shattered lives, resuscitated, led, taught. I handed out the key to the room where lovers met, consoled the deserted ones, restored faith, aroused the intellect, opened new worlds. Ecstasy. I gave the key to it too, and I feel it now because my lame ducks are dancing.

In America, I can see, it is all survival of the tough. The sensitive, the tender are trampled down. Mass moulds, loss of individuality, confusion between individuality and the ego. So there has been a loss of individuality and respect for the self, a loss of identity.

Met Norman Bel Geddes at the Ritz bar. Later we went to the Kit Kat Club. He tells me he ran away from home to become a magician in vaudeville.

Everywhere we go everybody knows him. The entertainers come and sit at our table. Norman says: 'When you get one of those performers in bed they have nothing to give you. They have given all of themselves to their performance.' He is generous, friendly, promiscuous. Names flash in his conversation like names on a marquee. 'When I saw Reinhardt . . . Miriam Hopkins . . . when Eva Le Gallienne and I had dinner in Paris . . . when I produced . . .' His fraternizing with the world was enjoyable. It was the way Henry would behave if he had Hollywood and Broadway at his feet. He left me at my hotel at 3:00 A.M. murmuring: 'You're marvellous.'

In Harlem I realized Negroes are natural and possess the secret of joy. That is why they can endure the suffering inflicted upon them. The world maltreats them, but among themselves they are deeply alive, physically and emotionally, and it is possible that their tormentors are jealous of this quality, they are the withered and bitter ones.

Rank misses the gaiety of Paris, its cafés, its humanity and warmth.

He said jokingly that he wished he could be analysed by me.

'Half of the effectiveness of analysis lies in the wish of the analyst to heal and to help. This wish is contagious, and often does half of the work. Every analyst has it at the beginning and then gradually loses it. If analysis becomes mechanical, it suffers. The neurotic feels it. You have kept your genuine interest in human beings. Freud began to analyse me. He believed every analyst should be analysed himself. But we could not go on. He was not objective. Or at least, I did not feel he was. Too much wisdom prevented me from living out my natural self.'

Schizophrenia looks so much like indifference that it is difficult to tell them apart. I am not sure at times whether Henry has moments of total indifference, non-caring, or moments of splits caused by the violence and brutalities of American life.

The danger of schizophrenia is that the neurotic in a state of shock seeks another shock to awaken himself, seeks pain. And the pain he feels gives him momentarily the illusion of being fully and wholly alive.

Henry is writing about Attila and Christ, both in the end conquering the world, one by force, the other by love and both doing as much harm.

Henry is contented with a flow of people who are not vital to him. To this flow he gives his time, his energy, his ideas, talk, letters, but he does not give himself. He feels he is communicating with the world. He thinks I am aloof, but does not understand that I cannot give superficially, can only form vital, deep attachments to a few. I hold back from the casual flow.

I lost weight, sleep. I was haunted by the troubles of my patients. Their nightmares became my nightmares. I could not enjoy my own life. I thought about them and how to help them day and night. I was ill with their illness, in sympathy, in empathy. I felt submerged, and desperate not to be able to save all the wounded. I went as far as I could in giving of my strength. I was depleted and drained of all I had to give.

Rank was asking for another sacrifice: to give up my writing and rewrite his books. He saw me thin and worn and yet he disapproved of my leaving New York. I knew the time had come to leave New York or I would be consumed in service and healing.

The gift Rank made me was that of being understood, justified, absolved.

He would always ask me what I had been doing during the week. It was at this moment his magic would begin to operate, because no matter what I told him, from the most trivial: 'I bought a bracelet,' to the most important for me: 'I found a job for my first patient,' or 'I wrote a page on minerals for *House of Incest*,' Rank would immediately pounce on this fact with the joy of a discoverer, and raise this fragment to a brilliant, complete, dazzling legend. The bracelet had a meaning, the minerals had a meaning, they revealed the amazing pattern by which I lived which only Rank could see completed and achieved. He would repeat over and over again: 'You see, you see, you SEE.' I had the feeling that I was doing extraordinary things. When I stopped before a window and bought a bracelet I expressed the drama of woman's dependence and enslavement. In this obscure little theatre of my unconscious, the denouement was this spontaneous purchase of a bracelet. According to Rank I was not seduced by the colour and shape and texture of it, by my love of adornment. It was much more dramatic than that! Rank's interest was concentrated on unravelling the mystery of this ritual. 'You see, you SEE.' Not only the moment spent on Fifth Avenue was revived, intensified, but all I had done during the week was like a perfect play, or a novel, fostered by Rank's revelation. I felt like an actress who had not known how moving her voice and gestures had been, their tremendous repercussion, but also like a creator preparing in some dim laboratory a life like a legend, and now reading the legend itself from an enormous book. And this was certainly a part of the legend, Rank bowing over each incident, explaining, marvelling at this miracle which had not seemed a miracle to me but a whim, my walking along and buying a bracelet, as miraculous to Rank as liquid turned to gold in an alchemist's bottle. The more I talked, the more stories I poured out, the more Rank convinced me that I had not only filled the world with a multitude of little acts but that all these acts were of deep significance and to be admired for the very act of their flower-

44

ing. To please him, I would go back and find little actions I might have missed or lost down the dusty streets of my rich life, which, touched up by the illuminating wand of Rank's interpretation, acquired a new depth, a patina, a glow I had never noticed before, and which Rank feasted upon as if it were one of the most colourful tapestries he had ever seen. Coloured lights played upon insignificant acts? Nothing was insignificant. I had gone back to the same place and bought a second bracelet. Why? I often bought two of everything I liked. I felt the danger of loss. I wanted to be prepared against the loss of a dress I loved which might wear out, the loss of a sandal of a unique design I might never find again. But two bracelets. Duality? Two loves? One representing the woman who wanted to be enslaved (slave's bracelet), the other to bind the other, the one I loved? Was I going to wear them together, like twins, or was I going to save one against the possibility of loss, or was I going to give the matching one to someone else? Nothing was insignificant. Even when I told Rank a lie, it was to expose the blindness of science, of psychoanalysis, to prove that it was not like the eye of God in my Catholic teachings, able to see everything that happened on earth.

Rank laughed. I was always glad to make him laugh. He laughed at my understanding of the games. He said I did not want to make things too real so they would not turn into tragedy, or die as they so often did in reality. I liked *play*. I did not want tragedy, destruction. I had cultivated elusiveness, means of escape, magician's tricks.

There was a meeting of psychoanalysts, and there were seven of us in the train going to Long Beach.

The long, sad boardwalk, with its scraping noise of feet on wood. Crowds. Discord between sea and voices, voices screeching like owls, discord between the colourlessness of the sea and the crude raw colours of movie advertisements, between the smell of hot dogs and the smell of fish, angry flying clouds and grit of sand. The crowd walking, chewing, the wind stirring up dyed hair, the salt so bitter in the bite of the wind on the lips, bold houses which should have been hiding, exposing diseased façades, open-jawed shops with loud-speakers deriding the hiss of the sea, announcing the sale of furniture, of horoscopes, of dolls. The long boardwalk, gritty to walk upon, a fair of monsters exposed without charge, faces of owls, rictuses of walruses, the eyes of sting rays. A hotel which looked like a penitentiary on the outside and like a brothel inside, all red and gold. The sea was there, its rhythm broken by radios blaring. The vast dining room where everyone had passed, no one had passed, all bearing names on their lapels. Conventions. The sea cannot enter. Dusty curtains are drawn, and there are too many waiters, too many signs on the doors, too many bells, too many mirrors, rugs, cigar butts in vases filled with sand. The sea was concealed and silenced.

It was that day, at a dinner, with a tag on my shoulder, that I discovered I did not belong to the world of psychoanalysis. My game was always exposed. At the door there is always a ticket collector asking: 'Is it real? Are you real? Are you a psychoanalyst?' They always know I am a fraud. They do not take me in. It seemed to me that day that all of them were examining fragments which should never have been separated except in a laboratory. I was not a scientist. I was seeking a form of life which would be continuous like a symphony. The key word was the sea. It was this oceanic life which was being put in bottles and labelled. Underneath my feet, moving restlessly beneath the very floor of the hotel, was the sea, and my nature which would never amalgamate with analysis in any permanent marriage. I could not hear the discussion. I was listening for the sea's roar and pulse.

It was that day I realized once more that I was a writer, and only a writer, a writer and not a psychoanalyst.

I was ready to return home and write a novel.

A few days later I sailed for home. When I left, New York was covered with fog. I could only hear the ship's sirens.

[JUNE, 1935]

Louveciennes. Home. Rush of memories. Sleeplessness. I miss the animal buoyancy of New York, the animal vitality. I did not mind that it had no meaning and no depth. Here I feel restless. The Persian bed. The clock ticking. Time slowed down. The dog barking at the moon. Teresa bringing the breakfast. All the electric bulbs are missing, the tenants took things away. The books are dusty. My coloured bottles seem less sparkling after the sharp gaudy colours of New York. The colourful rooms seem softer, mellower. The rugs are worn. Where is the jazz rhythm, the nervous energy of New York? The past. The glass on my dressing table is broken. The curtain rods are missing. Where are the garden chairs? France is old. It has the flavour, the savouriness, the bouquet, the patina of ancient things. It has humanity, which New York does not have.

I had traumatic fears on the boat. Dr Endler would be waiting for me at the pier to take me back to the hospital to go through the stillbirth again. Or I would picture my father's house all in brown (brown, said Oswald Spengler, is the colour of philosophy). Brown is a colour I hate.

Louveciennes is old and tranquil. I once loved its oldness, its character. Now it seems to have the musty odour of the past. New York was *new*.

The garden wall is crumbling from the weight of the ivy.

My mother thinks it is beautiful.

But I am sad. I do not seem to fit here any more, or am I in love with feverish activity, intensity, excitement? The silence of Louveciennes, the stony peasant faces behind the windows. Peace. Home is peace. The village bells are ringing. The smell of honeysuckle enters through the window. A new me does not belong here any more, a new me is an adventurer and a nomad. People around me do not change as I do, do not sprout new branches. To come back was like being caught in a circle. I struggle against monotony and repetition.

I spread out on my bed all the gifts I brought from New York. A set of wooden dishes with astrologic symbols against blue-painted edges. We will have a dinner and invite Antonin Artaud and René Allendy.

It is the sameness of everything which makes me feel I have not moved at all. That is why adventurers take a ship and go to Africa, walk through Tibet, climb the Himalayas, ride on camels through Arabian deserts. To see something new.

Face to face with a gentle, diminutive Paris, all charm, all intelligence, the new Anaïs feels: But I know it already. It is familiar. I am in love with a new, as yet uncreated world, vivid colours and large scales, vastness and abundance, a synthetic vast city of the future.

How surrealistic it was to go up as fast as a bullet to the top of the Empire State building, to look down at New York as from an airplane, and find canary birds singing in a cage. Incongruous. In New York you feel you are living in space, with no earth under your feet.

In Louveciennes the sheets smell of mildew, there are thousands of old autumn leaves to rake and burn. Anaïs, rake the leaves, you are at home, no more adventures.

I had expected too much: great expansion, tremendous outward changes to match the inner changes in me, voyages to India, Spain, China, new friendships, new sensations, new rhythms.

I am trying to land gently. From the fantastic voyage through all the levels of American life, the exploration of Rank's vast, cosmic mind, the intoxication of freedom, the adventure of analysis, to the isolation of Louveciennes, its sleepiness.

I have to grow in a different way, not cover mileage, but in depth. I have to sublimate my love of adventure.

My father is in the South, taking a cure for rheumatism. Joaquin is competing at the Paris Conservatory.

I dream of a printing press, of publishing.

There is a barn next to the house which once served to store wheat on the top floor, and horses and carriages on the ground floor. Everybody loves the idea of setting up a printing press there, and to become independent of publishers.

China again, as Henry calls it, the China of the artist. The house began to awaken, to shed its magic again. People came and said it was like the house of Alain-Fournier's *Le Grand Meaulnes*.

Henry is working blissfully. Visitors. Slow meals in the garden. I create an inner whirlpool.

I am not a patient craftsman in writing. I like to keep the aliveness and the freshness of writing. I like the first spontaneous version, the explosion of seeds, the opening of new roads. Lively talk last night.

We all write about the same people, but so differently. I am always true to life, as a woman is. Henry, [Michael] Fraenkel and [Fred] Perlès invent, fictionalize.

Fraenkel came, appropriated the printing press project, dominated Louveciennes, talked uninterruptedly all day and far into the night. The ego! A small, frail man, nervous, ill, but the *will* and the ego immense, filled the house. He made outrageous statements, that *Black Spring* was the result of all the talks that took place between Henry, Walter Lowenfels and Fraenkel. Even Henry laughed at this. Finally he lost patience and said: 'This talk is wonderful, isn't it? Well, I've had better ones with Anaïs right here in this room.' But Fraenkel was drunk on himself. He would not take the train back to Paris. He moved in. I left them in the garden talking and went back to my work.

I was writing when Fraenkel came into my room. He was humble and gentle because he had found a copy of his book marked by me and he liked the notes I had made. He said: 'You know better than anyone what this book means.' He touched his own book fondly, tenderly.

After this incident I told Henry I thought the printing press should be set up at the Villa Seurat.

Henry wrote about France:

Physical deterioration, but the soul expands. Things are rotting away on the outside and in this quick rot the ego buries itself like a seed and blooms. Here the body becomes a plant which gives off its own moisture, creates an aura, produces a flower. I see one big globule which swims in the blood of the great animal MAN.

This globule is Paris. I see it round, and full, always the whole globule at once. The globule will stretch and expand, it will permit him the most fantastic movements, but will not break. Suddenly I am inside the globule. I entered by osmosis. I seeped through between late afternoon and midnight. I am inside now. I know it. I had managed to get inside all together, a complete man, including my soul.

Fraenkel was talking about how we became tired of logic, of rationalism, how surrealism, humour and chaos came to break down logic which was unlike life and uninspiring. The living thing, as Henry puts it. I recognized this quality in Henry and followed its influence. It is closer to the feminine way of perception, which I gave up when I had to take care of my mother and my brothers, when I tried to take the place out the missing father and my mother would say: 'Now tell me what to do, with that clear, logical mind of yours.' I went back to intuition and instinct when I turned to D. H. Lawrence, and then to Henry, who represents the non-rational. The very fact that he is all paradox and contraries, unresolved and without core, is like life itself.

What makes people despair is that they try to find a universal meaning to the whole of life, and then end up by saying it is absurd, illogical, empty of meaning. There is not one big cosmic meaning for all, there is only the meaning we each give to our life, an individual meaning, an individual plot, like an individual novel, a book for each person. To seek a total unity is wrong. To give as much meaning to one's life as possible is right to me. For that is a contribution to the whole. For example, I am not committed to any of the political movements, which I find full of fanaticism and injustice, but in the face of each human being, I act democratically and humanly. I give each human being his due. I disregard class and possessions. I pay my respects to their spirit, their human qualities or their talents. I fulfil their needs as much as I am able to. If all of us acted in unison as I act individually there would be no wars and no poverty. I have made myself personally responsible for the fate of every human being who has come my way.

I miss the electric rhythm of New York; it was like riding a fiery race horse. I was drunk on liberty, on space and dynamism. Where are the dazzling lights, the roar of airplanes, fog horns, fast cars, wild pace? I am restless. Adventure is pulling me out. When a man feels this, it is no crime, but let a woman feel this and there is an outcry. Everywhere I look I am living in a world made by man as he wants it, and I am being what man wants.

I was happier when I was selfless, but now that this growth and expansion has started I am unable to stop it.

I feel so strangely released, I feel no boundaries within myself, no walls, no fears. Nothing holds me back from adventure. I feel mobile, fluid.

I do not miss Rank. I think I have finally conquered the need of a father. He played the role generously, but he also tried to dominate me and absorb me into his work. He wanted me to devote my life to the rewriting of his books, a lifelong task which would have destroyed the artist in me. He will never forgive me my return to Paris.

Walking from the Opéra to Parc de Montsouris, I realized that Paris was built for eternity, and New York only for the present. A documentary film on Egypt portrayed their obsession with eternity.

We planned to do our own publishing, even though we do not own a press yet. Fred baptized the press Siana, reversing the spelling of my name.

Fraenkel makes a list of books we will publish and omits me.

All I have been suffering from is falling from a quick rhythm to a slower one. I cannot sit in a café for hours, or talk for ten hours as Henry and Fraenkel do. I crave action and motion. It is as if my heart were beating faster than theirs and I had broken into the running pace of New York.

I come back with relief to Louveciennes, after the café life, to a certain order and discipline in work, a certain seriousness which I conceal from the world. The world prefers clowning, jokes, and vaudeville shows.

Henry is not concerned with insight. He is not troubled by paradoxes and inconsistencies. He accepts contradictions, irrationality and chaos. He is working on *Capricorn*.

I asked Henry if he would like to visit Brancusi with me. He said no, he didn't like prophets, it was a pose. So I went to visit Brancusi with Dorothy Dudley's daughter.

It was late afternoon. He lives in a little house with a courtyard. He opened a huge iron door to us. He wore a white mason's suit, and his beard was long and white like Father Christmas. His studio was white, his statues white or silver. I liked his *Bird Without Wings*. One long lyrical flight, piercing space. His dark eyes closed completely when he laughed. He looked like a Russian muzhik, a peasant. His face was healthy and rosy in his white beard. He cooked shish-ke-bab in his open fireplace, and served this with big bottles of red wine.

His statues watched us, but by contrast with the statues of Chana Orloff, they all had a lightness, a capacity for flight, and their abstraction made them unobtrusive, disappearing into the shadows as the big studio darkened. To laugh he threw his head back. Red wine, laughter. He danced, and he explained the stories he told with gestures, he acted them out. Time passed, but when time came to leave, he complained. We said we had to leave, it was very late. He said he could not bear for anyone to leave, he could not bear separation.

We laughed and said we could not very well sleep in his studio.

Dorothy's daughter and I began to back towards the door, and Brancusi began to talk volubly as if to distract us from leaving. As he had sculptured so many eggs, I teased him about introducing him to Chana Orlof who sculptured pregnant women. 'Or perhaps you have met already, and it is the sight of your eggs which made her sculpture so many pregnant women.' Brancusi responded that he would never impregnate a realist. Only young women like us, beautiful young women. Then, as he had sculptured the famous 'Colonnes Sans Fins' I asked him if he also believed in 'Nuits Sans Fins' (Columns Without End and Nights Without End). We finally left, laughing, teasing, but when we stood on the outside of the iron gate, and Brancusi behind it, with his hands on the bars and such a wistful, lonely expression in his dark eyes, we felt that we were deserting him.*

Henry is writing about June.

'My interest in the past is almost scientific, like a detective's, not human. It just happens that I am struggling with several mysteries. And I want to be truthful.'

He was describing his first meeting with June, their first kiss, her first lie.

'I am writing coldly, so slowly. I am not in love with what I am writing. I have not returned to the past to hug it. It is only my mind which is working. I feel that I was asleep during my whole life with June, that it was a dream, that I was somnambulistic.'

'She wanted you to be asleep, she needed you to be asleep.'

'I realize that she was my creation. I realize how much I learned from your novel, how much I learned from your sincerity.'

Fraenkel is living on the ground floor of the Villa Seurat. Fraenkel and Henry talk a great deal about Spengler, about the end of the world, war, revolutions, destruction, death. The world of death. When I object to this as a philosophy, Fraenkel says that being a woman I am taking a hurdle over and beyond war, into life, because I stand for life. I do not believe Henry is interested in the theme of death, either, but he likes these ideological wrestling matches.

I have just finished Dr Esther Harding's book *The Way of All Women* and Fraenkel was interested in hearing that it was

*When Brancusi died he bequeathed his studio to the City of Paris asking that it be kept as a Brancusi museum. The City of Paris neglected it, and it remained closed. People broke in through a transom, and stole the smaller sculptures. The rain was allowed to fall into the studio. – A.N.

because of the loss of polarity between male and female that we had so much of man seeking man in order to re-enforce his masculinity, and woman seeking woman to re-enforce her femininity. But polarity will come again as it comes at the end of psychoanalysis, when both men and women have found their separate sexual identity, sexual core. How it became weakened, Dr Harding does not say.

All the world suffered from the sterility of consciousness, and had to be cured by tapping the unconscious to find the true sources of life again.

Fraenkel said that would be impossible because the whole world would have to be analysed.

'Oh,' I said, 'it will be, not individually, but by infiltration, contagion, through new arts and new philosophies, new ways of criticism and new ways of interpreting history. Everything that happens to a small group ultimately happens to the masses, to the world.'

Visited Chana Orloff, Richard Thoma, and Fujita, in the Rue des Artistes.

As I walk down the Villa Seurat with my red Russian dress, I feel in love with the world again, in love with the whole world.

Jack Kahane [of the Obelisk Press] agreed to publish *Winter of Artifice* and made me sign a contract. Yes, I have a contract in my pocket.

Henry is becoming a celebrity. He receives letters from T. S. Eliot, a review by Blaise Cendrars, and 134 copies of *Tropic of Cancer* were sold to date.

Our own press will publish Henry's *Scenario* first, inspired by *House of Incest*, which I see as a parody of it. *House of Incest* will be published after that. The third book will be Henry's one-hundred-page letter to Fred.

[JULY, 1935]

Reality. When you are in the heart of a summer day as inside a fruit, looking down at your lacquered toenails, at the white dust on your sandals gathered from quiet somnolescent streets. Looking at the sun expanding under your dress and between your legs, looking at the light polishing the silver bracelets, smelling the bakery odours, *le petit pain au chocolat,* watching the cars rolling by, filled with blonde women taken from pictures in *Vogue,* then you see suddenly the old cleaning woman, with her burnt, scarred, iron-coloured face, and you read about the man who was cut into pieces, and in front of you now stops the half-body of a man resting on a flat cart with small wheels.

Henry said: 'When I am depressed, I go to sleep.'

And suddenly I realized that when I get depressed I have to act. New York cured me of depression by intense activity.

We read this definition in Arnaud Dandieu's book on Proust: *'Le tempérament schizoïde peut s'exprimer par une fuite dans l'action aussi bien que par une fuite dans le rêve. Le Docteur Minkowski a très bien montré qu'un des symptômes les plus clairs de la perte de contacte avec la réalité était la perte du sens de repos.'**

*'The schizoid temperament manifests itself either by flight into action or into the dream. Dr Minkowski proved that one of the clearest symptoms of the loss of contact with reality was the loss of ability to relax.'

In the diary I cannot include the endless talks on art, philosophy, literature, because I am more concerned with human beings and their intellectual life is usually a part of their masquerade. The big themes left out of the diary can be found in the books of Spengler, Otto Rank, Antonin Artaud, André Breton, and recently in Denis Seurat's *Modernes*.

Artaud once said to me: 'The difference between you and other women, you breathe in carbon dioxide and exhale oxygen.'

Dorothy Dudley writes me: 'I felt inside of nature in *House of Incest*, a poem. Poets are rare. You are one of them.'

I suggested to Henry that he give up the impossible effort to synthesize his book on D. H. Lawrence, to accept its impressionistic fragments.

I am the young mother of the group in the sense that I am giving nourishment and creating life. All of them now in motion. When I look at the changes, the transformations, the expansions I created, I grow afraid, afraid to be left alone, as all mothers are ultimately left alone. To each I gave the strength to fly out of my world, and at times my world looks empty. But they come back.

Henry gives me a summary of a three-day discussion of schizophrenia. Henry is worn out, nervous, affected by his own story of how he broke down Fraenkel and made him weep (we all reproduce in one form or another the process of psychoanalysis for each other: confession, exposing the self behind the masks, absolution, faith, new faith and new vision).

Fred came with ten pages of his translation of *Winter of Artifice* into French.

'We are not happy,' I said, 'we're joyous, that's a different thing.'

We all went to have coffee together. Henry was still talking about his analysis of Fraenkel, telling me how the description of schizophrenia also applied to him.

'*Tropic of Cancer* was a book of cannibalism and sadism,' he said.

As I know him now, it was a mask, a disguise of the sensitive Henry to parry the blows of the world.

*

Yesterday I went to Elizabeth Arden's to shed my fatigue. I was lying down with cotton over my eyes. This induced a half-asleep state, a kind of half-dream such as Proust described so well. Then I saw both outer realism and inner realism of the subconscious, saw how they could be fused or alternate harmoniously as they do in life. The state of passing from fantasy to realism, from reverie to action, that was what I wanted to do. In our life they are interwoven. In literature they were treated as separate activities. I began to monologue about my father. I rushed home to my typewriter and swiftly wrote five pages about my father's feet and the drama of projection. Now I know how I will write that book. It is a full recognition of the influence of the subconscious on the vision. In and out of the tunnel of consciousness and subconsciousness, with all the realistic details as well as the waking dream.

Then came an enthusiastic letter from Rebecca West, who gave my book to her son-in-law, a publisher, and he was in accord with her opinion.

So to work.

Copied ten pages of the diary I kept in New York. Enjoyed reliving the feverish activity. Then I wrote the ten pages on the orchestra in *Winter of Artifice*. Music. That was the key word. Music. He, the musician, did not make the world musical, rhythmic, lyrical for me. 'I never could dance around you, my father. No one ever danced around you. As soon as I left you, my father, the whole world swung into a symphony.'

Joaquin sent me the first royalties he earned on his sonata, published in London.

Henry's first royalties went into the printing of his *Scenario*.

Finding the motives for the actions of human beings is my way of justifying their behaviour. I am like the keeper of the python in London. When asked how he managed to feed the python without endangering his life he said: 'Oh, I feed him on a stick, he is fond of me, but he does not have enough sense to see the difference between my hand and a piece of meat.'

*

57

Henry believes in love, money, fame, as a child does. 'It will always come from somewhere.'

Fear of the world produces crystals in writing. One seeks the faultless, crystallized phrases, perfection, the hard polish of gems, and then finds that people prefer the sloppy writers, the inchoate, the untidy, the unfocused ones because it is more human. To jewels they prefer human imperfections, moisture of perspiration, bad smells, stutterings, and all the time I keep this for the diary and give the world only jewels.

[AUGUST, 1935]

One afternoon in Fraenkel's studio we composed a charade on the theme of Fraenkel's death. He asks us to believe in his death, just as people were asked to believe in Christ's death, because he says until we believe in it he cannot be resurrected. I cannot share Fraenkel's madness as I shared and understood Artaud's. I think because in Fraenkel the madness is intellectual, and in Artaud it was rooted in real emotional pain. And besides, Artaud is a great poet.

Writing more and more to the sound of music, writing more and more like music. Sitting in my studio tonight, playing record after record, writing, music a stimulant of the highest order, far more potent than wine. In the interior monologue there is no punctuation. James Joyce was right. It flows like a river.

Henry calls me '*Schneewittchen*', the German word for Snow White.

I wrote about a hundred pages on my father (*Winter of Artifice*). I copied the diary I wrote in New York and returned the original to the vault in a bank where I keep them. I took a taxi to the Villa Seurat and ran into Fred carrying milk for his breakfast with Fraenkel. Fraenkel invited me in and Henry joined us. Henry was in a very good mood because he received a letter from a new admirer and we all sat down to work on mailing subscription blanks for *Black Spring*, to be brought out as part of the Obelisk series. I wrote a lot of letters to arouse interest in the book. Then Fred and I marketed for lunch, and after lunch we all went back to work. Fraenkel's *femme de ménage* washes the dishes. Richard Thoma arrives. He brings me back the copy of *House of Incest* I loaned him. He has designed a dress for me.

He tells fantastic stories of voodoo curses and black magic, which are prolongations of his romantic writing. He is not a surrealist.

We all went to the Café Select. We talked of how we are all victims of obsessional patterns and themes. Fraenkel always wants the woman he cannot have, who belongs to somebody else. Henry loves the prostitute but let a whorish aspect show in June or any woman he loves, and then he becomes critical.

I cannot rest in Louveciennes. The beauty is not enough. I have to keep racing to avoid my past catching up with me and strangling me. I have to live very fast, place many people and incidents between my past and me, because it is still a burden and a ghost.

Last night a frivolous night with friends from New York. Bright lights, savoury dinner at Maxim's, Cabaret aux Fleurs to watch Kiki, but it was not Kiki who seemed attractive to me, Kiki with her bangs and short tight skirt, but her aide-de-camp, a woman so humorous and alive she vivified the entire place. I told her she was wonderful, and she answered me: 'Please tell that to the *patronne*.' 'Where is the *patronne*?' I said. 'She is there, counting the money.' So I went up to the *patronne* and told her. From the Cabaret aux Fleurs we went to the Boule Blanche. Mr W. was very red after a month of hunting in Scotland. When the Negro hostess bent over Mr W. to serve his drink, he stared at her so intensely that she simply pulled her breast out of her dress and offered it to him. His face was wonderful to see. If he had been riding one of his thoroughbreds, he would have fallen off.

We are sitting at the Café Select. Dorothy Murphy joins us.

She never quite knows where she is. She looks at times like a Pomeranian. She recognizes certain people, certain foods, certain drinks. But the rest of the time her eyes look on the world as from a rolling ship, and without any sense of recognition. She knows where the Coupole is, but only with her nose. But once there, on her chair, she does not know why we are sitting on those chairs, talking an unfamiliar language. Whereas it is our lips which move, it is her nose which moves and twitches. To form words as we do demands a long effort on the part of her tongue and all her phrases end in a question. We should understand the language of her nose. The syllables in the form of a perpetual question are a caricature of our talk, but the twitch of her nose is truly Pomeranian. Each vein on it bears clearly the year of vintage. One can detect the blue of Beaujolais Supérieure, the sun colour of Pouilly-Fuissé. Whisky has formed little craters. Rum has designed a fine grain like the seed of figs. The entire nose, though lacking in prow, is not as pointed as a submarine, but widens in imitation of what as a woman she lacks. It is a nose which testifies to drinking valour. Sitting in her café chair with the same bewildered air of a dog in a strange place, she sniffs the smell of rain on raincoats, of rain on rubber boots, of rain on umbrellas, in puddles, the indoor air of Paris, apéritif and charcoal burners, fog and gasoline, tobacco and *café au lait*, and she is silent. Her dress has not dragged in the mud, but looks as if she had slept on the sawdust, as if the starch had been boiled out of it, as if it had been pressed through a clothes wringer. Her hat drooped like cock feathers after a fight, but one feather on it remained pointing and alert. By the time I left my chair she had opened her mouth to say something. But what she says has already been said by the feather. What it says is that if instead of one feather sticking up resolutely she had none at all, her friends would not have all abandoned her. But it was this last feather, this feather posing a question, rebelling against doom, protesting, anguished, anxious, heroic, this heroic feather rising from a cemetery of crestfallen sorrows, which dismayed, haunted and estranged people. The last tower of a castle in ruins, the last cry of a turkey condemned by the cook to die, was like that outrageously arrogant feather, surviving drunkenness, proclaiming a gaudy past, the stubborn gallantry of a flag-bearer in a battle of bottles. It was this which made people turn away.

Brassaï is never without his camera. His eyes protrude as if from looking too long through a camera lens. He appears not to be observing, but when his eye has caught a person or an object it is as if he became hypnotized. He continues to talk without looking at you. (Later, Brassaï, who was Hungarian, suffered much during the war. The Germans entered his workshop and went through all his files of negatives. Looking for what? They carried away many of his photos of Paris at night, many mementoes, many prints he had found on the quays, many old and irreplaceable negatives of erotic subjects.)

Marcel Duchamp sat down with us, and talked about Brancusi. He said he was 'arrested'. He had found his philosophy and would not budge away from it, would not be dislodged.

Marcel Duchamp thought that an artist should never crystallize, that he should remain open to change, renewal, adventure, experiment.

Yet he himself looks like a man who died long ago. He plays chess instead of painting because that is the nearest to complete immobility, the most natural pose for a man who died. His skin seems made of parchment, and his eyes of glass. A different death from Fraenkel's, not obsessional, but noble and classical.

Inside of me I feel the microbe of jazz. It entered my blood. It is neither white nor red, this microbe which causes my agitation. Rhythm. I am aware that the rhythm of New York was external, and here it is analytical and conversational. I have a feverish need of novelty, renewal.

I am now writing on the eclipse of my relationship with my father for *Winter of Artifice*.

The mysterious theme of the flavour of events. Some pale, weak, not lasting. Others so vivid. What causes the choice of memory? What causes certain events to fade, others to gain in luminousness and spice? My posing for artists at sixteen was unreal, shadowy. The writing about it sometimes brings it to life. I taste it then. My period as a debutante in Havana, no flavour. Why does this flavour sometimes appear later, while living another episode, or while telling it to someone? What revives it when it was not lived fully at the time? During my talks with my father the full flavour of my childhood came to me. The taste of everything came back to me as we talked. But not everything came back with the same vividness; many things which I described to my father I told without pleasure, without any taste in my mouth. So it was not brought to life entirely by my desire to make it interesting for him. Some portions of my life were lived as if under ether, and many others under a complete eclipse. Some of them cleared up later, that is, the fog lifted, the events became clear, nearer, more intense, and remained as unearthed for good. Why did some of them come to life, and others not? Why did some remain flavourless, and others recover a new flavour or meaning? Certain periods like the posing, which seemed very intense at the time, violent almost, have never had any taste since. I know I wept, suffered, rebelled, was humiliated, and proud too. Yet the story I presented to my father and to Henry about the posing was not devoid of colour and incidents. I myself did not feel it again as I told it. It was as if it had happened to someone else, and the interest I took in its episodes was that of a writer who recognized good material. It was not an unimportant phase of my life, it was my first confrontation with the world. It was the period when I discovered I was not ugly, a very important discovery for a woman. It was a dramatic period, beginning with the show put on for the painters, when I was dressed in a Watteau costume which suited me to perfection, and received applause and immediate engagements, ending with my becoming the star model of the Model's Club, a subject for magazine covers, paintings, miniatures, statues, drawings, water colours. It cannot be said that what is lived in a condition of unreality, in a dream, or fog, disappears altogether from memory, because I remember a ride I took through the Vallée de Chevreuse many years ago, when I was unhappy, ill, indifferent, in a dream. A mood of blind remoteness and sadness and divorce from life. This ride I took with my senses asleep, I repeated almost ten years later with my senses awakened, in good health, with clear eyes, and I was surprised to see that I had not only remembered the road, but every detail of this ride which I thought I had not seen or felt at all. Even to the taste of the huge brioche we were served at a famous inn. It was as if I had been sleepwalking while another part of my body recorded and observed the presence of the sun, the whiteness of the road, the billows of heather fields, in spite of my inability to taste and to feel at the time.

Today I can see every leaf on every tree, every face in the street, and all as clear as leaves after the rain. Everything very near. It is as if before I had a period of myopia, psychological blindness, and I wonder what caused this myopia. Can a sorrow alone, an emotional shock cause emotional blindness, deafness, sleepwalking, unreality?

Everything today absolutely clear, the eyes focusing with ease, focusing on the outline and colour of things as luminous and clear as they are in New York, in Switzerland under the snow. Intensity and clearness, besides the full sensual awareness.

Neurosis is like a loss of all the senses, all perception through the senses. It causes deafness, blindness, sleep, or insomnia. It may be that it is this state which causes anxiety, as it resembles death in life, and may seem like the beginning of death itself. But why do certain things come to life, and others not? Analysis, for example, reawakened my old love for my father which I had thought buried. What were the blocks of life which fell completely into oblivion? What was lived intensely sometimes disappeared because the very intensity was unbearable. But why did things which were not important return clear and washed, and suddenly embodied?

Neurosis causes a perpetual double exposure. It can only be erased by daylight, by an isolated confrontation of it, as if it were a ghost which demanded visibility and once having been pulled out into daylight it dies. The surrealists are the only ones who believed we could live by superimpositions, express it, layer upon layer, past and present, dream and actuality, because they believe we are not one dimensional, we do not exist or experience on one level alone, and that the only way to transcend the contradictions of life is to allow them to exist in such a multilateral state.

I come back to Louveciennes to read letters from my ex-patients, all swimming in life, grateful and happy.

To escape depression sometimes, I walk all through the city, I walk until I am exhausted. I call it '*La fête des yeux*'. Antiques on Rue des Saints-Pères, art galleries, fashions on the Rue Saint-Honoré. Or I buy *Vogue* and live the life of *Vogue*, all luxury and aesthetics which I gave up. I could have attended the ball at which everyone went dressed as the portraits of Velásquez. I sit at the Lido, watching the rich old ladies pick up the young Argentine dancers. I go skiing or yachting as in *Vogue* pictures. I buy a transparent cigarette case and a *chapeau auréole*. I really attend the dress show of Schiaparelli which is a magnificent work of art. I can well believe she was a painter and a sculptress before she designed dresses. But I could wear none of her things at Villa Seurat, or at Louveciennes.

I never buy for duration, only for effect, as if I recognized the ephemeralness of my settings. I know they are soon to be changed to match the inner changes. Life should be fluid.

My father, on the contrary, builds for eternity. He has such a fear of life that he struggles for permanency, to defeat change. He wants the strongest, most lasting woods, closets full of medicines for possible future needs. He is pained when I send him a letter without waiting for the chronological order. The creator's love of change and mobility does not inspire human confidence. I think in all this I am motivated by such a passion for life that the idea of not moving is for me a death concept. I shiver when people boast of having been born in the same bed in which they hope they will die. The quest for fixed values seems to me a quest for immobility and stagnation. I think of museum pieces, embalmed mummies. Whatever is not alive I want to cast away, even if it is an old chair. Whatever is not playing a role in the present drama is good for the attic. The Spaniards have a ritual: once a year they burn the old objects, in the street, in a big bonfire.

I believe in avoiding constructions which are too solid and

enclose you. The same with the novel, if you catalogue too completely, the freshness and the life withers.

Colette Roberts comments on *Winter of Artifice*: 'Your novel touches me. It is human and real. But because it happens more deeply than the level on which people usually experience life, there seems to be glass around it, like the glass over the paintings at the Louvre. One sees the real painting, all right, one almost feels it, but there is glass.'

When I was analysing I observed clearly that the fear of death was in proportion to not-living. The less a person was in life, the greater the fear. By being alive I mean living out of all the cells, all the parts of one's self. The cells which are denied become atrophied, like a dead arm, and infect the rest of the body. People living deeply have no fear of death.

[OCTOBER, 1935]

For the winter I rented Jeanne's furnished apartment. At first I enjoyed living in her atmosphere, slipping into the décor of her world, but soon I had to hide the porcelain figures, the eighteenth-century gold-and-mosaic clock, eighteenth-century paintings. I had to pin back the heavy white brocade curtains with their gold tassels. But I loved the white telephone next to my bed, the white satin sheets embroidered with Jeanne's initials. Since her divorce she stays in the country and comes to visit her children, who live with their father at the other end of the apartment. This apartment is separated from mine by a long glass hallway planted with hothouse tropical greenery and has a separate door.

I see the Tour Eiffel from my bedroom. In the apartment above me someone studies the piano haltingly.

Perhaps if I do not succeed in living June and Henry's chaotic life, fail to enter into it completely, I may succeed in living a life like Jeanne's, while carrying into it all that differentiates me from them: depth. Luxury is sweet and beautiful. Luxury helps to dream.

How well I dreamed in New York under Rank's protection! Flowers every day. Taxis. Beautiful restaurants. I loved shooting letters down the glass tubes, elevator doors opening magically, maids in starched light-green dresses, elegance, soft lights, radiators boiling, whistling, snow on the window sills.

The rhythm of New York was what I felt in harmony with.

My room at the hotel flooded by the sun and snow reflections. White flowers in a vase. A phrase from that immense and wise soul of Rank's to guide the day.

I worked all morning on *Winter of Artifice*. Walked along the Seine after lunch, so happy to be near the river. The hum of cafés. No money, so I close my eyes when I pass a shop.

Henry is working too. He cut out some pages I did not like about 'I snooze while you work, brothers.' Ranting and moralizing. Trivial passages. It is clear now that I have more to say and will never say it as well, and he has less to say and will say it marvellously. It is also clear that surrealism is for him, not for me. My own style is simple as in my father book, direct, like the diary. Documentary. Henry's rich and meaningless to the mind. Turning inward, to write all day.

Certain pages on my father are deep and moving. I have been thoroughly honest. My style is bare. I never think of how I will say it, only to say it as spontaneously as possible.

I wrote the last pages of *Winter of Artifice*. About the last time I came out of the ether to see a dead little girl with long eyelashes and slender head. The little girl died in me and with her the need of a father. The great emotion with which I wrote the last pages, and the last lines, was so strong that it was only much later that I understood their meaning.

The book is not finished, only half done, because I write the emotional pages first, without order, and then I have to fill in and construct. I have been in a serious, solitary mood, withdrawn, knowing only the austere joys of work.

The key to Henry's work is contained in the word burlesque. What he writes is a burlesque of sex, a burlesque of ideas, a burlesque of Hamlet, or Bergson, or Minkowski. A burlesque of life.

What I feel is too deep and too human for that. I write my book on my father and I feel lonely, for I am detaching myself from the Villa Seurat life.

When I lost my necklace of blue stars which I loved, all Henry could say was: 'That's good, that's one less object in your life.' Henry makes Fred throw away a tuxedo, a suit, shoes, manuscripts so 'he will travel more lightly', and they throw them in the rain so that nobody will use them, profit by them.

Conflict between my feminine self who wants to live in a man-ruled world, to live in harmony with men, and the creator in me capable of creating a world of my own and a rhythm of my own which I can't find anyone to share.

My desire for adventure, expansion, fever, fantasy, grandeur.

A visit from Jeanne. We transported ourselves into fantasy. She read *House of Incest* and was completely affected. She read me from her second book. Unreality. The fairy tale. Enchantment. Out of life. Her life has the grandeur I love, she has wings and power. Her talk is imaginative. The mistake I made before, which put an end to our friendship, was that my timidity and my love for a human connection did not harmonize with her incapacity to connect with anyone, her schizophrenia. 'I construct nothing durable,' she said.

I have learned to do without this human warmth, to accept these floating icebergs, these remote non-human species like my father. To live in fantasy without human closeness. Her freedom and mobility in space carried me away. A few hours before, at Villa Seurat, I felt my worlds crumbling because I could not accept mediocrity. When I saw Jeanne I realized in what realm I can always sail freely, the realm of the dream. I have decided to become reckless, to do and try everything because nothing holds me on earth, and I am not afraid to die. I will live out my fantasies, intoxicate myself with people, life, noise, motion, work, creation, even if it means a shorter life, for life is not truly worth dragging out too long. Perhaps all this which lies outside of reality is what gives joy.

Jeanne is coming back soon to change her dress here and go out for the evening. *Les métamorphoses*. That is very important.

What is it that pulls me away from what others call happiness, home and loved ones, why does my love for them not hold me down, root me? Games. Adventures. The unknown.

I have finished writing the emotional pages about my father in *Winter of Artifice*.

I have finished struggling with the dualities and ambivalences of Henry's writing. He expresses an idea and almost simultaneously a burlesque of it. We had a vigorous argument in which I tried to prove that a man can be contradictory but not ambivalent because then creation is impossible. Creation is taking sides. There is a distinction between relativity and destructive contrariness.

'Burlesque,' answered Henry, 'is a means of destruction.' His instinct is to destroy. But what? The world of ideas? Then the best way to destroy the world of ideas is to live and write about life, the passions. But he does not turn his back on ideas. At the moment he is interested in the theme of death because he is stimulated by Fraenkel as well as D. H. Lawrence. Yet in his preface to Fraenkel's *Bastard Death* he begins with four very serious pages, and ends up with twenty pages of burlesque.

From the day I talked with Jeanne I began to create a whirlpool again, a ballet, a symphony. I saw René Lalou, John Charpentier, Salvador Dali, Anne Green. I visited Le Verrier. Dancing from one to another so as not to fall into depression. Charpentier saying about Blake's head: '*Quelle belle caisse à résonance*' unleashed pages on orchestra in *Winter of Artifice*, in which I include the violinist who played violin with her own body, passing the bow between her legs. The idea of an orchestral piece in writing had been fermenting in my head. I wrote ten pages without stopping.

Something takes place at the Villa Seurat which I cannot share. It is a kind of dadaism.

The doors are closing on me. I cannot earn my living as an analyst without the presence of Rank. I cannot start publication because Fraenkel would dominate it. I cannot travel for lack of money.

Henry said: 'I feel depressed about the inertia of the world.' He cannot get the response he wants. We were talking as we walked along the Seine. There was a fog and we felt lost in it. It seemed like an outer representation of my mood.

I met the poet Jules Supervielle. Wet, dreamful eyes. A

haunted man, with human roots. He is partly South American and writes delicate lyrical fairy tales, and delicate poetry. He is in love with mystery and fantasy. I love *L'Enfant de la Haute Mer* and *Voleur d'Enfant*. I could hear the voices of children in another part of the apartment, a lively household, laughter. He read me his new poems with wistfulness. We talked about surrealism. He does not like it. He is trying for utter simplicity, humanity. He agrees with me that dreams have clarity, luminousness. Supervielle dreams day and night. He hates surrealism because it is chaos and absurdity.

'*Ce sont des farceurs.*'

Supervielle creates a world of his own which never strays too far from reality, filled with children, humour, whimsicality, with the sea, houses, gardens, animals.

He said he was always trying to catch up with the man he wanted to be.

When Henry wrote a fan letter to Kay Boyle she thought it was a letter from a very young writer, who, while admiring and praising her, could not help imitating her own style.

I once coaxed Allendy to give me a hashish pill.

I decided this was the time to try it, as I felt weary of my mother role but could not find a new one. Perhaps the hashish pill would bring some revelation.

I was fully awake and yet dreaming. And my dream was bigger and more overwhelming than my ordinary dreams. It filled the whole room. There was an immense black ocean threatening to engulf me. A big wall protected me, but as I examined it, it was made of books, thousands of enormous books. Books. Books. But the ocean was beginning to shake this wall and I was in danger.

Such an obvious symbolism made me laugh.

I do not belong in the Villa Seurat. I do not belong in Jeanne's world. I will have to make my own world.

[JANUARY, 1936]

Letters from patients asking me to return to New York come every day. When I hear jazz I feel a tremor of adventure, as if the analysis I am going to do if I return there were an adventure, a romance. I dream of the miracles I will perform. Inside of myself I feel ready for a new rhythm, the rhythm of New York. The monster I am going to grapple with is the machine which mechanizes people. I am not a victim of it, so I can stand outside of it and challenge its power, defy its standardizations, dehumanizations, depersonalizations. I can even enjoy its loud mechanical heartbeat, the mechanical beat of New York.

Pain at parting from my loved ones. The human Anaïs feels pain and wonders why she is possessed by this need for fruitful activity, for an expenditure of herself, for fullness.

The Christmas tree is withering. Joaquin is playing a Beethoven concerto with the Havana Philharmonic. My mother writes joyous letters. Thorvald may be in New York. James Bond sent me his novel.

The life here too tame. The pretty apartment. Pastel-coloured friends. Money restrictions, publishing restrictions. Open the window! Let's have the immensity of New York, its magnetism and forces, jazz, smiles, tempo.

I will be leaving for New York in a few days.

*

Arrived in time for Joaquin's U.S. debut at Town Hall. It was a shock to me, for it brought out all the ghosts from the past, from life in New York before Paris, life in Richmond Hill, and I never like to be thrust into the past. I had come to New York for its life in the future.

People began to come for strength and wisdom, and I felt my own weakness. All of them getting well but saying: 'I need a friend.'

Met Dr Conason again, a friend of Henry's, a tireless monologuer. He is one who weaves a net around himself, a net of words, and they paralyse him.

Henry seems numb and remote. For him New York is the past, too painful and he wants to shut it out. I understood his suffering.

He is working on *Tropic of Capricorn*, to alchemize the past. The pain became creation.

What a fear of relationship there is here. No talk. Drinking together. Blurring all feeling and senses. No sense of richness, fullness, expansion. Terrified of intimacy. And consequently alienated. Lonely.

Sunday supper at Mrs Thomas. Raymond Massey, Adrienne Allen (he is acting in *Ethan Frome* and she in *Pride and Prejudice*). John Huston, the Middletons. Aesthetic surroundings. Exquisite food and conversation. Mrs M. has a porcelain face, but her mouth trembles, and I was told she had had a breakdown. Later the talk became glazed and cynical, scathing and acid about people I did not know.

Norman Bel Geddes said: 'Ferdinand Bruckner's play *The Criminals*, which I admire, was too Russian for Americans.'

'What do you mean, too Russian?'

'Americans do not understand tragedy.'

Slowly the fullness I came for was there.

Snowstorms, streets like the *mer de glace*. One patient is weeping while remembering the cruelty of his playmates. Another overflows with the bitterness of a passionless life. Another weeps because the poems she was writing in secret were discovered, read aloud to the class and jeered at. One says: 'You have given me more than one human being can

73

give to another.' In one there is an artist who has been brutalized. In another a child who has been neglected. I am rescuing the individual who is submerged by the power of the masses here.

One of my patients calls me in Russian his 'holy secret'.
Rank is in the South, lecturing.

Last night, Hilaire Hiler's studio. I was in a gay mood. I danced satirically, dialogued in a south-of-France accent with Hiler and he said: 'You're the only one who has come here who is not grey.' They were all smoking marijuana. As I do not inhale it had no effect on me, but I decided to pretend it did and really put on a performance which convinced everyone I was riotously intoxicated. Wild improvisations.

Then I went dead. Too much illness around me, too much sorrow. For the first time I understood indifference. Suicide of a soul. Not to care. I wanted to convince myself that I did not care. All my patients are getting better, writing books, giving concerts, taking sides in politics, getting married, but I am dead. Freedom and recklessness. Perhaps because I have fulfilled my responsibilities, I feel free not to care any more.

[APRIL, 1936]

Visited Rank. He was settled in an apartment on Riverside Drive. When I arrived he was standing at the door, gentle, eager, sad. He was thinner, younger, sunburnt. A knowing smile. The river flows under his window. We have an hour to talk, as if I were a patient. He seems resigned to be working intensely as before, with little time for life: 'But it is just as well, I am too much of an absolutist for life. It would be better for life if I were less total. You have escaped from the obsession of analysing. I am glad for you.'

'But I am still in conflict with my feminine self. I am afraid to lose my personal, intimate happiness in this drive towards growth and fulfilment.'

To a great deal Rank asked me, I answered: 'I don't know, I don't live by analysis any more, but by a flow, a trust in my feelings.'

'I envy you,' said Rank.

Perhaps it was this I had saved from his intensive obsession with analysis, my emotional life. I did mind his never letting things be. It seemed to me that living by my feelings and impulses I was happier.

To flow, to drift, to live as nature. I felt that Rank was sad and wished he could be free, discard the doctor. I went to the limit and to the end of this experience, finished with it.

*

My brother Thorvald arrived from South America. I waited for him a long time at the pier. He did not come walking down the gangplank. Then an officer came to tell me that he was still aboard, detained by an error in his passport. He said that Thorvald had to stay aboard all night and then would be taken to Ellis Island for questioning. But that I could come aboard and visit him. In fact I could have dinner with him and stay the night if I wished. So I sent a message that I would like to come. And on the deck we faced each other after an absence of ten years. He had left us in Paris, my mother and Joaquin, saying he could not live there, that he preferred to try his luck in South America. He was twenty-one when he left. How different he was now! A man's voice, blue candid eyes behind dark glasses, poised, trim but no taller, the same height as my father. His face a mask too, like my father's. Brusque gestures. Somehow, I could not tell why, he seemed to me like a very young man trying to play the role of a man. It may have been my vision of him from childhood, my remembering him as an adolescent. Thorvald the tease, the only one of the three who had decided to become thoroughly American, to dress like the other boys in school, to be practical, businesslike, to toughen himself. When a child he played the violin well. Soon he cut his hair short, learned baseball. He was going to make money, be a success, etc. Surreptitiously he must have been proud of me, for he took me to games instead of taking his girl friends and pretended to his boy friends that I was his 'girl' of the moment. Later he became a Don Juan and collected handkerchiefs to show how many girls he had taken out or kissed. Thorvald was secretive as a boy, estranged from the rest of the family.

We both wept. And talked. Talked all through dinner.

'Do you remember, Anaïs, how you shamed me by fighting the boys who attacked me, they all piled up on me because I had long hair and I was a foreigner, and you came and beat them off with an umbrella?'

'Do you remember how you shamed me by saying it was because I was an artist that I could not learn mathematics?'

'You bossed me, and I only emancipated myself when I became a boy scout. But you look swell.'

We were having dinner in the empty dining room. A ghostly ship. Already being scrubbed, washed, vacuumed, all the doors open, the beds rolled up, the people scurrying to polish and tidy. Empty rooms, empty salons, an empty dining room, empty decks.

I was rediscovering my lost brother. My brother who cut himself off from all of us, by not writing letters. He will not show feeling. He talks only of money and practical matters. He is reticent. He is afraid to be misunderstood. He is afraid of gossip. He likes to act in amateur theatricals. The hard shell over him I interpret as a cover for his sensitiveness. But then I always interpret the hard shell thus and I have often been wrong.

The ghostly ship, not sailing, without any other passenger, was so much like the ship of our childhood. We took a journey through the past.

The boat became the room of the *Enfants Terribles* of Cocteau. The whole rest of the world was left out. It was a strange and unique boat, loaded with the past, with socks to mend, tennis shoes, quarrels, chewed pencils, homework, dishes washed in unison, service to my mother. We did not talk about today. Only about yesterday. Yesterday. Childhood. He remembers that we both went to work very young, that he wanted to go to college and could not, that we both worked.

So we are on the boat of our childhood which is not allowed to steam away, which makes other voyages overloaded with the past. A hiatus. A bridge. A suspense. An entr'acte.

My father had written to Thorvald that I had become interested in the queer science of psychoanalysis, and that I had become filled with strange ideas.

Thorvald expected not to be able to talk to me, but when we met we understood each other.

A trip to Morocco. A short but vivid one. I fell in love with Fez. Peace. Dignity. Humility. I have just left the balcony where I stood listening to the evening paper rising over the white city. A religious emotion roused by the Arabs' lives, by the simplicity of it, the fundamental beauty. Stepping into the labyrinth of their streets, streets like intestines, two yards wide into the abyss of their dark eyes, into peace. The rhythm affects

77

one first of all. The slowness. Many people on the streets. You touch elbows. They breathe into your face, but with a silence, a gravity, a dreaminess. Only the children cry and laugh and run. The Arabs are silent. The little square room open on the street in which they sit on the ground, on the mud, with their merchandise around them. They are weaving, they are sewing, baking bread, chiselling jewels, repairing knives, making guns for the Berbers in the mountains. They are dying wool in vast cauldrons, big cauldrons full of dye in which they dip their bunches of silk and wool. Their hands are emerald green, violet, Orient blue. They are making sienna earth pottery, weaving rugs, shaving, shampooing and writing legal documents right there, under your eyes. One Arab is asleep over his bag of saffron. Another is praying with his beads while selling herbs. Further, a big tintamarre, the street of copperwork. Little boys are beating copper trays with small hammers, beating a design into them, beating copper lamps, Aladdin's lamps. Little boys and old men do the work. They hold the tray between their legs. The younger men walk down the street in their burnouses, going I know not where, some so beautiful one thinks they are women. The women are veiled. They are going to the mosque, probably. At a certain hour all selling, all work ceases and they all go to the mosque. But first of all they wash their faces, their feet, their sore eyes, their leprous noses, their pock-marked skins at the fountain. They shed their sandals. Some of the old men and old women never leave the mosque. They squat there forever until death overtakes them. Women have their own entrance. They kiss the wall of the mosque as they pass. To make way for a donkey loaded with kindling wood, I step into a dark doorway. A choking stench overwhelms me. This stench is everywhere. It takes a day to get used to it. It makes you feel nauseated at first. It is the smell of excrement, saffron, leather being cured, sandalwood, olive oil being used for frying, nut oil on the bodies, incense, muskrat, so strong that at first you cannot swallow food. There is mud on the white burnous, on the Arab legs. Children's heads shaved, with one tuft of hair left. The women with faces uncovered and tattooed are the primitive Berbers from the mountains, wives of warriors, not civilized. I saw wives of one Arab, five of them sitting on a divan, like mountains of flesh, enormous, with several chins and several stomachs, and diamonds set in their foreheads.

The streets and houses are inextricably woven, intricately interwoven, by bridges from one house to another, passageways covered with lattice, creating shadows on the ground. They seem to be crossing within a house, you never know when you are out in a street or in a patio, or a passageway, as half of the houses are open on the street, you get lost immediately. Mosques run into a merchant's home, shops into mosques, now you are under a trellised roof covered with rose vines, now walking in utter darkness through a tunnel, behind a donkey raw and bleeding from being beaten, and now you are on a bridge built by the Portuguese. Now admire lacy trelliswork done by the Andalusians, and now look at the square next to the mosque where the poor are allowed to sleep on mats.

Everywhere the Arab squats and waits. Anywhere. An old Arab is teaching a young one a religious chant. Another is defecating carefully, conscientiously. Another is begging, showing all his open sores, standing near the baker baking bread in ovens built in the earth.

The atmosphere is so clear, so white and blue, you feel you can see the whole world as clearly as you see Fez. The birds do not chatter as they do in Paris, they chant, trill with operatic and tropical fervour. The poor are dressed in sackcloths, the semi-poor in sheets and bathtowels, the well-to-do women in silks and muslins. The Jews wear a black burnous. In the streets and in the houses of the poor the floor is of stamped earth. Houses are built of sienna-red earth, sometimes whitewashed. The olive oil is pressed out in the street also, under large wooden wheels.

I had letters of introduction. First I visited Si Boubekertazi. He sat in his patio, on pillows. A beautiful Negro woman, a concubine, brought a copper tray full of delicacies. And tea served in tiny cups without handles.

At the house of Driss Mokri Montasseb I was allowed to visit the harem. Seven wives of various ages, but all of them fat, sat around a low table eating candy and dates. We discussed nail polish. They wanted some of mine, which was pearly. They told me how they made up their eyes. They bought kohl dust at the market, filled their eyes with it. The eyes smart and cry, and so the black kohl marks the edges and gives that heavily accented effect.

Pasha El Glaoui de Marrakesh offered me a military escort to visit the city. He said it was absolutely necessary. He signalled to a soldier standing at his door, who never left me from then on except when I went to my hotel room to sleep.

De Sidi Hassan Benanai received me under the fine spun-gold colonnades. But he had just begun a forty-day fast and prayer, so he sat in silence, counting his beads, and tea was served in silence, and he continued to pray, occasionally smiling at me, and bowing his head, until I left.

From outside, the houses are uniformly plain, with high walls covered with flowers. One cannot tell when one is entering a luxurious abode. The door may be of beautiful ironwork. There may be two, or four, or six guards at the door. But inside, the walls are all mosaics, or painted, and the stucco worked like lace, the ceilings painted in gold. The pillows are of silk. The Negro women are simply dressed but always beautiful. One does not see the children or the wives.

The white burnous is called a *jelabba*.

Mystery and labyrinth. Complex streets. Anonymous walls. Secret luxury. Secrecy of these houses without windows on the streets. The windows and door open on the patio. The patio has a fountain and lovely plants. There is a labyrinth design in the arrangement of the gardens. Bushes are placed to form a puzzle so you might get lost. They love the feeling of being lost. It has been interpreted as a desire to reproduce the infinite.

Fez. One always, sooner or later, comes upon a city which is an image of one's inner cities. Fez is an image of my inner self. This may explain my fascination for it. Wearing a veil, full and inexhaustible, labyrinthian, so rich and variable I myself get lost. Passion for mystery, the unknown, and for the infinite, the uncharted.

With my guide I visited the Quartier Réservé. It lay within medieval walls, guarded at each gate by a French soldier. The houses were full of prostitutes. Only the poor Arabs go there because the others have enough wives to satisfy their need of variety. Dark, dramatic, tortuous streets. Bare cellars which have become cafés. Arabs slinking in and out. Negroes. Beggars. Arab music heard now and then. The walls, ceilings covered with shabby rugs and potteries. *Thé à la menthe* served, or beer. No wine drinking but much drug traffic. Bare, cellarlike rooms. Doors covered by muslin curtains, or beaded curtains. Front room is the bar or café where the men sit and the musicians play. Back room is for the prostitutes. The muslin curtain was parted and I found myself before Fatima, the queen of the prostitutes.

Fatima had a beautiful face, straight patrician nose, enormous black velvet eyes, tawny smooth skin, full but firm, and the usual Arabian attributes of several folds of stomach, several chins. She could only move with difficulty on her enormous legs. She was both queenly and magnificent, opulent, and voluptuous. She was dressed in a wedding costume, a pink chiffon dress embroidered with gold sequins laid over several layers of other chiffon petticoats. Heavy gold belt, bracelets, rings, a gold band across her forehead, enormous dangling gold earrings. Over her glistening black hair she wore a coloured silk turban placed on the back of her head exposing the black curls. She had four gold teeth, considered beautiful by Arab women. The coal-black rim around her eyes exaggerated their size, as in Egyptian paintings.

She sat among pillows in a room shaped like many bedrooms in Fez, long and narrow. At each end of the room she had a brass bed, a sign of luxury and success. They are not used as beds, they are only a symbol of wealth. In between the two brass beds lay all the pillows, rugs, and low divans. (In rich homes the floors are tiled but the brass beds are displayed there too.) Fatima not only collected brass beds but also cuckoo clocks from Switzerland. One wall was covered with them, each one telling a different time. The other walls were covered with flowered cretonne. The atmosphere was heavy with perfume, enclosed and voluptuous, the womb itself. A young girl came in with an atomizer and lifting up my skirt gently atomized my underclothes with rose water. She came once more to throw rose petals around my feet. Then she came carrying a tray with glass tea containers, sheathed in copper holders with handles. We sat cross-legged on vast pillows, Fatima in the centre. She never made a vulgar gesture.

Two blind, crippled musicians were invited in and played monotonously, but with such a beat that my excitement grew as if I had taken wine. Fatima began to prepare tea on the tray. Then she passed around a bottle of rose water and we perfumed our hands. Then she lit a sandalwood brazier and placed it at my feet. I was duly and thoroughly perfumed and the air grew heavier and richer. The Arab soldier lay back on the pillows. The handsome bodyguard in his white burnous, white turban and blue military costume conversed with Fatima, who could not speak French. He translated my compliments on her beauty. She asked him to translate a question about my nail polish. I promised to send her some. While we sat there dreaming between each phrase, there was a fight outside. A young Arab burst in, his face bleeding. 'Aii, Aii, Aiii,' he cried. Fatima sent her maid to see what could be done for the young Arab. She never lost her composure. The musicians played louder and faster so I would not notice the commotion and my pleasure would not be spoiled. I spent two hours with Fatima, as it is impolite to hurry here. It is a mortal insult to leave too soon or to seem hurried. It offends them deeply. Relationship does not depend so much on conversation or exchange as in the creation of a propitious, dreamy, meditative, contemplative atmosphere, a mood. Finally, when I was ready to leave, my escort made a parting speech.

It was after midnight. The city, so crowded during the day that I could hardly move in it, was slient and empty. The night watchman sleeps on the doorsteps. There are gates between different quarters. Six gates had to be opened for us with enormous keys. You are not allowed to circulate at night except by special permission and with a pass which the soldier showed to each watchman.

The frogs were croaking in the garden pools behind the walls, the crickets were announcing tomorrow's heat. The smell of roses won the battle of smells. A window was suddenly opened above me, an old woman stuck her head out and threw out a big rat she had just caught, with many curses. It fell at my feet.

Fez is a drug. It enmeshes you. The life of the senses, of poetry (even the poor Arabs who visit a prostitute will find a woman dressed in a wedding dress like a virgin), of illusion and dream. It made me passionate, just to sit there on pillows, with music, the birds, the fountains, the infinite beauty of the mosaic designs, the teakettle singing, the many copper trays shining, the twelve bottles of rose perfume and the sandal-wood smoking in the brazier, and the cuckoo clocks chiming in disunion, as they pleased.

The layers of the city of Fez are like the layers and secrecies of the inner life. One needs a guide.

I loved the racial nobility of the Arabs, the pride, the love of sweets instead of alcohol, the gentleness, the peace, the hospitality, the reserve, pride, love of turquoise and coral colours, dignity of bearing, their silences. I love the way the men embrace in the street, proudly and nobly. I love the expression in their eyes, brooding, or fiery, but deep.

The river under the bridge was foul. Men held hands while talking on the street. A dead Arab was carried on a stretcher, covered with narrow white bandages like an Egyptian mummy. Over his feet they had thrown a red rug. Silence and quietism. Contemplation and chanting. Music. Tea served on copper trays with a samovar kettle. Glasses have coloured tops. On another tray a big silver box with big rough pieces of rock sugar. Trays with perfume bottles. Trays with almond cakes covered by a silk handkerchief or copper painted lids.

I met the Arab women walking to their baths. They went there always in groups, and carrying a change of clothes in a basket over their heads. They walked veiled and laughing, showing only their eyes and the hennaed tips of their hands holding their veils. Their full white skirts and heavily embroidered belts made them heavy and full-looking, like the pillows they liked to sit on. It was heavy flesh moving in white robes, nourished on sweets and inertia, on passive watches behind grilled windows. This was one of their few moments of liberty, one of the few times they appeared in the street. They walked in groups with their servants, children, and bundles of fresh clothes, laughing and talking, and dragging their feet in embroidered mules.

I followed them. When they entered at the mosaic-covered building near the mosque, I entered with them. The first room was very large and square, all of stone, with stone benches, and rugs on the floor. Here the women laid down their bundles and began undressing. This was a long ceremony, for they wore so many skirts, and several blouses, and belts which looked like bandages, so much white muslin, linen, cotton to unroll, unfold, and fold again on the bench. Then there were bracelets to take off, earrings, anklets, and then the long black hair to unwind from the ribbons tressed into the hair. So much white cotton fallen on the floor, a field of white petals, leaves, lace, shed by the full-fleshed women, and as I looked at them I felt they could never be really naked, that all this they wore must cling to them forever, grow with their bodies. I was already undressed and waiting, standing, as I would not sit naked on the stone bench. They were waiting for the children to be undressed by the African maids, waiting for the maids to get undressed.

An old woman was waiting for us, a completely shrivelled old woman with only one eye. Her breasts were two long empty gourds hanging almost to the middle of her stomach. She wore a sackcloth around her waist. She gave me a little approving tap on the shoulder and smiled. She pointed to my finger nails and talked but I could not understand, and I smiled.

She opened the door to the steam room, another very large square room all of grey stone. But here there were no benches. All the women were sitting on the floor. The old woman filled pails of water from one of the fountains and occasionally poured one over their heads, after they had finished soaping themselves. The steam filled the room. The women sat on the floor, took their children between their knees and scrubbed them. Then the old woman threw a pail of water over them. This water flowed all around us, and it was dirty. We sat in rivulets of soapy, dirty water. The women did not hurry. They used the soap, then a piece of pumice stone, and then they began to use depilatories with great care and concentration. All of them were enormous. The flesh billowed, curved, folded in tremendous heavy waves. They seemed to be sitting on pillows of flesh of all colours, from the pale Northern Arab skin to the African. I was amazed that they could lift such heavy arms to comb their long hair. I had come to look at them, because the beauty of their faces was legendary, and proved not at all exaggerated. They had absolutely beautiful faces, enormous, jewelled eyes, straight noble noses with wide spaces between the eyes, full and voluptuous mouths, flawless skins, and always a royal bearing. The faces had a quality of statuary rather than painting, because the lines were so pure and clear. I sat in admiration of their faces, and then I noticed that they looked at me. They sat in groups, looking at me and smiling. They mimicked that I should wash my hair and face. I could not explain that I was hurrying through the ritual because I did not like sitting in the darkening waters. They offered me the pumice stone after using it thoroughly all over their ponderous bodies. I tried it but it scratched my face. The Arab women's skin was tougher. The women chatted in circles while washing themselves and their children. I could not bring myself to wash my face with the soap they all used for their feet and armpits. They laughed at what they must have thought was a European woman who did not know the rules of cleanliness.

They wanted me also to pull out superfluous eyebrows, hair under the arms, and to shave my pubic hair. I finally slipped away to the next room where pails of cooler water were thrown over me.

I wanted to see the Arab women clothed again, concealed in yards of white cotton. Such beautiful heads had risen out of these mountains of flesh, heads of incredible perfection, dazzling eyes heavily fringed, sensual features. Sometimes moss-green eyes in dark sienna skins, sometimes coal-black eyes in pale moonlit skins, and always the long heavy black hair, the undulating tresses. But these heads rose from formless masses of flesh, heaving like plants in the sea, swelling, swaying, falling, the breasts like sea anemones, floating, the stomachs of perpetually pregnant women, the legs like pillows, the backs like cushions, the hips with furrows like a mattress.

They were all watching me, with friendly nodding of their heads, commenting on my figure. By counting on their fingers they asked was I adolescent? I had no fat on me. I must be a girl. They came around me and we compared skin colours. They seemed amazed by my waist. They could enclose it in their two hands. They wanted to wash my hair. They soaped my face with tenderness. They touched me and talked with volubility. The old woman came with two pails and threw

them over me. I was ready to leave, but the Arab women trans-
mitted messages of all kinds with their eyes, smiles, talk. The
old woman led me to the third room, which was cooler, and
threw cold water over me, and then led me back to the dressing room.

On the way back, landing at Cádiz, I saw the same meagre
palm trees I had carefully observed when I was eleven years
old, on my way to America. I saw the cathedral I had described
minutely in my child-diary. I saw the city in which women did
not go out very much, the city, I said, where I would never live
because I liked independence.

When I landed in Cádiz I found the palm trees, the cathedral, but not the child I was. The last vestiges of my past were
lost in the ancient city of Fez, which was built so much like my
own life, with its tortuous streets, its silences, secrecies, its
labyrinths and its covered faces. In the city of Fez I became
aware that the little demon which had devoured me for twenty
years, the little demon of depression which I had fought for
twenty years, had ceased eating me. I was at peace, walking
through the streets of Fez, absorbed in a world outside of myself, a past which was not my past, by sickness one could
touch and name, leprosy and syphilis.

I walked with the Arabs, sang and prayed with them to a
god who ordained acceptance. With the Arabs I crouched in
stillness. Streets without issues, such as the streets of my
desires. Forget the issue and lie under the mud-coloured walls,
listen to the copper being beaten, watch the dyers dipping their
silks in orange buckets. Through the streets of my own
labyrinth, I walked in peace at last, with an acceptance of
myself, of my strength, of my weakness. The blunders I made
lay like garbage in the doorsteps and nourished the flies. The
places I did not reach were forgotten because the Arab on his
donkey, or on his mule, or on his naked feet, walked forever
between the walls of Fez. The failures were the inscriptions on
the walls half effaced, and those books eaten by the mice, the
childhood was rotting away in the museums, the crazy men
were tied in chains and I walked free because I let the ashes
fall, the old flesh die, I let death efface, I let the inscriptions
crumble, I let the cypresses watch the tombs. I did not fight

for completeness, against the fragments devoured by the past or today's detritus under my feet. What the river did not carry away nourished the flies. I could go with the Arabs to the cemetery with coloured rugs and bird cages for a little feast of talk, so little did death matter, or disease, or tomorrow. Night watchman sleeping on the stone steps, or mud, in soiled burnous, I too can sleep anywhere. There were in Fez, as in my life, streets which led nowhere, impasses which remained a mystery. There must also be walls. The tips of minarets can only rise as high because of the walls.

It was in Cádiz that I lay down in a hotel room and fell into a dolorous, obsessional reverie, a continuous secret melody of jealousy, fear, doubt, and it was in Cádiz that I stood up and broke the evil curse, as if by a magical act of will, I broke the net, the evil curse of obsession. I learned how to break it. It was symbolized by my going into the street. From that day on, suffering became intermittent, subject to interruptions, distractions, not a perpetual condition. I was able to distract myself. I could live for hours without the malady of doubt. There were silences in my head, periods of peace and enjoyment. I could abandon myself completely to the pleasure of multiple relationships, to the beauty of the day, to the joys of the day. It was as if the cancer in me had ceased gnawing me. The cancer of introspection.

It seemed to have happened suddenly, like a miracle, but it was the result of years of struggle, of analysis, of passionate living. Introspection is a devouring monster. You have to feed it with much material, much experience, many people, many places, many loves, many creations, and then it ceases feeding on you.

From that moment on, what I experienced were emotional dramas which passed like storms, and left peace behind them.

[MAY, 1936]

Louveciennes. But I am living outside. First there was Fez outside, the sun, the sea, and the city which was shaped like the brain, a city externally like the cities of the soul, and then there was Paris outside, and I on the streets. And then there was *House of Incest* arriving in huge bundles from the printer's, there were letters to be written, turquoise paste for the eyelids to be sent to Fatima. There is Henry passing through an air pocket, as he calls it. Lost, dispersed, disconnected.

Then there was coughing all night to the choking point, loss of weight. The little French doctor saying it was chronic bronchitis. After a few weeks, someone mentioned a German refugee doctor recently arrived from Germany. I went to a modest apartment, and as soon as I entered the room I felt in the presence of an unusual personality. He was Dr Max Jacobson (who later became so famous in New York). He had dark, piercing, brilliant eyes. He took one glance at me and said: '*Toi, ma fille*, you have whooping cough. I'll fix you up in a minute.' And with one injection he restored me to sleep and health.

He was so vital, so keen, so alert, mentally and physically. It was as if he were making diagnosis while flying. He never sat down, or listened. It was as if he did not want the patient's talk, list of details, to obstruct his intuition which worked swiftly, like an arrow. He was handsome, with curly dark hair, a healthy rosy face, and always ready to laugh. He did not listen, but *watched* with such intensity and then pounced upon the symptoms. From that momoment on I had a blind faith in him (which was never to change). We became friends. He came to dinner with his wife.

No money from New York, although much is owed me. There is shopping to do for the new apartment on the Quai de Passy, which I want to be modern. A psychic need for new surroundings. I found a clock made of sea shells, a white wool rug from Morocco.

Outside, red flags are waving. Newspaper headlines: 'C'EST DONC UNE RÉFORME? NON, SIRE. C'EST UNE RÉVOLUTION.'

Workmen in the streets. Strikes. Strikes ended. New strikes. Strikes in progress. A tumultuous, restless, brooding, dark season.

Fraenkel left for Spain, saying that Henry is faithless to ideas and to friendships. Henry quickly forgot him.

Charpentier praises *House of Incest*. 'Absolutely beautiful.' Stuart Gilbert says: 'It is music, it is a symphony. And I love the irony. A unique use of language. Like Scriabin.'

I cling to the world made by the artists because the other is full of horror, and I can see no remedy for it.

Roger Klein asked me to lunch. A friend of his, Émile Savitry, a photographer, talked all through lunch about his Peruvian friends. One was a dancer I once saw dancing in a small theatre on the Rue de la Gaité. She did strange and wild dances, like voodo dances, and ended with the dance of the woman without arms which I wrote about in *House of Incest*. It was a very small theatre. She left me with an impression of a nightmare. 'Her husband accompanied her. You did not notice him?' No, I had not noticed him. Henry had met the couple later at a party. He had described her dances, and his conversation with Helba's husband, Gonzalo. 'He and I were drunk, we got along very well, we agreed that what neither one of us wanted was to work.'

Roger added to the story: 'They are dreadfully poor, unbelievably poor. She has grown deaf and can no longer dance, and he drinks. But they are extraordinary people.'

He said this in a tone of awe. The contemplation of them sent him into a fit of silence, as if he could find no words with which to describe them. He aroused my curiosity. He promised we would meet.

He gave a small party in his new, small workman's apartment near the Villa Seurat. The night before I met them I had a dream of a pale, haggard woman who looked so ill, as if about to die.

And it was this very pale and haggard woman who appeared at Roger's small apartment in the crude light of naked bulbs. And right behind her, a very tall, very dark man, with long black hair. He had a round, full laughing face, and he carried a guitar. Their friend, the photographer, was not there. Gonzalo explained: 'We can never both go out at the same time because we have only one good pair of pants between us. Tonight was my turn.' The contrast between Helba, who had a bilious-coloured skin, faded eyes, faded hair, and the fiery, alive Gonzalo was striking. He played the guitar and sang. We danced. Gonzalo had a rich, husky voice. When he laughed the high cheekbone of the Indian made his eyes close and seem Oriental. He had heavy coal-black eyelashes. A tiger who dreams, a tiger without claws.

Jonathan Cape of London rejected *Winter of Artifice*.

The world gets Henry's joyousness, enjoyment of food, generous talks. I get the revelation of his anxieties, fears, guilts, and discontent. I have to fight his ghosts, which haunt him whenever he is not writing. While he seems to be enjoying cafés, parties, it is then he feels emptiest and saddest. I pull him back always into himself. We had an argument one day after I had disentangled him. He accused me of not letting him be sick, but of trying by artificial means to help him, against nature. I said: 'A sick animal is not nature. Analysis is not artificial because in the end it frees the animal from his sickness. You know very well you are not a man of nature, or you would not be sick occasionally with ghosts and fears.'

Henry fears starvation as much as I fear losing those I love.

When I fall into a reverie among people, my voice becomes remote. Henry noticed the contrast between my warm voice and my remote voice. Some people are natural only in public. Henry breathes, lives, talks better among a lot of people. For me the most sincere and natural moment is either alone or with the one I love.

[JUNE, 1936]

30 Quai de Passy.

A new background created without hope or joy, without feeling of permanence or with a conviction of its rightness. But inevitably beautiful. Modern, simple, joyous, light. Orange walls, white wool rugs from Morocco, chairs of a natural pale oak and cream leather, a huge table of pine wood with a sand-blasted surface which looks like pale sand on the beach. Luminousness, lack of formality. Created during the hot days of summer and the mood of estrangement from the Villa Seurat.

Villa Seurat seems like sand, a sponge, dissolution.

I gave a big housewarming party and invited a group of Tahitian singers and dancers. I hung orange paper lanterns, and filled the place with pots of tropical plants. The doors to the balcony were open. The Seine was flowing and shining below, while the Tahitians danced and sang (the men play music, the women dance). It was a truly tropical-night fiesta, with sensual dancing and voices, the lanterns, the exotic plants and the river sparkling below.

Stuart Gilbert was reminded of his life in the Gold Coast. A friend had told me about a remarkable poet-astrologer, Conrad Moricand, who had known and written about Picasso, Louis Jouvet, Max Jacob, Blaise Cendrars. I had invited him and he came, a pale, aristocratic figure. He told me: 'When I heard your voice over the telephone I thought it was a voice from another planet.'

Gonzalo towered above everyone, *le tigre qui rêve*, the Inca with his coal-black eyes, his black hair wild. A shock at his dark intensity, through which a radiant, childlike smile flashed now and then. Mystic, dreamer, full of nobility and depth, a mysterious quality. And with all that, earthy. He whispered while we danced: 'You are so strong, so strong and so fragile. What an influence you have on me. I fear you. Your voice, it is so strange. You're all sensitiveness, you're the flower of everything, you're stylization, the perfume and essence of all things.'

His voice was low and husky. He spoke in Spanish. In Spanish I hear things with my body, my senses, my blood, not with my mind. It reaches me through subterranean channels of atavistic memories. It touches a different Anaïs, one I scarcely know.

'Anaïs,' he continued, 'you have bruised your head against the world's reality, you don't see the city, houses, men, as such, you see *beyond*. Anaïs, I have seen thousands of women but never one like you.'

His eyes like the night, a night without moon. I fear him as much as he fears me, because I fear the dream.

The Seine glitters outside as we step on the balcony to cool. Couples come to kiss in the darkness of the balcony. Dr René Allendy fascinated by the Tahitian girls, De Maigret dancing, Henry Leigh Hunt scandalized, because this is becoming a Bohemian party, and yet he cannot walk away. 'Aloha, Aloha Tahiti'; soft and sensual faces; sensual ambiance, one of those evenings when everyone comes out of his shell, expands, lives fully.

The Spanish Civil War is in the air. It is as if Gonzalo had come in answer to my question: 'What does it mean, what can I do, as an artist?' Perhaps he can answer, for he knows what it means, and what to do.

Gonzalo went to sleep with *House of Incest* under his pillow, reading it over and over 'like a drug'.

I went to Fez without the diary. I wanted to lie in a hotel bed, in a strange place without the diary, to break the flow of self-examination, of the diary as mirror, as assurance, diary in place of talk. I wanted nothing to ruminate over, nothing to chew over. Life passed in Fez as I passed, leaving no trace or shreds. The sun was on the water of the Seine. I breathe and love without need to say: 'I am breathing, I am loving.' When I was caught in the dark cellars of the cathedral as a child I was afraid of being shut in within the walls of my own terrors. Later I was bound and bandaged by my traumas like a mummy, by a twenty-year calvary of doubts and fears. A long circle of struggle with a crippled self. And now, I am free.

Gonzalo took me to a big party at Alejo Carpentier's, the Cuban novelist. His vast studio also overlooks the Seine. The Tahitians are dancing and singing. Helba is sitting on one of the couches looking at an art book, withdrawn. That she is deaf is not the reason, for there are things she does hear. Gonzalo is taller than anyone, his golden-brown arms are bare, and he is still talking in my ear: 'Anaïs, what a force you are, spiritual and vital, though you are all wrapped in myths and legends, you are like a whip on me. When I first saw you I felt a shock, you aroused my pride, for the first time I am shedding the fumes of alcohol; I want to *be*, Anaïs.'

He talks about Peru, his hacienda, his Scottish father who married an Indian woman, the Inca culture, legends, the great distances between haciendas, the crushing immensity of nature, his hunting, the Jesuits who brought him up, the smell of his father's cigar boxes, and the smell of the furniture made of cedarwood. Days spent on horseback riding along narrow paths, beside huge gorges and waterfalls which put the Incas to sleep and often caused their death. Chewing coca, necessary at that altitude, his Inca nurse, and his first love, the statue of a fourteenth-century Madonna, and the day he swore to find a face which resembled it, and now it was my face.

He talks like a chanting Indian, poetry, myth, tales.

'With cruelty, with cruelty, you can whip me into action, we are so old we Incas, we cannot reach for the food. Did you know about the seven mystical circles? Seven circles had to be broken through to reach the core.'

The curled black hair has a few strands of white in it. His

eyes are more brilliant than those of the Arabs, the brow high. He has grandeur, nobility.

He has pride and intransigence. When he is thirsty he places a glass of water in front of him and does not drink it. (The Jesuit's theory of self-chastisement?)

He talks disconnectedly and feverishly, as June did.

He says he is too old to live in an ordinary way, too old, too subtle, to reach directly for things.

By his talk he leads me back into the medieval life of Peru, and at the same time he gives me Karl Marx to read, and explains the meaning of the strikes.

He tells me that he came merely to rescue me from what was going to happen. The whole world was going to erupt. There would be a revolution in France.

He wanted to see Louveciennes because I talked about it. So we took the train and I showed it to him. Louveciennes dying, the wood rotting, the rain falling, the ghosts creaking, the odour of ancient houses, the threadbare velvet cover. We visited the garden, all tangled and filled with weeds. We walked along the river and sat at the workmen's café.

Here he talked about the revolution again. He accused me of living only in the world of art and artists, of not knowing the political life. 'When the changes come I will be able to rescue you.'

Now we are in Notre-Dame. He seems to live in several worlds, one the Catholic, another the Inca world of his childhood, pagan, violent, and a third, the Marxist world of today.

The organ is playing. Purple light falls from the stained-glass windows.

Into the past, and then into the future.

The world of politics, until now, had seemed one of corruption and ugliness. Nothing for me to do there. Of what use could I be? Gonzalo talks to the workmen. After visiting Notre-Dame, we went to Rue de la Gaité and I bought a ten-dollar tailored suit in grey, I took the polish off my nails and I went with him to a political meeting where Pablo Neruda was speaking. Neruda was fat and very pale, and he recited poetry in a rather colourless voice, but the speeches afterwards, in Spanish, were vehement and I did not know what they were about. With the workmen, Gonzalo is familiar, cheerful, fraternal. They love him although they do not understand his bad French. He drinks with them. They trust him. His big hands are rough, his body is rough and he is dressed as they are. He is so much taller than they are, and as black as a Negro.

Letter to my mother:

I was in Notre-Dame yesterday afternoon and I heard Vespers, and I wept and found my old soul again, I don't know where it was. I had found it once at the Hospital, remember? I found it again yesterday. I stood there in the Church and cried and today I am happy, it is all so good, the house is sweet, the cat is funny, and I have a bicycle and will go to the country soon, but there is no sun at all, no heat, and I was not able to rent Louveciennes because of that. I will pay your rent tomorrow, and let Joaquin read this too, it is for him, it is what they call the modern style in writing, with all the phrases running close together, I am doing it to make you laugh, because you like surrealism so much. I hope Alida liked my book, you will like it too someday, I don't know when, when you realize *la vida es sueño*, and that dreams are necessary to life; and you know not all our dreams are holy, are they, you had some which were not so holy, our dreams are not holy but that does not hurt or change the fundamental soul, maybe some day you will believe so firmly in my fundamental soul you won't mind my fantasies, you won't frown, you will just listen and smile as I imagine you smiling and listening when you are far away, I never imagine you cross or displeased with me, or disillusioned, when you are far everything is sweet and as it was before and always when I was wholly devoted to you as you were to your children, and this devotion has remained even though my life split up, only you did not believe it as much and you drove me away a bit, scolding me for being different than I was as a girl, but fundamentally, little mother, nothing has changed, if one is good, nothing ever really changes, I love you as much.

Henry states in seventy-eight pages of his book the most tragic of all truths: 'Life does not interest me, what interests me is what I am doing now (this book) which is parallel to it, of it, and yet beyond it.'

The river of Henry's life is anonymous, amorphous, and whoever wanted to make it personal or intimate drowned in it. He denies the life of feeling which he corrodes by angers, contrariness, denials and role-playing, by fragmentation, dispersion.

Henry's definition of human is the one who drinks, forgets, is irresponsible, unfaithful, fallible. Mine is the one who is aware of the feelings of other human beings.

When I left the Villa Seurat I went to visit Gonzalo's home, which I had never seen. He met me at the door of an old apartment house, and we walked down some dark staircase which seemed to be leading to a cellar. There had been a fire once, the walls were charred, and I felt them crumbling under my fingers as I leaned against them because it was so dark. The staircase opened into a studio with a big window so dirty that one could not see out. The light was diffuse as if coming through frosted glass. I could not see well at first. And then I saw Helba lying on the couch, covered with old blankets and coats. Her black uncombed hair fell around her face. She smiled with her lips but not with her eyes. On the chair next to her lay many bottles of medicines, boxes of pills. She had two expressions, which followed each other almost without transition: One was dolorous, pleading, like that of a beggar. Pleading for pity. In pain perhaps. Almost a grimace of agony. But it was followed by, or almost alternated with, a shrewd, foxy, uncanny suspicion and mockery. I responded to the plea for pity. I sat on the edge of her bed, there was no other place to sit on, and took her hand. I told her how I had seen her dance once, years ago. Behind her I could see the greasy walls of the studio, shining with dampness.

Gonzalo had come back with wood and was lighting a fire in the fireplace. After a while he placed a deep iron pot over the fire and started to boil potatoes.

It was growing darker. Then Gonzalo began to place on dishes little pieces of fat, which he had melted beforehand, and planted with a wick, and this was their candlelight. Later a young girl came in, who resembled Helba, and Gonzalo introduced her as Elsa, Helba's niece. She was pale and wore a handkerchief tied around her neck. She was suffering from goitre and was soon to be operated on for it.

Then Gonzalo led me into another dark passage to a darker room, a real cellar room with two small windows which might have appeared in any of Dostoevsky's darkest poverty stories.

97

I had Dostoevsky in my mind, the mood of his life, of Siberia. And it startled me when Gonzalo as if he had known what I was thinking: 'I want to introduce you to Ivan. He is just out of jail for stealing a set of Dostoevsky's works. The French judge was sympathetic. He had good taste in literature. He said: "If you had stolen a bad writer's books I would have given you sixty days. Now I will give you only a week." And the day he left jail he received from the judge a set of Dostoevsky wrapped in brown paper.'

We were standing in front of an opaque glass door, and Gonzalo was knocking gently. But we had to wait. 'He is always afraid to open the door. He has to make sure it is me. He was so often in jail for revolutionary activity. Finally it unbalanced his reason, that and starvation. In the madhouse he met his wife. They are making a new start together.'

The door opened. Ivan was standing before us, staring at me. He was unshaved, emaciated. He looked as if he no longer understood what was happening around him. His eyes had no life in them. We entered. In a corner of the room, his wife was sewing by candlelight.

The walls were damp too, perspiring. There was hardly any furniture. The bed had no sheets. It was like a prison, and it was as if Ivan could no longer live in the daylight, but had to cower away in a dark, humid place. I shivered. Neither one of them smiled. Ivan was studying. He asked Gonzalo if he had any fat left, as the candles were about to peter out.

I could not talk. But when we returned to Helba there were visitors. There was Désirée, a voluptuous-looking Russian woman, with magnificent blonde hair piled on top of her head, magnificent ice-blue eyes, a sensual heavy voice. She was the mistress of Balthus, the painter. And there was Pita, a Cuban adolescent with the eyes and skin of a young girl, who was gay and talkative. He took my arm and made me dance all around the room, and Gonzalo looked darkly at us like Othello, Helba was laughing at Pita's antics, and then Désirée, taller than Pita, suddenly stopped his dancing and clowning and led him away.

When she left Gonzalo said: 'Those two are inseparable, incongruous as it may seem.'

*

How lost Gonzalo is, drinking, drifting, trapped in poverty As soon as Helba stopped dancing because of her deafness, they fell into poverty.

Now he said as he walked me home: 'You have aroused my pride. I did violence to my true self, I begged, and drank, and accomplished nothing. *I was dying*. Now I want to *live*. You give me a desire to live. *Quiero vivir*. All this for your face which is the face of ancient Spain. Spanish women move their heads in two ways, one the *manola* way, which is vulgar, which I don't like, and the other as you move it, with pride.'

Later he added: 'I have always pursued the unreal, the marvellous. I have a thirst for danger, heroism. I want to go to Spain and help the Republicans.'

Such contradictory wishes! He talks about Marx. All this ancient Inca poetry, mysticism, and now Marx. At first I did not understand.

But I did understand that Gonzalo's fervour was the opposite of Henry's: 'I never cared enough, it made life painful, just didn't care a hang,' but then he also talks of how June killed his faith, gave him such a terrible shock: 'When I see pain again I'm paralysed, fatalistic. I can't act.'

The world is shedding blood. With the taste of Catholic wafers, distilled bread on my lips, offered to me by Gonzalo, I lose the taste for ordinary bread which Henry handed me.

The death of the Republicans in Spain wounds me like the death of flesh I love. I am sensitive to every face I see in the street, every leaf, every cloud, every form of love, and is it the universal one waking in me? The poetry of Moricand, the girl face of Pita (to whom Gonzalo says roughly: 'I will lift your skirts up and spank you if you go on').

The voyage of dispossession began when I met June and Henry. I walk dispossessed as June did, without hat, underwear, stockings, walking poor to better feel humanity's closeness, to be nearer, less enveloped, less protected, dropping falsities, forms, continuity, desiring to be poor like the others, giving all I have, the dress I love, my jewellery, money because I am given so much, enriched, fecundated, possessed by life.

I have not been unaware of the political drama going on, but I have not taken any sides because politics to me, all of them, seemed rotten at the core and all based on economics, not humanitarianism. The suffering of the world seemed to me to be without remedy, except by what we could give individually. I did not trust any movement or system. But now the drama is going on, and Spain is bleeding tragically, and I feel tempted to engage my allegiance. But I must find a leader I trust and would die for, seeing only betrayal and ugliness so far, and no ideals, no heroism, no giving of the self. If I met a revolutionary who was a great man, a man, a human being, I could serve, fight, die. But meanwhile I help in a small radius, and I wait. The 'people' will destroy me anyway because of my birth ('shoot everybody with clean nails,' they shouted in Spain), because of my individual and personal giving, and so I don't know if I can be useful. It was not the Kings we valued, but the symbol of a leader. Now we seem to have no leaders, no rituals, no ceremonies, no direction, only a struggle for bread. We are very poor indeed.

Gonzalo, in his childhood and youth saw the Catholics lashing themselves until they reached ecstasy. He calls for the same violent ways to reach ecstasy. Sacrifice.

He says I am a Pagan and he a Christian. He says he likes red wine like Christ's blood and I like white wine which is Bacchus' drink.

Black Spring is out, dedicated to me.

[JULY, 1936]

We live on top of a crumbling world. The more it crumbles the more I feel like asserting the possibility of an individually perfect world, personal loves, personal relationships, creation. I may be trying to place an opium mat on top of a volcano. The world in chaos. Panic. Hysteria.

Gonzalo has not yet left for Spain.

My mother and Joaquin arrive home safe after my struggles to get them out of Majorca.

I met Denise Clairouin, the literary agent. Small stature, beautiful face, large blue eyes and classical features.

She asked me to give her as many volumes of the diary as I had copied.

I took to Henry my favourite books, Moricand's *Miroir Astrologique*, Blaise Cendrars's *L'Eubage* and *Transsibérien*.

I sent the remaining copies of *House of Incest* to Frances Steloff of the Gotham Book Mart in New York, in case we have to leave France. She wrote me a warm, welcoming letter.

Henry unable to work. All the artists quitting. I place all my diaries in the bank vault where this one will go too when I finish writing in it.

Gonzalo talked about his childhood.

'One of my first memories is of watching an anaconda devouring a cow. Another vivid memory is of walking through my father's hacienda and coming upon a condor preparing to eat a dead donkey. I looked on, petrified with horror. The condor is immense, with almost seven feet of wing span. He has a hairless head, with two white balls protruding from the back of his neck. He bows his head quickly, many times, as if he were saluting, and bowing, and chatting. Then he plants his enormous claws into the swollen belly of the animal. I grew to know about their organization. When an animal or a man died, they seemed able to telegraph this to all the condors in the neighbourhood, and arrange a meeting. They would appear in groups, and sit around the carcass in a circle, bowing their heads but not touching it until the King arrived, the biggest of them all. He made as much noise as an airplane. All the shaved heads bowed and scraped their claws. The *condor real* let them sit in an orderly fashion around the carcass like guests at a banquet. They would not dare to eat until the King had eaten. Men in the mountains are afraid of the condors, because they follow caravans, watching to see if any of them show illness, weakness, and might fall down and die. There was also a tree whose shade killed whoever fell asleep under it. It had gigantic leaves which gave shadow and coolness, and the Indians would lie under it for a siesta and die. There were carnivorous flowers, and a bread tree which gave both a breadlike substance and water. I lived in an atmosphere of utmost cruelty. Fifty or more Indian families lived on my father's hacienda, in great poverty. Of the products of their farming and cattle raising, they were allowed to keep just enough to eat, but all the rest went to the master. The servants were treated like members of the family, but if they were caught stealing, or guilty of any other minor offence, there was a formal court made up of members of the family, and a judgement and punishment was meted out right then and there. The offender would be tied to a post and whipped. When I was a child I saw many flagellations, and not what you might know about a flagellation, just blows which may leave a long scar, but a very expert kind of flagellation by which it is only the tip of the whip which lashes the flesh and tears it off, a whole piece at a time. With eleven or fourteen blows a man would die. His muscles, tendons all torn out. The Jesuits were the first humanists I knew who tried to abolish such punishments. They awakened my compassion. My father was Scottish and my mother an Inca. Perhaps this gave me compassion for the Indians, or perhaps my Marxism came from this. I don't know. The Jesuits, to gain the conversion of the Indians, had to let them flagellate in church. My own violence was tamed first by the Jesuits, then by America, then even more by France.'

Is the primitive in Gonzalo tamed? Is his spirit broken, his blood thinned by his life in America and his life in France? Seven years in America, seven years in France. Today, when he is angry or mutinous, he drinks.

Gonzalo said: 'When I first saw Europe, I was amazed at the smallness of it. After Peru, the giant country, after the size of our mountains and rivers, France seemed like a garden and a vegetable patch. Here we are sitting amongst the gardeners. But now a war or a revolution may swallow France. In Peru we had revolutions all the time. When my mother was pregnant with me, there was a revolt of the Indians, and her nurse had to disguise her in Indian clothes so that she could run away from the hacienda and hide. I was born in a humble Indian hut, to the sound of gunfire. The first word I learned was *guerrillero*.'

Gonzalo is torn apart. 'When I place you and Helba on one side of the balance, and the world on the other, you seem worth more to me and I cannot tear myself away. I must be a coward.'

'You are not a coward, Gonzalo. It may be you do not have absolute faith, an absolute belief in the side you're on, or else no wife or friend could stop you. I think you are not sure. Sometimes it takes more courage to stand by one's personal convictions than to follow a line of action one can share with many.'

Ambivalence. Duality. A part of Gonzalo cannot act.

'Perhaps I am an artist after all.' As if to prove this, he spent all afternoon drawing at the Académie Julien. He is slowly breaking with Montparnasse and drinking. He wants his strength back. In the café he talks on. 'I cannot sleep on a Western bed. I like to sleep on a mattress on the floor, or on a bench out of doors. Sleeping on the floor reminds me of the opium dens in Lima, where I lay on straw mats with the Chinese, behind curtains, in dim lights.'

After so many years of Bohemian life, he still has modesty and pride. His pride is intact. I have to find all kinds of circuitous ways of helping him and Helba, through other friends, complicated ways.

'Anaïs, you have the same passion I have for creating human beings. I created Helba. I would like to have known you when you were ten years old, before you went to America. At ten years of age I am sure you were more Spanish.'

Last night I had dinner at Henry's. We talked over his last pages. They are the most terrible descriptions ever written of dissolution and void. I talked about his Gargantuan appetite, his seeking of quantity, his drama and conflict against the loss of the self, of the core. Quantity and the impersonal are symbolical of the American drama of the spirit unable to master so much matter. I said the personal experience with June overshadowed the crowd experience, proved that everything else was worthless. Have I helped Henry to transform his material? Have I breathed meaning into his crowded streets? I have tried to put the core back inside of him. Even today. Now in this book, Henry's disease lies revealed, terrifying, his dispersions, his atrophied emotions, the loss of his self in the city ('shattered by the city,' he writes). But it is the crowd, the gigantism, the shiftless wandering which produces emptiness, the void, the split, the schizophrenia.

But what an interesting world, his world. How ever-changing, disquieting. I was walking through it, rediscovering its monstrosities, its perversities.

Henry says: 'You're not just a woman – you're more than a woman.' I laugh, because I am both. I can live sometimes in a larger, impersonal world, and at other times I find all that cold, and I return to the personal, intimate world. The big world, in which woman sometimes swims with a bit of human apprehension, human loneliness, a stellar world of magnitude and mutation by which woman is fascinated and wounded at the same time. Up there, I swim in planetary deserts where I find no trace of Henry at all, but a kind of fevered monster spilling out legends, myths, anathemas, or the plain story of a Brooklyn boy, Max the Jew, Claude the whore, a strange Henry who made love impersonally, all women and woman rolled into a universal orgasm, a schizophrenic maniac, absent altogether, removed from daily life, butting his Capricornian horns into the same turning windmills like Don Quixote, or a rag-picker sticking his forked cane into all the debris junk, and excrement of the world, philosophically, a man skating on icy drolleries, a man with long-sightedness who can see much better the sleeping princes she read about in the newspaper, lying asleep in some Chicago suburb, than anyone standing next to him.

Henry distended, expanded, multiform, boundless, transformable, transmutable, dissolving.

Gonzalo says: 'I am not a creator.' That is why he is in life, why he has acted in the world, risked everything, experienced everything. He throws his whole self into the present. Like a child, he has no memory of yesterday, no thought of tomorrow.

The artist, like Henry, is a gambler who saves his biggest throw for his writing.

In my own life there is a perpetual struggle to unite life and art. When I go out into the world, to the cafés, to parties, I am looking for deep experiences, friendships. When I find them, I pause. I stop to taste, to deepen by reflection, to give my whole attention to it. Henry goes on, more cafés, more people, more movement, no selection, no deepening, no evaluations.

The world of man in flames and blood. The world of man disintegrating in war. The world of woman alive as it is in this book, as it shall be forever, woman giving life, and man destroying life. Death and carnage all around me, death and hatred and division. I continue to make an individually human world for Joaquin, my mother, Helba and Gonzalo, Henry and other friends.

Gonzalo seeking drunkenness and the dream. Gonzalo with a bottle of red wine in his torn pocket, rushing into political meetings, and I weeping before the film of the sailors of Kronstadt. Heroism, the heroism to die, but never the heroism to live, to defend the personal world, the soul. My personal world unshattered, but it becomes harder to keep it alive. We are all going to lose each other as people lost each other in the Russian Revolution.

[AUGUST, 1936]

Gonzalo still has not gone to Spain. Out of a thirst for greatness, for the holocaust, he would die. Exaltation leading to dissolution.

Joys pierced with melancholy. I look tired, nervous, struggling to love in a world full of destruction. Where is my joy?

I am walking home with Gonzalo and he is talking about the need to sacrifice and to die for the world.

'I will die shot, Anaïs.'

Out of the world of art and creation into a world of death. I can only see it as death. What will his death give birth to? I cannot pull Gonzalo out of his world of action, of political action. He believes in it.

Art has been my only religion. I do not believe in politics.

Meanwhile, Henry's book grows immense, written with sperm and blood, and Henry grows each day more delicate, more frail.

The weather is grey. No summer. No sun. Tragedy and death. *Black Spring* is out and Henry is saying: 'I am getting old.'

At twelve o'clock I am bicycling through the Bois. Wondering whether war is coming here, and who will die, and who will be saved, and where will we go?

*

Conrad Moricand.* He is about forty years old, and looks like a white Indian. He has narrow Oriental eyes. He believes himself to be the last of the Mohicans, a faded, high-cheeked Indian transplanted from lost continents, whitened by long research in the Bibliothèque Nationale, where he studied esoteric writings. He has a slow walk like a somnambulist enmeshed in the past and unable to walk into the present. He is so loaded with memories, cast down by them. Out of his researches, his calculations, he extracts nothing but the poison of fatality. He sees only the madness of the world, the approach of a great world-engulfing catastrophe. For Moricand all life is a minor crystal phenomenon on the surface of a planet. As a result people appear to him without their density. He sees their phosphorescence. He speaks of the intensity or the feebleness of the light in them. He offers the world first of all an appearance of legendary elegance. His coat is handed to you with the care of a man who refuses to be weighed down by a speck of dust. This coat must be hung up with care, he asks, so that no wrinkles would form on it. His white collar is incredibly starchy, his cuffs dazzlingly white, his buff gloves have never been worn. His clothes show no trace of being lived in. Somnambulists make so few gestures, never knock against objects, never fall. The trance carries him through all obstacles with an economy of gestures and the dream interposes itself between him and all he wants to touch and feel. He himself passes invisible, untouched, unattainable, giving at no time any proof of reality: no stain, tear, sign of wear and death coming. It seems rather as if death has already passed, that he has died already to all the friction and usage of life, been pompously buried with all his possessions, dressed in his finest clothes, and is now walking through the city of Paris merely to warn us of the disruption of Europe.

He has the armature of the aristocrat, this strong armature which not only upholds his clothes, but which forbids him to complain, to beg, to loosen or slacken either physically or spiritually, that extraordinary armature which is the only redeeming characteristic of nobility, the very last of the erect and stylized attitudes vanishing out of this world. Now he lives

*See also Henry Miller, *A Devil in Paradise* (New York: New American Library, 1956). – Ed.

at the top of a hill overlooking Paris, near the white Sacré-Cœur. He lives under the slanting roof of a very small hotel room, where the ceiling touches the floor behind his bed. He gives to his room the order and barrenness of a monastic cell. He covers his books with cellophane, the blotter on his desk is white and spotless. On the walls hang horoscopes designed with geometric finesse. The planets in finely drawn lines of blue and red and black, traversing the 'houses'. The opposition between them outlined in red ink, the squares in black, the conjunctions in blue.

Moricand sits in his little room under the roof, hot in summer and cold in winter, and from there he watches over all our lives and makes predictions. All he needs is the hour, date, and place of birth. Then he vanishes for several days into his laboratory of the soul, and we only see him again when the horoscope is, as he says, properly infused. Does he really know when disease and madness will strike? Does he know when we are going to love, unite, separate? Moricand believes that he knows.

Now he sits reading Henry his horoscope. He talks at times like a child, at times like a homosexual, at times like a drug addict, at other times like a schizophrenic. But he is more than an astrologer, he is a poet. His horoscopes are poems. He has a natural access to invisible, subtle worlds. What he describes as the Neptunian world is all that I cannot find words for, states of consciousness, metamorphoses, intuitions, illusions.

A need for a stoical attitude. So I keep working, housekeeping, writing, copying, while everyone sits in cafés and suffers anxieties, fears, disintegration.

Everyone has quit working, loving, living.

Ideas are a separating element. Love is a communion with others. Mental worlds are isolators. Love makes one embrace all races, the whole world, all forms of creation. The artist really seeks a universal language, and artists from all parts of the world can understand each other.

When women rush up to Henry today and say: 'Who's your latest cunt?' Henry blushes and moves brusquely away from them.

Gonzalo wants to burn *Tropic of Cancer*.

'All that ugliness is in him, in his mind.'

'But ugliness has character, Gonzalo, it is like George Grosz caricatures, like Goya.'

Everyone is full of fissures, dualities, contradictions. Gonzalo's drawings of prostitutes are like Henry's descriptions, Helba herself is wallowing in ugliness. In all of us, flashes of understanding, flashes of lucidity, and blind spots. Gonzalo's blind spot is the idea that all art is an ivory tower. When it is art which made tolerable a condition of the world for which the artist is certainly not responsible.

'Gonzalo, if you want me to come out of my art world, then to me that means action. Your own conflict between your individual and your collective life is not solved. You are hesitating to act.'

'I'll tell you honestly, Anaïs, I don't know what to do. I have a feeling of responsibility towards you as an artist, towards your work. I hesitate to drag you out of your art world, your creative world, into chaos and the making of a new world. At times I feel I should serve you, that you are doing something important, and I should help you.'

'It seems to me that the real issue is of what use I can be in the making of a new world. I can see how you can be of use, you are strong, you are trained in Marxism, you can talk to workmen, they like you, listen to you, but what can I do?'

Gonzalo knows that once my faith is aroused, I act. I will not lie back and write books.

We are sitting in the café at Denfert-Rochereau. We are having coffee. We buy a newspaper. Blood. Massacres. Blood. Tortures. Cruelty. Fanaticism. People burned with gasoline. Stomachs ripped open in the shape of a cross. Nuns stripped naked. French surrealists have gone to Spain to fight. Gonzalo, at three in the afternoon, is sketching at Colarossis. I call for him. I watch him work, showing the grave side of his nature. A minute later he may be drunk and laughing at the Dôme.

Only you, my diary, know that it is here I show my fears, weaknesses, my complaints, my disillusions. I feel I cannot be weak outside because others depend on me. I rest my head here and weep. Henry asked me to help him with his work.

Gonzalo asks me to join political revolutions. I live in a period of dissolution and disintegration. Even art today is not considered a vocation, a profession, a religion, but a neurosis, a disease, an 'escape'. I titled this diary 'drifting'. I thought I too would dissolve. But my diary seems to keep me whole. I can only dissolve for a little while, but ultimately I become whole again.

'Henry's corruption,' says Gonzalo, 'is a *fleur de peau*.'

Mine is deeper. I am not shattered by a city, history, or outer events, but by the one I love. I now understand the anguish I feel in certain places where there is laxness, drunkenness, abandon, corruption. It is not my kind. I dissolve into relationships, empathy, sympathy, projections, identifications with others, but do not lose myself, do not descend into failure, masochism, defeat, death.

Henry is writing now in *Tropic of Capricorn* the very best descriptions of void, disintegration, corruption. He symbolizes and represents the disease of modern man. He is at one with the chaos of the world, of cities, of streets. His anonymity is collective, the lies of the self. I do not lose myself. His dispersion seems more dangerous to me than mine. When I pass from one life into another, from one life into many lives, it is an expanded life, but not dissolution, although I skirt dissolution every instant.

Henry admires the Chinese lack of sympathy.

Gonzalo sings softly at the café table: '*España, que te mueres. No has sabido que te quiero.*' (Spain, you are dying without knowing I cherished you.)

Roger Klein has been in Spain. He came back last night. We sat in his room and talked. Gonzalo had stolen a little construction lantern which gave off a dim yellow oil flame.

Roger talks about Spain and what he has to tell is so terrible that I went into his bathroom and broke into hysterical weeping.

Roger is not staying. He was bringing back a young Spanish girl he married, who was left alone by the war. He wanted to leave her in someone's care. She wanted to return to Spain with him.

The Chinese say the future is only the shadow of the past.

There is a shadow lying on my path, and it is the recurrence of the moment when I am asked to give up my life (first to my father, then my mother, then my brothers, then others, Henry's work, Rank's work, Spain).

And each time I enter fully into the giving, giving up, the selflessness, until I feel that something is being destroyed (me, as a woman, or the writer?). I don't know. Then I am forced to stop. I do feel I have something to accomplish, a destiny to fulfill, but, like Proust, I am not sure that what I am doing is important.

The two pulls are there. Selflessness, and work.

Gonzalo attacks the world I live in. Henry destroyed my bourgeois virtues, Gonzalo my art world.

Yet what has Gonzalo made of his life, while he preaches Marxism?

How is he living out his Marxism?

It is true he is fighting off his drinking, and keeping away from his alcoholic friends.

It hurts Gonzalo when I confront him with his life. He said: 'With cruelty you can make me create.'

But I do not wish to exert cruelty. And if this will be another duel with destruction, against destruction, as with Henry's world, then I cannot really bear it. I want unity, wholeness.

Gonzalo says: 'I want to make you class-conscious!'

And all my life I tried to erase class barriers, admitting only qualities of mind, or feeling, or courage, or talent.

'I only believe in poetry,' I said. 'I want to live beyond the temporal, outside of the organizations of the world.'

'But the mystique of Marx . . .'

'Marx is no mystic.'

'You have no religious mysticism.'

'Art is my religion.'

'We are talking Chinese.' We always say this, when arguments become meaningless.

'Yes, you talked Chinese, we talked Chinese, you and I talked Chinese.' He laughed. 'And everything is Chinese and meaningless.' We were sitting on a bench, and looking down at the shadows of the branches. I told him what the Chinese said about the future.

Gonzalo sneered at Cocteau's trip around the world because no one should be writing about Greece, Egypt, India, and China, while Spain is on fire.

When I meet Henry, the news of this trip is the only item he has read in the newspapers.

Gonzalo took me to visit the rag-pickers' village. They live just beyond one of the gates of Paris, close to the gypsies, on a vast expanse of bare earth in shacks made of tin, cardboard, newspapers. The gypsies live in their own colourful carts.

After the rag-pickers have searched the garbage cans and filled their hemp bags with odds and ends, they come here to sort it all out and arrange their wares for the flea market.

The paths are a yard wide, with fences on both sides made of black rotted wood from the railroad tracks. Shaky, lop-sided shacks, open to cold and wind. Men and women living in the mud, sleeping on piles of rags. Babies sleeping on potato sacks. All the discarded objects of the city lying about in piles, rags, broken dolls, broken pipes, bottles, objects without shape or colour, detritus, fragments of furniture, of clothes. The women are feeding their babies from withered breasts. Children fetch water from the fountain in leaky pails. When they come back the pails are nearly empty. Between the shacks are gypsy carts overflowing with big families.

Among them was a pretty red-and-black house, a toy-size house with a miniature garden, enclosed by a fence. In the garden grew giant sunflowers, and it was filled with pigeons, birds in cages, doves. This was the house of Django, the guitarist, whom Gonzalo knows well. He plays magnificently with hands crippled in a fire. Gonzalo had stayed with him, eaten and talked all night with the gypsies. We rang the bunch of cowbells but there was no answer. In the back of the house stood Django's gypsy cart. We found him there, playing. The cart was red outside, inside it had an orange ceiling and dark leather walls. They looked like the walls of an ancient frigate. Django's bed was hung at the back of the cart, like a ship's berth. The cart had small Arabian windows. Gonzalo could not stand up so he sat on the floor. It was so dark I could not see Django's face. One oil lamp burnt in the corner, covered by a red lampshade with gold tassels.

One of the gypsies had covered his shack with sea shells. Another had a gypsy cart, green on the outside, and inside also lined with Cordova leather. The dark, blood-red leather, worn, its carved surface smoothed by the touch of hands, was soft and sensuous. The curtains had gold tassels. The gypsy had a dark beard and fierce eyes, but soft white hands, well manicured. He never worked. The gypsy women do all the work, bartering, cheating, stealing. The men play the guitar or sit in cafés. Gonzalo and I wanted to buy a gypsy cart. We talked it over with the gypsy and his soft hands were still. 'I know a cart you might have bought, but it is now occupied by a *mutilé de guerre* who has no arms and no legs. And I would not put him out for anyone, not even for you, Gonzalo.'

We went to visit the man without arms or legs. He had difficulty manoeuvring the ladder which led into the cart. Gonzalo offered a solution. We went to the empty lot beyond, the one which skirted the railroad tracks. Gonzalo found two planks and carried them back. He placed them over the ladder steps, secured them to the ground. Now the war cripple could easily and smoothly slide down to the ground. This cart had red curtains. No beds. Just mattresses which were rolled up during the day. It was laundry day, and the multiple skirts and petticoats of the women hung on a wire. They danced in the wind, red, yellow, white, orange, purple and blue. One gypsy was brushing her long black hair. She gave Gonzalo an inviting glance, but he murmured: 'If I responded I would soon get a knife in my back.'

The merchandise collected by the rag-pickers was strewn on the ground, every conceivable object from pins to automobile tyres, bird cages, broken records, and most touching of all, mismated and unmated objects, a single glove, a single earring, a cup without saucer, a basket without a handle, eyeglasses with only one glass, etc. Cigarette butts and holy medals, feathers and torn lace. Clocks without hands, shoes without laces, half a toy, half a book, family photograph albums (an orphan could find ancestors there), pincushions, buttons, shoelaces, dolls without heads.

'I could write here,' I said.

Gonzalo said: 'I could draw here.'

We stayed until dark. Watching the oil lamps being lit, the food being cooked on open fires, watching some of the carts preparing to travel, watching the fortunetellers counting their earnings, watching the children playing with fragments of toys, in fragments of clothes. One child wore a coat which was completely ripped in the back, so he was only protected in the front.

'In Peru,' said Gonzalo, 'they cure madness by placing the madman next to a flowing river. The water flows, he throws stones into it, his feelings begin to flow again, and he is cured.'

So I look at the Seine flowing, but the madness continues. I hear the cries of the people: '*De La Rocque au poteau!*' (To the guillotine!)

From the train window, on my way to an innocuous dinner, I had a vision of trees uprooted, with their heads in the ground, and roots gesticulating in space. A vision of war?

Hilaire Hiler wrote me from New York: '*House of Incest* is very sad, at the same time comforting, in the way some drug stimulates and calms at the same time ...'

I say to people that I am not writing, but I keep on writing in the diary, subterraneously, secretly, a writing which is not writing but breathing.

'*De La Rocque au poteau!*' they shout in the streets.

Denise Clairouin. Her classic face does not seem to belong to her small stature. It gives her the appearance of a Greek head placed upon the body of a pudgy child. She has an expression of innocence and lucidity, a straightforwardness unusual in a French-woman. She is Breton. There is something mystical, or fanatical, about her, though no fire shows in her clear features, in her large blue eyes.

She lives near the Étoile, in a beautiful, old-fashioned but comfortable apartment. High ceilings, fireplaces, bric-à-brac, silver and crystal, gold and tapestries, fine wood, and many books. Her mother sits like a queen in a high-backed armchair.

She wants all the diaries to be published. 'A Proustian work without disguises, a relief from literature, from the boredom of other manuscripts,' she says.

[Denise Clairouin worked for the Resistance during the war. She was caught by the Gestapo and tortured to death. In her honour a fellowship for writers was set up bearing her name. – A. N.]

Moricand says: 'You are in a state of grace. The fairy tale is possible for you. You make it happen.'

He understands me. He understands the larger wave lengths of my life, what he calls '*les ondes*', like some divine radio, with special antennae.

At night, in front of my window, workmen are laying the foundations for the 1937 Exposition, a mosque from Timbuktu, Algerian palaces, Indo-Chinese pagodas, a Moroccan desert fortress, and around the piles will be moored Chinese junks, Malayan proas, sampans.

Quai de Passy is on the edge of the aristocratic quarter, near a bridge which carries me to the Left Bank, to Montparnasse where Gonzalo lives, to Denfert-Rochereau where Henry lives. The subway carries us back and forth across the river, the poor, the rich, at all hours of the day. Gonzalo stands at night on that bridge after he has left me and watches my window and waits for the light to go out.

The wide window of the living room is open before me, leading to the balcony. I see the lights on the Seine, the illuminated Tour Eiffel, the red moon, and across the river the communists are holding a meeting to hear La Pasionaria, the woman communist. Gonzalo is there. In a little while he will come and get me. He wants me to see, to hear. My heart tightens. I heard them singing an hour ago, as they marched in. Taxicabs passed by, filled with people singing, waving red flags.

I try to understand. I went to the communist meeting. I heard La Pasionaria. I heard André Malraux. I was sitting in the front row. She with her ardent face and powerful voice, he with a nervous intensity, another kind of fire, his hair fell over his eyes, he was perspiring, the crowd like one voice, one heart, singing, shouting, stamping, applauding. I wanted to respond, and I couldn't. It was fierce and angry.

I was reading in the *Cabala* about crystal-gazing. All forms of trances, it did not matter which one, produced the same magical effect of unity. The whole being drawn together, fused entranced, and capable then of ecstasy. Ecstasy is a moment of exaltation, of wholeness.

I am like the crystal in which people find their mystic unity. Because of my obsession with essentials, my disregard of details, trivialities, interferences, contingencies, appearances, façades, disguises, gazing into me is like crystal-gazing. They see their fate, their potential self, secrets, their secret self.

I do not yield to small talk. I am silent. I skip so much. I turn away. I am always absorbed by the core of people, looking at it, interested only when *it* speaks. The miracle I await, the miracle of clarity, always happens.

Was the meeting to help Republican Spain another kind of unity? A faith in revolution, in change? A willingness to kill for it, to annihilate those who do not believe? The words which were uttered, strangely, were meaningless. Clichés. Banalities. But the feeling . . .

A day and a night. Opened my eyes with the usual desire to sing and dance without ever knowing why, but there is already the dancing of light from the river on my ceiling, walls and bed. It is the refracted sunlight on the Seine.

After the meeting I walked with Gonzalo until dawn, talking, dreaming, sitting by the river, eating at the market, watching the rag-pickers searching garbage cans and the hoboes still asleep on the doorsteps and benches, clutching empty wine bottles.

Janine comes softly with the breakfast. With the newspaper and with the mail. Letters from my 'children': 'I am soon to give a concert. I am writing my book. I have written a story. I am writing about my childhood. I am lonely. I have no friends. Do not abandon me. I am getting married, thanks to you. I did not break down this time. I wish I could be in your little room at the hotel talking to you. You have freed me. I feel stronger.'

Towards them I feel an impersonal love. I have no personal tie with them. I love the moment of the miracle, the instant Sasha sobbed on Fifth Avenue at the revelation of the meaning of his life; Dorrey weeping at her deliverance from the nightmare; Emily falling on her knees because she could believe again; Will's first pages of writing and the first flash of joy and life in his eyes.

To keep Moricand alive, all of us go about selling horoscopes. I talked about him to Denise Clairouin.

I have dust on my feet when I arrive at Villa Seurat. Henry has been writing feverishly and he says he is afraid of going mad.

He went so far and wide, into a new way of using language, into whirlings, turning worlds, to give the flavour of Broadway, that he felt lost. He was dazed and lonely.

'Women,' he said, 'have not liked my books as you thought they would. You were wrong in that.'

It is true. Women do not like to be de-poetized, naturalized, treated unromantically, as purely sexual objects. I thought that they would, that they were tired of idealization. I thought I was, and yet Gonzalo's troubadour romanticism out of the Middle Ages revived me after the blight of Henry's absence of romanticism.

La Voie Lactée.

Constellation of ideas.

Conflict with diary-writing. While I write in the diary I cannot write a book. I try to flow in a dual manner, to keep recording and to invent at the same time, to transform. The two activities are antithetical. If I were a real diarist, like Pepys or Amiel, I would be satisfied to record, but I am not, I want to fill in, transform, project, expand, deepen, I want this ultimate flowering that comes of creation. As I read the diary I was aware of all I have left unsaid which can only be said with creative work, by lingering, expanding, developing.

Henry said that I did not permit the geological change to take place, the transformation achieved by time which turns carbon into a diamond.

'No, that is not true, I think. I like the untransformed

material, I like the thing before it is transformed. I am afraid of the transformations.'

'But why?' asked Henry.

'Because it is a going away from the truth. Yet I know it is attaining reality because I recognize there is a greater truth today in your fantastic description of Broadway than in my instantaneous sketches I made in New York while staying there. When I was a child I wanted to see how the plants grew. I used to stir the earth away from the growing pod, to see the process.

'Fear of transformation has something to do with my fear of loss, change and alteration. I write to combat this fear. For example, Henry, I used to dread your cruelty. I took meticulous care to record your moments of kindness, understanding, like something which could be used later to conjure away the evil, the fears. It is like this. A marvellous thing would happen to me and it would seem like the lighted match to a primitive – a miracle. Like the primitive, I did not know it would be repeated, that other matches existed, that the power to produce a little flame lay within me. In this I have made no progress. This fear I confessed to Rank. It is like the fear of change in a face. Now it looks beautiful, human, near, and now contorted, evil, and cruel. But in the diary I can keep track of the two faces of reality. I have a record, I can balance one vision against another. As I write, I can dissipate the fear of alteration and loss. My instantaneous vision of the world I believe in. It is my reality. It is born of intuition, of feeling. The transformation required of creation terrifies me. Change, to me, represents tragedy, loss, insanity.'

Henry was surprised by this. 'This is your malady.'

'Well, if it is my malady, Henry, I should express it to the utmost through the diary, make something of the diary, just as Proust made his work out of his disease, his malady for remembering, resuscitating the past, his obsession with recapturing it alive. I should give myself wholly to the diary, make it fuller, say more, live out my neurosis and see where it will carry me. Whereas until now I fought it, I tried to cure it, you tried to cure it, Rank tried to cure it.'

'The problem,' said Henry, 'is one of arithmetic. You will never catch up with the days. And the record of the days will not satisfy you. A day is not everything. The record of a day goes on and on, and sometimes something bigger is left out, postponed, lost. It will be like a big web which will strangle you. Art requires indifference. You're yielding to your primitive cult of life, to your adoration of it. And each day of record arrests the flow. The flow would gather in mystery, cause an explosion, a transmutation. You're also concerned with completeness. You say, for instance, you're worried about a certain portrait. It isn't complete, like one of Proust's characters. There you talk as an artist.'

'I do feel that the portraits in the diary are only done at the moment a person is important to me. The person rises and sinks, appears and vanishes only in relation to the range of my vision, in relation to what I see of him. It's like a statue without arm or head, unearthed, and having to be deciphered, divined. Why am I not satisfied with a day? Perhaps only because I did not make it full enough, so that it would contain the infinite? A day of the diary should be complete like a book, and all the spaces I skip, all the arms missing, all the layers not illumined because I did not touch them with my own warm fingers, love or caress them, should be there in the dark as the mystery of life itself. What is this bigger thing I captured in my book on my father that was not in the diary? A day so full. Is it that the record prevents the supreme flights? Every day of record counts against this bigger thing or can it be made so big and beautiful that it can become the whole thing – the infinite? Is the flowering possible only with forgetting, with time, with the rotting and the dust and the falsities? If I wrote in the diary for fear of loss, then, as Nietzsche said, it was for the same reason that the artist created. For the artist without his vision of life – of the tragic and the terrible – would go mad and only art can save him.'

An hour later I was walking along the Seine looking at houseboats.

Ever since my visit to the people who bought the house which once belonged to Guy de Maupassant, I have longed for a houseboat.

This was his house in Étretat, near enough to the sea so that one day, during a wild storm, the sea came as far as the house and dumped on the garden a fishing boat which remained there. This was the house so often described in his stories, letters. An alley of poplars led up to the entrance. It was a double alley, so that on each side of it there was an alley covered by the arch of branches. It was said that Maupassant could observe his visitors from there and decide whether or not he wanted to see them. Many women must have walked along that alley. Many carriages driven up to the door. We had dinner in a dining room paved with tile. I saw the room he used as an opium den. I saw the platform covered with a straw mat, and the opium table and utensils. But what I remembered best was the derelict sailboat, deep and wide, planted in the back of the garden. It was used as a garden tool house. I asked my hosts if I could not spend the night in it. They laughed at me, and said I would be more comfortable in the guest room. The boat had a strange effect on me. It reproduced exactly my most recurrent dream of a boat stuck in the ground, unable to sail for lack of water. Here it was, stranded and static, in an old garden. Never to sail again. Rotting in the earth, like a flower pot. With moss growing over it instead of barnacles, with the smell of earth on it instead of sea.

The sight of it gave me a dream that night. I dreamed that I was spending the night in the fishing boat at the bottom of the garden. I feel asleep, and it began to sail down a river. I had no control over its journey. People called to me from the shore, distressed, or ironic, or critical, or mocking, or pleading. Where was I going? How long would I be? Why didn't I return? Why did I not moor with them for a while? The flow, once begun, was uncontrollable. Waving at those on the shore, husband, friends, I myself felt happy to be in motion. The journey took twenty years. For twenty years I sailed continuously in my dream.

When I returned from this weekend at Étretat, I wrote a short story. The journey ended in a circle. I returned to my point of departure. My friends were unchanged.

As I stood leaning over the parapet, the policeman on duty watched me. Did he think I was going to commit suicide? Did I look like someone who wanted to commit suicide? He watched me going down the stairs to talk to the owner of

Nenette, a lovely bright-red houseboat, the deck flaunting not a flag but a string of coloured laundry fluttering, flower pots being watered. On the little windows there were beaded curtains. They had a nostalgia for their little suburban cottage, their garden. And I for the water. *Nenette* was not for rent or for sale. It was still young enough to carry coal, to work for its living. The owner advised me to go and visit the discarded barges, the unseaworthy houseboats being repaired for resale.

Walking along the quays, near the Tuileries, I gathered information and advice.

My father came, egotistically, egocentrifugally, egocentripetally delightful and clear and clean as a Frigidaire and tender and lying, pathological and incurable mythomane.

Thursday, Henry and I visited Moricand. He has no interest in the present. He monologued on Max Jacob and Blaise Cendrars, his two idols. He has too much to remember, and his only pleasure was to re-create it. There are some whose past life helps to illumine the present, to flow into the present enriched, loaded with treasures but still avid for more. There are those, like Moricand, who give the impression of having closed the locks so that the water is held static in one place and no longer flows into one continuous river. Did he see Henry? Did he see me? We were spectators. His room has a meticulous order, a geometric precision and form, in spite of poverty, of illness, of anguish. No chaos. No explosions. 'Explosions of Neptune,' said Moricand, 'are all internal, no one is aware of them.'

For the writer, it seems as if the past never died. Gonzalo is jealous of my past friendships. To console him, I talk about my dead love for my father. I say: 'Your jealousy is necrophilic, past loves are dead loves.'

'But you're constantly visiting tombs, with flowers. What a love you have for the dead!'

I said playfully: 'Today I have not been to the cemetery.'

Moments when the universe seems profoundly harmonious, when Henry is writing magnificently, when Gonzalo is effective politically, when Moricand has been commissioned a horoscope and is therefore sure to eat.

Henry's pages on Blackie and their climax, an insanity produced by life, as I wrote about him early, and now he says himself: 'My surrealism is born of life. That is true surrealism.'

Juxtaposition of the poetic and the ugly. Henry is to me the only authentic surrealist. The others are the theoreticians. He is a surrealist in life, in his work, in his character. What I enjoy in him is his surrealism.

When I visited him yesterday he had been writing intensely and he said: 'I've been working madly and I don't know whether it is good or not. Tell me. Am I utterly crazy or utterly right?' I read the pages and told him he was utterly right.

After I wrote here the other day on art versus diary, I felt the danger of putting art into the diary. It might kill its greatest quality, its naturalness. I must split up and do something apart – it is a need. No consciousness of perfection must enter the diary. Good-bye completeness. My plan of writing up a Day and a Night until I reach perfection.

[SEPTEMBER, 1936]

My father came to say good-bye before going to Spain. As he was leaving, my mother arrived and they collided at the elevator. My mother was weeping when I opened the door. She was carrying a market-bag full of things for me. She sat in the balcony and cried. She murmured: 'Thief! Thief!' I consoled her with deep feeling. 'No,' I said, 'he did not steal your children from you. We love you more and more, the more I know him, the more I love you.' I felt her suffering deeply. 'He means nothing to me. I do not love him.' I talked this way until she was consoled.

At night my mother's suffering haunted me. I walked to her apartment to see if her light was out, and she asleep. I was tormented by pity, by the image of her as devoted mother carrying a market-bag, and her weeping. Her light was out. I could sleep now. The next day I found out that she had gone peacefully to sleep thinking that it was my father who had looked scared! Yes, he looked scared! I am sure he had not noticed the market-bag, I said.

She left for Italy to join Joaquin, who was giving concerts in Milan and Rome. We had a farewell lunch, and we sat together working on a rug.

Before she left, my mother told me a story about myself: at age nine, when I was carried on a stretcher with an appendix about to burst, I said to the doctor: '*Docteur, ne croyez-vous pas que je suis une malade imaginaire?*'

At seventeen I wrote in my diary: 'I would like him to be poor, very poor, and that he should need me . . .' It was true of Henry and of Gonzalo.

Gonzalo the laughing, the lazy, the debonair, with a love of the bottle. I envy those who can drink, disintegrate, grow loose, slack, careless, ragged, sick, because I can't. Something pulls me up always. I go there only to find myself a friend, and then I come out and entice them into my world, away from theirs. Gonzalo's cigarette butts and ashes strewn all over. He makes drawings of me, writing, reading, sitting on a pillow in the balcony, by the river. He made fifteen drawings of my ears.

'Your ears are quite incredible. They do not look like ears, they are so delicate. I never saw such ears. All my life I have looked for ears like that.'

'And looking for ears you found me!'

'Anaïs, I understand your life. You are a great explosive force. You have such freedom in you, such fearlessness. But you never let yourself explode. You put all kinds of obstacles in your own way, they are all obstacles, lids, restrictions, all your loves are devotions, services, keeping you from exploding. You have drowned your strength. You hamper and block yourself.'

'It is not compatible with being a woman. Within all these boundaries, restrictions, I do what I want.'

'Yes, you do, magnificently. You do all you want except to live for yourself. Your care not to destroy anything takes all your energy and ingenuity and imagination.'

'I understand your life, Gonzalo. A great force is asleep in you, curled up inside of you like a snake. You pretend to be asleep – absolutely asleep – lazy and dreamy and nonchalant. But I feel the dynamite in you. You drowned yours in wine.'

I saw the houseboat which belongs to Maurice Sachs.

I walked along the quays which face the Gare d'Orsay, walked up a gangplank and knocked on the door. Maurice Sachs is a pale, tall and rather flabby-looking man with striking dark, soft eyes. He had advertised that he wanted to rent his houseboat.

He led me inside. It was a long coal barge which had once served as an ambulant theatre and had travelled down the Seine River, stopping at every small town to give a show. It was very long, very wide, black and tarred on the outside, unpainted wood inside. Except for the studio in the prow, the whole length of it seemed one long table covered with sketches, manuscript pages, opened books, photographs. Maurice Sachs was going away for a few months and was packing some of his belongings. The light fell on all this from opaque windows. He seemed vague, abstracted, and anxious too. The walls were papered with tar paper, and I loved the smell they exuded. One window on the river was like a trap door held open by chains. At the stern, the water showed under widely separated beams to indicate how much pumping the barge needed. The wood was covered with soft green mildew. The huge chain which held the anchor gave the whole place a medieval air.

There was only one big coal stove to keep the whole place warm. Maurice Sachs himself suggested it was not the right place for me, it was too big to take care of.

But the visit to his houseboat barge left me with an even stronger desire to find one I could live in.

I was sitting waiting for Gonzalo at a café when my eyes fell on an advertisement. 'Houseboat for rent. *La Belle Aurore*. Quai du Pont Royal.'

I rushed down to see it. This time the owner who opened the door was Michel Simon. His face looked battered and distorted, but he had the most beautiful hands I ever saw on a man, slim, white and sensitive. He took me into the glass studio he had built above the deck. It was beautiful, with windows through which I could see up and down the river, and the Quai d'Orsay as well as the Tuileries gardens.

He began to tell me the story of the houseboat. He had intended to live in it with his monkeys. He loved his monkeys. 'They are kinder to me than human beings. They love me. One female, when I went on a tour of the provinces, went on a hunger strike and died. Do you think a woman would love as deeply? But the houseboat was not right for them, because they could escape onto the quays, and frighten people, and the police were alarmed. I had to take a house in the country.'

Meanwhile he was showing me the interior. On the same floor as the glass studio were two cabins. One was inhabited by an old one-legged man with a beard, wearing a captain's cap; the other by a sullen-looking young man who did the heavy work, pumping the water, running the electric battery for the lights, fetching water from the fountain, lighting the fire, cleaning the deck, etc.

The third cabin was the kitchen, with a huge coal stove for cooking which also heated the water for the radiators, and for the bath. And then there was a bathroom with a tub. The place was warm, beautiful. We walked down the stairs to the bedroom, which was as big as the studio, and which had small ogival windows on both sides like the windows of an old galley.

I said I would take it immediately. The only condition Michel Simon insisted on was that I keep the old ex-captain. And René, because he was an orphan.

I came back that very evening with the first month's rent. The boy René called out: 'Hey there, who are you?' The old man, grandfather of the river in his blue peasant blouse and captain's cap, peered through the glass window and muttered: 'Oh, it's you, wait, I'll open.' I could hear the clump clump of his wooden leg.

There were sounds of beams creaking, those which held the houseboat tied to the quays, and sounds of rusty chains from the anchor pulling in the swift evening tide. I smelled the familiar tar. Dim lights came from the street lamps on the quays, and from the other boats passing by. The old man and René went back to sleep, and I sat and talked with Michel Simon and signed a contract.

I listened to the lapping of the water.

Now and then a boat passed, stirred up the river, the water heaved and the old barge swayed. It was like being at sea, sailing.

'We are navigating,' I said.

The next day when I came with Gonzalo, he was enthusiastic.

He said: 'The Incas always had a small subterranean passage in their home which led to a secret garden, a garden which was called in Quechua, *Nanankepichu*. That means "not a home". That is what you should call your houseboat.'

The river was alive and gay. The tar on the walls shone.

I will move in in a few days.

Henry was sitting at a café. He had been writing so deeply, so sincerely about his childhood. He said: 'You spurred me on the other day to continue.'

He is sober, thoughtful, swimming in creation and imagination. We talk about dreams, languages, childhoods. I am aware all at once of his loneliness, that nobody understands him as a whole, of his greatness, of his genius, of his ageing, of the worlds in his head, of the fact that as he gets deeper and deeper into his book his sincerity, the real Henry, the creator, his illuminations spread over and around and beyond the Henry of everyday, the prosaic Henry, touches his baldness, his hands, his housework, he gets nearer to the truth.

And as the train stops [he writes], I put my foot down and my foot has put a deep big hole in the dream . . . I have gained nothing by the enlargement of my world: on the contrary, I have lost. I want to become more and more childish and to pass beyond childhood in the opposite direction. I want to go exactly contrary to the normal line of development, pass into a super-infantile realm of being which will be absolutely crazy and chaotic but not crazy and chaotic as the world about me. I want to pass the responsibility of fatherhood to the irresponsibility of the anarchic man who cannot be coerced nor wheedled nor cajoled nor bribed nor traduced. I want to take as my guide Oberon the night rider who under the spread of his black wings eliminated both the beauty and the horror of the past: I want to flee towards a perpetual dawn with a swiftness and relentlessness that leaves no room for remorse, regret or repentance. I want to outstrip the inventive man who is a curse to the earth in order to stand once again before an impassable deep which not even the strongest wings will enable me to traverse. Even if I must become a wild and natural park inhabited only by idle dreamers, I must not stop to rest here in the ordered fatuity of responsible adult life. I must do this in remembrance of a life beyond all comparison with the life which was promised me, in remembrance of the life of a child who was strangled and stifled by the mutual consent of those who had surrendered. Everything which the fathers and the mothers created I disown. I am going back to a world even smaller than the old Hellenic world, going back to a world which I can always touch with outstretched arms, the world of what I know and see and recognize from moment to moment.

Any other world is meaningless to me and alien to me and hostile to me. In retraversing the first bright world which I knew as a child I wish not to rest there but to muscle back to a still brighter world from which I must have escaped. What this world is like I do not know, nor am I sure that I will find it, but it is my world and nothing else intrigues me.

When I am sewing buttons I am not only sewing buttons, I am playing the mother to all of them, sewing together the fragments of the words they want, mending their tattered dreams, sewing together their shattered souls, so that they can feel it there, sewing together anti-poisons, to cure their bitterness, sewing the wounds where the *banderillas* were stuck in their enraged bodies which the world taunted and made so hopeless. When I first met Henry all he could do was to hurl insults, to spit, to lie in the gutters of *Tropic of Cancer* and drink, but now he can talk about having found the language of the night, and all the treasures he finds in his madness, a madness I cannot luxuriate in because I am the mother of them all, of their dreams, and I am obliged to sew buttons on torn coats when they return from their bouts, jousts, challenges. I am obliged to prepare the drugs of life to cure Gonzalo of the heroin he took until he fell almost dead in the street and was taken to a hospital, his heart breaking, exploding inside of him. I gave them what their mothers and fathers could not give any of them, Henry, Gonzalo, Helba. Their own parents put them all in the wrong world from which all of us had to escape. I helped them to escape.

The large wheel turning, the wheel of three-days-within-one, three-nights-within-one. At ten-thirty in the evening I am sitting in the studio of Annette with friends. Henry reproaches me for not liking Fred, for not being amused by his *'veuleries'*, and Annette is babbling her French suavities, puerilities which sound intelligent and fall apart in my hands. Annette's husband is like a dog who shakes himself in a dream now and then, but never remembers any of his dreams. When he awakens he awakens as a good domestic dog, a watchdog. I look for the exit. I slip away. Outside, it is drizzling. It is only ten-thirty. I decide to visit Helba and Gonzalo.

Gonzalo is breaking wood to feed the stove. The works of Marx lie open on the table, by the light of two candles. It looks like a Dostoevskian setting. Gonzalo's charcoal drawings lie scattered among the books. They are sketches of river people, the tattered hoboes who sleep under the bridges, on top of newspapers, clutching their bottles of wine. Hoboes washing their sore feet in the river, fishermen sitting on the edge of the quays, in a trance. Old women sit under the trees. Others ply their trade behind the trees. The policeman is leaning over the wall to see that all is well.

Gonzalo sketched a hobo who collects all kinds of hats from garbage cans. The first time we saw him he was wearing a Scotch beret and we asked him where he came from. The second time a policeman with a sense of humour had given him a discarded police hat, frayed and faded.

Gonzalo talks again of Marxism. I read him my story of the rag-pickers which I wrote in one morning and one afternoon.

At midnight he walks me home. The river is enveloped in a mist.

Gonzalo found in the rag-pickers' story some of his own feelings about the love of fragments, of the unfinished, of the imperfect. Henry found it 'strange and whimsical, very strange and wonderful'. With Gonzalo as well as with Henry I explore a kind of underworld, the caves of Pluto, *clochards*, hoboes, rag-pickers, scamps, parasites, vagabonds, rogues, anarchists. When Gonzalo was young and his father the mayor of the city, he was sent with a posse to capture a bandit who had hidden in the mountains (Wild West of Peru). When he found him, he made a friend of him, they drank together all night, told stories of their lives, and Gonzalo returned saying he had not found him.

Gonzalo can't keep his wild mane of black hair combed, his nails clean, or his shirt buttoned. He says very proudly, looking around at *Nanankepichu*: 'I will paint that door. I will get oil for the lantern.'

Nothing happens. The door remains unpainted, the lantern unlit.

Henry Chinese, indifferent to everything, sly, humorous, tolerant, mellow. Gonzalo fanatical, fatalistic, Oriental.

Negative. Gonzalo is always saying: 'This is bad, this book is weak, that person is vulgar. Montparnasse is rotten.' He tears down, mocks, demolishes, exactly as Henry did. Gonzalo says: 'I would give my whole life for three months of fulfillment, creation.' His arms fall at his side.

As he complained once of the great effort he had to make to open the bottle of wine, pull the cork, find a glass, and sit up to drink it, jokingly (because the subject of his drinking has never been openly discussed), I turned up once with a small barrel of red wine. I placed it on his table. I said: 'All you have to do now is lie under it and turn on the faucet!'

It was this, he says, which cured him. Every time he saw the barrel he thought of me, of my teasing, joking, and it made him stop. He realized the wine was making him inert, supine, killing his energy.

Gonzalo and June resemble each other. No creativeness, but all their gifts blossoming in talking, in living. I like him as he is, with a bottle-opener in his pocket, his timelessness, his slackness.

I once said to Henry: 'I don't like clowns, I like madmen.'

Henry said: 'Madmen are too serious. I like clowns.'

Artistically, Gonzalo has infallible taste. He saw the flaws in the rag-pickers. He pushes me into the fantastic, for which, he feels, I have a gift.

Gonzalo is all devotion and care. He is devoted to Helba's work, to Elsa's, he takes care of them, cooks their food, runs errands, lights fires, does everything except work for a living.

Gonzalo tells me stories. I can see him as a child. Vital. Overflowing with energy. Up at six in the morning with his eagerness to live. In his father's hacienda. Spanish furniture, leather coffers, cedarwood chests, the smell of fine cigars. The father makes each son take over the managing of the hacienda one day a week. He must get up early and learn to run the entire estate. When Gonzalo gave money to the cook he said: 'Buy a leg of lamb for the family, and one for me.' And he ate it. Immense solitude around them. Indian servants. Indian *peones* (farmhands). Miles and miles of land. Learning *Quechua* from them. Then eight years of Jesuit school. Then military service. Then Lima, where the students and the intellectuals boasted of associating only with boxers, theatre actors, dancers, and drug addicts. Gonzalo boxed and was a good runner. Lima had a large Chinese population, and many opium dens. Gonzalo took all the drugs, until they nearly killed him. He was saved by Helba. He was writing sports columns for the family newspaper then, and was sent to write about her, and when he met her he dedicated himself to her dancing. She was a mixture of Spanish and Indian. She had been married off at the age of fourteen to a brutal man. Gonzalo and Helba decided to run away to New York. First they went to Havana, where her Indian dances were ridiculed. Then at Tampa she fell ill and Gonzalo went on alone to New York. They struggled against starvation. Gonzalo had to wash dishes in restaurants. He could get no help from his rich family, having run away with a dancer! Then Helba was taken up by Shubert, and starred in a Ziegfeld show. Three years of money, success, travel, but Helba's 'illness' developed. Eccentricity, then neurosis, then the beginning of deafness. She behaved more and more strangely. They went back to South America where the Latins laughed at her. She was no longer dancing Indian folklore dances but inventions of her own. Gonzalo thought she would be better understood in France. In France she was appreciated as an original, inventive dancer, but they starved. Helba's deafness became total. She withdrew into herself. Gonzalo drank.

When I tell Henry about Gonzalo's nursing of Helba, who, like Job, is stricken with every kind of illness (Henry remembers seeing her dance and being impressed by her vitality), he says: 'Does he like that nursing business? I don't. If anybody is sick I guess I would run out of the house. When people are sick I think they ought to be left to die, that's what I think.'

Helba tells me: 'In Lima everybody knew about Gonzalo's irresponsibility. He worked for his brother's newspaper, he covered sports and theatre. That is how we met. When he began to manage my appearances, I was earning a great deal as a dancer. When my first concert was planned, and he started to advertise it, the announcements and the placards did not carry the date, place or hour of the performance! He never kept appointments with journalists or other managers.

He had a horror of commercialization and success. It was always mañana. The Latin god Gana. *No tengo ganas.* I feel like it, or I do not feel like it. Gonzalo destroyed my career and my health. He is a Bohemian.'

Gonzalo wears out a suit in three months. He burns everything. He spills the wine. He breaks forks and knives. His papers are soiled. He forgets everything, the letter he is going to mail, Helba's messages to me, the book he wants to read, engagements, appointments.

The houseboat is homely from the outside. As it was made of a barge cut in two, it looks like a boat drawn by a child, fat and stumpy. The studio was built on top of the deck, making it slightly top heavy. The upper half is made of grey painted wood, the lower of dark old wood. The studio has a glass roof, and windows on three sides. The lower half is dark, sooty, worn by many voyages carrying coal down the Seine. The prow is thick and wide. It is anchored to the quays by a heavy chain tied to an iron rivet, and two enormous long poles tied to iron rings. They creak with the strain of holding the houseboat close to the quay. There is a drawbridge which leads to a small door. The studio is on the right. I can see the Gare d'Orsay, the Tuileries gardens, and up the Seine. As one enters, to the left there is a small cabin and the kitchen. Narrow, curving stairs lead to a large bedroom, as large as the studio, with many small casement windows, and to the left a bathroom and a storage room.

By day the river throws sunlit reflections on the walls and ceilings, by night reflections of the lights on the quay. Day and night the river laps at the wood, and rocks the houseboat gently. It gives me a feeling of departure. What a strange coincidence that I wrote on the title page of this diary: ‹*Les Mots Flottants*›. The Floating Words. A prophecy.

Les Mots Flottants led me to the *Belle Aurore* on the Seine. I sit in it now, writing. The Sunday I moved it to be near the Pont Royal, I telegraphed Gonzalo to come and help me navigate, but he was too late. I sailed alone, pulled by a tugboat.

When Moricand came he was astonished by the atmosphere of the place. He was sure it was an opium den. Even a poet like Moricand does not understand that there are ways to stimulate dreams without artifice. He associated boats with opium. Always thought I took drugs and that *House of Incest* was a product of an opium dream. I laughed at this concept. I said: 'There are experiences which come from living out one's dreams. I once dreamed about a houseboat and was not satisfied until I had one.'

So beautiful the bedroom, low-ceilinged, with heavy wooden beams. The old furniture from Louveciennes, which did not fit in the modern apartment on Quai de Passy, seems made for the boat.

Outside, on the quay are the hoboes, the alcoholics and the homeless. They sleep under the bridge, they light fires and cook their dinner there.

Moricand had brought me a revolver. He thought I would need it living by the river. To show me how it worked, he fired a shot into the river.

He also brought me the books of Léon-Paul Fargue, a poem by Max Jacob.

We talked by candlelight. The English poet who looks just as an English poet should look, David Gascoyne, came, bringing me the books of Pierre-Jean Jouve and a poem he had written for me, called 'The City of Myth'. Gonzalo came and David Gascoyne said: 'He looks like Othello.' The houseboat enchanted them. It took them away from a tortured world, into a poetic voyage. In my bedroom at night I am in a medieval galley. The Byzantine copper lamp swings like an incense holder. The shutters bang against the windows like the wooden wings of a giant seagull.

The rain falls heavily into the letter box and my letters look as if my friends had been weeping.

Moricand is perverse, full of ruses and destructiveness. He has frequented sadists, prostitutes, criminals. He has used the revolver he gave me. When I felt it in my hand I became aware of death. I never think of death. It seemed terrible to be capable of causing death.

Moricand told the story of the flower created by sand in the desert of Africa. It is a kind of petrified dust rose which falls apart if one touches it. I had imagined such a flower in the mirror story long before I knew of its existence.

*

I fell in love with the poetic novels of Pierre-Jean Jouve. They sustain one in a trance of poetic living. *Paulina, Le Monde Désert, Vagadu, La Scène Capitale*. I could not stop reading him all through a busy day, in the subway, in the café, on my way to Villa Seurat, while my hair was being washed. *Paulina* opens with this quotation from Saint Teresa: '*L'amour est dur et inflexible comme l'enfer.*'

His poetic-psychological novels are masterpieces. Analytical insight wrapped in poetry is far more potent than bare analysis. The drug of poetry makes truth and lucidity more absorbent. The intellect cannot resist its invasion. Language becomes the magic potion. Rhythm becomes the instrument of contagion, and the fluidity of the images flows directly into the subconscious without interference. Pierre-Jean Jouve has described a world in which visions, hallucinations, symbolism, usually relegated to our night life, operate in full daylight, and in unison with the body, fusing desire and fantasy, dream and action, reverie and passion. He does not pretend to illumine everything. He does not construct all the bridges, chronology, sequences, to which we usually cling because they are not a part of life. In life we have these sudden illuminations, sudden blanks, sudden shadows, sudden abysses, and incoherence according to a logic which has been proved pseudo-logic. We do not synthesize experience, nor sum up every day the meaning of our acts.

We often live moved by impulses which our wide-open eyes of consciousness know to be dangerous, perhaps fatal. We rush into ecstasies before lucidity overtakes us, and paralyses us. Illusion gives us heightened joys unknown to pedestrians and realists. And these people who resist intoxication by the drugs of imagination or aesthetics are those who seek it out of wine bottles, or drugs like opium.

After I have washed a pair of stockings, the tank is empty. When I have heated a cup of coffee, the coal is finished.

As the tugboats pass, their occupants wave at me. The men are at the tiller, and the women hanging out the laundry.

At times the current is too swift. I have nightmares of storm-tossed boats.

[OCTOBER, 1936]

Last night there was a rehearsal for war. We all went out in the streets to watch the airplanes simulating air attacks and defences.

Novalis wrote: 'Poetic life is the only absolute, the only reality.' That is what it is. I may be able to escape the fatality of historical time, the tragedies of daily life, the cruelty and destructiveness of the world into poetic life, the eternal.

Gonzalo, with his pockets bulging with newspapers and news of the monstrous world, often breaks the dream, but then draws strength from it and goes off again to work. One must not be afraid. One must know how to float as words do, without roots and without watering cans. One must know how to navigate without latitudes and longitudes and without motor. Without drugs and without burdens. One must learn to breathe like a wind-measuring instrument. The cord must be made of sand, the anchor of aurora borealis.

As a child, on the ship bringing me to America, I noticed that we moved towards a horizon line we never touched. The slippery, evanescent contours of illusion. When words and feelings have learned to float they reach the poetic *mouvement perpétuel*. To float means to be joined to some universal rhythm. The absolute means the pulsing moment of rhythm.

It is while floating, abandoning myself to experience that I became tied to the whole world. I let myself be pushed by everything that was stronger than myself, love, pity, creation. I floated thus into unity. The boat is carried by something, by a water many times deeper than itself. I am now in the current. I fear no grounding, no sudden dislocation.

The studio is the sun room. It is pierced, saturated with sun and light. It is a bower of light. I love to work in it, typing on a huge table. The bedroom is the mystery, the bower of night. The Hindu lamp throws designs all over the walls, trellises, cactus flowers, lace fans, intricate arches, circles, iron grilles, cages, plane trees, orange leaves.

I know where I have seen such windows before: in illustrations from Grimms' fairy tales.

How prophetic my description of the labyrinth. 'The spider web was broken by a foghorn, and by the chiming of hours. I found myself traversing moats, gangplanks, while still tied to the heavy straining cord of departing ships.'

The old grandfather of the river, the ex-captain of sumptuous yachts, had been for a long time the captain of *La Belle Aurore*. He resented if anyone took care of the houseboat. Occasionally Gonzalo would repair the pump, or the electric light batteries. Or he would stir up the stove, and break up wood. The old captain would come out of his cabin and spit, and curse under his moustache, and bang his pipe loudly against the walls.

Gonzalo's dark skin frightened him, his six feet of height, and although Gonzalo wore workmen's clothes, battered corduroys, the captain was still more in awe of him than of my other, better-dressed visitors, such as the immaculate Moricand.

Every day, it seemed, the old man drank a little more. And when he was drunk at night, he banged on the walls with his pots and pans. He spat, snored, cursed.

One of his chores was to fetch drinking water from the fountain on the quays. He carried two pails, strung on a stick, Japanese style, but he was so drunk that by the time he reached the houseboat the pails would be empty. If I ran out of water at night, I was afraid to fetch any because the hoboes slept under the bridge. The walk back and forth was very dark. Prostitutes plied their trade behind the trees.

One evening Gonzalo arrived with a friend, and I asked them to get me a pail of water. The old man came out on his one leg, and watched what he considered a taking over of his duties. He stirred up the stove angrily, and muttered something about black men. Gonzalo is quick to anger. He told the old man to go back to his cabin and stay there.

While we talked he banged on the walls.

The barge, the black-tarred walls, the shadowy beams, the slapping water at the bottom, began to seem haunted by the shadow of the old man.

René said: 'I have seen that old man knock a man out cold, he's tough, that old man.' ('*Je l'ai vu descendre un homme comme rien, il est costaud, le vieux.*')

When he climbed up and down the stairs on his one leg, with his crutch, he made a loud thumping which would wake me at dawn, or late at night.

Helba always tells the story of when her mother first saw Gonzalo and said: 'Aye, how black he is. *Dios mío*, how black his sins must be!'

When he is angry he looks like a demon. His curled black hair flies about his face, his eyes blaze.

It was eight in the evening. Gonzalo was making a sketch of René with his apache cap, his dirty yellow scarf around his neck, and his hands blue from the loading of cabbages at dawn in the market. The stove was snoring. The boat moorings were creaking, like wood about to tear, the water was lapping the sides of the barge. Shadows. The street lamps were twinkling between the tree branches on the boulevard above.

The old man began to throw pots against the walls, and to shout.

Gonzalo leaped up, furious, and banged on the old man's door. 'Keep quiet,' he shouted. 'If you don't keep quiet you'll be thrown out of the boat.'

The old man continued his songs, and insults. Gonzalo was becoming angrier. He threw himself against the old man's door, kicked it with his feet and demolished it.

The old man appeared half-naked, lying on a smelly pile of

potato sacks, with his beret on, holding his crutch like a sword. Gonzalo said in his muddled French: 'You're a bad old man, get out of here. Now you're going to get out or I'll fetch the police.'

René had already done that, fearing a murder. The old man was hazy with drunkenness, too frightened to move. Gonzalo held up the oil lamp. René said: 'Get dressed. The lady wants you out. Get dressed.'

'Who broke down the door, I ask you, who? It's not me who should be taken to the police station.'

He lay there. He could not find his pants. Gonzalo and René talked. The policeman talked. They could not dress him. He kept muttering: 'Well, what do I care. Suppose you do throw me down the river, it's all the same to me. I don't care if I die. I'm not bad. I run errands for you, don't I?'

'You make too much noise, all night, singing and knocking your pots and pans on the wall.'

'I was sound asleep,' said the old man, 'and you knocked the door down. Then you come for me. I'll not get out. I'm too old. I can't find my pants.' For an hour, thus, innocence, haziness, drunken logic, until finally the humour overwhelmed us all, and we all began to laugh; everyone laughed, including the old man.

'*Je ferais la mort*,' he said, and lay down and closed his eyes, docile, bewildered, and frightened. The policeman left, laughing. René went to bed, laughing.

At the café one day, Gonzalo began to ask me questions about psychoanalysis, the great enemy of Marxism. I talked about Rank's ideas, in relation to Helba's neurosis. He said after a while: 'I want to read those books.'

Then suddenly he banged his forehead with his closed fist: 'Curse all intellectual worlds. Literary worlds. Burn those books. Nobody would be neurotic if the economic problem were solved. Neurosis is for the rich. It's a luxury. The poor need bread. Did those books of yours solve the problems of the world?'

'Not all problems are economic,' I said gently.

Gonzalo commented on the mellow ending to the old hobo in the boat. He said a Spanish hobo under the same circumstances would have set fire to the boat, or poisoned the water he brought for drinking, or murdered Gonzalo in the dark.

Gonzalo said: 'I could easily kill a man in a moment of anger.'

It is only alone that I find my head again, cooler philosophical regions, where I seek explanations of what baffles and wounds me, where I question all the wisdoms, oracles, interpretations in order to achieve balance again.

But it is only a pause. The rest of the time I am living as fully as anyone ever did, on many levels, in many languages, with many people, in many worlds, with a poignancy and freshness as if each day were new, each human being new, and ultimately faithful only to life, always to life.

A sombre day. Everyone weighed down, oppressed.

Gonzalo receives letters from his mother, old and sick, calling him home, promising him that if he comes he will get his inheritance, which would solve his poverty.

Helba confesses that she never loved Gonzalo with passion, that they are like brother and sister, that his fatalism destroyed her.

All the time I feel that I am fighting a dark, engulfing force. I feel that within a thousand walls I managed to create an illusory paradise for all of us by selecting only the high moments.

The dark, cavelike dwelling where Gonzalo, Helba, and their friends sit like defeated, passive, tragic figures in a Chekhov play. Helba in her rags, wearing Gonzalo's discarded shirt, his socks, and several coats. Elsa, after her goitre operation, sitting in a brown dress touching her scar constantly, as a pianist touches his keyboard, and the violinist, stealer of Dostoevsky's complete works, who looks like the young man in *Doctor Caligari*. There the food is served on a bare table, stained with wine, covered with cigarette ashes and bread crumbs.

Was my rag-pickers' story a humorous, fantastic acceptance of futility?

Is my life dangerously balanced over a precipice? The

further I soar into fantasy and live by my selections, the tighter does the cord of reality press my neck. The more I move, the more I feel the suffocating hand of a nameless anxiety.

Seeking the absolute only in multiplicity. An absolute in abstractions, dispersed elements, many lives. An absolute in fragments. An absolute which does not flow serenely but which I have to grasp by sheer wakefulness, and as elusive as the ecstasies of the poets, the marvellous sought by the surrealists. An absolute in flight always.

This absolute is like dynamite which has not exploded, but the cord is lit, the little flame runs up and down the cord, with a kind of Dionysian joyousness, keeping me breathless, nerves bristling with their tips awakened like eyes, necks stretched, eager, hungry, eyes open, ears peaked, all the little nerves waiting for the climax that will send the blood running through them and make them sleep.

Ecstasy and anxiety are twins. Anxiety is a sentinel which sees in a yellow face at the café the face of a criminal, a drug addict, a premonition of disaster. A knife? Poison? A pause of some kind. But the taxi did not smash against another. The walls did not fall, the past did not crumble, and I wait for an absolute which does not shoot through the sky, a fugitive absolute, uncapturable.

Do all burning fires have a hundred flames pointing in all directions, was there ever a round flame with one tongue? Why does anxiety rush like quicksilver through the veins, take typhoon shapes, round up each monster walking through the streets to question its intuitions, to imagine its perversities, to slide between the lovers. This man with his little girl on his arm, why are his eyes so wet, his mouth so wet, why are her eyes so tired, why is her dress so short, his glance so oblique, why this malaise I feel as I pass them; why is this young man so white, his eyes so haggard, is there scum on his lips, the scum of veronal I first saw on Artaud's lips; why does that woman wait under the lamplight with a hand in her muff – a revolver? Why did the two sisters murder their crazy brother, living many years with him alone in a big house?

Ivan's wife sits absolutely still, with a wrinkle between her eyes as if she could not understand anything we say. Elsa traces the line of her scar as if discovering it for the first time.

Helba puts on her two coats sewn together, she pins on a brooch without stones, all the stones in it lost, torn off.

And I am still seeking the fairy tale, while the man who sold us stockings and cigarettes at the café, at half-price, carried cocaine in his wooden leg, Gonzalo tells me. I did not guess it, I never guess at these things, that is my brand of innocence. I do not foresee evil or danger, but even while I am dreaming my life, I see the dead leaves floating down the gutter, I see the old drunken hobo waiting for Gonzalo at the bottom of the stairs to stab him, I see the rust on the coffee pot Helba is holding, the leak in the roof, the rain falling on Gonzalo's drawings, the fire that has gone out, the sour wine dried up at the bottom of the cup, and continue to descend trap doors without falling into a trap, passing through as if invisible, so that I can dash across the street and the car does not knock me down, I am still listening to those who are weeping. The fairy tale wears a gown that makes a breeze, makes a space between the feet and earth, wood, and rust.

What I call heaven is when none are suffering. If one suffers, my joy is spoiled.

The night we had dinner at Helba's, Gonzalo was counting the people to set the table and did not count himself.

Evreinoff from the Moscow Art Theatre, with his hair combed like a page, a page with a bald top, the face of an old woman, the mobile eyes of an actor, interchangeable, amorphous, his clothes hanging loosely on him, as if they had been borrowed, not espousing his body, like a man in an old-fashioned lithograph, exactly as if his hard collar reached to his ears and his tie was flowing, saying: 'There is this man of today, the self of today, the modern man, but then there is the archaic self, the archetype in terms of psychology, and it is *this* self which remembers millions of years, which requires art to nourish this self. Dramatization, theatricality, is necessary to bring out the meaning.'

Conrad Moricand, who is an '*homme de salon*', but who stands like a young virgin shy of her body, dropping his hand in front of what requires protection, who has the face of a white Indian, a very diluted one, is saying: 'The real condemnation to death will come the day I am forced to sell all my belongings to pay my back rent. I shall have to take a job, know all the ignominious cruelties. I am about to take veronal.'

Ivan's eyes dance like the eyes of those Bali dancers, of the possessed. The first thing the spirits do when they enter a body is to unhook the eyes, as one might do to bad pictures.

Those who cannot follow all my swift rotations, who see me vanish at strange hours, reappear at strange hours, should see me sitting on the floor working on a rug, actually knotting the white wool at each opening of the tapestry backing, snipping the wool at the right length, making sure the knot is secure and the cut even, as the Moroccans do. And although this rug has taken me years to make, I do not undo what I have already done each night. The rug shows signs of having been worked, of time, and dust, and fatigue.

Helba makes drawings of houses which have no point of gravitation, like Chagall's flying horses; she buys a dog collar to wear as a Peruvian headgear and tries it out before an indignant merchant who angrily reminds her it is a dog collar.

In Havana, when Helba danced there, the public advised her to drink olive oil and gain weight. She chased them out of the theatre with a broom. It was a broom made of twigs, used for the stage, and it made her look even more like a witch.

Gonzalo draws Goyaesque figures, three old women sitting on a bench, weighed down, as if magnetized by the earth, towards its fiery centre, as are all those who are not gravitating upward towards magnetization from the stars, the dreamers, the artists, who seek to elude the earth's downward pull.

In Helba's studio, there is the presence of dampness, the breath of the buried seeps through the walls and the floors. The breath of the buried always seeps in, sensing the approach of death in the living, those who are already of their fraternity. No need of art to remind man of the past, a soiled greasy wallpaper sweating will render centuries of melancholia better than a face on a painting. But the painter teaches us to see it. Their walls give off the sweat and grease of the earth we come from, the dampness of roots and of cemeteries, the moisture of birth, agony and death. There are walls which impede breathing, flying, escape from the earth. The thickness of such walls upon which bodies have left grease, breath, and dampness, is something no destroyers can pull down. When the house is pulled down, it is this stain which will remain, like the stain of blood, and when this stain is removed, stone by stone, layer by layer, there is still the odour in the air, an odour of death. Helba has just washed her walls with a solution of ammonia and her hands have swollen. She was trying to erase the presence of death, she said. Ivan helped her, half-naked, while all the while he explained Einstein and geometry to her, shouting with the hope she would hear him. Gonzalo shakes his head like a lion, impatient under a harness of knowledge, closes his eyes as if he were meditating, charging into the delicate framework of logic and science, snorting fire. He looks for the wine to forget how happy he was in the jungle, on his horse, and what a blight it was the day he was taught to read. He curses the aunt who played the piano all night in the hacienda, a maiden aunt whose loved one had deserted her, was dying of love and committed suicide by playing the piano day and night and not eating. She left Gonzalo a treasure of music, and the haunting sound of the piano, so that when she died, with her hand on the keyboard, he felt compelled to continue, to study the piano. At that time, no man ever studied the piano. It was an art for women, like embroidery. When he arrived at the music school, fresh off his horse, still in white boots and leather coat and vicuña fur, all the little girls laughed at him. He seeks a state of being, a state of consciousness which is far from the intellectual conversations held around him. He sought it in opium, in cocaine, in chewing coca as the Indians did, and taking the mysterious beverages given to him by his Indian nurse, the concoctions they took at church to achieve an ecstasy not known to the Catholic priests.

I would like to take care of them all, to break into my father's unused, silent house and let them live there, because they have the courage to be, to act what others only dare to dream of at night.

Gonzalo passed by a bookshop on the Boulevard Montparnasse and saw *House of Incest* open in the window. Underneath it was a reproduction of Cranach. He said he did not know if it was intentional on the part of the bookshop, but that there was a resemblance between the Cranach figure and me. I came home and opened a copy of the *Minotaure* Gonzalo had just given me. It had a full reproduction of Cranach's woman. I opened the New York *Times* the next day and found the reproduction again.

Henry is a celebrity now, due greatly to his own efforts, his sociability, gregariousness, correspondence, his boundless energy and ambition.

Dream: Sitting on the roof of a house in China waiting for the darkness. Sitting among the roof tiles made of broken Chinese cups and saucers, with the last of the tea leaves still at the bottom of the cups. Sitting among the cups and saucers and waiting for the darkness when I could slip down and enter the city secretly. Sliding down the sandalwood beams, finding that the walls were made of sliding panels. A Chinese woman, with a porcelain face, slid open the panel and showed me the way in. I was kneeling before a meal, an immense round plate on my knees, filled with pearl-studded slippers, angel-hair, *filigrane*, icicles, melted gold. I looked intently and lovingly because I knew that I would be only once in each room, and that all I saw I would see only once, so I looked lingeringly at the carved panels, at the dish, I smelled the incense odour of the room, I saw the light filtered through parchment paper. Each panel I moved led me through the Chinese house but also out of it, and once I would be out of it for good, and so I pushed the panels slowly, passing through each room with regrets, meditating in the soft filtered light, and on the carving on the wood, which was so precise I thought, given time, I could read it like a book. I began to decipher the carving but its meaning eluded me, it reminded me of many things, none of which I could remember entirely, and the last panel which I pushed gently found me out in the street of China with doorless houses, windowless, with lanterns swinging, all alike, and dolls sitting on the sidewalk.

Ivan was sitting on a park bench. A hobo addressed him. He

did not answer him. The *clochard* said: '*Et moi qui croyais que tu étais de la cloche.*' ('And I who thought you were one of us.')

When I was thirteen I wrote in my diary: 'What I call making a heaven for myself is making a heaven for others.'

Henry is in a blaze of activity. People. Letters. Hopes. Reviews. New friends. Ideas, Tired eyes. Cannibalism: 'What was it you read me the other day about a brooch without stones? That was a marvellous image.'

'Don't steal it, I need it for my portrait of Helba.'

'I won't,' said Henry, but he made a note of it.

He is collecting addresses. He wants to communicate with the whole world. Like a telegraphist, I said. Laughter. Lao-tze Miller, I call him. The Chinese rogue. He was having dinner at some Dutch people's home. I asked: 'What are they like?' He answered they were boring, but they knew a lot of people.

In the morning I write letters, I try to sell my Indian sari dress because I am out of money. I continue to copy diaries for Denise Clairouin.

I get deeply tired because everything touches me, I am never indifferent. Indifference or passivity are impossible to me.

Louveciennes is dead. It was dismantled. I never wrote about its last days. When I wanted to enter a new cycle and move to Paris, into a modern apartment with modern furniture, I had to part with Louveciennes and its furnishings. I was told there was no other way but to sell everything at auction. When I arrived I found the auctioneers had moved everything out in the front yard, and were holding the auction out of doors. I had no clear idea of what an auction meant. I was appalled to find it advertised in the local papers and by the village town-crier, the man in uniform who drums to attract attention and then reads the local news on the square. The gates were wide open. A crowd had gathered to look over everything.

Beds, curtains, carpets, tables, desks, chairs, bookcases, pillows, bedspreads, all the intimate furnishings of a house so much loved and lived in, so saturated with memories. It seemed to me that when strangers opened the drawers, words would come out, that when they shook the curtains, one would hear the voice of Artaud, Allendy, Joaquin, Henry and June, my father, Jeanne, others. I was standing in the courtyard, in the crude daylight, while the auctioneer stood behind my desk and banged on it to obtain silence. The crowd was composed of neighbours, workmen, peasants, and a few big-house owners. They had always been curious about my life and my house. They touched the curtains, felt them, opened all the drawers. What I minded most was their lying on my bed, the big Spanish-Moorish bed I had first seen in an antique shop on the Rue de Seine, wanted to have for years and could not afford, watched through the window fearing it might be sold, and was able to buy only a few years ago. Its nacreous-pearl and copper inlay shone in the sun. People tried it out for softness and for size. It was as if they had invaded my house, my life, pried into my intimate secrets. I began to feel that the furniture was an extension of my body, that it still contained the imprint of those who had touched it. It seemed wrong to be selling it to strangers. I could not bear it. To the astonishment and horror of the auctioneer, I began to bid against the buyers. I was buying back my bed, my bookcases, my desk.

There was a murmur of anger in the crowd. They had come to pick up bargains, and to amuse themselves, and I was not playing the game properly!

By the end of the afternoon I found myself the owner of some of my furniture again, which I kept in storage until I found the houseboat. It was perfect for the houseboat.

But what a tragic-comic day. Each object auctioned off contained a fragment of my past. I had regrets for the passing of time and the death of homes, objects, and the change and passing of feelings and attachments. When it grew dark, and the sale was still going on, the empty house lit up by naked bulbs shone out once more like a mosque, with its gorgeous colours in contrast to the grey muted village, shone out once more, warm, sparkling, and then died. Everybody was carrying away the furniture I did not dare to keep, mirrors, lamps, curtains, and all the traces of my life here were scattered in different homes, never to be seen again.

It was a sacrifice to the need of those I take care of, and to my desire for giving, stripping my life down to essentials, and Louveciennes had become a luxury.

*

Last night Moricand was talking about astrology and saying: 'There are large wave lengths, and small ones, there are short wave lengths and long ones, in people's psyche.' He talks of the psyche in terms of ocean, waves, vibrations. He does possess the language of the poets.

At the same time Evreinoff is gesticulating. One can see in the mirrors the faces and candles repeated to infinity. Colonel Cheremetief is the *entremetteur* who delights in mixing people. He murmurs old dates of Russian history while new history is being made across the river Seine by the left wing. We can hear the shouts, the fermentations, the songs on the loudspeakers. Gonzalo is there. He is an idealistic Marxist. He defends the downtrodden. I could be there if I could accept bloodshed and violence. Gonzalo saw the Indians of Peru maltreated by the whites. The half of himself which is Indian takes the side of the oppressed always.

Gonzalo has gestures like an animal. He never rubs his face with open hands, but with closed fists as a cat does with his paw. His eyes are slanted like a cat's. He wrinkles his nose as cats do.

Gonzalo tells me about the Russian Revolution.

I do not understand him when he says: 'Moricand is a victim of capitalism. Artaud is a victim of capitalism.'

He talks about dynamic as against static philosophy. Marxism as a dynamic philosophy. He paints the world in constant evolution and revolution.

'Gonzalo, I hate injustice. I am in sympathy with your Marxism because it is idealistic. I can die for any faith which is idealistic. But now the Russian Revolution is split, corrupt, divided. The organization of the world is a task for realists. The poet and the workman will always be the victims of power and self-interest. No world will ever be run by an idealistic team because by the time it begins to function it ceases to be unselfish. When the Catholic Church became a force, a power, an organization, it ceased to be a religion. The realist, the man of power and greed, always conquers over the humanist. Greed wins out. The world will always be ruled by the materialist.'

Gonzalo does not believe this. He talks about Spain. For him, to go or not to go and fight in Spain is a constant conflict. 'The wounded are coming back. Roger is wounded. I must go, I must go.'

Later he points to my need of giving, and tells me it would be more effective if it were impersonal. He thinks the way I do it now is self-destructive and ineffectual. 'You're just palliating misery which must come to a head, get worse, or no one will solve it.'

He left me to meet Artaud. He is helping Artaud translate a book on the Tarahumare Indians' rituals.

After listening to Gonzalo talk about Peru, I wrote:

One never walks along level paths, one is always rising as upon a stairway, an eternal and wearisome stairway towards black skies, made of gigantic stones, square stones, set one on top of another, a stairway which wears one out because the stones are cut higher than a man's footstep can encompass, they are made for giants, those whose faces are carved in granite, those who drink the blood of sacrifices, those who laugh at the efforts of Lilliputian men. Men tire, taking such tall steps, and the Indians walk downhill with their shoulders bowed down by invisible maledictions. Everywhere, he finds footsteps, traces of large footsteps. Could they have been made by men wearing white boots? Up there, where I lived, the world began, and the world ends. Here were drowned continents, men who never saw the daylight. There is no sea, but because of the altitude one hears the rhythm of the blood. The wind is sharp enough to cut off a head, and the clouds are pierced by windstorms. The lava from the volcanoes freezes in the shape of dead stars, the dew burns where it falls. Clouds of smoke and steam rise from the earth's cracks. Here the world is born.

I have a superstitious belief that when Gonzalo has finished telling me about his childhood, he will get up and go and fight in Spain.

Henry says about what he has written on the diary, on *House of Incest* and on *Winter of Artifice*: 'I don't know whether it has anything to do with the books, but it's damned fine writing!'

*

I wrote about *Black Spring*, that it represented an effort to seize life on all levels, including the dream which obsesses the poet.

Henry leaped, shouted, said it made him feel like sitting at the typewriter immediately.

Gonzalo tells me that one of the secrets of his attachment to Helba is how much she needs him, all that he had to do for her, for her work which he admires, and I ask him if he believes that devotion to a few human beings is less important than dying in Spain. We have both sought devotion to others.

He loves the pages on Peru which I wrote in Spanish, as he told them, but I add something to them which he does not understand. I see him as a mythological character, torn out of nature, planted incongruously in Paris.

When I enter a roomful of people, I feel a strong malaise which warns me that I cannot stay, a real anxiety. Places and people I am not made to be with, because I cannot stop feeling. I cannot be with cynics, with debauchees, with callous, hard-boiled, or superficial people. I may see below the surface of Henry, I may know there is a tender Henry, but that does not obliterate the brutal and insensitive people he likes around him.

I can see myself walking into a roomful of people, and the one who will come towards me is the one troubled, unable to attend the function at which we are both present.

This time, at the apartment of Denise Clairouin, it was a young man who wanted to travel through far-off countries and who could not achieve his desire. He was sad. He spoke to no one, until he selected me as a confessor. Did he guess that I would say: 'Do like the Spanish dancer, who can dance her entire dance on a table. Choose a table to dance on, to travel on. Keep dancing on the same spot. One does not have to travel. There are other voyages. Right in Paris, one can go anywhere. You can live with the gypsies, as Blaise Cendrars did, you can fall in love with a Tahitian girl, you can live on a houseboat and get the same ecstasy from imaginary travels.' He began to laugh. 'You think so quickly. You answered me even before I formulated my question. I love the Orient.'

'There are veiled women right here in Paris. You can live in the mystery if you refuse the European habit of puncturing all the mysteries.'

'Are you happy?'

'I am happy, but I would be happier if it did not take so many separate things to make me happy.'

'I want to run far away, to get away from the "self".'

'The self will follow you everywhere. It is your shadow.'

'How do you get rid of it?'

'Give it to another. Give yourself up.'

We looked around the room to find who he could give himself up to. Ponisowski and his Russian cousin. Britton Austin, an Irish actress, Beltran Masées, a blonde model, a timid young writer, a Japanese woman. The rooms were full of wonders from all over the world. I heard Spanish, Russian, German. Mrs Stuart Gilbert has the delicate face of Marie Laurencin's women. When she talks, her eyes are fixed on you, but her lips modulate, sensitive and tender.

I have the power to abstract myself totally from my immediate surroundings and to throw myself into an imaginary life at will.

Moricand, with a folder of horoscopes, is saying to me and to Paul Fort, the young man who wants to go to the Orient: 'There is something so soft and smooth and non-resistant about Pisces that it often gives a wrong impression. Pisces does not believe that the truth is the best thing to tell and consequently, since they hate to hurt, they substitute what they believe to be a cosmic truth for lesser truths. The connection of this sign with enchanters and with enchantment is very plain. Unworldliness, self-sacrifice, romantic ideals, inspiration, because of glimpses of a larger consciousness.'

Paul Fort was amazed. He began to guess how I entertained myself 'on a table'. 'So that is how you travel,' he said. I left him talking with Moricand.

[NOVEMBER, 1936]

Gonzalo has definitely entered into his activities as an agitator, writer, talker, leader of eighty South American intellectuals. He is close to Pablo Neruda, to José Bergamín. I heard Neruda read his own poems. José Bergamín, a Catholic philosopher, is trying to balance Catholicism on one hand, and Marxism on the other.

Gonzalo's passion about politics, his vehement speeches, his sincerity are not without effect on me. I was won over to his Marxism.

'Strange,' said Gonzalo, 'that even though you were so far from all this, it was you who urged me to fulfil myself, and brought on my desire for action.'

I sat down and typed twenty-four envelopes of propaganda for Republican Spain. I took the envelopes to him. But I cannot share his faith. It seems utopian and naïve. Gonzalo has the illusion that Marxism will rearrange the world. I do respect his illusion. I will help him. I have been a spiritual anarchist.

If I still cannot believe in systems, I do believe in people. I believed in Henry, and I believe in Gonzalo's deep desire to cure the evils of poverty.

Gonzalo is hungry for heroic living. His strength and pride are aroused. I do like those who are willing to turn the world upside down for a new faith, a new effort, a new attempt to cure corruption.

He will stop cooking for Helba and Elsa, stop listening to their whining, stop washing laundry for them. It was because of the puerility of his personal life that he drank, to forget.

Gonzalo's vision is affecting mine. Before I knew Gonzalo, dinner at Maxim's with wealthy people was an aesthetic experience. The place all in red, sensuous plush, exquisite crystals, candles, crockery, the courtesy of the waiters, the elegance and beauty of the dresses. I never really saw the people close up. I saw them as one sees a Viennese waltz in a film, or on a stage. Crystal chandeliers, music, animation, rhythm. Lyrical moments. This time my eyes opened and I saw their faces, their gestures, saw expressions I had never noticed. The rich and the *nouveaux riches*, the aristocrats and the tycoons. I saw irony, arrogance, greed, malice, mockery, self-satisfaction, shallowness. And when I questioned the value of each person at the table as individuals, I could not find any.

Gonzalo plans to hold a meeting in the houseboat. He and Pablo Neruda are inviting all the Latin Americans to come. Anaïs, go out and rent chairs for the plotters!

Men think they live and die for ideas. What a divine joke. They live and die for emotional, personal errors, just as women do.

The monster I have to kill every day is realism. The monster who attacks me every day is destruction. Out of these duels come transformation. I have to turn destruction into creation over and over again.

Letter to one of my patients in New York:

I understand your desire to know me. Analysis forces one to wear a mask of objectivity. The effect of it depends on one's detachment. Only sympathy is permitted. I feel that you pierced through that mask very well. I feel that you knew me as well as I knew you. Even if I answered your questions and told you more about my life, it would not add to your intuitive knowledge of me. Besides, I suspect there is a lot of affinity between our emotional attitude towards life, and towards love, because I always seek, as you do, to realize as fully as possible all that I imagine, or carry within myself. I seek richness and fullness. I like the Gide quotation. But notice that he says: 'He can do nothing for the happiness of others who does not know how to be happy himself.' Which is precisely it. That is why it seems paradoxical sometimes to see that the joyous and egotistical man can make others around him joyous by contagion, not by giving. But that is joy. Happiness, which is deeper, and vastly different, is what one can give without possessing it oneself. I never helped so well, or gave as much life to others, until I myself had conquered whatever blocked me. You know, I went through a real hell, five or six years ago, I only count for myself six years of human fulfilment. All the rest was a struggle. You now want to know if I am happy. I am very happy. It is a precarious and dangerous happiness, because of what is happening around me. I am always tightrope dancing. I need abundance, and I want to hurt no one. I live in a furnace of affections, activities, and reveries. The happiness does not lie in the factual happenings, or what I do, but in what is aroused in me and what is created out of all this. I live simultaneously a physical and a metaphysical life. You write me that the world of the poet and the world of political action seem to conflict. If the poet is working, writing, creating, that is his job for the moment, and there lies his strength. Neruda has power today only because he is Neruda, the great poet. But I see no reason why, minor poets, or idle poets, or writers who are not writing, I see no reason why, if they have any blood inside of them, why they should not participate in the re-construction of the world. But if Proust had delivered speeches, written propaganda and talked all night with his comrades, he would have accomplished less for the destruction of false values than he did by satirizing a decadent society. Today in Russia they are reading Proust. It is a question of semantics. There are two kinds of dynamite. One invisible, one visible. Men who are not metaphysical need to employ concrete dynamite. The artist is right to employ satire. Those who are not effective in their art do well to learn how to use real dynamite.

I am in sympathy with Marxism. I respect efforts, and illusions. Certainly I have no use for capitalism, and I hate the systems which exist now. You will receive an envelope asking you to sympathize with the Iberian-American group. I find myself surrounded by miseries I can no longer cope with. So I want to try a vaster, more encompassing remedy. I would have preferred a collective analysis, but since that is not possible, let us try Marxism. You ask me to explain what you felt at the Writers' Union. You experienced the unbreakable isolation of the individual. To be a part of a group one has to become a void, a sheep, a sort of gelatinous substance.

Remember D. H. Lawrence: 'It is harder to stick to one's own soul than to die with others [go to war].'

Stuart Gilbert on *House of Incest*:

In an earlier age the author of *House of Incest* would probably have ended her career at the stake – in good company, needless to say, beginning with Joan of Arc. For there is something uncanny in her clairvoyance. It is as if she had drunk a potion or contrived a spell giving her access to that underworld whose entry bears the prohibition: 'All consciousness abandon, ye who enter here!' Courage was needed to embark on such a quest, and, with courage, shrewdness and a delicate sense of balance, enabling the clairvoyant to walk the tightrope between self-analysis and self-abandonment. All these qualities and with them no ordinary skill in the manipulation of words and rhythms, are manifest in the work of Anaïs Nin.

My father took a house on the outskirts of Madrid.

Letter to Father:

The atmosphere of Paris is oppressive and heavy with political unrest. We are not yet condemned to live in the subway, but it will come. For the moment we only take it to visit friends. The assaults of reality are more and more violent. It becomes more and more difficult to maintain an individually beautiful or integrated world. I have to kill one dragon a day, to maintain my small world from destruction. Unfortunately the dragon of reality is too tough to eat, or we would be saving money spent on steak. An impossible flesh, reality, gelatinous and at the same time fibrous, nervous, drooling, frightened.

[DECEMBER, 1936]

The magazine returned my review of *Black Spring* because it was not an analysis of its contents.

Christmas Night at the Poisson d'Or. Caviare and vodka. Tzigane songs, fiery dances, emotional orgy with Russian friends and Hélène R., until five in the morning. A Russian breaking glasses against his own head. They are not ashamed to weep. Five-thirty and we are out in the boulevards, wide awake. Hélène wants to walk. We will go and have breakfast. Where? We are sitting in Melody's bar. The orchestra is Argentine. Only a few Negro women and a few men left. It is six-thirty in the morning. The orchestra plays a *paso doble*. I get up and dance alone, incited by the musicians and the Negro women. It is seven in the morning. The dawn is blue. The feeling always that this may be the last night of pleasure, the last night of drinking vodka, dancing, laughing. That soon it may be cannons, and alarms, and bombardments, war, and blood, and horror.

Chinese ideal: 'To make even a poor scholar's room artistically satisfying: show the large in the small, and the small in the large, provide for the real in the unreal, and for the unreal in the real.'

Quality in painting the Chinese call *kingling*: 'Empty and alive, extreme vitality and economy of design.'

*

Hélène tall and full-blown, with perfect features, a classical bearing, and eyes of such light green that the sockets at times look almost empty, as in old statues. Magnificent and impressive, yet the first story she told me when I met her at Henry's was about herself as a child. She liked to crouch in a corner of the room, covered by a shawl. Her family would call her, search for her. She pretended not to hear. Once they found her thus, and shook her angrily. 'What are you doing there?'

'I am travelling,' she answered.

Hélène is sitting on my couch. She is saying she would like to be a man because a man can look at all things objectively, he can be a philosopher. When she found herself married (in Brazil) and the mother of two little girls, she was terrified, almost insane. She did not know it then, but she did not want to be a mother, the mother of children. She wanted to be the mother of artists, of creations. She suffered from terror, terror of nature, of being swallowed by mountains, stifled by the forest, absorbed by the sea. She has a horror of the actor and metamorphosis. She suffered from claustrophobia. She had a dream which recurred, of being carried away by a centaur. When she mentioned the centaur it was very easy to situate her in the myth. She is larger than nature, and stylized, perfect in face and body. I thought of the Olympians and the myths of large people, larger than human beings. I call people who are larger than nature myth people. But because they have also a symbolic significance, I separate those who are ordinary from those whose lives are significant, symbolic. They have a grandeur. In their world I breathe freely. Enters Hélène with her many dreams, her strength and positivism, the power to act out her dramas, as Gonzalo has. She belongs with June.

We were talking about Henry. I said: 'He helped me to accept life, and I helped him to accept the power of illusion which he had ceased to believe in because June's illusions were built on air. Mine were creative and real. I am not the illusionist at the fair, with only cardboard around and behind me, playing tricks. I am an illusionist with real power, the power to make things come true. I promised Henry he would not be a failure, that I would make the world listen to him, and I kept my promise. Much that I have wanted for myself did not come true, but I suppose the day the creator wants something for himself, his magic ends.'

Red wax fell on the floor last night. Red wax from the candles on the tables and from the lanterns. Red wax on the table. Empty bottles of champagne and vodka.

Last night around the table, Gonzalo, Helba, Elsa, Grey, a Javanese girl, Carpentier, his wife and mother.

I believe something magical happens when I wipe the furniture, praying that others may enjoy it, when I lay the table thinking others will enjoy it, when I cook food and wish they would enjoy it, when I light the candles saying: 'Enjoy them.' When I serve the wine saying: 'Enjoy it.' There was a glow of joy in the orange walls, the guests enjoyed each other, enjoyed Gonzalo's dark beauty, Helba's long black hair, Elsa's slanted eyes, Grey's slender dancer's figure, the Javanese girl's high cheek bones. They enjoyed the roasted pig, the almond paste from Spain. When it came to drink a toast to the New Year Gonzalo drank to *Nanankepichu*.

When Henry is writing he is divorced from life. Gonzalo is in life continuously. He reads very little. He has a big friendship with Artaud without knowing Artaud's work, the same with Neruda. He worked with Artaud on his theatre. When Gonzalo talks about them it is about them as human beings. What he hears and retains is the essence of what they give in their talk or in their actions. He has read very little of my writing. His world is an entirely personal world.

Henry had a lively correspondence with Lawrence Durrell, the English poet who lives in Greece. He admires *Tropic of Cancer* and sent Henry the manuscript of his *Black Book*. I wrote him about my response to *The Black Book*. We corresponded. He sent me for Christmas a story dedicated to me. It is called 'Asylum in the Snow'.*

*Reprinted by Circle Editions, Berkeley, California, in 1947, without the dedication, together with a story, 'Zero', which Durrell had dedicated to Henry Miller. – Ed.

I wrote to him:

DEAR LARRY:

You have done something amazing in 'Asylum in the Snow', reached a world so subtle, almost evanescent, caught a climate so fugitive, the dream life directly through the senses, far beyond the laws of gravity. You use a language which is surrealistic and full of echoes. Magical phrases. You wrote from inside of the mystery, not from the outside. You wrote with closed eyes, closed ears, from inside the very shell. You caught the essence of what we pursue in the dream, and which most of the time eludes us. You wrote about the incident which evaporates as we awaken. In answer to 'Asylum in the Snow' I am sending you *House of Incest,* which I consider a woman's *Season in Hell.*

[JANUARY, 1937]

I mastered the mechanisms of life the better to bend it to the will of the dream. I conquered details to make the dream more possible. With hammer and nails, paint, soap, money, typewriter, cookbook, douche bags, I created a dream. That is why I renounce violence and tragedy. I have made poetry out of science, I took psychoanalysis and made a myth of it. I mastered poverty and restrictions; I lived adroitly, intelligently, critically; I sewed and mended, all for the sake of the dream. I took all the elements of modern life and used them for the dream. I subjected New York to the service of the dream. And now it is all again a question of dream versus reality. In the dream nobody dies, in the dream no one suffers, no one is sick, nobody separates.

Now politics. What shall I make of that? Will Gonzalo put my name down on the list of people working for Republican Spain? He is proud of this. He tore me from tradition, he awakened me politically. Let him put my name down, I say. If I can make a poem out of rag-pickers, I can make a poem out of an economic revolution.

Gonzalo asked me if I would come to the meeting Wednesday evening.

I entered with impunity the world of psychoanalysis, the great destroyer of illusion, the great realist. I entered that world, saw Rank's files, read his books, but found in the world of psychoanalysis the only metaphysical man in it: Rank. I lived out the poem and came out unscathed. Free. A poet still. Not all the stones tied around my psychoanalysed and analysing neck can drown the laugh. Life, for me, is a profound, a sacred, a joyous, a mysterious, a soulful dance. But it is a dance. Through the markets, the whorehouses, the abattoirs, the butcher shops, the scientific laboratories, hospitals, Montparnasse, I walk with my dream unfurled, and lose myself in my own labyrinths, and the dream unfurled carries me.

It is because of my insistence on the dream that I am alone. When I take up my opium pipe and lie down and say: politics, psychoanalysis. They never meant to me what they mean to others. Nor New York. Nor nightclubs. Nor anyone around me. Nor Montparnasse. It is my mystery. They always want me to become serious. I am passionate and fervent only for the dream, the poem. Whether I ally myself to the analysts to find that I am not an analyst, or to the revolutionists to find out I am not a revolutionist, does not matter. I feel my solitude at the instant I make my greatest connection with human beings, the world. When one practices witchcraft one practices alone. One interviews the devil alone. Something is happening to me of which I am not afraid; it is an expansion of my consciousness, creating in space and loneliness. It is a vision, a city suspended in the sky, a rhythm of blood. It is ecstasy. Known only to the saints and the poets. Ecstasy before life. Before all things, the growth of a seed, Durrell's Christmas story, Hélène's Chirico face, the orange in her voice. I may explode one day and send fragments to the earth.

I cannot believe in Gonzalo's dream. I feel deeply for people's hunger and needs but I do not believe any system will save them.

Henry, contrary to all appearances is not *in* life, not inside.

Underneath the cult of the dream, I sense the inexorable destruction and separation in life which I rebel against. I rebel against change and evolutions. So it is the exactness I keep here, the breath and the odour, to keep everything alive! But we cannot bear to keep everything alive. That is why death was given us, and gradual death in life. Because we cannot feel so much. Parts of us must die, must die to free us, to lighten us. How well parts of Henry die in him because he possesses the gift of destruction. I can only gather together until it becomes unbearable. To hear too much, to see too much, to have no detachment or protection or refuge from being alive.

First political meeting, *Comité Ibérien pour la Défense de la République Espagnole*. The big studio is lit with one lamp. The men arrive. Mexicans with long black hair, gold rings, coloured shirts. Chileans, Nicaraguans, Cubans, poets, medical students, law students. The stove is lit. It is a foggy night. But we can see the policeman on guard at the top of the stairs. His presence gives anxiety to those whose papers are not in order. Neruda is uneasy. He is pale and flabby. His nickname is Yoghurt, because of his colour. Gonzalo is physically the biggest, the most fiery, dynamic one there, talking with his deep husky voice. The others are rather pale, prosaic. The main theme is how to utilize, exploit the death of a Mexican poet who died in Spain for the cause. A pamphlet should be written. Some of his poems should be published. How much money is there in the cash box? Forty francs. How do we get the money? Neruda rubs the soft white hands of the politician. Gonzalo looks like a man about to throw a bomb. His hair is wild. The height of his brow gives him a romantic air. The dark Indian in him cursed with a soul.

Later at the café, when everyone had left, he said: 'I know that until now your problems were purely artistic, and how to take care of a few people around you. I realize that I bring you into an entirely different realm. Yet I can't help feeling that it is good for you, that you are too vital a woman to live in ivory towers, I can't help feeling that today the artist cannot stand apart. He must have a political conscience.'

When he talks about the artist's role in the transformation of the world I ask with gentleness, 'But of what use can I be? I thought of transforming the world, abolishing poverty when I was fifteen and sixteen. Afterwards I realized the futility of it and I worked obstinately to build an individually perfect world. That I have done.'

'Yes, but there comes a moment when this perfect world is destroyed by what happens in the bigger world. Now you cannot go any further. You are blocked. Your work cannot be published because it outrages bourgeois ideals. You cannot live your own life because too many people are dependent on you.'

This is true. Somewhere, at a certain point, my individual world touches the walls of reality. I am faced with outer catastrophes, wars, revolutions, economic disasters, decadence, and I cannot protect my world and its dependents from them.

I have built a rich private world, but I fear I cannot help build the world outside. Deep down, I feel, nothing changes the nature of man. I know too well that man can only change himself psychologically, and that fear and greed make him inhuman, and it is only a change of roles we attain with each revolution, just a change of men in power, that is all. The evil remains. It is guilt, fear, impotence which makes men cruel, and no system will eliminate that.

But Gonzalo is sincere. And I want to believe.

A printer, brooding on the loss of the woman he loved, set her name in type and swallowed it.

A gangster who attacked a man to rob him drove a nail through his hands to tie him to a bench.

The horrors of Spain. Who can cure man of cruelty? They have bullfights. But instead of a bull, it is a rebel, and the others stick *banderillas* in him, explosive *banderillas*.

They place dynamite in the wombs of women.

Hélène so strong, emphatic, unyielding. Yet in her confessions, all she tells me is fear, indecision, fear of solitude, fear of being enslaved by man, made again into a wife and mother. She has guilt, for having walked out of her life. She has a lover who is a famous conductor. She deliberates over marrying him. She likes best his occasional visits. He is there, but not all the time. She is studying painting with Fernand Léger.

'I want to live *within* meaning, not outside of it.'

She is a friend of Maruca's and my father. Hélène says: 'From all I hear about him he is a complete and absolute child. How could you expect him to play the role of father?'

Gonzalo attended a meeting with Gide and Malraux.

*

Last night a visit from the Carpentiers, the Stuart Gilberts, Hélène and Moricand. Friends start a review called *Civilization* to resist the savagery and bloodiness of the time. We read their manifesto. It was scholarly, serene, noble. What a contrast. I promised to write reviews for it. To work for pacifists, and to work for Spain. Duality? No, I believe in a philosophical detachment from violence, savage destruction, and I also believe in action and rebellion.

To Hélène I say: 'You could be happy with Henry. You have strength and the ability to laugh at everything.'

In Spain the blood is flowing.

Henry is getting admiration from everywhere. He wants to go to Denmark. A woman writes him that she can be a thousand women to him. He cut out a picture of Mae West because she was born in Brooklyn. Henry is waiting for the plumber. 'Everything is fine. The stove is hot. I got a fine letter from the lady in Denmark, a stupid letter from England ("the role of art as sterilizer," says an English critic).'

I walk around the Cité Universitaire. I sit at the Dôme where everyone looks soiled, as if they had not gone to bed and had slept on a park bench.

At seven-thirty I am at Hélène's because she called me saying she had terrible nightmares. A cry of distress. No matter how rapidly I live, I always hear the voices of those who lag behind me. Hélène lags behind me in life, choked by fears, guilts and conventional scruples. I thought that she was ahead and strong.

She has been thinking about Henry. Was he the type of man she needed?

'I decided against it. He is an intellectual. I'm too selfish for that. I don't want to be sacrificed to a work.'

'I promise to reconcile you to yourself,' I say, and then remembered these were Allendy's words to me.

I like her honesty and sharp wit.

Gonzalo obtains help from the Spanish Legation. They will supply money, stamps, paper, printing facilities. Gonzalo has written the first manifesto. He is glad. I ask questions. I listen.

He says: 'The capitalistic world killed the artist in me.' He sees as coming from outside all that comes from inside. I know the artist in him must have been very weak to be defeated by this obstacle at all. Limitations, restrictions, defeats, come from within. I am fully responsible for my own restrictions.

Hélène became really ill, choking with anxieties. She has already been described in *House of Incest*. It took me four hours to illumine the darkness. To chase away the evil spirits. So as the day grew dark, Hélène's eyes green and gold again, she appeared more and more like a woman in a myth. No matter how fast I run, the tail end of others' ghosts pursues me, and I am fated to hear the same words: 'I never found anyone I could lean on, anyone who understood me. What strength you give me. I am well again.' Hélène lying in bed, and the bed covered with the sheets of Moricand's horoscope of her. His handwriting spidery, but the letters large and clear. I saw the title he had given it (he liked to give titles to his horoscopes from lines of poetry). This one was labelled: '*Du Sang, de la Volupté et de la Mort.*'

Blood, Sensuality and Death.

This line made her ill. She thought it was prophetic, that it applied to her.

'It is a line from a poem by Maurice Barrès,' I said. 'It is not meant literally. It is symbolic. Didn't you tell me that in Brazil you saw much bloodshed, much sensuality and much death?'

The dark stars were shining upon her, they dug their fatal points into her sun-coloured flesh.

Hélène said she wanted to paint me as Daphne, in the act of becoming a plant.

'Anaïs, so many people say things I never hear or remember. I remember everything you say to me.'

Gonzalo talks about his childhood. He talks about the beautiful Jesuit school amidst gardens and woods in a valley surrounded by volcanoes. The discipline of the Jesuits was severe. At home and in school, Gonzalo always wanted to sleep naked. He hated pyjamas, kimonos, clothes. The Jesuits watched him. Gonzalo would get into bed naked. A Jesuit father would come in late at night and lift a corner of the blanket and look. The Jesuits created an idealized image of themselves by never showing themselves at the table or at work. They appeared unreal and stylized. At fourteen and fifteen Gonzalo was sexually timid while his schoolfellows were already sleeping with maids and prostitutes. At sixteen a girl sent him a note to meet her at the park. He went, but hid behind a tree and at the sight of her he ran away. He talks about the Indians and his desire to lead them into rebellion against their oppressors. Peru, in those far-off ranches, was still medieval. The Jesuits must have had a hard time civilizing him. His family found it natural to whip the Indians for trifles. The Jesuits put an end to that and made Gonzalo aware of the inhumanity of these floggings. They must have had enough strength to awaken in Gonzalo a social consciousness, so it was he who went to help a nearby village suffering from an epidemic of meningitis. He nursed the people until he himself came down with a raging case of it.

Gonzalo said: 'Ecuador and Peru are nearer to the moon. And high up on Lake Titicaca, fourteen thousand feet up, we were still nearer. The moon is so immense it frightens the white man. It appears with a blood-red halo, takes half of the sky, and everything is stained red. There is a bird we hunted whose life is so powerful that even after he is shot he does not die, and the Indians have to tear out one of his feathers and plunge the hard tip into a certain part back of his neck. Then there is the long-beaked bird who only feeds on brains which he sucks through the ears of dead animals. I remember a tame eagle who stayed on the roof of our house and was fed chickens. I remember big formal dinners at our house on Sunday, and the visit of the monsignor in his sumptuous embroidered robe. Masses and prayers said in the house. My mother recited the rosary every morning for the entire household. An atmosphere of sixteenth-century Spain overlaid the Indian life. I still remember the taste of lamb cooked over hot stones while we hunted, and our Scottish father teaching his three sons to run the hacienda.'

What I like most in Gonzalo are the Inca Indian contemplative moods, the twilight zones, the trances he falls into watching the river, or a tree, or a bird.

He can be silent for hours. I like his suspicion of the intellect. 'Jesuitical,' he says. Europe seemed shabby, diminutive, puny after the immensity of his country. A toy, a toy moon, toy gardens, little people. But the immensity of Peru caused sadness and loneliness.

He talked so much about the moon being larger and nearer and more powerful in Peru that I finally confessed that when I was sixteen I took moonbaths because I thought they would influence my destiny, grant me a more mysterious life, a night life. I had heard that the effects of the moon were dangerous. This tempted me. In Richmond Hill, in my bedroom, I would lie naked where the moonlight shone through my open window, in the summer, bathing in it and dreaming of the kind of fantastic life it would create for me.

I did not think at the time that both the moon and the sea are symbols of the subconscious, and that this was the realm which would appeal to me, which I would be driven to explore, to live in, to write about.

Gonzalo, when he tells me his stories, gives me the feeling of a dream already dreamed, of a being I have already known, of one making the gestures, creating the atmosphere, images already imprinted in my blood, in the Spanish blood of my father's race which flows in me. Is it memories of Don Quixote, of romances, of novels of the Middle Ages, of books read on the Spanish conquest of Peru, or blood memories? What he awakens in me is contact with a world so far away, like the world a man may see when he watches the sun rising from a mountain and looks down at valleys, rivers, mountains he has not seen the night before. The world is so expanded I reach the jungles of South America, the deserts of Arabia, the skin colours of the Hindus, the Balinese, the Tahitians, the mysterious life of the Incas. It is not in this life that I have seen Gonzalo, because I was torn away from Spain too young, before seeing or tasting it, it is not in this life that I have seen Gonzalo on horseback. But I have seen him. It is like those obscure memories which assail one while travelling through lands to which one did not know one was bound in any way, and then one feels the roots of familiarity stirring. Some roots in me were buried in sixteenth-century Spain, with its severity, its rigid forms, the domination of the Church, the confinement of women, the sensuality of religious rites, the intensification of passion by restrictions and obstacles.

Gonzalo is always re-creating his childhood. He talks constantly about the Jesuits, their efforts to 'civilize' the Indians. True, they destroyed the culture of the Indians. But these Jesuits, the teachers, were also the ones who preserved the manuscripts from destruction, who imposed humane laws on the ranchers, who took care of the sick and taught the talented children medicine and law, music and literature. They were also the ones who taught Gonzalo to play the piano and to read poetry.

His father's ranch was as big as a village, with a main house, a church, a gun room, a vast salon for parties, many Indian servants, and the Indians' huts all around.

The Jesuits could not eliminate all the Indian rituals, and to win the Indians over to the Church they allowed them to combine rituals. In church, they listened to the Mass, the organ, watched the incense spiral and the stained-glass windows shine, and also practised flagellating each other. The Church let them use drugs which brought states of ecstasy.

Gonzalo, very young, had assisted at some of these spectacles. He had seen Indians, like Orientals, carry vivid-coloured rugs, cages, and festive food and coloured candles to the cemeteries on feast days. They refused to take death sombrely. It was the music and the spectacle which attracted them to Catholicism. The jewelled reflections of coloured windows on tile floors. The purple robes of the priests, the gold mitres, the gold cup of communion wafers, the silver candelabras, the gardens of white lilies embroidered in gold thread on the white damask capes, the choir boys' blouses with white lace sleeves, the chalice like a symbol of the sun god, the multiple folds and veils of the nuns' robes, tissues of black night, folded for centuries into undulating waves of mystery, the body a ciborium, a chalice in niches of shadows. The priests stiff and heraldic in their robes, pale with remoteness. The Indians enmeshed in incense, soothed by seas of silk, lace. Came the procession on feast days, moving with the sinewy contours of a long dragon tail, swaying heads of men reeling in the hammock swings of ecstasy. Came the procession of flames from giant candles and torches, the tongues of the holy ghost burning in the night on its sacrificial pyre. Men prayed with tongues of flame, and with swords and whips in hand. The procession moved like the spiral currents of men's blood, flesh chanting in the turmoils of guilt and the heads bowed as if cut by the sword of punishment. Knees on the dust of the past and the dead, knees on the doorsteps of the church, door open like a coffer of velvet exhaling incense and jewels. Came the procession like an aurora borealis spanning the church, then swallowed as by a crater by the shadows and the darkness, entombed under incantations, flowers, organ designs. The procession came to rest, the candles and torches were placed before the altar, the white eucharist was locked behind the golden door, and priests and people struck their chest three times in contrition for the God they killed and turned into a wafer, bread and wine for all to partake.

Gonzalo's childhood was the paradise of nature, mine came from books. But the stories he tells me I recognize. And I understand his indifference to art.

The paradise of my childhood was an invented one, because my childhood was unhappy. It was by acting, pretending, inventing, that I enjoyed myself. Reality gave me no joy. Gonzalo had no need to invent. There was a mountain of legendary magnificence, lakes of fantastic proportions and depths, extraordinary animals, tales of witchcraft of the Indians, drama, and colour and excitement, and romance. He took his ecstasy from the air he breathed, his drugs from religion, his sensual pleasure from battle, danger, physical power, domination, his poetry from solitude and the Indians. He rode horseback all night to visit the girl he loved, he leaped walls to meet her, he risked her parents' fury, it was all written in the *Romancero*.

The paradise of my childhood was under a library table covered to its feet by a red cloth with fringes, which was my doll house, and the little piece of oil cloth I was given which I used as a doormat on which I wiped my feet ostentatiously. The paradise of my childhood was music, which filled the house, books which filled my father's bookshelves, in games drawn from books and music, such as operas sung and acted, or act-outs of history such as the 'Journey of Marie Antoinette to the Guillotine' on a chariot made of chairs piled on top of each other. It was like the world I once saw through the knob of a coloured-glass window through which trees, houses, skies, people, became kaleidoscopic jewels.

Henry says: 'My letters to Emil Schnellock are as good as Gauguin's letters to his brother.'

Read Carlo Saurès *La Procession Enchaînée*. The maddest book I have ever read, truly schizophrenic.

Letter to Durrell:

I thank you for seeing Henry as a whole. Few people do. They nibble at him. Your letter to him and about him was the only one I liked. It was strong in its vision. All you say about *House of Incest* is true. Its opposite is the diary, where lie the roots, the peaty soil, the compost, the blood, the flesh, the stuttering. *House of Incest* is the smoke, 'the neurotic fulguration', as Henry says. Yes, I want to change the title too, but it is too late. I pass from the human, soft, truthful, natural diary to the stratosphere, from the least artificial to the artificial. I use a pair of rusty scissors to keep them apart. Duality. They would hamper each other, otherwise. The immediate destroys the transformed. And you get the smoke by mail. From the first I liked your heraldic world. Behind it I sense faith, symbol, meaning. The opposite of narcissism, since each one of us must be himself plus the symbol, a greater himself.

Henry took me to visit Hans Reichel. His studio was cold and dilapidated. He is always hungry. He carries a tiger-eye stone in his pocket. His clothes are tattered.

His paintings are beautiful, delicate and full of mystery. They are also full of eyes staring at you, sometimes more than one eye in a painting. There are eyes in the fishes, in the eggs, bulbs, snails, on the planets. Floating eyes sunk in houses at bottom of the sea, eyes on the moon. There is a bell which laughs, a flower petal with an ear. The boats, the fishermen's nets, and houses are sunk by a revengeful fish who comes to look at the silence. In this silence and communion all things are in a state of metamorphosis. Plants are turning to flesh and flesh into plants. Fishes are becoming fans, and leaves water. Inside of a snail there is a treble clef, the moon is resting on sand, and the sea coral grows in the sky. A man looks out fixedly, out of fluidity, but he is a man only for an instant and he is soon decomposed into a medusa, a swordfish or a tower. A man with eyes which can only see in the water, bulging left and right to displace the water. The nearly full moon rotates on a sky of lava, the stars are like a spiderweb, without fulguration but piercing and evanescent. Fixed are the eyes inside of roots, hanging from branches. The snail that romped through Spain in a cloud of blood carries an accordion. Hans Reichel says with great gentleness: 'This is the *Poisson Furieux* and that is me.' His self sits with a tiny bird like the bird of Saint Francis, a frightened tenderness sustains the bird immobile, asking for no food and singing no song. He is at the centre of a flux of communion, all the elements intermingling and marrying in deep silence. The branches bear little eyes and the fish grow little branches. The stained-glass window is webbed like a beehive and inside of the beehive there is music. The fish nets swell like mountains and the electric storm has eyes too. One eye like a frozen teardrop hangs at the top of a quaking tower, a tower without a window but a tower that is looking at me with fear of dissolution. A great terror paralyses the clouds, despair pursues the fishes at a trembling pace, the branches are heavy with the intensity of this growth. The eyes of fish are like the eyes of man and the eyes of man like those of fish. The eyes, all of them, see too much. They cannot close because here there is neither night nor day. The light they see is filtered through the tissues of an unbroken womb, through the slabs of nameless tombs, through the eyes of fish, plant, and man confounded and confused in communion and metamorphosis.*

Walking back from Reichel's, Henry said to me: 'Now you will quietly write the whole thing in your diary. Then you must read it to me so I can get inspired. Give me some of those finite phrases!'

'You are too modest. You know no one can write as well as you do.'

But I do see my role as the *eye*, the third eye, the eye of

*See the story 'The Eye's Journey', in *Under a Glass Bell*. – Ed.

vision. For Henry was talking wildly about Reichel, and then he took me there and it was I who saw all that Reichel wanted people to see: I saw the importance of the eyes in his work, the emphasis on communion, metamorphosis.

Henry wrote a big, sonorous, rich description of Reichel. I wrote my own.

'You give me ideas,' said Henry, chuckling.

In Henry's own water colours there is a childlike quality. I am adept at catching the presence of this child in adults. Its fleeting appearance in a too open, surprised look in the eyes, surprise at the harshness of the world. I could see it in Henry's water colours, in Gonzalo's round-cheeked, closed-eyed laughter, in Helba's *sonate pathétique* and constant plea for devotion and compassion. In Henry's water colours there is levitation. He is not tied to the earth as he is in his work. It is a game, a world without monsters.

Depression.

Meeting to help Republican Spain with Gonzalo. Alberti's poems were read. All these words I hear, lyric speeches, romantic flourishes, wreaths, prayers, poetic lamentations, irritate me. I see in revolution a vital life-and-death matter, a struggle one must enter directly and violently, by action. Why do they talk so much, recite poetry?

And Gonzalo who hunted, fought, boxed, and killed in his wild land of Peru, is shocked by the realism of the birth story.* He tells me horrors about Spain, describes tortures, and he winces at my description of a stillbirth!

*See *Diary, 1931–1934*, pages 340 *et seq.* – Ed.

[FEBRUARY, 1937]

Began a sketch of Moricand. Was perplexed by the fact that he does not arouse compassion. Why? Is it that by stylization and formality he has effaced from his life all human traits? In spite of poverty, tragedy, he has maintained a façade which repels intimacy and therefore compassion. He conceals the human being. He acts like a prophet or a clairvoyant. His speech is so poetized, and he talks so much about the past that one does not situate him in the present at all, it is difficult to believe he is cold or hungry.

When I found him a rich patron he looked mysteriously satanic, but he never confessed what happened. He conveys that he has many secrets but he never shares them. He intimates and suggests but never confides.

Henry said: 'If things go bad in France I will go away. I will go to Holland. Escape. Above all, I do not believe in struggle.'

Talking about friends he made this statement: 'The truth is that I have a lot of friends who love me, but I love no one. If only they knew how little I care.'

He appears to care. He becomes soft, sentimental. Everybody is taken in. He creates an illusion of warmth. But if any of them came with a real need, they would find out.

I appear not to care. I create an impression of remoteness, but if anyone has a real need, they discover I love.

*

He said: 'Like a mollusc. I want to live like a mollusc.'

Met Jean Carteret. He is tall, thin, with pale-blue eyes, long straight light-brown hair. Upper half of his face that of a poet, high brow, an air of spiritual illumination, the lower half marked with pock marks, heavier and sensual, almost gross. His eyes, though pale in colour, throw off sparks. When I opened the door he *saw* me instantly. I felt instantly unveiled. His vision was even quicker than mine. A few moments later he was saying: 'You are a personage out of a myth, you live in the myth. I see you as a fine, flawless mirror. A pure mirror in which others can see themselves. The mirror is important for you. The day a large mirror is delivered to you, given to you, will be a fortunate day. If a mirror breaks you will be unfortunate. You wear your bracelet on your left arm: you are dependent on your affections. But doors and walls do not exist for you. You are ultimately independent.'

He tries to channel his gifts and intuitions in the form of astrology, or the analysis of costume, mannerisms, handwriting. But I feel that it is all intuition. He has lectured at Allendy's '*Idées et Tendances Nouvelles*'. He said: 'But all the slides I showed kept coming out upside down. I think I wanted to keep all my knowledge for myself – a mystery.'

Over the absorbing glance that could drink and never be satisfied fall gentle eyelids of the most delicate skin, and in the gentle way they fall there is goodness. In the length and softness of his blond eyelashes there is a silken yieldingness, but over the delicate eyelids fall savage eyebrows, wild like a Bushman's. The small nose is vulnerable, the brow spiritual, the mouth full and sensual, and the hands those of a peasant asserting his strength. As he stands there, he is constantly in mutation between fierceness and yielding, between assertiveness and sudden eclipses of his whole being which cause him to pale and vanish before certain people who are not of his climate. Constantly oscillating even in the same moment between a physical appetite which his mouth demands and some secret flame of a dream sapping at his strength.

Hélène returns and tells me about a conversation she had with my father in the south of France. He made her translate

House of Incest for him. She explained it to him, how it came to be written, out of dreams, etc. My father said: 'Anaïs lives in fantasy. I like logic and rational order.'

She said: 'Anaïs lives in another kind of reality. She can do without order and logic because she has a core of her own. It is you who are the romantic one, and possibly chaotic because you cling so fiercely to outer order. Her life is a kind of metaphysical play.'

I loved Hélène enough to save her life a few times, to restore her appetite for life, her faith in herself. But I cannot sustain this, and I beg her to see C. G. Jung. As soon as I help her out of her illness, I see the demon reappear in her, the mocking, sensual, selfish woman in her. Her sexual hunt begins anew, but it is an appetite, an enthusiasm, and she wants only pleasure.

Each one of us has his demon. Gonzalo's demon is a revolutionary one.

He reads me from *Libro de Chilan Belam de Chumayel*, which contains all that is left, all that we know of the Inca civilization.

Stuart Gilbert on the diary: 'Remarkable. Never read anything like it. So much feeling. Of course, you magnify. Everything is six times larger, but your feelings are so real that one has no feeling of exaggeration but of sincerity. Divided lives. Living most excitedly, passionately, and at the same time aware, detached, cool. You *see* everything. Small portraits of people you are not intimately involved with very humorous. One can see everybody as well as yourself. You have the makings of a Proust. This is too natural and will never be published. You ought to write a novel. You can be mocking without meanness, and you tell the truth without hatred. There is an absence of hatred.'

Gonzalo begins to understand the stillbirth story. Says it is out of the frame of epoch, social world, consciousness, beyond moral, the present. Beyond time. It is woman facing nature.

Denise Clairouin said: 'The diary will never be published. People can't bear such nakedness. You are so much in life.

Never write for intellectuals. The childbirth story will immediately be censored.'

Henry writes about the incident of his trip to London after the break with June, and gives it a completely different twist. Instead of being (as he told me) a victim of June's anger, he and June sit drinking merrily and in a fit of drunken sentimentality, Henry gives her the money, etc. It is all written in a hard, brassy manner. This perplexed me, set me wondering on the shifty aspects of truth. Which version was a lie? This one, or his version in his letter to me?*

Henry said: 'This is fiction.'

There is always a superimposition of a hard Henry over a tender Henry. The two often get confused in my mind.

Comes the moment when I choke, when all I have lived, seen, heard, felt, overwhelms me, comes up in my throat, drowns me. Comes the moment when over-abundance bursts the cells and I have to shout. Life comes to a climax, an orgasm. Everything pointing to an orgasm. *'Poème de l'Extase'* of Scriabin, dream of Gonzalo saying the flame of his life was Helba's dancing, the dancing of Uday Shankar, Lawrence Durrell's *Black Book*, talk with Henry and David Edgar, work on diary, while Henry writes about the three volumes he read, talk on playing roles with Evreinoff, the Russian actor, and with Jean Carteret. Evreinoff says you can become anything or anyone you wish merely by playing the role, but it has to be thorough, an immersion into the role, a profound study of all its details.

Mrs Green writes me: 'Come and give a lecture in Estonia.' She sends me the photograph of the most beautiful boy of eight I have ever seen. He seems made of velvet, from the soft light of his enormous eyes, to the softness of his features, the tenderness of the mouth, the pose of the neck, his hands, a soft-focused child, a dreaming child, who reminds me of Joaquin at his age, except that Joaquin added great liveliness and sparkle.

*See Henry Miller's story 'Via Dieppe–Newhaven', published in *Max and the White Phagocytes* (Paris: Obelisk Press, 1938).

Joaquin's piano-playing applauded by the King of Spain, Joaquin and Mother climbing the sixty-five holy steps in Rome, on their knees. Spring sketching a pale appearance.

People throw themselves from the Pont Royal. The coldness of the water awakens them from their hypnosis with death, and they begin to shout lustily for help. They cling to the rusty chain anchoring the houseboat. The policeman on guard at the top of the stairs runs down and pulls up the chain with the help of a hobo. The suicide clings to it. He (or she) is hoisted on deck, or on to the quay. He is almost always ashamed. Ashamed not to have had the courage to live, or ashamed of not having had the courage to die? I cannot tell.

Everyone is jealous. Some admit it, others do not. It is a perversity to be jealous of the past because the past is usually made of ashes. But with the artist the past survives in another form, and I can understand those who are jealous of the past of an artist. It becomes a monument. Examine the past of most people, and you find a neat cemetery or an urn with ashes. But examine the past of an artist and you find monuments to its perpetuity, a book, a statue, a painting, a symphony, a poem.

Helba said: 'How could I not love you, Anaïs, we are sisters. You have saved my life. When you came I wanted to die. You saved my life. I do not love Gonzalo as a man. He is a child. He has done me so much harm. He is really an Indian, he just wants to drink and talk with his friends. I have to sew for him continually. He tears everything. He sticks wine bottles in his pockets and they are always torn. He does nothing for me. He is full of wild ideas, full of candour. He cannot think of tomorrow. He is just a child. If you are fond of him, I am glad, because of the kind of woman you are, because you are full of quality and you are an artist.'

We kissed.

Dinner for Moricand, Jean Carteret and Hélène, the Medusa. Moricand was telling about the auction sale of his belongings, how much he suffered, how outraged he was by the rapaciousness and lust of the people fighting over his drawings, paintings, books, intimate souvenirs, trophies, symbols, magic gifts, tokens of love. 'They bartered and handled things I would scarcely handle myself with the greatest tenderness. I had poems of Max Jacob, letters, the garter of a woman, hairpins, handkerchiefs with perfume still clinging to them. Seeing them bartering over these things, I felt calcinated, like those trees one sees in the South still standing but with their entrails burnt out, ashes. Perhaps it is true that those who unveil the mysteries have tragic lives. I was born of well-to-do parents in Switzerland. I came to Paris and rented a beautiful studio and gave beautiful dinners. I knew Picasso, Louis Jouvet, Max Jacob, Cendrars, Henri Michaux, and made drawings of them all. Then I became interested in occult sciences, and concentrated on astrology. I did a whole series of erotic drawings. When Max Jacob became a converted Catholic he would tell me: "Conrad, burn those drawings, or else God will punish you." I did not burn the drawings. My parents died. My older brother, who was a businessman, took all of the inheritance, swindled me, with the excuse that I led an immoral life in Paris. I fell into the most abject poverty. I was incapable of earning a living. From the days of my wealthy past, I knew many ladies in society who wanted to invite me as their house guest. I could have lived indefinitely on their property. All I had to do was to converse brilliantly in their salons. They live in castles and manor houses in the country and get bored. I could bring them stories of life in Paris and revelations of intimate adventures. But they wanted me alone, and not with Blanchette.'

I could imagine how Blanchette seemed to Moricand's aristocratic hostesses. Blanchette was a young woman he had met on the Rue Godot-de-Mauroy, behind the Madeleine, where she picked up clients. She was pale, as if she had never breathed any air but that of the street and the cafés where she plied her trade. She was passive, quiet, expressionless. She had big tired, faded eyes, hair badly dyed by herself, which she wore in bangs, in the style of 1920. She never talked. She had a white dog. The white dog was never very white, more often brown with dust and mud. He was neither combed nor brushed. There was a strong resemblance between Blanchette and her dog. The dog never barked. Blanchette endured Moricand's visitors. She never looked at his books or horoscopes. She never joined in the conversation. I believe Blanchette was there as a *trompe-l'oeil*. Because the delight Moricand took in telling about Max Jacob's love of boys and their exploits at night when they went searching for boys in a carriage was too genuine. He always told the stories as if they were the life and loves of Max Jacob, but the expression of his face was one of such enjoyment that it betrayed him. Memories of pleasure illumined his face. And in his drawings there were exact reproductions of these pleasures. As he told them his body lost its rigidity, its almost hierarchic poses. It began to undulate gently, like the body of a woman. He would raise his left shoulder, and lower his right hip as if to show its flexibility, yieldingness, its pivotal talents. His hand would be placed where Venus de Milo, if we had found her arms, would have hers placed, to hold her robes with a modesty which indicated where she had hoped eyes would stray.

Did Moricand want Blanchette to protect him from the over-protectiveness of his Muses, Egerias, patronesses? Or to veil his interest in boys?

Thinking again of what Moricand had said, that all those who unveil the mysteries have had tragic lives, I asked him if he thought this applied to the psychoanalysts too.

'All the unveilers,' said Moricand.

And I thought of Allendy's life.

Moricand looked at Carteret and said: 'You are Rimbaud *gai*.'

And Carteret said: 'There is something non-human about you.'

'Don't be afraid to say it,' answered Moricand. 'There is something fatal.'

The Medusa came in, with her hair done by Antoine, in a white toga, and said: 'Last night I dreamed about a temple with columns made of people, and I could not get to it because there was an abyss under my feet.'

Evreinoff said: 'People were almost afraid to clap at the dancing of Uday Shankar. The feeling of a magic ritual was so strong they felt as if they were in a temple.'

Everyone at this moment looked at my cotton Persian dress

and I knew I was a part of that world in which everything was said by a symbol. I could easily forget all the thought of the Western world, all the analysis of the West, the intellectual overgrowth, and take all the meaning into the body and give it out in gestures only. That was the miracle of Uday Shankar. There was not even a need of music. The *'sommeil lucide et sans durée de Siva . . .'*

In the middle of his talk Moricand stopped. There was a complete blank. 'That happens when I suddenly begin to watch myself talking.' The Medusa said: 'I call that my absences.'

Moricand was telling her about the stigmata of Theresa Neumann.

This is the nearest one can come to magic in the West. Moricand, Allendy, Carteret, Rank. Western magic.

Evreinoff points to his toes, leaning over, explaining: 'In the Moscow Art Theatre one was taught to conceal the outward marks of timidity. For example, a singer, instead of twisting her hand, was taught to twist her toe.

'There are so many things lying within one, potential, unconscious, that if you are acting a role, and this role corresponds to a dormant self, this self awakens, becomes reality. But if you act a false role, something entirely outside of one's self, you get sick, uneasy. As in the Gilbert and Sullivan musical, the poet who was not a poet, who pretended to be a poet, got a terrible cramp.'

Pepe-le-Moko, the Siamese cat, made a sound like a dove.

During lunch I ask myself: was it pure hazard that in Spanish, English and French the words *passion* and *compassion* are almost the same. Add the *con*, which means 'with'. So compassion – with passion.

Henry represents violence, and chaos, which I could not express, and I represent a Henry he could not express, a tender Henry.

The rest of the world arouses him to combat. It is thus one arrives at one's own balance, in relationship to others. Henry expresses my martial self. A strange paradox. I who never fought, fought in defence of Henry. And Henry who never yielded, yielded to me.

*

I must continue the diary because it is a feminine activity, it is a personal and personified creation, the opposite of the masculine alchemy. I want to remain on the untransmuted, untransformed, untransposed plane. This alchemy called creation, or fiction, has become for me as dangerous as the machine. Feelings and emotions are diverted at the source, used as the fuel to other purpose. What comes out of the factory: painting, sculpture, pottery, rugs, architecture, novels, I now regard with fear. It is too far from the truth of the moment. Perceived by feeling, during the life, not after.

It resembles the moment when I felt that with Rank I saw too much, unveiled too much, the psychological terminus. Too much awareness, without accompanying experience, is a skeleton without the flesh of life.

Analysis has made three errors:

1. Idealism. In struggling against the negative, destructive element in relationships, it also sets up a falsely idealistic one, a perfect balance, an absolute, which is humanly impossible.

2. It considers all escape as bad, as evasion. Some of these escapes are mobilities into creative areas, towards light or sun, new growth, new departures or renewals.

3. The desire to get back into the womb can become, in a creative way, a making of a womb out of the whole world, including everything in the womb (the city, the enlarged universe of *Black Spring*, of *The Black Book*), the all-englobing, all-encompassing womb, holding everything. Not being able to re-enter the womb, the artist becomes the womb. Analysis does not take into account the creative products of neurotic desires.

My story 'Ragtime' accepted by *New Directions*, New York.

I burnt my eyelids severely under the sun lamp, did not wear glasses. Eyes swollen and painful. I wear scarves to hide my oiled eyes. Picturesque effect. A Moslem woman, a veiled madonna. But for me a week in darkness, fear of blindness. Deprived of the opium of intensity I fell into an abyss.

Henry was hot blood and a cold soul. When he saw my eyes he said: 'Now you will have time to meditate.'

He and his friend David Edgar move in icy objective

worlds. Ideas. New words. Technique of water colour. Analysis. Henry gave a conference on *'La Vie Intégrale'*. He read me a review of *Tropic of Cancer* in *Le Mois*. Fan letters. He read me the thirty pages he wrote on my diary. They are magnificent, but not about the diary. Edgar is all mind, all ideas, as Lowenfels and Fraenkel are.

To construe? To misconstrue? What? The whole universe? All life suddenly looks monstrous again, and yet is it a monster? How many days and nights have I expected catastrophes which did not happen, how many hours during the last years have I expected the loss of love? What is this pall of anxiety, the expectation of the nerves, the fears in full sunlight, compared with my life as others see it? The envy of women for my life and loves. The days when I am outside of the monster, days of peace, normal vision, when Henry does not look like a rogue without scruples, when I can laugh, those are the days which make me doubt the monster, its presence, its reality. It is only a nightmare. That is why I cannot rest, cannot be idle, I cannot sleep as much as others, that is why I seek my joys, my activity, my creations, my loves, my friends.

I awake joyous. The world is clear and soft, at peace. The trees, the sky, are peaceful. Leaping out of a taxi in the sunny morning I meet Joaquin just back from Italy. We have breakfast together. We buy music paper on which to type my text on the orchestra from *Winter of Artifice*. No time to meet Eugene Jolas, who asked to meet me. Stuart Gilbert, ensorcelled by the diary, asking: 'Are you writing?' I take notes in the bus. Henry says joyously: 'I will die of tranquillity.' Enjoying his life, living with a deep enjoyment of peace. Writing steadily. Content.

My moments in the bath are the only moments I have for meditation. I love the richness.

Helba so sick I took her to see the doctor. I translated what she said in Spanish to the French doctor. The man she was married to at fourteen had given her syphilis. She had been pronounced cured years ago. 'When was the last blood test made?' asked the doctor. 'What kind of cure were you given?'

'Two months ago my blood was tested. I was given injections of mercury.'

He turned to me and because she could not hear us he said plainly: 'That explains the deafness.'

'Were your parents strong?' asked the doctor.

'My father died insane. My mother was half-crazy too.'

Poor Helba. I kissed her with sudden pity. She was frightened to have spoken. She lay on the couch, half undressed. A sick body.

'Degenerate,' the doctor said. 'The mixture of Spanish and Indian is bad. The Indians are degenerate. The Spanish father may have died of syphilitic madness.'

In the taxi Helba was terrified. 'I beg you to tell no one, Anaïs. Gonzalo will be furious if he knows I have told you that. He has begged me not to tell you. He hates disease, he says it is so ugly, he puts you always as someone in a dream, he does not want you to know about these things. Today I said the Turkish woman might come to see me at the same time as you. He was furious. He said he didn't want you to meet her, she was vulgar, and she talks about operations. He thinks you are a dream.'

'Helba, don't be afraid. It will be our secret. Between women. I won't say anything. Naturally. But I am not a dreamer, I am a human being, I feel pity for you, I am not disgusted. You were a victim. I want to help you get well. I will get you well . . .'

'Oh, Anaïs, why do you do all this, nobody has ever done this for me. Gonzalo does nothing for me, he is a child, he dreams his time away . . .'

Helba's suffering touched me, and I was also touched by Gonzalo's need to dream, our need to dream while cooking, chopping wood, cleaning stoves, posing, modelling, dancing, playing the piano, dreaming while serving, healing the sick, dreaming in the middle of ugliness and a monstrous reality.

Helba's story: Her father ran away from her mother and she never saw him again. He took away her two brothers. He left

Helba with her mother, who hated her. At seven years of age she was placed in a convent for orphan girls. It was housed in what was once a prison. The nuns who entered it never saw the street again. There were no windows on the street, only transoms. The girls were awakened at five in the morning by a nun shouting: '*Viva Jesús.*' Then they went to Mass before breakfast, and breakfast consisted of a piece of pig meat. Helba could not bear the fat of the meat and when the nun observed this she served it to her over and over again, even after it was covered with ants. The girls were only allowed to urinate at certain hours. Helba could not control herself and would feel the need much later during class. The nuns said she was possessed by the Devil. They punished her by braiding her hair very tight, first in many small braids and then all of them tied together in an even tighter knot. She would be left two or three days with her hair pulled this way until congestion set in and Helba would faint. The girls were not called by names but by numbers, like prisoners. Helba discovered that by putting a piece of black paper behind a window pane it made a mirror. All the girls wanted to see what they looked like. The nuns caught them and said it was a mortal sin. They were bathed once a year, wearing their long white cotton nightgowns and rubbing the soap over the nightgown. When the nuns flogged them they kept muttering: '*En nombre de Jesús, en nombre de Jesús.*' Helba's mother did not believe in these stories, she felt that Helba must be possessed of the Devil if the nuns punished her.

The atmosphere of the houseboat now darkened by René. Because René was an orphan, I began to give him more and more, and he did less and less work and demanded more and more help.

We had an accord that if I came after dark I would throw a stone from the quay to the roof of the barge and René was to come out and meet me and walk with me back to the barge, because at first I was frightened by the hoboes sleeping under the bridge (it was not until later I realized they considered the houseboat occupants as brothers and themselves as protectors in exchange for a bottle of wine, cheese and soap). René often pretended not to hear and when I ran all the way and arrived at the houseboat I would find him asleep. The houseboat began to look like the site of a crime. René's sullen angers penetrated the walls. He grew careless about pumping the water and I could see it seeping through the floor. In the darkness and the isolation, the mood of the world and the mood of the river mingled, immense and threatening.

The Seine became swollen and angry. It inundated the quays. To reach the houseboat now I have to climb over the wall, down a rope-ladder, get into my rowboat and row to the houseboat. On rough windy days René has to do the rowing.

The people walking along the quays watch me climb down the ladder. It amuses them. Once I dropped a volume of the diary, and it fell to the bottom of the rowboat and was soaked.

Soon after that René left for a job at the market place, and I took on Albertine, a little servant girl from the country.

[MARCH, 1937]

Henry is writing about surrealism. I feel most of what the surrealists write is artificially produced by the mind, not by the unconscious. To place an umbrella on an operating table is incongruous but it is not an image from the unconscious. The only fecund chaos comes from dreams, fantasies, from the unconscious. Absurdity is the reaction of the intellect to events, it is not poetry or fantasy. We talked about psychoanalysis. I said it would have to invent a system of integration for those who could not be integrated by life. But this system only heals those who have faith in it. We have not yet found a way to implant faith. What will replace the faith religion was once able to give?

Henry finished his 'Via Dieppe–Newhaven' story. Does not want to go to Denmark.

Gonzalo has no confidence in his luck. When we gamble with twenty-five centimes in a slot machine in one of the cafés, he turns his back to the machine before awaiting results: he is sure he will lose. When he wins he can hardly believe it.

Hélène's magic wears off. I do not know why. My friends call her 'the vampire' and are tired of her.

A day: The light from the swollen, turbulent Seine reflected on the ceiling. It is dawn and I am half awake. It is the fourth of the month and my allowance is all gone. Rent, food, doctors, clothes, dentists for my orphans. I have seven francs in my pockets. I own two pairs of stockings, mended, two pairs of worn-out shoes. I owe money to everyone. My jewels are at the pawn shop. There is no more wine in Gonzalo's barrel. Everybody needs coal because it is cold. The light awakens me fully, and the money problem. I have lived like an ostrich.

Hélène's concierge telephones me she is concerned about her because she did not come home last night.

Gonzalo says over the telephone: 'Don't worry about her, she probably slept with somebody.'

'I do worry precisely because she does not have anyone to sleep with. If she did I would not worry.'

I find her unbalanced after two nights of insomnia, of walking through the city, sitting in cafés. She says: 'I feel that nobody loves me, that they regard me as a monster. All but you. I feel unwanted everywhere.'

'It is your guilt which makes you appear unlovely in your own eyes. There is something you can do to attract people. They feel you do not care about them. Show them that you care about them. Love attracts love. Moricand did your horoscope and he felt you did not help him in return, and he is so desperately poor.'

What an ambulant diary. At times behind desks, under a mattress, in an unlit stove, in trunks, in valises, iron boxes, buses, subways, taxis, lecture-hall desks, brief cases, in doctors' offices, hospital waiting rooms, park benches, on café tables, hairdressers' salons. The pages often stained with coffee, wine, tears, lipstick. It has travelled in canoes, ships, hidden among dresses, underwear, and once lay on the window sill outside of a hotel window, once on a fire escape in New York, on top of closets, etc.

Albertine, the new maid, is a small woman with thin legs, big breasts, and frightened eyes. She moves furtively, taking care of the houseboat, sometimes silently, sometimes singing a fragment of a song from her native Brittany, a song always accompanied by the clashes of pots and pans. She wears a mouse-coloured sweater, and mouse-coloured felt slippers. On her night table there is a photograph of her future husband, in a soldier's uniform.

Her greatest fear is of going to the fountain after dark. During the day the hoboes helped her carry her pail of water in exchange for a bottle of wine now and then, and she laughed and talked with them. But at night she feared them.

The days turning, the wheel turning, a burst of green foliage, the days so full they burst almost from fullness and richness. New dust in the air, gold dust.

Helba is talking as we walk: 'Gonzalo loved me as I loved him, not as a man and wife, but as friends. He was not jealous. I never responded to a man really, all through my life. My first experience was too much. Married at fourteen to a sadist, who forced himself on me and beat me.' Helba and Henry, both born of ignorance and poverty, of the 'people', both have genius in their art but cannot live poetry in their lives; in life they are prosaic and homely. Is this art and magic in life bound to disappear from human life, killed by communism which says: 'Do not dream. Attend only to the needs of food and house, concentrate only on the need for bread.' No matter how deeply Gonzalo and I concerned ourselves with others' human needs, there remained a secret world closed to them, to Henry and Helba, the need of beauty, the need of a shelter from ugliness.

I cannot remember what I saw in the mirror as a child. Perhaps a child never looks at a mirror. Perhaps a child, like a cat, is so much inside of himself that he does not see himself in the mirror. He sees a child. The child does not remember what he looks like. Later I remembered what I looked like. But when I look at photographs of myself one, two, three, four, five years old, I do not recognize myself. The child is *one*. At one with himself. Never outside of himself. I can remember what I did but not the reflection of what I did. No reflections. Six years old. Seven years old. Eight years old. Nine. Ten. Eleven. No images. No reflections. Feelings. I can feel what I felt about my father's white mice, the horror they inspired in me, the revolting odour, the taste of a burnt omelette my father made for us while my mother was sick and expecting Joaquin in Berlin. The feel of the beach in Barcelona, the feel of the balcony there, the fear of death and the writing of a testament, the feelings in church, in the street. Sounds in the Spanish courtyard, singing, a memory of a gaiety which was to haunt me all my life, totally absent from America. The face of the maid Ramona, the music in the streets, children dancing on the sidewalks. Voices. The appearance of others, the long black moustache of Granados, the embrace of the nuns, drowning me in veils as they leaned over. No picture in the mind's eye of what I wore. The long black stockings of Spanish children I saw in a photograph. I do remember my passion for penny 'surprise' packages, the passion for surprise. Yet at the age of six the perfection of the blue bow on my hair, shaped like a butterfly, preoccupied me, since I insisted that my godmother tie it because she tied it better than anyone else. I must have seen this bow in the mirror then. I do not remember whether I saw this bow, the little girl in the very short white-lace-edged dress, or again a photograph taken in Havana where all my cousins and I stood in a row according to our heights, all wearing enormous ribbons and short white dresses. In the mirror there never was a child. The first mirror had a frame of white wood. In it there is no Anaïs Nin, but Marie Antoinette with a white lace cap, a long black dress, standing on a pile of chairs, the chariot, riding to her beheading. No Anaïs Nin. An actress playing all the parts of characters in French history. I am Charlotte Corday plunging a knife into the tyrant Marat. I am, of course, Joan of Arc. At fourteen, the portrayal of a Joan burning at the stake was my brother's favourite horror story.

The first mirror in which the self appears is very large, it is inlaid inside of a brown wood wall in the room of a brown-stone house. Next to it the window pours down so strong a light that the rest of the room is not reflected in the mirror. The image of the girl who approaches it is brought into luminous relief. Against a foggy darkness, the girl of fifteen stands with frightened eyes. She is looking at her dress, a dress of shiny worn blue serge, which was fixed up for her out of an old one belonging to a cousin. It does not fit her. It is meagre. It looks poor. The girl is looking at the worn shiny dark-blue serge dress with shame. It is the day she has been told in school that she is gifted for writing. They had come

189

purposely into the class to tell her. In spite of being a foreigner, in spite of having to use the dictionary, she had written the best essay in the class. She who was always quiet and who did not wish to be noticed, was told to come up the aisle and speak to the English teacher before everyone, to hear the compliment. And the joy, the dazzling joy which had first struck her was instantly killed by the awareness of the dress. I did not want to get up, to be noticed. I was ashamed of this meagre dress with a shine on it, its worn air, its orphan air, its hand-me-down air.

There is another mirror framed in brown wood. The girl is looking at the new dress which transfigures her. What an extraordinary change. She leans over very close to look at the humid eyes, the humid mouth, the moisture and luminousness brought about by the change of dress. She walks up very slowly to the mirror, very slowly, as if she did not want to frighten reflections away. Several times, at fifteen, she walks very slowly towards the mirror. Every girl of fifteen has put the same question to a mirror: 'Am I beautiful?' The face is masklike. It does not smile. It does not want to charm the mirror, or deceive the mirror, or flirt with it and gain a false answer. The girl is in a trance. She does not want to frighten the reflection away herself. Someone has said she is very pale. She approaches the mirror and stands very still like a statue. Immobile. Waxy. She never makes a gesture. Surprised. Somnambulistic? She only moves to become someone else, impersonating Sarah Bernhardt, Mélisande, *La Dame aux Camélias*, Madame Bovary, Thaïs. She is never Anaïs Nin who goes to school, and grows vegetables and flowers in her backyard. She is immobile, haunting, like a figure moving in a dream. She is decomposed before the mirror into a hundred personages, recomposed into paleness and immobility. Silence. She is watching for an expression which will betray the spirit. You can never catch the face alive, laughing, or loving. At sixteen she is looking at the mirror with her hair up for the first time. There is always the question. The mirror is not going to answer it. She will have to look for the answer in the eyes and faces of the boys who dance with her, men later, and above all the painters.

*

I am still wearing the chiffon scarf over my burnt eyelids. The Abbé Lancelin rang the bell. He is collecting for his poor. He stands amazed when I open the door. A nun? No. A woman veiled with a long chiffon scarf. He has a grey beard. We talk. I tell him immediately that I no longer believe in Catholicism, because there is too much cruelty in the world, but I will help his poor. We talk. He wants so much to see the face behind the veil. It must be an association. Nuns. Veiled women, whose faces he cannot see behind confessional windows. But here it is permitted to have curiosity, to wonder at the face. He began to come every day, to convert me. To convert this mysterious veiled woman. He was hypnotized by the mystery, the nun that is not a nun, a rebel.

Pierre Bresson says that symbolical writing, stylized language impedes human participation. People admire *House of Incest* but they explode over the birth story.

Lawrence Durrell writes me:

I feel a pig if I don't write you and tell you what a splendid writer you are – though of course you know. It was that last thing you sent, the Dionysiac little birth scene. That rang the bell and returned the penny: as you know, only a real strength will do that. I tell you what really thrilled me. I have always dreamed of a sort of hypothetical goal which the woman writer would reach one day in her art. It would be something so positive in its quality that one would immediately stop criticizing it according to male standards. Rather, it would set up a new standard, a sort of man-woman fusion, an unalterable furlong to the present standard of miles. What or how or when this positivity would be, I could never imagine. But in this thing of yours I feel that foretaste which tells me that you are the woman to do this thing. I have always felt resentful of women writing up to now. I felt that their footrule was a male footrule: and by male comparison they suffered. What I think you are doing (possibly have done) is creating a new Art: if you like, a new sensibility which a man can accept totally: as a man; and not qualify by his own standards. A new experience, where the only bond again – as between the true artist and his age – is faith. This is the shadow your birth story throws before it – and I am happy because it is a real novelty. You are the novelty and your work through you achieves a status, a totality, which no longer concerns me as a man meeting a woman – but as a man meeting his maker. This is very good because it spells an emotional freedom we have all got waiting for us: a new IS. Salute!! If I have expressed this badly I'm sorry – though again an apology is stupid. You will get the meaning – which lies universes beyond mere ink. So salute! A salute of 400 guns.

Post Script:

DEAR ANAÏS NIN:

I am speaking for myself, for Nancy, for Patrick Evans, Leslie my brother, for the two dogs Roger and Puke: MARVELLOUS. ABSOLUTELY MARVELLOUS. CORUSCATING. Worth a million 'Carols' and 'Zeros' and *Black Books*. We groaned with the pain of it, a physical pain. A birth reading it. Marvellous. All my most violent congratulations and admiration. All my jealousy in fact.

Writing as a woman. I am becoming more and more aware of this. All that happens in the real womb, not in the womb fabricated by man as a substitute. Strange that I should explore this womb of real flesh when, of all women, I seem the most idealized, the most legendary, a myth, a dream. And it is this descending into the real womb, luring men into it, struggling to keep men there, and struggling to free him of woman to help him create another womb, which fascinates me. The diary ended in Fez, in a city, in a street, in a labyrinth for me, because that was the city which looked most deeply like the womb, with its Arabian Nights gentleness, tranquillity and mystery. My self, woman, womb, with grilled windows, veiled eyes. Tortuous streets, secret cells, labyrinths and more labyrinths.

I talked with Gonzalo. We talked about madness. I said: 'No one becomes mad except from loneliness. While there is someone near you who sees what you see, hears what you hear, you do not go mad. So many artists were saved from madness by the faith of a wife, when all the world was against them. See, Gonzalo, the lamp hanging there has the colour of the moon. Yes, it has the colour of the moon you say, then you see it too and we are both sane, but with the artist often he is one against the whole world.'

The rain is falling. I am faced with money problems, debts,

even though Henry got paid 3,000 frs royalties on *Cancer* and Kahane gave me a part of what I paid for the printing of it. Henry gave Osborn 100 frs, gave Reichel 100 frs on account for a painting he is buying, paid a debt to Edgar, 300 fr. debt to Durrell, bought a shirt and a tie, and when I arrived two days later Henry was eating red beans for lunch, heavy red beans. When I met Betty Ryan at the Dôme I told her about the red beans and ordered Vichy. How we laughed! I never worry about money, but I often have to play desperate tricks, like pawning every pawnable object, borrowing, juggling. And at the blackest moment, something happens, a cheque comes, a patient from New York pays me, debtors relent.

I don't know why I cannot feel humanly close to Hélène. At moments we do. When she is at home, quiet and serious, sitting in an armchair covered with a tiger skin, and we talk about our lives. But soon I feel as I did with Jeanne, that we are playing a game. I see the coloured balls of our fantasy floating over our heads, I see the non-human eyes, and I do not trust her. People sense the non-human in her, and are afraid of her, as one is of a person who ultimately does not feel for others, and only obeys its own obsessions. Yet she talks about her life in tragic terms, but it does not move me. She does not move me. She seems unreal. A brilliant, multicoloured Medusa, capable of destruction. A vampire, one feels, who takes one's substance to nourish herself. Yet her conscious role is maternal, she is generous, imaginative, creative. She really has two faces: one at home, sewing, serious, tragic, the Catholic woman who is afraid of sinning, and the other outside, with mocking eyes, a sardonic mouth, a daring and voluptuous appearance. This aspect freezes people, or amuses them. 'Which is my real self?' she asks me. Absolute duality. As there is in me. But perhaps what is frightening is that the different aspects of her personality are like women on a revolving stage, there is a wall between each rotation. If you are enclosed with one, the other does not hear you. Her heart is not there. There is only an actress, bent on seducing you. One could not call out to this Hélène in a moment of distress.

Her tallness, her statuesque proportions, her larger-than-nature head, strong neck, her green eyes, her powerful voice, give a feeling of strength and invulnerability.

Henry is all paradoxes. He loves the ordinary, the natural aspects of Paris. He is disillusioned when he travels because nothing is extraordinary as he expected it to be. I tell him his search for the natural, the ordinary, stands in the way of his finding the extraordinary. This he does not understand. One finds the extraordinary in proportion to one's rebellion against the ordinary. It would seem as if Henry fears the extraordinary, dodges it, in order to be forced to caricature the ordinary, or to create the extraordinary. I seek it unashamedly, and I find it. Rank, Moricand, Jeanne, Hélène, Carteret, Gonzalo, Fez. Henry enjoys the familiar and fears the unknown: Corfu, Durrell, etc. The extraordinary in life makes him uncomfortable, he does not recognize it, he does not like it until it becomes familiar, human, natural. You cannot have great adventures and your bedroom slippers at the same time. I am at home in the marvellous. Absolutely at home. The unknown, the mysterious, the exotic, the strange, the never-lived-before, the difficult. I am uncomfortable and paralysed in the common. The common is unfamiliar to me. What Henry enjoys are the people who are not picturesque, not striking, the common street, the face of a clock, a homely house, a sloppy café, mediocre people. Faced with the marvellous in life it frightens him. I think now that June was like André Breton's Nadja, only Henry did not accept her. He tormented her for being a mythomane, yet he is a mythomane in writing.

Gonzalo and I, leaning over the parapet, saw the hoboes asleep under the trees, the Seine undulating.

I was telling him about Albertine, the Mouse, as I call her, how nothing I could do or say would dispel her fear, her suspicion of my friendliness. When she breaks a dish she laments: 'Madame will take it out of my salary.' Gonzalo thought she must have been ill-treated in the past.

Gonzalo talked about rituals. The sumptuous Catholic rituals in Peru. When he is describing this, and the Indian rugs and tapestries, the colours on the textiles and pottery, the rules of courtesy, I feel I am recovering a lost world.

When Gonzalo raves against the vulgarity of the Western world, I understand. When Gonzalo says we are tainted with self-consciousness, unable any longer to dream, or to enjoy beauty, to achieve communion with nature, and the Peruvian Indian's collective humanism, I understand.

I try to live out this sense of ritual in my life, by the way I dress, the places I live in, by the symbolism of my gifts, by my power to dream, to move out of realism by exaltation, away from violence, into the unconscious. A sumptuous world of grandeur and hierarchy, of faith and worship, which the Western world has lost. A lost world. Religion as poetry. Artaud attempted to recapture symbolism and ritual, to break with realism in the theatre, but I think he had too much anger. He was insane with anger. Or is all insanity anger?

Helba took a black cat under her protection. The cat vomited a worm. Helba went into convulsions. I saw her with her face twisted and her eyes protruding. 'The worms are inside of me. That is why I am sick. They have eaten into my intestines and the food does not nourish me. Take the cat away.' Worms. Fear of death. She does not recognize me.

At the same moment Osborn haunts Henry's studio. He lies on the couch and sticks his tongue out, and tries to chew the tip of it. Or he stands before the mirror cutting his hair with his left hand and contemplating his unshaved face. Or he comes out with his sex in his hands showing it to Henry and Edgar saying: 'It looks quite healthy, doesn't it, it doesn't look like syphilis.' And later: 'Henry, how would you go from Littlefield, Connecticut, to Boston?'

He has built a legal case against an imaginary man who has stolen his manuscripts, sold them for a fabulous price to a Hollywood producer. He thinks he was ejected from his job because he drank Pernod, frequented Montparnasse and had a mistress. He wants Henry to hold his money and deal it out to him in small sums.

Henry is haunted, uneasy about Osborn. He wants to leave Villa Seurat. He hides. He is afraid to type because Osborn might hear him and insist on coming into the studio. Yet he will not go to Corfu where Durrell invited him. I have to hold the money for all of them. Henry hands it over to me. He does not trust himself. I have to send envelopes with a hundred francs to Osborn by way of other people. Osborn is staying in some squalid hotel.

Henry looks tired and serious. He wants to eat in restaurants quite far from Villa Seurat.

I get tired of Edgar's acrobatics. Henry likes mental acrobats. Henry urges me again to talk. I stop as soon as I feel misunderstood. Edgar, like Fraenkel, talks geometrically, mathematically, in abstractions. I do not understand abstractions. I am not ashamed of that.

What I failed to say to Edgar was: 'Self-analysis is destructive. It only generates introspection. It is usually based on a false premise. It is paralysing. Analysis of you by a professional healer is objective, dynamic. It unifies. Self-analysis dissects and disintegrates. Analysis should only be used by professionals. Self-analysis is anti-creative. It is passive.'

Gonzalo says: 'Strange, the effect you have on me. Although you drug me with poetry, you have a dynamic effect on me. I want action.' I helped him once to take a firm attitude towards a man who was a politician and who wanted to use Gonzalo's romantic revolutionary spirit. I help him with clairvoyance about people.

Waiting in the café, I write these words: 'On *being* the womb.' And it unleashes a tremendous feminine universe. I am completely divorced from man's world of ideas. I swim in nature. On *being* the womb . . . englobing. My pity looks like love, and often is taken for love. All the artists, intellectuals rushing to find their blood rhythm in war and revolution. I go wherever there is life-pulse. Nothing can shatter my individual world, no collective action. No storm on earth. Communism they call it.

But to me it is the drama, the poem, and rhythm of personal hatreds, desires, lusts, and war, passions, greed. Someday, these same downtrodden workmen will become the tyrants, the same greedy inhuman 'bosses'.

My madness is that of perpetual identification with others. As human beings, not as members of races, parties, or classes. People mingle within me. There is a flow between them all, an absence of separateness.

Carteret and I went to the place where they question madmen when they first are brought in. A psychiatrist does the questioning. A few students, a few friends of the doctors make up the audience.

They brought him in in a strait-jacket, with legs tied together. His hair, which was very thin at the top, was damp with perspiration. The doctor was smiling at his clear eyes, at the childish mouth, at the puzzled way he looked down upon his crossed arms and his bound legs.

'Why are you so violent? Why were you afraid of coming here?'

'You are going to take my strength away, you had everything ready to take my strength away.'

'Why should I want to take your strength away?'

'Because of the *merle blanc* [white sparrow], which is born every hundred years. The *merle blanc* is the friend of the good. And the man with the white tie who warned me of the danger, was of the order of the *merle blanc*. The white sparrow is now inside of me and the *aigles fins* [foxy eagles] are envious, the foxy eagles are the friends of evil, and they are against me. They come, six of them in grey suits, and they pursue me. I see them sometimes in a coach, that is when it was a long time ago, in a print I saw; of course today they come in an automobile. The President died today, or else I would not have been brought here.'

'The President did not die today.'

'Not he, perhaps, but then the other, the one who is like him.'

'There is one like him?'

'Yes, just as there is one who is exactly like me, who thinks everything that I think, it is a girl, it is my betrothed, but I can't find her.'

'Does she know you are here?'

'Not yet.'

'Who else goes after you?'

'A monk who is castrated and who sometimes takes the form of a woman.'

'Where do you see this personage?'

'In the mirror.'

'Do you see anything else in the mirror?'

'This monk who was castrated and who sometimes takes the form of a woman.'

'You know I don't wish you any wrong, don't you?'

'Yes, yet I know you had everything ready to take my strength away, like Abélard.'

'Why should I want to take your strength away?'

'Because I desired my fiancée, this girl who thinks as I do.'

'How often do you see the white sparrow?'

'It is born only once in a hundred years so you see there are many more *aigles fins* than there are *merles blancs*, and so the good is always persecuted and followed by six men dressed in grey in a coach as in the print I saw, or if you prefer, in an automobile as it would be today.'

'How do you recognize the white sparrow?'

'By my thoughts.'

'You tried to commit suicide did you not?'

'Yes, because nobody loved me. I was sent to live the life of Musset and as you know he suffered a great deal and nobody loved him, and as you know he drank a great deal because nobody loved him. I was sent to live the life of Musset and explain the prophecy he made in the café before he was hanged.'

'He was hung?'

'Yes, nobody knows that and I have to save his honour.'

'How can you save his honour?'

'By explaining the prophecy he made in a café before it was closed which I got from him as I stood in front of the mirror waving a white rag at the sound of the angelus.'

'The angelus?'

'I was born at noon when the angelus was ringing. White is the colour of the *merle blanc*, and the *aigles fins* think they are superior to him, they think they have all the power, but this power is in me now, and that is why you want to take my strength away.'

'That was why you got so violent when I wanted to bring you here?'

'No, that time it was just to show off to you because you expected it, you were expecting it so I did it, because I know all that I tell you you think comes out of a detective story, and you know it is true that I have read one hundred thousand novels.'

'Why did you want to die?'

'I have the blue love, the blue of love, because the woman who was in every way reciprocal to all that I thought did not love me, so I threw myself into the Nile in Egypt. She wanted to know where my strength came from. I have many enemies.'

'Why?'

'Because when one is white like the white sparrow and the others are black, one has enemies. It is always the same. It is the white sparrow you want to take away from me.'

The doctor turned away from the man in the strait-jacket to his audience: 'You see,' he said, 'nothing that he says makes any sense whatsoever. There is no logic and no continuity. It is a clear case of schizophrenia, with disconnected statements, chaotic and meaningless dissociation of ideas, and an obsession with persecution.'

He watched the man in the strait-jacket, who was laughing softly and who said: 'I knew you would think it was a detective story but I knew all this would happen to me and I had seen it in the mirror, I took the warning of danger from the man wearing a white tie, and so all you take away from me you cannot take away because I am living the life of Alfred de Musset, which was full of suffering, and there is a monk in the mirror who is now watching the six men in grey suits who wanted to shoot me.'

The two aides, who were there to see that the madman did not become dangerous, stood beside him. The doctor bade him goodbye and said he could leave the room. The madman got up. The two aides, who knew his feet were bound and that he could not walk without help, looked at him and made no gesture to support him. They let him make two steps by himself on his way out of the room. The doctor turned towards his student audience with an ironic twinkle in his eye, an accomplice look which seemed to say: how intelligent I am, the doctor, and how intelligent my students, how superior to this degenerate.

The madman took two steps and fell forward. He was permitted to fall. And the doctor sat there with a leer on his mouth, with pride in his lucidity and logic, and he was permitted to smile, and the gods permitted the madman to say deep things, things which a poet could understand, which any poet could have deciphered for the doctor, and everything was permitted, this mockery of a man lost in his unconscious labyrinth, asking for the way, and being treated with contempt.

After hearing this, Carteret and I walked away from the Palais de Justice (Justice!) along the Seine. Would human beings ever learn the meaning of symbolism? Poets and dreamers and madmen, using a language which was clear, clear, clear. A language necessary to the life below our consciousness.

We commented on the cruelty of the doctor who thought himself so superior, and on the poetic imagination of the madman, and how meaningful his fantasies were. If symbolism were something to be banished, then why does everyone dream in symbols?

Jean Carteret.

His face reminds me of the faces I saw in Fez. The brow, the eyes, almost always beautiful, and the cheeks, chin, mouth, almost totally ruined with pockmarks, the smile ruined with gold teeth. Like faces carved in stone part of which is ruined by weather. Jean's brow, eyes, eyelashes, with a spiritual beauty, illuminated as one imagines Rimbaud's brow and eyes. But the rest of his pock-marked face revealing anxiety, and the smile sorrow.

He loves zippers on all his pockets, which are full and inexhaustible. He carries books, photographs, notes, magazines, pipes. He lives like a heavily loaded snail. His eyes are innocent, pale blue, yet he attracts and seeks underworld characters, adventurers, circus performers, guides to Paris at night, people from the Fair, sharpshooters, gamblers, prostitutes, pimps. He arrives late for everything. He cannot finish anything, realize or fulfil his wishes. An overcrowded, chaotic life. Every day new explorations, new appetites, new enthusiasms. Everything is interesting. He writes letters he never mails, promises visits he never makes.

But Gonzalo has initiated me to this world of unkept promises, of great literary productions volatilized in talk night after night in cafés. Gonzalo says: 'I will fix your radio. I will show you what I wrote on *House of Incest*.' I have learned not to believe it, not to wait. For I am the kind of dangerous dreamer who executes all his reveries, wishes, words, promises, plans. The wildest and the lightest. A wish for me is not a game: it's a creation. If I lie on my bed and dream of the pointed sea-shell necklace I might sew on my black dress, I have to get up and sew the sea-shells.

One has to walk very lightly on the waves and vibrations of ecstasy to keep the mood of poetry, with eyes half-closed not to see deterioration, ravages, illness, ugliness. This is a state easily achieved by the gurus in Tibet. They can walk barefoot over the snow. Can I not walk without seeing pockmarks and gold teeth. The *merle blanc* of the poor madman was singing in our ears, for he was right; there are many enemies eager to destroy purity, innocence, or the visionary who sees what they cannot see. And if their vision were faulty? The doctor limited in his vision?

Carteret falls away, lost in the traffic, waving from his bus, and I am sitting in a café with Gonzalo, who is describing the tortures inflicted upon the communists in Peru, how they were left standing in water until their flesh cracked, the blood coagulated, the legs swelled, and the men went mad with pain.

'Gonzalo, I cannot live in such a world. That is why I turn away. Unless I can act, save them, fight the cruelty of the world, I have to turn away and live in another world. I cannot see it as one political party, or another, I see it as the cruelty of man.'

Gonzalo's torment was slowly calmed. I gave him medicines for Helba, and I took the subway to meet Henry at the café. Henry has been signing his contract with Éditions Stock for the translation of his books. When he arrives he talks excitedly, but he says he is not excited because it has all come too late.

It is always too late for the artist, when it does not come instantly, the moment he has finished his work, for after all he does not want an answer which comes years later.

It is raining. His friends, the Rattners, were invited to celebrate. Abe Rattner paints like Rouault. Bettina writes about fashions.

Henry knew Gonzalo years ago, Artaud knew him, and yet I did not meet him until years later. Why? I would not have understood him before.

What is destiny? Henry introduced me to Gonzalo when the right time came, when the impersonality of Henry's life and friendships seemed cold to me.

How each friend represents a world in us, a world possibly not born until they arrive, and it is only by this meeting that a new world is born. With Gonzalo I rediscovered my Spanish world, my Spanish blood, warmth and personal involvement, direct passionate response to experience, fire, fanaticism, fervour, faith, the power to act *whole*, wholeness, caring. Henry does not care. Gonzalo cares. He could die for a cause, for the workmen, for the poor. Henry only seeks his pleasure and his self-glorification. Gonzalo wants to give himself.

Ironically, Henry is saying that he is becoming a saint, and that his life was an error. 'Write this in your journal, Anaïs.' Henry says he likes to be with himself now, not outside, he is collecting himself, concentrating.

And I am dispersing myself, as I learned from him, to give myself, waste, live blindly. People pass into other planes, exchange qualities, change. Henry discusses analysis with Edgar, I am moving away from analysis into action.

Ever since Osborn came, haunted Henry's studio, borrowed money and food, Henry, while acting with compassion and wisdom, became more and more depressed. His own passivity, acceptance, inertia ties him in a knot. I tried to help him. I suffered his bad moods, fatigue, despondency. I understood. Henry was far away.

When Henry is faced with a conflict he simply goes dead. When he is faced with the need to take the lead, to act, to free himself, disengage himself, he is paralysed.

He gets sick. He sleeps. He hibernates. He cannot act. He sleeps all day, as if this would solve the problem of Osborn.

He says he feels shattered inside, tired, in need of concentration. We had dinner in a café, and talked quietly. He said: 'I feel I have never lived on the same level as the level I write from, except with you and now with Edgar.'

'Did you do that not to be alone, to be like others, with others, not to go mad? You sought out mediocrity in people, in life. Why should Osborn's state depress you so? Are you afraid to be cut off from reality as he is?'

Dream: A long winding path of ice. I am walking on it with great terror of the ice breaking. I run in a panic. Henry begins to walk over it and I hold his hand. I tell him not to try because he is heavier and he will fall through. The ice breaks. I am holding him so he will not fall into the pit but I feel the heat that comes from it and I pull Henry out of hell. We all have to pass through a narrow aperture to reach a certain place. I feel the usual anxiety before a hole, and decide to take another route. I leap over lakes, bushes, hills, like a deer. I reach an isolated castle, very old and ravaged. It has many rooms locked with huge keys. The rain is pouring in through broken windows and the floor is rotting. I open all the rooms. I come upon a room and through a glass door I see a man sitting with his back turned, sitting in an absolutely empty room. He is blond. I get panicky and I run away, carrying one of the keys. When I join the others, the manager of Helba has decided I am to dance an Indian dance with my body painted in gold and feathers. I say to Gonzalo: 'I think Helba would do this far better than I.' Gonzalo agrees. A man says: 'If you got inside of that castle, can you prove it?' I say: 'I have one of the keys.' 'Then you are a hysterical woman,' he answers. Cocteau, Chirico, and Dali!

Durrell writes:

Your little Dionysiac birth story. That lives and shines, I tell you ... I have no doubt, not a shadow of a doubt about you as an artist. The sense of dislocation proves that to me more fully. Loneliness is the password ...

To Durrell:

When I read your letter the word *faith* loomed immense and I was struck with the warmth, the summer softness of the letter. When I read about the 'spiritual atrophy of Gregory', I said no, the only trouble with Gregory is the emotional conflict, the English conflict. It is feeling which England is ashamed of, which bothers Gregory. Difficult to say all this in English. The taboo on feeling. I don't mean that Gregory is English, nor has he atrophied feelings, but they are coiled inside, indirect, they move obliquely, they romp in the dark only, they manifest themselves perversely, through irony, hysteria, and fully in the poetry only. That is what is entirely lacking in Huxley [to whom he had been compared – A. N.] and why I see no affinity whatever. Huxley is no poet to begin with. *Ca ne chante pas.* And *you do.* Why must Spandrell commit a crime? It's to leap out of paralysis created by abstractions. People jump into crime, to bring the blood to life when they are bloodless. Emotion is again left out. Sensation is mistaken for it. See the leap from surrealism to revolution, war. Gregory, because he analyses, is aware, divided, but he is not paralytic. His instincts, nature, are alive. His feeling lies like an explosive. Waiting to show its face in ecstasy. At other times it is blinded, dazzled, muted by the vision. I could say to you what Henry said about me in the diary, living with eyes too open . . . And I see yours closing a bit, the metamorphosis. You are already somewhere else. You reached life by divination first, I take it, as I reached it. How much like Gregory and his sincerity and his cosmic reachings. I wonder where you are now, in your metamorphosis? I'm in the night looking for silence. The head is quiet and everything else, all the other cells are breathing tentacles. Wonder why you called me the submarine superwoman. That made me laugh, yet it is accurate. Only it took me many years to recover my fins and my swimming strides. I was trying to walk (like the penguins) and to think like a man. I was very impressed with man's thinking!

Eugene Jolas comes to visit. He looks like a bull about to charge. He is heavy with German mysticism. He is disillusioned with the poets' temporal concessions. He praises *House of Incest* as a marvel of language, beauty, and which 'gave him great fears'. I believe he felt that his life was dedicated to the discovery of a new language. Does he not feel James Joyce did it? He is disillusioned with the 'actual'. So we talk in harmony, a kind of opaque mystical language. I hear the semantic horses leaping over our heads, a bath of fogs and mists and his 'language of the night' with its red caves, and very black letters and mysterious hieroglyphs. In the face of Jolas I see a man tormented, with an anxious smile, and a mystical despair in a world becoming absolutely one-dimensional.

Visiting the Gilberts, I was in despair because I felt timid, there were too many people around.

Stuart Gilbert repeats that I am intense and emotional about myself but that when I describe others I have irony and humour. He enjoys my sketches. Has read all that is copied of the diary and says I have achieved my own style.

One can imagine him very well in the uniform of a colonial judge in Indo-China or Sumatra. The face of an English Buddha, dispensing justice, his small eyes alert for comedy, his 'tolerance' of the native, his learning, his detachment. When he retired, Caresse Crosby said to him: 'Translate this for me.' (I forget what it was.) 'But I'm not a translator,' he said. And he ended by translating Joyce into French, and writing about James Joyce.

The piano takes up a great deal of the salon, which has two windows overlooking the Seine. A big drooping tree makes a trellis through which the barges and boats pass and the river becomes like a shattered mirror, or a spilled necklace of diamonds. Mrs Gilbert has a tender and lovely face, the face of the ideal mother-wife, even though young, eyes ready to understand and to shelter, voice to assuage, smile to console, and with that a lovely laughter of the human being not lost among abstractions, creating the atmosphere in which books are like living sparkling guests, not objects. There are always books about, in piles, on tables. Deep armchairs, graciousness, and an unostentatious way of cultivating only quality. Their apartment on the Seine is a steadfast boat no storm can upturn. It is anchored in the world of intelligence.

My mother collected clothes for the Spanish Red Cross (for Franco's Red Cross). I asked her to give me one suit contributed by David Nixon, the violinist, for someone who was extremely poor and working for Spain.

'Not a Republican?' asked my mother.

'Not a Republican.'

I took it to Gonzalo, who had nothing to wear for the opening of an exhibition at which some of his drawings were being shown. I asked a friend to buy one of Gonzalo's drawings so he would be encouraged, promised I would buy it back later. Then came the day, and we all met on the Rue de Seine. Gonzalo appeared in his dark-blue suit and I could see what an effort it was for him not to run away. He is wild and timid in crowds. He looked continuously to the left and to the right for an opening, as if corralled and seeking a chance to escape. His eyes looked more sombre than usual, and he kept his head bowed. Although the suit was big enough he looked as if Western clothes were not intended for him. Heathcliff. The untamed Inca from Peru, too tall, too wild for this small gallery, for the narrow Rue de Seine. He did not fit in this diminutive world, between walls, in a crowd, listening to artificial compliments. He stood near the door and then stepped outside for a breath of air. I stood beside him, and we both saw, at the same moment, David Nixon walking towards the gallery, with my mother! David Nixon would recognize his suit, my mother would recognize a Republican! Gonzalo vanished with the speed of an expert magician.

When Henry talks about his impersonal relationships (one friend as good as another, interchangeable, they can come and go, he does not care), I try to explain to him my impersonal compassion which he does not understand. I am pushed by a force over which I have no control, to create, to construct, to give hope and compassion even when I do not care for the person.

Every now and then Helba says she is going to dance again. This means that her trunks with her costumes have to be hauled out of the cellar, that Gonzalo has to prepare paints to decorate her dresses and headgears which are tarnished, I have to buy some beads and spangles, tassels, gold thread, costume jewellery, coloured glass, mirrors. For days she will be in a fever of activity preparing her wardrobe. And then, just as suddenly, she forgets the whole attempt, closes the trunks, and Gonzalo drags them back to the cellar.

I watch Helba sewing rags. No matter what she is given, in her hands it soon looks like a rag. She sews rags and makes costumes for the theatre such as the ones children make for amateur theatricals. She makes clothes for herself which make her look like a rag-picker. All she touches seems like a rag-picker's object as soon as it has been kneaded by her hands. It turns old, faded, patched in a few seconds. As if her hands withered whatever they touched. Once after a party at which she admired my Persian flowered cotton dress, I took the dress to her as if I wanted to clothe her in some shining flowering garment in place of her rags, a magic garment. She promptly dyed it black. She killed its colours. Another time (as she says I have a nose like a rabbit), I took to her at the hospital a white rabbit-fur cape to lie in bed with, saying it was my own fur which would keep her warm. She never wore it. She cut herself a cape out of an old grey, moth-eaten blanket. She persists in dressing like a beggar imploring pity. She indulges more and more in her pitiable role until at times both Gonzalo and I feel weary as before professional beggars. She continues in this role long after it has ceased to be true. Was this the child in Helba refusing to die? All unfulfilled desires are imprisoned children.

She sits with shoulders hunched. Helba's dancing was a miracle, the opposite of her life. In life she limps, hunches her shoulders, sways awkwardly, has slow reflexes, dresses like a beggar and moves like a cripple. On stage she became fiery and satanic. Her Indian dances were violent and strong.

Her face is faded. Her skin is old, though she is only thirty or so. She has expressions like a shrewd peasant woman, like a beggar girl in the streets. As a very poor girl of the people she aroused Gonzalo's compassion, Gonzalo – Don Quixote, the defender of the poor. She was dancing in nightclubs then, and Gonzalo was the black sheep of his powerful and wealthy family.

In the fall of Helba's eyelashes, in the shape of her eyelids, there is suffering. She humiliates herself, makes herself uglier, poorer, she shrinks within herself, has no interest in anything but her dancing, cannot see others dancing, or read, or even turn her eyes outward. She has a yellowed, ascetic face. I gave her clothes, coats, everything I could possibly spare. Gonzalo would say: 'Helba has no coat.' Then one day, when they were moving, I had to help Helba pack, and all her trunks were brought from the cellar, her costume trunks. One of them had to be opened, and out spilled a fur coat, dresses of all kinds, underwear, shoes, stockings, all her finery from the days she danced with the Ziegfeld show in New York. Handbags, handkerchiefs, belts, combs, everything which she could possibly need and which she had been hoarding like a gypsy while I stripped myself of all I had to dress her.

Gonzalo's devotion to Helba touching. I feel the same pity when I see her smaller, shrunken, deaf, with hair hanging limp, her dead black hair, and no longer dancing but withering.

She says: 'My hair is falling off in bunches. My teeth are sore, and loosening. Gonzalo is mad. He seems changed only because he is leaning on you. He lets everything happen, and he says it's destiny. With his cigarette he nearly set fire to the apartment house. He threw the still-lighted butt down the garbage chute and it started a fire during the night. For a woman to love Gonzalo is not happiness. He is one who sacrifices woman to himself without knowing it, unconsciously. He is a child. I know why you want to give him a printing press. You want to keep Gonzalo from going to Spain to fight. You are thinking of me. The idea of Gonzalo at war, when I think of it, the whole beauty of this afternoon turns black.'

Sometimes I watch her gestures with horror. For at times she goes far beyond the dramatization which her dancer's training makes understandable. She is a theatrical character, she does express everything with her body, but in her dancing, when she danced with so much inwardness, I already recognized the gestures of insanity. She exaggerates her mimicry to express physical pain to a monstrous degree. For the pain of pleurisy, which I have known, she acted with her hands like the statue of the god whose entrails were being eaten by the ravens. For a stomach pain she mimics someone devoured by flames. Finally I recognized she had transposed her gift for theatre into a gift for dramatizing her illness so it would always seem like a state of agony just before death. This threat of her death hung over Gonzalo's head, giving him not a moment's rest. He could only forget her threats when drunk. To see these gestures border so often on the gestures made by the insane appalled me. There is insanity in caricature of gestures, grotesque deformations. If Helba's drama did not destroy Gonzalo, I could be moved by it, but I had to become the exposer of it to save Gonzalo's very life.

*

Distressed by my timidity. Was introduced to André Breton and almost turned away in a panic. He awes me, because I am fully aware that his ideas have influenced all of us deeply. And he is a great poet himself.

[SUMMER, 1937]

Poverty is the great reality. That is why the artist seeks it. It was my only reality as a child. It gave me a closeness to human reality forever. I sought it out afterwards, voluntarily, to remain close to all my friends, Henry, Helba, Gonzalo, Moricand, who were all poor. Poverty also has a religious significance. It represents sacrifice, it is usually the outcome of a choice between artistic, spiritual values and the material ones. It has a spiritual significance. To protect the poor I have denied myself voyages, luxury, clothes, comforts. I have kept only the barest necessities. I have stripped myself joyously. I feel great joy thinking of Henry working in his studio, with his water colours, Helba able to go to the doctor, Gonzalo with paper to draw on, suits to wear. The fewer possessions I have, the richer I feel. I seek poverty. But when I see what it did to Henry, Gonzalo, and Helba, I wonder. Their health destroyed, their work, their life. Without protection, their dream destroyed. No food. No materials to work with. No paper, no paint, no typewriter, no costumes, no medicines. Yet I seek this. Every day I come nearer to it. To be nearer to spiritual values? Nearer to the defeated, the failures, because I feel they have qualities the others do not have, the rich, the selfish, the flattered, the recognized, the decorated? I am born under the sign of the giver, Pisces, I will have to give even more. I have to give up visiting my father in Caux, staying in Corfu with the Durrells, Montecatini with Hélène or Venice with my mother and Joaquin, because I have to pay for Henry's rent, Gonzalo's rent, and to feed them all. No rest. No seashore, no travel, no vacation. Voilà. No Heine's beach costume, no mountain air, no sun on the body. But I get pleasure from seeing how my children live. Gonzalo is so good for the present, he is good for life, but that is why he may be of less value in the eternal, in art, than Henry. He is immediate, and that is why he lives in politics. He lives so much in the present that he has the beautiful gift of direct emotion, as a woman has, a beautiful gift of responding with all of himself, as Henry does not. Gonzalo lives so much in the present that when he gets cigarettes he forgets the matches, and he has to go out again. A moment later he thinks of coffee. As soon as creation begins there is a need for planning, for thinking of tomorrow. I have so strong a sense of creation, of tomorrow, that I cannot get drunk, knowing I will be less alive, less well, less creative the next day.

Gonzalo loves with devotion, fidelity, sacrifice, with a giving of the self. Henry loves in a primitive way, he enjoys, takes, uses, and never gives himself. It is all for him, for his work, for his benefit, for his career as a writer, for his appetites, his pleasures.

My father is talking about the marvels of the microscope, about the scorpion he saw and studied, about the minerals, the gold dust. And meanwhile I ask myself about the novel I wrote, was it the truth? Henry deformed June in his novel, did I deform my father? Art is a microscope, as you examine one aspect of a human being, you cannot give the whole, the entire picture. The diary is closer to the truth, because it paints my father each day anew, with changes, paradoxes, contradictions, growth, and in these oscillations lies the truth. *Here* alone is the human vision restored. The novel is an act of injustice. One is true to the *theme*, an aspect of relationship, not a portrait. I do not want to be a novelist. I want to keep the snapshots of the father I knew in Valescure. The novel depicts the conflict, not the human being separated from his conflict. It depicts the dangerous animals we are in relation to each other. As Lawrence once said, every human being is dangerous to every other human being. Now that we are no longer at war, I can see him differently. He likes to sit on the floor, as I do, and tell me about his dreams which resemble mine, about the ship passing through a waterless city, about a train leaving and his valise not ready, of flying, of cataclysms. I looked at him with sad eyes. Tell me more, Father, about the microscope. He is ashamed of all he wants for himself, of his thirsts, appetites, his whims, his games which he must pursue inexorably while people die and starve around him, of his need of luxury and show, of his need of gadgets, of new cameras, microscopes, and so he says: 'I bought the microscope during Maruca's illness, to amuse her.' When I know Maruca has no interest in the microscope, and even less in the best microscope ever made. Games.

Others' needs, real needs. Dark needs, vital needs. Games with poetry, costumes, music, guitars, charcoal, water colours, with words, the vital games of art. Bread and poetry. All the pleasures I might take in luxury, as my father does, I willingly surrender to the greater pleasure I get from creating life, hope, fulfilment all around me. I feel a deep pleasure when others enjoy. It is deeper than any other.

There is a drug in Mexico called *sinicuik* which helps one to remember the past. I could call my diary by that name. Taoist teaching: 'To get one's due is to remain in the whirligig of time; but not to claim one's due is to fly off at a tangent to eternity.'

'Importance of being a fool (to make others laugh). Foolishness, not knowledge, is power.' Henry's philosophy.

In China: Blocks of wood carved with printed texts used as walls of houses. People could come and rub paper against them and get texts of important documents.

'The fundament of Taoism is the subtle idea of the permeation or interpenetration of opposites.' 'In Tao the only motion is returning.' Chinese proverb: 'When a thing is pushed to its utmost limit it will return.' 'Another way of going beyond good and evil is the assiduous practice of what Lao-tze would call soft or feminine virtues.'

More and more revealed in the diary is my struggle against the scientific intellectual inventions of man. With my feelings and instincts I belie all the theories and psychological explanations of man. What I did with analysis was to use, transform, and finally reject all but the poetry.

At this point I was fortunate enough to meet the Inca, Gonzalo, who picks up Frazer's book, *Myths of the Origin of Fire*, and says: 'Why seek the origin of fire? Why not *be* the fire?'

I have a growing obsession with order, I organize my closet, my papers, create an unburdened atmosphere, no useless objects, everything ready to be found, lived with. Reduction. Papers classified, medicines in order, as if ready for a trip, clothes in order. To make living smoother, faster. Order gives me serenity. It is the philosophy of the Japanese. Order around you helps you to think clearly. I need this because my body is too keyed up, like that of a race horse, and I need sedatives. I have given away everything I do not need. No waste. No accumulation of belongings. Nothing around me torn or broken. I see in Helba's and Gonzalo's life the very opposite; they are always submerged and drowned by what they have not done, trammelled by small obstacles, laundry never done, nothing to wear, everything lost, torn, *dispersed*.

I was able to buy a printing press for Gonzalo. Gonzalo was in ecstasy. For him it meant financial independence, prestige, domination, propaganda for Spain. His pride is now aroused. I have awakened his energy, his love of leadership, dispelled his sense of guilt which makes him afraid to live for himself, ashamed to do anything for himself. We went to buy the machine together. We danced around it. It lies flat on a table like a proof-making machine. Henry wanted it, but does not really need it. His work is published and accepted. Gonzalo needs it and can earn his living with it. His joy was wonderful to see. Afterwards I thought a little regretfully that I would have liked the press for myself, to do with as I liked, but I can never do this while those I love have a greater need. I was enjoying Gonzalo's joy.

Lawrence Durrell writes me about the two novels I had sent him [*Winter of Artifice* and another, later incorporated in *Ladders to Fire*].

Postscript the following day; i.e. today. Dear Anaïs. I have read your two manuscripts, and I'm delighted with you. What a woman you are, my god. I'm a bit scared of meeting you, etc. The Father one was lovely, beautifully proportioned and written with a hot poker. Tremendously memorable; and the little girl portrait is moving for me. But the other is, I think, bigger in scope, though it lacks the objectivity of the Father one. You become a real female gorgon, double-headed. The only criticism, if you can call it a criticism, that occurred to me, was that in making it so subjective, so intensely personal, you were forced to make the characters transcendent, superhuman: mythical, as they were mythical in your world. I wept a bit, because this is the first book in Europe which belongs to a female artist; and it is bitter. I was not concerned so much with the interplay of the characters; but thought all the time how female it was, how the gift was total, always, unreserved, not withheld. And this is a crucifixion much worse for a woman artist than a man – because her world operates so intimately *through* man. Somehow the prime detachment for the female is not a rift with humanity, but a rift, an amputation from the male; whereas for me it works differently. Perhaps women have had more practice in involution; perhaps the deep sensitive biological nerve of the woman is more hurt by the snapping of the cord (perhaps I am simply talking rubbish). But the spectacle is more wounding, more painful, when a woman assumes the role of protagonist. Anyway, I find it so. I wish there were more of those mischievous, reassuring touches: like when Jay was talking so painfully about the whores, etc., to assure himself about the depths being as necessary as the heights and all that. When you put a feather in your hat and draw back the bowstring then you make me delight: because the male is so vulnerable to this kind of mischief. He is transfixed before he has any retort ready. He stands with his mouth full of bread and onions and shuffles his feet. And the magnificent edifice of his self-esteem simply totters! I love that! It is extraordinarily great. I'm glad I'm not a woman. How can you stand it? They are calling me to bathe. It is hot. I shall send you the novels back soon: Nancy is finishing them. Who is Jolas? Isn't he the chap with the dream-note-book. Is he any good? Awful the stuff in the last *New Directions*. Have met a wonderful painter called Ivy Langton. *I would like her to illustrate the heraldic madhouse*. In her funny little brain she keeps a menagerie of people as volatile and living as Breughel: but she has miles more feeling than he has: so much of the automatic art (Klee, Miró and Company) seems to me to be on crutches: somehow static: but in her paintings there is an incessant activity, though the little figures seem petrified on the canvas by their strength of colour. I wish I could buy a painting by her. She knows Reichel. Says he is always drunk, but admires his work. Lived in Paris ten years and *loathes the English*. This last trait is enough to make her an artist even if she had nothing else. A funny little Lincolnshire lass who is good because she does not care. More anon.

In Henry's writing there is a sonority, a fever, an amplitude. Cosmic Wind. The diary was once a disease. I do not take it up for the same reason now. Before it was because I was lonely, or because I did not know how to communicate with others. I needed the communion. Now it is to write not for solace but for the pleasure of describing others, out of abundance.

Someday I'll be locked up for love insanity. 'She loved too much.' This could be on my tombstone. What I feel intensely and always respond to is the aloneness of the others, their needs. Which love makes the great closeness, the fraternal, the friendship, the passion, the intellectual harmony, the tender one, devotion, the lover, the brother, the husband, the father, the son, the friend. So many kinds of fusions! What is it that annihilates the loneliness? The understanding of Rank, devotions, ardour, creative harmony?

Break and shatter loneliness forever!

I am never close enough; I want some impossible communion.

I must accept intermittences. Loneliness in between.

Letter from Faber and Faber to Denise Clairouin:

We have been having an exceptionally difficult time deciding about the diary of Anaïs Nin. As you already know from my request for the further material, we were very much interested; yet in the end, and after very great regret, we cannot see how to shape the material into book form which could be published in England. Much of what we should wish to use for the integrity of the book, we should be prevented from using by the restrictions on books in England. In the end the difficulties of the problem have defeated us, and I am sending the volumes back with a great deal of reluctance.

On loneliness. My connection with Henry is on a creative, an imaginative, a more impersonal level. It is not continuous because he shares himself with his work and with the world, he leads a collective life.

Gonzalo's talent is for the personal relationship. He is emotional, direct, personal, human. He is spontaneous, warm, loyal, devoted.

Gonzalo's dynamism and involvement in history, Henry's celebrity, Helba's returning strength, satisfy me.

My father writes me: 'I came away filled with peace and sweetness.'

Gonzalo expanding, blooming. I call him the *Dieu du Feu*, the god of fire, whom he used to drown in wine. I run between the Shangri-la of literature, Villa Seurat, and *Nanankepichu*, the Indian drug of poetry. I write about metamorphosis.

The Mouse is always given the same food I eat and not treated like a French servant. One day I ran short of money and I asked her to buy eggs instead of meat. She began to cry.

'Oh, Madame, I knew it could not last. We've had meat every day and I was so happy. I thought at last I had found a good place. And now you are acting just *like the others*. I can't eat eggs.'

'But if you don't like eggs, you can get something else. I merely mentioned eggs because I was short of money today.'

'It isn't that I don't like them. I always liked them at home, on the farm. We ate a lot of eggs. But when I first came to Paris the lady I worked for was so stingy – you can't imagine what she was like. She kept all the closets locked up, she weighed the provisions, she counted the pieces of sugar I ate. She bought meat for herself every day and eggs for me, until I got deathly sick of them. And today when you said . . . I thought it was beginning all over again.'

We cleared up that misunderstanding and all was well.

But I left the houseboat for a week and when I returned the Mouse looked more worried than ever.

A few weeks later the Mouse was grinding coffee in the kitchen when I heard her groan. I found her very white, doubled up with pain in her stomach. I helped her to her cabin. The Mouse said it was indigestion. But the pains grew worse. She groaned for an hour, and finally asked me if I would get a doctor she knew who lived near by. It was the doctor's wife who received me. The doctor had taken care of the Mouse before, but not since she lived on the houseboat. That made it impossible for the doctor to visit her because he was a '*grand blessé de guerre*' and on account of his wooden leg he could not be expected to walk across an unsteady gangplank. That was impossible, the wife repeated. But I pleaded with her. She finally gave a half-promise.

When he came the Mouse was forced to make some explanations. She was afraid she was pregnant. She had tried using something she had been told about, pure ammonia, and now the pains were terrible.

The Mouse had to uncover herself. I asked her why she had not confided in me.

'I was afraid Madame would throw me out.'

The doctor said: 'You risked a terrible infection. If it does not come out now you'll have to go to a hospital.'

'Oh, I can't do that. My mother will find out then, and she'll be furious with me.'

'Maybe it'll come out by itself but that is all I can do. I can't be mixed up in things like this. In my profession I must be careful. Bring me water and a towel.'

He washed his hands carefully. 'All you servants make trouble for us doctors.'

'Don't send me to the hospital,' pleaded the Mouse.

When the doctor left the Mouse said: 'To tell you the truth, Madame, it isn't worth it. I don't see anything to it at all. It only happened because you were away and I got terribly frightened. My young man came and I let him stay here, and that's how it happened.'

The fever mounted. I was forced to take her to the hospital. I packed her valise. She insisted on wearing her Sunday hat which she kept under her bed in tissue paper, and a piece of mouse-fur around her neck. She wanted her book with her. It was a child's reader. At the hospital they refused to take her in. I appealed to my own doctor. She was saved, and I kept the secret from her family. But I could not forget the woman bleeding there on the bench of the hospital while they asked endless questions. The little round moist eyes, the tiny worn piece of fur, the panic in her. The brand new Sunday hat and the torn valise with a string for a handle. The oily, soiled pocketbook, and the soldier's letters pressed between the pages of a child's reader. And this pregnancy accomplished in the dark, out of fear. A gesture of panic, that of a mouse falling into a trap.

This volume of the diary [No. 54] is large. A large, honest, expansive one given to me by Henry, on which I can spread out beyond the diary, encompassing more, transcending myself. The small notebook I could slip into my pocket was mine, this one I cannot clutch, hide, restrain or retain. It spreads. It asserts itself. It lies on my desk like a real manuscript. It is a larger canvas. No marginal writing done delicately, unobtrusively, but work, assertion. It so happens I am alone. I can leave it on my desk. The place is wholly mine. Perhaps I shall include the world. I neglect the world. Henry was right, what I write is less communicable than what he writes because he has a human love of writing, of words, he takes a sensuous pleasure in writing, it is flesh and food, whereas I have a sort of contempt for the sensuous joy of expression, I seek the meaning, the contents. A lonely quest, which isolates me. Henry is nearer to all because of the language, because he likes to talk, to formulate, to share. His concern is with communication, mine with exploration, discoveries, tracking down elusive states of mind, of feeling. We shall look around a bit, my diary, at the enjoyments. We shall dwell on the sensuous pleasures of language, the word made flesh, and have less concern with significance. Henry often does not care for meaning. He does not care if one paragraph contradicts and annihilates the other.

Sometimes in the street, or in a café, I am hypnotized by the 'pim' face of a man, by a big workman with knee-high boots, by a brutal criminal head. I feel a sensual tremor of fear, an obscure attraction. The female in me trembles and is fascinated. For one second only I am a prostitute who expects a stab in the back. I feel anxiety. I feel trapped. I forget that I am free. A subterranean primitivism? A desire to feel the brutality of man, the force which can violate? To be violated is perhaps a need in woman, a secret erotic need. I have to shake myself from the invasion of these violent images, awaken.

Henry's writing has that effect on me, his brutality of speech, his barbaric language, his primitive behaviour. Food and sex the primal needs for him.

In Gonzalo too, I like the man of nature. The poet Neruda said to him: 'Where is your horse? You always look as if you had left your horse at the door.' The times in his studio when he washed his hands and they smoked, for his hands were so warm and the water so cold. He dried his hands over the fire and watched the smoke running through his opened fingers. *Le Dieu du Feu*, I said laughingly. He cannot be submitted to time. He is chaotic. He does not know how much can be done in half an hour. Half of him is forever asleep, coiled in his Indian mother's womb, in reverie, in Indian laziness. Only half of him acts in the world, and the idealist is already nauseated by the political game, by the self-interest and the power-lust around him, by the writers gaining publicity for themselves under cover of the Spanish cause, by the men profiting from the blood sacrifices of others. 'I am doing dirty work,' he says. 'The work behind the front is filthy and unworthy. I would rather be fighting.' He is pure. He has the shyness of noble animals. He always refuses orgies, or exhibitionism at parties. We both like ancient, unreal qualities, we like heroism and passion, and these are vanishing from the world.

Gonzalo represents for me all that I inherited from Spain, mystic, ardent Spain, whose peasants are as polite and stylized as its aristocrats. Imbedded in my blood, in the blood of my race, was the figure of a romantic Don Quixote and I had to find him. Gonzalo, the Inca Don Quixote; only he fights for a cripple, and for Spain's revolution.

When Gonzalo read *House of Incest* he said several times: '*Qué sensual, qué sensual.*' He responded to the sensations and the images directly. For Henry *House of Incest* is 'esoteric'. He responds to the language; he is fascinated as by something very far from him. He likes the images as an artist. But he does not *feel* them. Gonzalo feels how deeply I am swimming, with gestures he tries to explain from what submarine regions I write. He knows. He senses things intuitively, as June did.

But the adventurer in him is tired, finds life too hard, too bitter, too terrible.

There is in him an anarchist, a naïve child who trusts and forgives, a Bohemian who does not care a damn, a fanatic who is ready to kill for Marxism, a drunkard who forgets all his responsibilities at a bar, a religious mystic who falls into a trance at Notre-Dame, an Indian with his secrets from all white men, his melancholy and inertia, a violent Moor, a Catholic nursemaid to Helba, an Indian slave, an Indian rebel. He has a lashing, Voltairian tongue when he is angry, he has sudden miraculous generosities, nobilities, he will give his life for a friend, for the weak, yet his own life is filled with mishaps, and at times great storms of bitter anger which take the form of long tongue-lashing monologues.

The only flaw I find in Proust is his generalization. If only he had written the following as a personal experience:

I understood the frustration of love. We imagine that the object of it is a being who is lying before us, enclosed in his body. Alas, it is the extension of this being in all the points of space and time which he will occupy. If we do not possess a contact with such a place, at such a time, we do not possess our love. And it is impossible for us to contact all these various points. If at least they were indicated to us, perhaps we could stretch ourselves towards them. But we fumble and cannot find them. And from this stems jealousy, suspicion, persecution.

If only Proust had spoken for himself, without saying: 'lovers, jealousy, all suspicion, all lovers'.

We can share all his moods, insights, and experiences because he is a great artist. But they are his. Every human being has a different way of achieving closeness, and of experiencing separation. Henry's is purely physical. It was centred on June's sexual activities, because his own relation to women is usually only sexual. His jealousy was centred on proofs. He only believed facts. Separations for Henry were caused by simple infidelities. But in Proust, Henry's opposite, separations were caused by his own intimate malady of doubt.

If only he had always said: 'the cheek of Albertine', or 'the colour of the Verdurin's sunset', but he would always start with an individual experience and from it generalize. Every jealousy, every fear, is different. In Proust himself there was an activity which constantly created unreality: one was hyperanalysis, the other self-doubt. So he spins the unreality from which he suffers. He dissolves life.

I want to describe the physical image just long enough to preserve it, but not long enough to reach dissolution.

Gonzalo touches the realms of creation, philosophy, psychology with occasional intuitions. There are moments when he understands everything. But he does not *live* there, he does not sleep, eat and walk there, he does not inhabit them continually. He gets on his horse and enters the forest. He quarrels, drinks, talks with workmen at bistros, fights for his ideals, can spend whole evenings with ignorant bar-room white trash, just as Henry does. I cannot do this. I cannot spend a day with empty friends without a sense of waste. I can't give myself to ordinary people. Henry says: 'But I don't give myself. That is why I can seem so human – just because I am not.'

But I have scruples. I feel guilty for the part of myself which I cannot share with just anyone. I feel guilty because being with them does not make me happy, but sadder. Humanly I do not get pleasure or comfort as Henry and Gonzalo do from ordinary exchange. Small talk at the bar, at cafés. I have no criticism. I have regrets, I would like to be near and like everyone. Woman is more alone than man. She cannot find the 'eternal moments' in art as man does, as Proust did, even if she is an artist.

Reading *Modernes* by Seurat, I take note of all he has to say about sensations. All he says about modern man's quest of 'sensation' applies to me, except the boredom which follows upon their fulfilment, from exhaustion. I have never known *ennui*. Perhaps because of the more meaningful quality of my sensations. They do not wither or die in me. I do not suffer from hangovers. My sensibility, response, vibration, exultancy enthusiasm are the same or deeper than when I first began to live. *Ennui*, which haunts modern man, is unknown to me. I only pray at times to feel less, to find peace and repose.

I awoke this morning with a song in my head, a poem of Éluard sung like a bird's song, the mechanical bird of paradise which was wound up by the handle of a phonograph. That which dies in modern man never dies in me, because my senses are alive, married to my feelings and to meaning, because my earth has roots in the infinite. It is the emptiness of their sensations which causes *ennui*.

I live so intensely for the *other*, I am so abnormally aware of others' feelings that I have fallen into the habit of lying about what I enjoy. I never say, for instance: 'I am seeing Hélène tonight because I enjoy seeing her, because we have such a mad, fantastic way of talking together.' I say: 'Hélène wants to see me tonight, she is so much alone and she gets depressed.' As if I were merely submitting to her need. This is meant at times not to hurt anyone by seeming to enjoy anything more than their presence, it is meant to convey: all my pleasures are here, with you. The rest is duty. But there is a deeper reason for all this. I live so much to give pleasure to others that after a while I am confused myself as to whether I see Hélène for her sake or for my own pleasure. The truth is that there is such a vast sum of things I do not do for myself that it has become the dominant impulse. True identification with others and the desire to give is erroneously confused with masochism in psychology. Psychologists say we give out of guilt, out of atonement, we give to suffer. But no account is taken of the divine pleasure which attends the giving and makes it a natural function of the pleasure-loving. I am far from Catholic hypocrisies, but I am returning to religion. Gonzalo last night was talking about Catholicism and the sensual life. He said: 'You're a true Catholic. You love sinning, and confessing, and obtaining absolution, and having regrets and then sinning again.'

Today I have to console Gonzalo for his great sorrow at hearing that his own elder brother in Peru runs a 'fascist' newspaper and is considered the *valet de plume* of capitalism.

'The house in which she lives,' says the mystical German writer, 'is for the orderly soul, which does not live on blindly before her, but is ever, out of her passing experience building and adorning the parts of the many roomed abode for herself, only an expansion of the body; as the body, according to the philosophy of Swedenborg, is but an expansion of the soul. For such an orderly soul, as she lives onward, all sorts of delicate affinities establish themselves, between her and the doors and passageways, the lights and the shadows, of her outward abode, until she sees incorporated into it – till as last, in the entire expressiveness of what is outward, there is, for her, to speak properly, no longer any distinction between outward and inward, at all; and the light which creeps at a particular hour on a particular picture or space upon the wall, the scent of a flower in the air at a particular window becomes for her, not so much apprehended objects, as themselves powers of apprehension, and doorways to things beyond – seeds or rudiments of new faculties, by which she, dimly yet surely, apprehends a matter lying beyond her actually attained capacity of sense and spirit.'

Watching the fish swim in the turquoise waters of the aquarium I experienced a suffocation. I had watched so intently, I had been so absorbed by their breathing, I had forgotten to breathe for myself. I had been so breathlessly attentive to their breathing, to imagine what it felt to breathe through one's flanks, through one's own groin, to breathe through a slit behind one's ear, to breathe through a slit on each side of one's neck, through an opening in one's ribs, to breathe with a wing of flesh open, to breathe with a part of the flesh curling up like the antennae of a sea anemone, to breathe with arms, trunks, legs, that I had forgotten to breathe for myself as the woman who stood there watching the aquarium. I had passed into the water, into the body of the fish. I was the fish breathing with my belly, and I discovered the multitude of cells inside of me which breathed in light, and sound, and colour, when I was asleep. I felt all the brusqueries of climate changes, all the incisions of colder airs, of hotter currents, of changes of level, of rarefied waters, of waters surcharged with air bulbs; and in passing into the fish I forgot to breathe as a woman. This happened to me so many times when I was watching the sorrows of others, their crumbling lives, the debris of their creations. I forgot to breathe as a woman, and for myself. I began to live the life of others, to gather the ashen fragments together, to weep at their despair, to share their rebellion, to enter into their struggle and fatigue, and I felt at times in the dark, the same suffocation of my forgotten self watching the aquarium. It is part of the Zen religion, to *become* what you are meditating upon, a tree, a flower, a human being in trouble.

The kiss in the taxi is the kiss which remains in the memory as perpetually unfinished and to be sought out again, for as the taxi moves it gives to the moment that physical proof of insecurity and ephemeralness of adventure, over swift, arousing resonances which cease at the first stop, the taste upon one's lips is a quick, deep lancination arrested by the sudden stop of a machine. The interference of the traffic is the recall to reality. Eyes out of the crowd rummage into the taxi to catch that flash of vertigo, that open mouth, the drunken look in the eyes. The street lights are the searchlights, opening crude ways into the smoky clouds of cigarette smoke, breath and perfume. And now the taxi is rolling again, the kiss is broken by fear of its termination. When the taxi stops, the adventure is broken. One steps on the pavement with a sound of a body falling from heaven. One pays with the sound of a harlot bartering. One opens one's foggy eyes to look for one's house, wishing an earthquake had devoured it and with it all sense of time. The adventure continues in the head, in the body. It evaporates, for it happened in mid-air, in unknown places, while in motion, there is no trace of the kiss, no surroundings to retain the flavour of it. It is uncannily removed from daily life. Perhaps it never happened. We were embarked and disembarked between midnight and dawn and perhaps we were asleep, as others were. Until the next taxi ride no kiss will have that flavour of life and time slipping by, uncapturable, unseizable. The thrust it made into us is unique, impossible to repeat. The taxi was moving towards an end, the kiss had no tomorrow, left only a wound of regret and the sound of a closed door.

I will write someday a long *Promenade en Taxi* describing all that takes place in a taxi. The reveries in anticipation of what is about to happen, the preparations, rehearsals to act, and then the retrospective analysis and reveries on what has happened, the moods of relief at escape, detachment, the exaltation and ecstasies relived, noted. The shift between levels of life, like a change of speed, gear shifts, now slow, now fast, now warm, now cold, now dissolved into others, now alone, now a thousand persons in one, now one. Such states cannot be achieved in subway or bus. Such isolation of the virus of life under a microscope.

One night I sat in Henry's studio pasting press notices of *Tropic of Cancer* and *Black Spring*. Henry was jubilating over them. It was a tangible proof of his progress as a writer, his communication with the world, recognition.

Henry is not in harmony with himself. He is full of confusion and paradoxes, and the conflict in him is so continuous that he projects it on all those around him. Each day he destroys what he has said the day before. He attacks the very qualities he praised the day before.

If a person is tranquil, he goads them to aggressivity. If they are aggressive, he squelches them. He is a sea of discord and contradictions.

He attacks my lack of interest in slang. Well, it is not my language. It would be phony for me to use it. I have found my own language.

Esther Harding's comments, in her book, *The Way of All Women*, apply to him:

Certain men seem to be dependent, almost like women, on the change in their inner feelings. The rational Logos functions have been relegated to the background, while the feminine part of the psyche, which is usually concealed, comes to the fore and forces their changing moods into undue prominence. This change results from a domination by the anima, the feminine spirit in man, which, however, should not rule the conscious but the unconscious. Consequently the domination by the feminine spirit has a peculiarly unpleasant quality. For such men are not really ruled by changes in the non-personal Eros, but by moods and whims which have as their chief characteristic that they are exceedingly personal. Domination by the anima produces a curious womanish quality, a dependence on personal likes and dislikes, on moods and feelings to the exclusion of all capacity to react with adequate feelings in accordance with any judgement of fact or the validity of an impersonal truth. This situation is a travesty of the woman's sub-mission to her inner law of change.

Gonzalo's language is the key to his nature. His favourite words are: 'Atmosphere', he liked or disliked the atmosphere (a word or feeling Henry could never use, because he is not sensitive to atmosphere, a more subtle climate). 'It has no quality,' says Gonzalo. '*No tiene calidad.*' Another word Henry never uses. He does not make such distinctions. Gonzalo says it even of a body, a body without quality. '*Calidad espiritual.*' Prodigious. '*Prodigioso.*' He uses extremes of enthusiasm. '*Qué prodigio!*' He has a sense of wonder, of the fabulous, of the miraculous. He often uses the words: 'unreal, vital, mystical'.

Gonzalo too is full of contradictions and confusions. He worships the old, he hates science, the machine, yet he embraces communism. He is religious, and he loves beauty, yet he goes to inaugurations, political meetings, he can listen to hackneyed speeches, sentimental speeches, he can go to mass meetings, walk the streets with workmen who will one day destroy all art, all aesthetics. He hates realism, but he makes naturalistic drawings of bums, prostitutes, drunks, hoboes. He loves beauty but he draws only deformities, cripples, etc. He loves poetry, and magic, but he does not believe a human being can be affected by a sorrow, a loss, a defeat, become blind or deaf for emotional traumatic reasons. He is aware of time passing; he can say it is five o'clock without looking at a clock, like all men who lived in nature, but he cannot arrive on time. He knows scientific statistics and he lives in chaos. He worships delicacy and quality yet he destroys everything around him. He lacks equilibrium, psychic or physical. He cannot draw a straight line (I can draw a perfect circle without a compass). He cannot frame a picture straight, he cannot cut a cardboard without mangling it. He cannot organize his day: he can make several trips through the city caused by lack of planning.

Henry never suffers from 'unreal' anxieties. Only from realities. His greatest neurosis is the fear of being left without food, so that to calm his anxiety I have to keep his closet stocked with provisions for a week ahead. He never fears the loss of a loved one, death, solitude, illness.

Esther Harding:

The moon-like character of the woman's nature appears to men to be dependent only on her whims. If she changes her mind, it never occurs to him that she changes it because of changed conditions within her own psyche, as little under her control perhaps as a change in the weather... Woman's nature is cyclic... apart from her personal or egoistic desires. The nature of woman is non-personal and has nothing to do with her own wishes, it is something inherent in her as feminine being and must not be regarded merely as something personal. The life force ebbs and flows in her actual experience, not only in nightly and daily rhythm as it does for man, but also in moon cycles, quarter phases, half phases, full moon, decline, and so round to dark moon. These two changes together produce a rhythm which is like the moon's changes, and also like the tides whose larger monthly cycle works itself out concurrently with the diurnal changes, sometimes increasing the swing of the tides and at others working against the tidal movements, the whole producing a complex rhythm hard to understand.

Neurosis, sickness, the malady consists in remaining fixed in a trend of thoughts which is destructive, a wallowing in all the negative, frustrating aspects of one's life. For example, dwelling on what one cannot obtain, on one's defeats, on a desire for unlimited power.

What is this malady which makes me dwell on the people who did not understand *House of Incest* rather than on Durrell's glowing letters? Meditating on my failures rather than my triumphs, joys, possessions, pleasures. Is it destruction which I do not carry out in life which expresses itself in self-destruction? In life I never destroy, I do not criticize, attack, punish, hurt others. Then this source of energy installs itself inside of my breast like some gnawing animal I am trying to keep locked inside and who tears at me. Would it not be better to free it, as Henry has freed his demons, and let it cause its ravages, to rebel as Henry does, to destroy the past, to hate, to spit on old fidelities, to plunder, to kill parents with words? How to liberate this demon of destruction I carry in my breast because I refuse to let it do others harm? It eats into me when I cease being active or living at a feverish rhythm. Solitude is forbidden me. Would creation feed the monster? Must I write with my demons?

*

Dreams, dreams. I arrive in a dilapidated taxi because I knew nobody else would take such a taxi. The floor of the taxi was so worn the street showed through the cracks. I could have counted the cobblestones. I wondered whether in the end I would fall through and be left sitting in the middle of the street like a new-born baby fallen out of a crib, or an egg from a hen. And there would be the street, suddenly, without time to have prepared myself for adventure. I was a believer in preparation. I liked to sit in a taxi and watch myself in the little mirror in front. I would talk to myself: I would say I need greatly to have heavy objects put on myself, on my head and feet, something like lead chains and boots. That way I would not leave the earth so easily. It is amazing with what facility I outdistance things, with what ease I float away, and soar away, and am carried thousands of miles from the spot where I stand, in such a way that I assure you I don't hear what is being said to me, I do not see the person who is there, and I am not aware of myself any more. I feel so light, so light at times, vaporous, like steam on a window which can be erased with a careless finger. Put a lot of heavy things on me so that I will stay on earth. Put warm blankets on me because heat attracts me and makes me want to stay where I am. Turn on a strong warm voice. A strong voice which comes from the stomach also makes me want to stay on earth. As a matter of fact, there are many things which might detain me, hold me down, like the smell of coffee in the morning and a mauve glass bottle with a neck like a man with a goitre, and the moment in the taxi when I am going somewhere and I have time to imagine what this somewhere will be like, time to invent it, time to prepare myself for it. I was going to say this to him, with a strange face in which the features do not seem to belong together, a face where the eyes seem to spark away from each other and the radiance of the cheeks depart in many directions, like a broken halo, and the smile falls apart. I made this face in the mirror, just like the face, I thought, you see sometimes on people when they are about to go insane. It is all unrelated. The eyes are not connected to the meaning of the phrase which is spoken, and neither does the expression conform to the contents of the phrase. There is a kind of panic through it all, they are all wavering as if in a panic, and each is saying a different thing. The eyes do not reflect the mood of the moment, but that blanket-like past hovering behind the present eternally, like the traces of an ancient disease, and the voice has in it still the terror of many years ago and not the courage of today. It is all confused, while the woman is saying with today's mood: I will say to him I happened to come here because when the bottom of the taxi fell out I found myself in front of your house. I would like life to be always as casual as that. There would never be any engagements. I dropped in here like a package left at the *consigne*. Will you give me a receipt please, give me a receipt. I have no confidence, you see, I like to hear from people what they think of me, how I look to them, even what I have said to them. You would have to write on the receipt at this hour there came a woman who looked exotic and talked with a foreign accent. I don't mean that she was born elsewhere, in another country, but that she has the intonation of never having been born at all to our language, to the language of other women. I received from her very grave words said in a bantering tone, a bantering uttered with a sadness I cannot understand. It was all very foreign because she made one feel so. She herself must have enjoyed feeling not at home. She liked to have the illusion of the uncommon, the never-lived-before. I really think she believed it. Now this receipt will prove to me that at five o'clock I was in your house and we did exchange words which you pretended not to have heard before, this receipt would be a great comfort to me. I will fold it and wear it against my breast. It is like a certainty. I would like also when you love me you should note it all down. I feel that from the very beginning life played a terrible conjurer's trick on me. I lost faith in it. It seems to me that every moment now it is playing tricks on me. So that when I hear love I am not sure it is love, and when I hear gaiety I am not sure it is gaiety, and when I have eaten and loved and I am all warm from wine, I am not sure it is either love or food or wine, but a strange trick being played on me, an illusion, slippery and baffling and malicious, and a magician hangs behind me watching the ecstasy I feel at the things which happen so that I know deep down it is all fluid and escaping and may vanish at any moment. Don't forget to write me a letter and tell me I was here, and I saw you, and loved you, and ate with you. It is all so evanescent and I love it so much, I love it as you love the change in the days. I would prefer to move away where I could not sense the movements of life passing, somewhere in space and distance where I might divine that ultimately it is I who will abandon life and separate myself from it, not life leaving me, and it will be like the old taxi that was falling apart and dropped its contents like an egg and maybe this egg is a book, and not me, and I am safe behind paper and ink and words and stories and only counting cobblestones, not having arrived anywhere yet because of the painstaking preparations involved, for you see in the mirror I am practicing a certain expression and when I arrive it is generally not needed. For the person is another from the one I invented, and I have to adapt my soul anew.

Another truth overlooked by psychoanalysis is that after they have classified a relationship as masochistic they never consider that what may seem to be the seeking of suffering may in some cases by one's spiritual salvation. They completely forget the fact of the soul's salvation.

There is, for example, the frustration I feel at Henry's lack of insight. But his lack of insight has forced me into self-expression, it has deepened my own and humanized me, for I always have to explain to Henry. Who is to say what is destructive and what is creative?

Henry perhaps helped me to find my strength by constantly challenging it. If it is true that I have the defect of being hypersensitive, it is also true that I have an uncanny divination of others' feelings. Gonzalo is perpetually amazed at how I guess all he feels, expose it, heal it. It is a penetration of the soul.

Henry is always admiring what is outside, external. Helba complains Gonzalo cannot live except with a group of people. He too, like Henry, moves in shoals. Gonzalo and Henry both arrive from the street with a glow on their faces. They come from the most innocuous places, a café, a talk with an anonymous, nondescript, colourless person, an exhibit of paintings. They denigrate what they have seen. But the glow is there. It is the glow of exercise, of motion, of pure physical circulation. It comes from flux and reflux, the waves. It is impersonal. It is the shoal-life pleasure, which woman cannot understand, because she gets this glow from intimate life. It is the health of collective exercise, of collective swimming. Woman looks for depth, and for intimacy. I should not say 'woman', and generalize as Proust does, I should say I, Anaïs, to be more exact.

[AUGUST, 1937]

I walked to Henry's studio to meet Lawrence Durrell and his wife. What first struck me were his eyes of a Mediterranean blue, keen, sparkling, seer, child and old man. In body he is short and stocky, with soft contours like a Hindu, flexible like an Oriental, healthy and humorous. He is a faun, a swimmer, a sail-boat enthusiast. Nancy, his wife, is a long-waisted gamin with beautiful long slanting eyes. With Durrell I had instant communication. We skipped the ordinary stages of friendship, its gradual development. I felt friendship at one bound, with hardly a need of talk.

When they left, Henry, Fred and I spent a quiet evening. We went to a movie. I saw workmen revolting, a fight with the police, injustice, suffering, hunger. At that moment, because the workmen were shot down by the police, because the machines left them without bread, I understood Gonzalo's talk about communism as a possible relief to injustice. I do not believe it can cure it, because injustice and cruelty are inherent in man, incurable, but it might control it somewhat.

It struck me again, that individual suffering should be merged into universal suffering. One should adopt the world's troubles in replacement of one's own. Of course, the personal life deeply lived always expands into truths beyond itself. My struggles with myself led me to understand the struggles of others.

*

When you write consciously, you follow the most accessible thread. Three or four other threads may be agitated like telegraph wires at the same instant and I disregard them. If I were to capture them all I would be cornering the nimblest of minds, revealing simultaneously innocence and duplicity, generosity and calculation, fear and courage. The whole truth! I cannot tell the whole truth simply because I would have to write four pages to each of the present ones, I would have to write backwards, retrace my steps constantly to catch the echoes and the overtones because of the slipperiness of embellishments, the vice of idealism which distorts the truth at every turn. The danger in carefully backtracking to pick up what fell out of the net is the danger of falling into introspection, that monster who chews too long upon a morsel, achieves only absolute mastication, and who withers all it touches rather than illumines it.

Gonzalo belongs to other centuries. What did he think of New York, of Paris, when he first saw them? They seemed small, crowded, and he had claustrophobia! Helba was the star of the Ziegfeld show, as an Inca dancer. She danced in Paris. He played the piano for her, he helped her paint her costumes. He played cards, he drank, and he took drugs. The women never left him alone. He had an extraordinary magnetism for women. He tells me this without vanity. He also tells me how being a Latin, a Moor, an Indian, he was not able to respond to women who courted him. He had to make his own choice. He was always in flight. The only force which unifies him, pulls him together is either love or politics. He has a gift for leadership and domination. He can talk to workmen, impress them. He is eloquent and fiery. There is power in him. But his weakness is like mine: he cannot use others. He can rule himself, drive himself, create, he has a vision, but he cannot use others, he does not know how to use others, make others work for him. He wants to serve communism, but he cannot bind himself by any contracts, he will not, cannot submit to anyone. He wants to do independent work, without obedience and discipline. He wants to work for the collective good, but he cannot, will not give up his freedom, his individual liberty.

He asks me: 'Is it possible that two years ago I was just a Montparnassian, just a Bohemian?'

'Never deep down,' I said. And I remember the first time I put my finger on the spring of his real nature, what it was I touched one day which exploded like dynamite: his pride, his aristocracy, his leadership, his devotion and compassion. I remembered how he awakened emotionally, like a man hit by a whip, whose manhood suddenly and violently asserted itself. I remember where we were sitting, in a small café by the Seine, when he had just said that I looked like a sixteenth-century virgin he had always loved, like the woman men went to the Crusades for, like his first ideal of a woman. It seems as if returning to his first ideal which he did not attain (he married its opposite) he suddenly had returned to the days when he was the lord of vast lands, owner of slaves, soldier, and mayor of his village. I awakened this in him, although when I met him he was as deteriorated as a hobo.

He said: 'I believe, *chiquita*, that our friendship was not only a personal friendship, but that we were thrown together to serve humanity.'

His ideal woman was the mother of Gauguin, who was a South American political heroine, one of the first socialists. I think he is confusing me with her. But why, if he likes heroic women, women of action, did he marry first of all a dancer, and then give his devotion to a writer, an artist?

I wanted to be of help to Republican Spain but I could not write letters full of platitudes, heroic bombast, sentimental propaganda, naïve humanitarianism such as Gonzalo does, collecting money, entertaining volunteers, attending meetings, listening to news on the radio and reading newspapers from cover to cover. Gonzalo said: 'All we want is your sympathy and faith. We do not expect political work or service from an Artaud, or an Erik Satie.'

Helba and I are walking in the Bois. I took her for a walk in the sun. We stopped at a model-dairy for a glass of fresh milk. And of all people, my father's snobbish mother-in-law came in, dressed in the latest model from Vionnet, with a toque by Trigère, a coiffure by Antoine, a new set of nails by Emil, false eyelashes by Gérard, a dog groomed by Cécile, gloves by

Hermès, a leather handbag by Chanel, perfume by Guerlain, face treated by Elizabeth Arden, and her chauffeur, costumed by Rue Saint-Honoré specialists, waiting near by with a Scotch plaid from Old England in case of danger from a breeze.

Helba was wearing Gonzalo's discarded torn red shirt, my green Majorcan sandals, a skirt made of a potato sack, and was blowing her nose with rag-picker's rags. She was carrying her sewing material inside of a tin box marked in large letters: OVARIAN SUPPOSITORIES, which she had rested on the table. Because Helba is deaf I had to raise my voice. Alta Gracia could have heard all of our conversation about the state of Helba's insides and her operations, about her test for syphilis, her constipation, etc. Alta Gracia decided it was best not to recognize me. The softness of the summer day like an ermine paw.

Everything seems miraculous, that the summer should be so soft, that fountains should play on the Champs-Élysées, that men and women are walking. A city never entirely known, yet which gives you the feeling of intimacy, of possessing it intimately. A sky which changes every day and yet keeps its opaline tones. Can life continue to unroll this way with a freshness never withered, new faces, new marvels? Can one arrive so many times at fullness without touching bottom, every year new leaves, new skins, new loves, new words. One day I weep at change, but then there is no death, there is this everlasting continuity, nothing is lost, it is transformed, or have I learned to walk magically over hot coals without burning my feet?

I have known Lawrence Durrell for a thousand years. He is a boy of ten playing in the Himalayas with the snow disease on him (the English disease of impersonality). He is an old man in some ways, who does not live impulsively but cautiously, he is a spectator, he is a boy who laughs.

When he came last night to eat out of my wooden plates, to watch the river below, he tasted the place, he let himself be ensorcelled by it, he sat at the centre of it, on the floor, like a Hindu, and enjoyed it.

We walked through the Exposition. He wanted to ride the

roller coaster, he wanted to travel on the train for children. We talked about everything, and at the same time there was no need to talk. How well he knows Henry. Talking about the Max story (the story of a Jew in which the Jew is exposed ruthlessly, X-rayed, caricatured, crucified forever),* he said: 'You are frightening, Henry. The way you cut the cord, the umbilical cord from what you describe – no pity or love – just the all-seeing monster, the savage vision, exposure. Something really outside of the human. If I were a Jew this story would kill me.'

A dimension without emotion. This in Henry I do not admire. Perhaps I have done it in the birth story, at times in the diary, but never without pity. Then Henry wonders why people are terrified, why Fraenkel got sick when he read the story, just as I wonder why the birth story has such a terrific effect on people.

Durrell is blond, fair-skinned. He has beautiful teeth, a sensual humorous mouth, blue eyes with northern lights in them, small stature, small hands, something childlike about the body. A fine warm laughter, easily brought on, a sort of uncanny knowingness mixed with hesitancy. This English obsession with impersonality makes him a spectator, makes him seem withdrawn, at the same time warm.

I sent him the metamorphosis story. '*Nous autres du Midi nous sommes très liants.*'

Patrick Evans, a friend of Larry's, writes me:

This is before breakfast, the air is full of sun but it's still fresh. I've just read your novel about your father [*Winter of Artifice*]. It's very moving. I admire it very much. And I'm enormously glad that Lawrence Durrell lent it to me to read. It's not the first thing of yours which I've read but it is, for me at any rate, the best. *House of Incest* I enjoyed very much; there are some staggeringly wonderful things in it; but I found it disconnected, there was no unity running through it, like the upward growth of a tree trunk. Or rather, there is unity there but it isn't on the surface, one has a remote presentiment of the drama but it never quite comes through, it's like seeing the tree trunk through a wall of many coloured fog. Or like a floating island – one expected the sea and in fact the sea is there,

*See Henry Miller, *Max and the White Phagocytes* (Paris: Obelisk Press, 1948). – Ed.

but one never gets to it, one is always on top of the island. The book is full of good things but they are all isolated and foreign to one another – the most amazing images, here a perfect line and there a perfect line, several of them on every page, a whole drawerful of gems; but they are all jumbled and disconnected, not strung together on one thread. The thread got lost somewhere. But in the book about you and your father it is different. There is the same excellent writing, the style quieter it is true but enormously good nevertheless – language used as the exact and spontaneous notion of experience; and there is also that collectedness and forward movement like the movement of a ship, which *House of Incest* hasn't got. Not merely a thread of drama, a dynamic wire running through the whole with accretions of undramatic, static incidents or descriptions clustered upon it like parasites; the whole thing *is* drama, with nothing superfluous. And it's alive, breathing. I'm very much moved by it and full of admiration for the honesty and aliveness and courage of it. (If I may say so without seeming fulsome and falsely complimentary, the sort of *cher confrère* stuff, fervid celluloid admirations designed for public occasions, which so infuriates me and disgusts me in French literary men.) I'm very grateful to you for having written it. In our age as in any other, there are so few works produced in which the writer relies simply on living experience, pure and unadorned (unaugmented), for the whole flesh and complexion of his art; it is so easy to mask the self, to produce a grandiose or elegant, or pétillant effect, empty of the sensation of living, by adopting a pose and by using petty devices by way of technique; it's very seldom that one finds a writer who is naïve and real, and frank, as genuine as food and as undeniable, as real, as the wind or the sky or a tree. Your work excites and pleases me and thrills me, and frightens me a bit too. I hope someday I shall be able to write something which approaches the same level. (As regards the *cher confrère* aspect – I'm still in the earliest stages myself struggling out of swaddling clothes. I've written a bundle of verses which are nine-tenths rubbish and the remaining tenth good. Just now I'm at grips with my first novel – got about a third of it done. Full of difficulties; it's wrestle, wrestle, wrestle, all the time.) And so out of the blue Ionian, on a creamy summer day with the sunshine blowing along, a salute and thanks.

DEAR PATRICK EVANS:

Your letter pleased me immensely, really. You are a writer and you know what happens when one writes. It is an arithmetic that takes place in the dark. It only becomes valuable, illumined with a sort of glow, a life glow, vital, when it creates a current, when there is someone at the receiving end, when there is an echo, an answer. Everything else is a sad affair, sitting alone, writing. The pleasure comes when Patrick Evans sitting before the Ionian writes back what he felt, saw, heard. Then the manuscript begins to breathe, really. We were talking about this the other night, with Henry, Larry and Nancy. Larry was rebelling against writing. Henry said: 'It does not take you away from life, it brings it to you, that is how we met.' When I wrote my book on D. H. Lawrence I met Henry. *House of Incest* brought me the Durrells. My father manuscript brought me a letter from you. Those are the pleasures. You should send me something of your work. One is repaid for the moment spent alone with paper, which Larry so much resents at times. I was repaid for the moments when I felt all the warm currents of life ebbing away, I, like a ghost, pale with absorption, far away from everything, out of contact, cut off, because the father manuscript was devouring me. Nancy, Larry, Henry and I are now enjoying the compensations. We like them in the present, we don't think much about immortality, we are sensual and human and we like it right now. When one gets a letter such as yours one feels one gets one's dues in the present, and it is humanly satisfying. I think all of us are lucky. I liked what you said about the sea, the sea is there but one never gets to it. Henry thought what you said about the drama, the forward movement, was very good. I am glad you thought the father MS. naïve, real and frank. I was a little anxious. Through timidity at times I get a little artificial. Instead of stuttering, I stylize. I thought that now and then in the father MS. I was artificial. I am glad you did not feel this. Seeing Larry has been a real joy. I value him greatly. For the softness and the ferocity and the clear vision, and the human quality he has. We talk a great deal, yet we don't need to. Last night we sat overlooking the Seine, and we talked in the dark, quite nakedly. We finally landed in the Heraldic Universe, installed ourselves there, rested, became whole again. For one evening. Do you live in Corfu? Do you make a copy of your novel as you go along? Do you like it to be read while it is being written, or only after it is finished?

Someday . . . Meanwhile, while we talk, we look at the Seine under my window, at the papier-mâché exposition, and the heat makes us a little lethargic. . . .

I am not sure what Lawrence Durrell means by his 'heraldic universe'. A poetic island? A place of nobility, a wholeness, a sign, a fraternity?

Curious that it should be Lawrence Durrell when Lawrence, the other D. H., was my first love as a writer.

Coincidences. That I should pass by the Café Zeyer and see standing there the proprietor of Louveciennes, and it was also at the Café Zeyer where I met Otto Rank, before Henry moved to the Villa Seurat. Gonzalo lives a few doors away from my first studio on the Rue Schoelcher. I once wrote about the Rue Jean-Dolent, which affected me mysteriously. I imagined myself living there looking into the Prison de la Santé and communicating with the prisoners by signs. Emile has taken a room on that street and is communicating with one of the prisoners by messages written on a folded-paper bird which they throw from window to window. The prisoners wanted to know who had won the bicycle *tour de France*. When the entire city of Paris will have been worn out by my experiences a day will come when I will have lived in every room in Paris, walked every street, sat in every café, eaten in all its restaurants.

The transposition of emotion made by the sincerest people when they are not aware of their subconscious feelings. This transposition of emotion women practice more than men.

Most women are unaware of this. I often become aware of it as I do it, and sometimes I do it consciously when I have a secret I cannot share, and yet my emotional state cannot be controlled or disguised, so I attribute it to another cause.

With me my unconscious is so vast, so tremendous, like a vast ocean which is constantly manifesting its presence, threatening to drown me, but which I can clarify and control as I live it out. It is very rare when I am not aware of what is happening to me, very rare when I live blindly. Chaos, storms, furies, anguish, they come as fiercely as in all women but very quickly I swim to the surface, and I can *see* with human eyes, and control the damage of primitive floods and eruptions.

The evening I spent with the Durrells and Henry seemed like a long voyage because we talked about so many things, stirred up so many feelings, awakened so many ideas. I had been in Greece, in their house, licked by the waves. I had been in the Himalayas, and in England. I had been in a new Paris with Larry visiting the Exposition as a playground of whimsical possibilities. His humour is poetic, delicate. He does not use Henry's language. I had dust on my feet, the song of Ravel's bird of paradise in my head, joy in Durrell's understanding of my writing, and of me. If he adopts Henry's dimension without emotion, and being impersonal he may, he will grow away from what I am doing. Even now he says one cannot write well without having written *Hamlet* once, as painters are supposed to have made copies of Rembrandt. I do not believe this. Not for modern writing.

An impersonal world. A glacier. So personal about himself, Henry, ruled indeed by the moon in him, but so impersonal about others. Yes, he never penetrates others, experiences empathy only if it is someone he can identify with. He observes. He does not penetrate. He cuts human beings open and exposes their vitals, but he does not feel for them. He can do this because he does not care.

And Lawrence Durrell, where does he stand? At times I feel he could have been, symbolically speaking, the writer child of Henry and myself. He likes Henry's ruthlessness. He calls it anti-romantic. He calls it the truth. He himself writes without feeling, impersonally. But there is something else there. I think he is a romantic seeking to repudiate or deny this. I think he is a poet and a painter, and that he will never open human beings in the way Henry does. But he will not go into them either, into their feelings as I do. He is too English for that.

I think he does not know yet where he stands.

Beautiful flow between Durrell, Henry, Nancy and me. It is while we talk together that I discover how we mutually nourish each other, stimulate each other. I discover my own strength as an artist, for Henry and Durrell often ally themselves against me. Henry's respect is also reawakened by Durrell's admiration for me. My feeling for woman's inarticulateness is reawakened by Nancy's stutterings and stumblings, and her loyalty to me as the one who does not betray woman but seeks to speak for her. A marvellous talk, in which Henry unmasked Durrell and me, and when Durrell said: 'And now we must unmask Henry,' I answered: 'We can't, because he has done it himself.' Henry is the strongest because he is not afraid of being alone. Larry is afraid. I am afraid. And we confessed it.

They suddenly attacked my personal relation to all things, by personification of ideas. I defended myself by saying that relating was an act of life. To make history or psychology alive I personify it. Also everything depends on the nature of the personal relationship. My self is like the self of Proust. _It is an instrument to connect life and the myth._ I quoted Spengler, who said that all historical patterns are reproduced in individual man, entire historical evolutions are reproduced in one man in one lifetime. A man could experience, in a personal way, a Gothic, a Roman, or a Western period. Man is cheating when he sits for a whole evening talking about Lao-tze, Goethe, Rousseau, Spengler. It would be closer to the truth if he said, instead of Lao-tze, Henry – instead of Goethe, some poet we know now – instead of Rousseau, his contemporary equivalent. It would be more honest if Larry said that it is Larry who feels irritation because symbolic wine does not taste as good as plain wine.

When they discussed the problem of my diary, all the art theories were involved. They talked about the geological changes undergone with time, and that it was the product of this change we called art. I asserted that such a process could take place instantaneously.

Henry said: 'But that would upset all the art theories.'

I said: 'I can give you an example. I can feel the potentialities of our talk tonight while it is happening as well as six months later. Look at the birth story. It varies very little in its polished form from the way I told it in the diary immediately after it happened. The new version was written three years later. Objectivity may bring a more rounded picture, but the absence of it, empathy, feeling with it, immersion in it, may bring some other kind of connection with it.'

Henry asked: 'But then, why did you feel the need of rewriting it?'

'For a greater technical perfection. Not to re-create it.'

Larry, who before had praised me for writing as a woman, for not breaking the umbilical connection, said: 'You must rewrite _Hamlet_.'

'Why should I, if that is not the kind of writing I wish to do?'

Larry said: 'You must make the leap outside of the womb, destroy your connections.'

'I know,' I said, 'that this is an important talk, and that it will be at this moment that we each go different ways. Perhaps Henry and Larry will go the same way, but I will have to go another, the woman's way.'

At the end of the conversation they both said: 'We have a real woman artist before us, the first one, and we ought not to put her down.'

I know Henry is the artist because he does exactly what I do not do. He waits. He gets outside of himself. Until it becomes fiction. It is all fiction.

I am not interested in fiction. I want faithfulness.

All I know is that I am right, right for me. If today I can talk both woman's and man's language, if I can translate woman to man and man to woman, it is because I do not believe in man's objectivity. In all his ideas, systems, philosophies, arts come from a personal source he does not wish to admit. Henry and Larry are pretending to be impersonal. Larry has the English complex. But it is a disguise.

Poor woman, how difficult it is to make her instinctive knowledge clear!

'Shut up,' says Larry to Nancy. She looks at me strangely, as if expecting me to defend her, explain her. Nancy, I won't shut up. I have a great deal to say, for June, for you, for other women.

As to all that nonsense Henry and Larry talked about, the necessity of 'I am God' in order to create (I suppose they mean 'I am God, I am not a woman'). Woman never had direct communication with God anyway, but only through man, the priest. She never created directly except through man, was never able to create as a woman. But what neither Larry nor Henry understands is that woman's creation far from being like man's must be exactly like her creation of children, that is it must come out of her own blood, englobed by her womb, nourished with her own milk. It must be a human creation, of flesh, it must be different from man's abstractions. As to this 'I am God', which makes creation an act of solitude and pride, this image of God alone making sky, earth, sea, it is this image which has confused woman. (Man too, because he thinks God did it all alone, and he thinks he did it all alone. And behind every achievement of man lies a woman, and I am sure God was helped too but never acknowledged it.)

Woman does not forget she needs the fecundator, she does not forget that everything that is born of her is planted in her. If she forgets this she is lost. What will be marvellous to contemplate will not be her solitude but this image of woman being visited at night by man and the marvellous things she will give birth to in the morning. God alone, creating, may be a beautiful spectacle. I don't know. Man's objectivity may be an imitation of this God so detached from us and human emotion. But a woman alone creating is not a beautiful spectacle. The woman was born mother, mistress, wife, sister, she was born to represent union, communion, communication, she was born to give birth to life, and not to insanity. It is man's separateness, his so-called objectivity, which has made him lose contact, and then his reason. Woman was born to *be* the connecting link between man and his human self. Between abstract ideas and the personal pattern which creates them. Man, to create, must become man.

Woman has this life-role, but the woman artist has to fuse creation and life in her own way, or in her own womb if you prefer. She has to create something different from man. Man created a world cut off from nature. Woman has to create within the mystery, storms, terrors, the infernos of sex, the battle against abstractions and art. She has to sever herself from the myth man creates, from being created by him, she has to struggle with her own cycles, storms, terrors which man does not understand. Woman wants to destroy aloneness, recover the original paradise. The art of woman must be born in the womb-cells of the mind. She must be the link between the synthetic products of man's mind and the elements.

I do not delude myself as man does, that I create in proud isolation. I say we are bound, interdependent. Woman is not deluded. She must create without these proud delusions of man, without megalomania, without schizophrenia, without madness. She must create that unity which man first destroyed by his proud consciousness.

Henry and Larry tried to lure me out of the womb. They call it objectivity. No woman died the kind of death Rimbaud died. I have never seen in a woman a skeleton like Fraenkel, killed by the dissections of analysis, the leprosy of egotism, the black pest of the brain cells.

Man today is like a tree that is withering at the roots. And most women painted and wrote nothing but imitations of phalluses. The world was filled with phalluses, like totem poles, and no womb anywhere. I must go the opposite way from Proust who found eternal moments in creation. I must find them in life. My work must be the closest to the life flow. I must install myself inside of the seed, growth, mysteries. I must prove the possibility of instantaneous, immediate, spontaneous art. My art must be like a miracle. Before it goes through the conduits of the brain and becomes an abstraction, a fiction, a lie. It must be for woman, more like a personified ancient ritual, where every spiritual thought was made visible, enacted, represented.

A sense of the infinite in the present, as the child has.

Woman's role in creation should be parallel to her role in life. I don't mean the good earth. I mean the bad earth too, the demon, the instincts, the storms of nature. Tragedies, conflicts, mysteries are personal. Man fabricated a detachment which became fatal. Woman must not fabricate. She must descend into the real womb and expose its secrets and its labyrinths. She must describe it as the City of Fez, with its Arabian Nights gentleness, tranquillity and mystery. She must describe the voracious moods, the desires, the worlds contained in each cell of it. For the womb has dreams. It is not as simple as the good earth. I believe at times that man created art out of fear of exploring woman. I believe woman stuttered about herself out of fear of what she had to say. She covered herself with taboos and veils. Man invented a woman to suit his needs. He disposed of her by identifying her with nature and then paraded his contemptuous domination of nature. But woman is not nature only.

She is the mermaid with her fish-tail dipped in the unconscious. Her creation will be to make articulate this obscure world which dominates man, which he denies being domina-

244

ted by, but which asserts its domination in destructive proofs of its presence, madness.

Note by Durrell: 'Asaïs is *unanswerable*. Completely unanswerable. I fold up and give in. What she says is biologically true from the very navel strings.'

The birth of the magazine the *Booster*, inherited by Fred and dominated by Henry, reawakened my rebellion against Henry's atmosphere of begging, stealing, cajoling, school-boy pranks, slap-stick humour, burlesque.

Gonzalo is working hard at the press, will begin to earn a living from it soon. He has plenty of orders.

Durrell writes me: 'You are sweet the way you spread your wings and we all climb under them for help. I don't know how you do it. You must have the wing span of an albatross.' This note came after we had a sparkling talk together, mainly on what seems to be irresponsibility in the artist is deeper down a responsibility towards his work, first of all.

Henry, Nancy, Larry and I. A soft summer evening. The illuminated city. Larry's movements slower than his awareness. His eyes arrive quickly, transcend, possess in a flash. His body lags behind, natural, indolent, easy-going, but a little bound. He has written with despair about the spontaneous act. He makes his double, Gregory, an Englishman. This may be the secret of his fascination with Henry. The new Larry emerges, animated by a creation that is not entirely in harmony with his athletic body, his love of sailing, his laughter, his pranks. 'Let's get on a bus and then ask for a cup of coffee. Let's walk into this Indo China restaurant, order food, and ask for the "indo" in it.' He is a little amazed at himself, as someone who discovers a disease in himself. Under the golden tanned skin, the blond hair, the sea-bottom eyes, behind the poetic gestures, mellow and human, he has found a cataract of words, a universe of nuances, shadows, quarter tones. Not by way of neurosis did he discover the imagination he has. He is like a sailor, a mountaineer who has been visited by revelations. There is a miracle about his creation. He is a bit amazed. He walks the familiar streets with a vague uneasiness. The wine bottle has become symbolical. This expresses all he is fighting against. He does not want to lose the warmth, the flesh, the odour, the reality.

There is no doubt that we flow as individuals through a non-individual world to which we are connected, the world of writing.

I felt that Larry and Nancy were a little uneasy, a little lost, a little ready for flight, after ten days at the Villa Seurat and the Dôme circus. I felt their loneliness. I asked them to come and see me last night. We sat on the floor, by the large window. We had coffee in the dark, sitting on pillows. All the lights came from the river. And we talked intimately. They recoil from what I recoil from. They wanted Greece again, after walking through the greasy, slippery, putrid world of Montparnasse. 'It is not a moral repulsion,' said Larry, 'it is heraldic.' The love of the 'heraldic' world in Larry excludes the other. Not in Henry.

Afterwards, Henry laments that he does not live on the level of his creation. He does not even live on a level with himself. Enjoyed Larry and Nancy's contempt. I enjoyed Larry saying as I so often do: 'I get impatient. I can't stand idiots very long. One should not have contempt, but this chap . . .' I felt less alone. In the dark we seemed able to say everything. Larry exposed his fear of going mad if he continued writing. He said I was unique and he did not want to lose me. He danced around when I showed him my diary and his letters pasted in it. 'You are important,' I said. He did not know it. He is afraid of what I will write about him but I said: 'So am I of what you will write, yet I can't stop talking, because you know me anyway.' We shared a malaise in disintegrated, dissolute surroundings, a nostalgia for wholeness, a need of wholeness. We shared the conviction that certain experiences are not necessary.

I remembered Larry's first mention of his 'heraldic universe', which caught my attention. Nancy and Larry were contemplating evasion, escape from Paris. I dispelled their fears by naming them. I conjured up the demons and we exorcised them. We had a moment of wholeness, of repose, of Oriental serenity.

Helba talks for hours about Gonzalo's paralysis. She is obsessed with his procrastination, his blocking himself, defeating himself. He builds up a thing and just before it materializes he stops. The press, all ready, is not used because he won't call the workman who will teach him, because there might be days when he has no work for him. And all the orders his friends have given him are waiting. Everything at a standstill. He says: 'I will do the work,' but he does not do it because the paper has not come. Why has it not come? 'I don't know. I was to call up the man yesterday about it.' 'Shall I get it Gonzalo?' 'No, it will be delivered tomorrow.'

'I will work with you tomorrow, Gonzalo.'

'No, not tomorrow. Tomorrow I have to see Neruda about his poems.'

Helba nags: 'Gonzalo, you're so awkward, you're stupid, you break everything, you can't do anything well.'

I say: 'Gonzalo you are so adroit with the press. Why are you timid about getting a workman to help you the first week?' Destruction. Creation. Destruction. Creation. Infernal duel. Continuous. If I had kept the press for myself I would be producing, printing, publishing. When I ask Gonzalo: 'How would you like your life to be?' he answers: 'A revolution every day.'

Nancy says courageously to Larry: 'Perhaps you are dissatisfied with me.'

Larry answers: 'I am, but that does not mean I want to change, or that I want anyone else.'

The incredible force of stagnation in Helba and Gonzalo which swept them into starvation, disease, death. Gonzalo uses rags for handkerchiefs. I gave him some handkerchiefs. He said: 'But I have dozens of them at home. For a year I have piled them up to take them to the laundry. I can't bring myself to wash them. The package is still there.'

Larry says: 'I hate Bohemianism.'

Henry was having dinner with some nondescript character.

The Dôme at nine in the morning. Antonin Artaud passes by. He is waving his magic Mexican cane and shouting.

'I don't want this rotting-away while I am alive' said Gonzalo.

I said to Gonzalo: 'Do you know what it means, desiring and not desiring, acting and then stopping yourself? You are afraid of realization, materialization. You want power and yet you are ashamed to take the lead. You want to serve communism but you reject discipline. You want a freedom which in the end results in the greatest slavery, the greatest helplessness and humiliation. You would rather die than risk defeat. You would rather starve than sacrifice an hour's sleep.'

I worked for an hour and a half at the press, to help Gonzalo. Elation at seeing the printed words appear.

We work in a small, low-ceilinged room with two windows on a very old French garden on the Rue de Lille. It is the abode of *Paix et Démocratie*. There are two enormous tables, one with the press on it. I printed two thousand strips for pamphlets. Cut them. Gonzalo was writing letters. It was pride and possessiveness which prevented him from getting the workman. He wants to be in control of everything. A personal universe. When the work becomes too heavy then we will run into trouble.

DEAR DJUNA BARNES,

I have to tell you of the great, deep beauty of your book *Nightwood*. The last half above all, moved me so much that I am almost afraid to write you. The true poet in you who isolated the Doctor, Nora, Robin in a world surcharged with meaning, and makes them talk with a clairvoyance and humanity, a depth I have rarely seen touched, how that moved me. The relationship between Nora and Robin, which you not only describe in reality, in the world we see, in the street, in the house, the city, the café, but which you enter through the most mysterious of all penetrations, to reveal its most elusive, its most poetic, its most symbolic and human significance. Blinding. While I read I felt: she knows too much, she sees too much, it is intolerable. It was intolerable. It was unforgettable. The language, the knowingness, the beauty, the tragic quality, the transparent power of touching depths . . . The most beautiful thing I have read about woman, and women in love. I am very much afraid to write you. You will know why. I would like you to know what your book has touched, illumined, awakened. But it is not in a letter, to someone I only know in her created world, that I can say

248

it. I would like to install myself in your created world, which I feel so keenly, and from there address you. I would like to break through the barrier of the exterior you. It is strange, several years ago our names were on the same page, I heard about you, one of your books and mine on D. H. Lawrence were announced by a 'barker' called Drake. Once you were pointed out to me in a café. I saw a beautiful woman. But had I known then you were the woman of *Nightwood* . . . I have been truly haunted by *Nightwood*. Haunted really by the emotional power, the passionate expression. A woman rarely writes as a woman, as she feels, but you have.

Even today when I am most deeply installed inside of life, I cannot hear music and gaiety from a neighbour's house without sadness, without feeling outside. To be inside or outside was my nightmare. I feel born on the rim of an eternally elusive world. When I was poor, when I was at an awkward age, when I was combing my long hair before the mirror of the pantry in the brownstone in New York, I can understand why the music that came from the house in front of us filled me with yearning, jealousy, envy, despair. It seemed to me inaccessible. It seemed to me to come from a forbidden, an impossible world. I thought it was because I was poor, because our life was not beautiful, because I was not beautiful. I thought it was because as I stood there in my nightgown with my hairbrush in hand, brushing my long hair, I was aware of the timidity of this body which only danced in the dark, of the fragility of this hair which seemed to shine only in the dark, the paleness of this face which seemed to shine better in solitude. I shone in solitude, that was the mystery. And I could not reconcile this black self shining to the brilliancy of the day, the day brilliancy of the neighbour's room on a gay evening and the music. It was not poverty, it was not the awkward age. The day came when I shone in daylight, when I wore the dress and danced in daylight, and the glow, the smile, the familiarity and the triumphs. The gaiety was mine and for me. But the moment of insideness, of participation, of belonging, was swift and left me outside as much as when I stood as a girl watching the neighbour's window. There was always this being outside at some moment or other, alone. I could not remain inside, I did not live inside. The glow, the familiarity inside of music, with people and gaiety, was there, but so was the moon-glow of solitude, the pale-faced watcher. At first I was altogether the lonely girl watching and feeling unfamiliar, *dépaysée*. Afterwards, I was both. Now I am often inside and I dread the moment when I will see the pale face at the window watching from another world. I do not want to be robbed of the present. Was not this yearning girl finally buried in the woman fulfilled? Why should the moment of music ever stop? Why must it come, the moment when I am thrust out on the periphery again, separated, and I hear the neighbour's music, I hear festivities, I hear dancing of which I am not a part, and I am sad, still yearning as someone doomed to feel this edge, this rim, this distance. Everything will not happen in my own home. There is always music coming from elsewhere, always a yearning, always something imagined to be lovelier and warmer. Always a colour that is inaccessible, a room that makes me feel poor and ragged, a music that makes me dance in the dark. Always a music that makes me glow in the dark, a different glow than the colour of the neighbour's gaiety. This violent desire to be *inside* of all warm, live, breathing pleasures, to sleep in them, to be always a part of them, never to be alone, to break the apartness forever, a mad desire.*

*It was this mood which inspired the party pages in *Ladders to Fire*. And one of the strangest incidents of recurrence took place some ten years later, when *Ladders to Fire* was published. I was invited to read at the University of Chicago by Violet Lang, then the editor of the *Chicago Review*. It was in the middle of winter and there was much snow on the ground. I gave my reading and talk and then friends took me in their car to the home of Violet Lang, where there was to be a reception. The snow was falling heavily. We arrived at the address given to us. But we could not find the apartment. Someone directed us towards the back of the apartment house. We saw some lighted windows of a basement apartment. We looked in. The party in my honour was going on, lively and animated. I knocked on the window. No one heard me. I was wet, cold and tired. The incident brought on the old feeling of being left outside. I would have gone away if I had been alone. Finally someone saw me at the window and came out to guide us through a labyrinth of cellar hallways.
– A.N.

[FALL, 1937]

My tragedy is that I love deeply but I cannot yield my integrity or live wholly in anyone else's world. I cannot yield. Part of me remains always Anaïs Nin. The desire to be with others, to amalgamate, to make concessions, compromises, kills me. I want to be at one with political work and I cannot. The work at the press done wastefully, erratically. For example, next to Gonzalo's apartment there is a big printing-shop where Gonzalo was to buy the tray for the type. He planned to get up early, get the tray, and asked me to come and help distribute the type. I came. But Gonzalo got up at eleven, did not get the tray, came to the office, forgot the wrapping paper, so I had no work to do. Then in the middle of the afternoon he takes an hour's trip by bus to go and get the tray while the office fills up with people waiting for him by engagement. He cannot organize, plan, and creates a vast confusion, wasted efforts. The immediate thing he cannot do. He has to circumvent. That is Gonzalo. But I cannot work that way. So I run away.

Someday I must have a press of my own.

It is symbolic that all Gonzalo does is lopsided, even to cutting paper. Henry is useless with his hands. I turn out work as if magically, quickly, merely because I don't want to be submerged, drowned in details. I don't take pride in this. Gon-

*

zalo cannot construct anything. If he went to war he would fight wildly, like a maniac, and probably die uselessly, blindly, out of an error.

The sculptor Henghes says to me: 'When I was poor and worked in restaurants, I thought and felt like those I worked with.' I envy him. When I was poor and worked as a model and as a mannequin, I never became like the others. I remained myself. I played roles, but I remained myself.

This incapacity to alter myself, remaining myself, deep down, is painful to a woman. Woman should be born blind so that she may serve blindly. Unquestioningly.

For this reason I had to give up my association with the *Booster*. Too much slapstick. Reichel, who was being praised by Henry, did not sleep for several nights wondering how he could tell Henry that he was ashamed to be so crudely 'boosted'.

When I said to Gonzalo: 'I wrote all those letters this morning because I want to feel free and light,' he said: 'And I postponed making those packages I have to make for days, knowing it will weigh on my mind, preoccupy me for days, as if I sought not to feel free.'

At times, by contagion, he does the immediate thing, is happy, but I know in an hour he will find another way to tangle himself up, botch himself, bind and enslave himself.

Why do I ally myself to destructive forces? And combat them? When I met Henry and June, it was the same. I walked into an inferno of dark destruction. And why, if I am drawn to them, do I not yield to their ways, become destructive, abandon the struggle to change them?

Hans Henghes sends me a letter with a rock crystal. 'It is the first time I live something pure, Anaïs. I feel I can see something new in my work. I was nauseated by the world, and weak, and lost. But not any longer.'

He went from his visit to me to the Princess de San Faustino, with my *House of Incest* under his arm. She read the book, bought it, wrote me a letter: 'I want to know you.' She is coming tomorrow.

Meanwhile all my time is given to the press.

*

The Princess de San Faustino turned out to be an American woman. She came to see me because she has known much anxiety and a sense of displacement. These she recognized in the book. Anxiety. No one writes about it. Yet it is today's drama. Not events. The suffering about incidents which never take place, sufferings of the imagination. By removing concrete identifications and X-raying the state itself, anyone, even Princess San Faustino from Illinois, can recognize how she feels, in no matter what place, country, time.

So many imaginary relationships, so many imagined scenes which never take place.

Henry's growing celebrity has created an inflation, an expansion and effusiveness which is followed by bad humour, fatigue, irritability. His week with the Durrells, a week of intoxiation, sleeplessness, was followed by depression.

H. H. brings me a green beetle with a gold-rust stomach. Two poems. We were sitting at a café. A group of workmen came in on a picnic. A huge woman unloaded her basket beside us, on our table. I said to H. H., laughing: 'Why didn't you tell me you had invited another woman for lunch? I feel *de trop.*'

'There is nothing between us,' said H. H. 'She is just a very old friend.'

Talk with Henry. I feel he is created now, as a writer. He is published, accepted, known.

I can now work for myself.

With writing it is this way. One says: 'I feel good, too good. I don't need to write. I want to live.' One is inside, enjoying life, living without formulation. No echoes, no registering. Then one day, without reason, life is split into two channels: being, and formulating. An activity resembling a motion picture starts to run inside of one's head. (One can hear the purring of the machine.)

I am writing. It is not analysing, or meditating, or a monologue, it is writing. It is living in terms of immediate phraseology, with great excitement as before, a discovery of appropriate words, an anxiety to capture, retain, to be precise, felicitous. It comes on unexpectedly, like a fever, and goes away, like a fever. It is distinct from all other activities.

All this month I have been writing in my head, I am coming

nearer to the realization of what I must do.

But I don't want to begin yet, because life is sweet, laziness is sweet. I am writing in my head about New York, Otto Rank, Henry's writing, the death of a dress. I am not detached enough to begin my big work.

Humorous, ironic things are happening with the publication of Henry's *Scenario*, which he had printed in a limited edition of two hundred copies with his first royalties.

We had started out by wanting to write a scenario together around *House of Incest*, which was not yet in its final form. I had shown Henry all my material. As soon as we began to work I realized Henry was obeying his own imagination, that *House of Incest* was becoming something entirely different, that our styles could not fuse. The very atmosphere, texture, contents altered. To me it seemed more like a parody of the original. I did not want to tell Henry I did not like what came out of our talks. I quietly left out of my final version the themes Henry had developed in his own way and in his own language. Henry felt he had been stimulated by *House of Incest* material and insisted on saying it was inspired by it.

In its present form, as Henry's *Scenario*, it will be read and liked by thousands who will never read *House of Incest*, or understand it.*

Hélène gives me a fierce description of her husband's jealousy. 'He was like Othello. He seemed to take a perverse pleasure in these scenes, and I tried to learn from him, but I must confess I have learned nothing. If there is any pleasure in them, I have not found it. It always began when we were most happy, lying in the dark. After caressing me he would lie silent and withdrawn. I would say: "What is it, *querido*?" He would strike his head with closed fists. "That image of you talking with the sculptor at the party, I have that image nailed into my brain, I cannot get rid of it."

' "But it was a casual conversation."

' "Then why were you so interested, so animated?" At such

*This prophecy turned out to be accurate. Many years later, *Scenario* was read over the French radio, acted out, and recorded. It was read in many languages. *House of Incest* was not translated into French and published in France until 1963. – Ed.

injustice, I would always become angry, and say things to hurt him, unconsciously, arriving always at what hurt him most deeply: "Why don't you let me study painting?" knowing that this unhinged him completely, the idea of my going to an art school with other art students, and painting naked figures. His emphasis on physical jealousy also incensed me. Why was he not jealous of my thoughts, of my love of painting, of my emotional and artistic life? We would fall into inchoate arguments. To reassure him I said I knew that I could never feel any sensual attraction without love. "How do you know?" he asked, violently. "How did you find out?" He reproaches me for appearing so lax, and free in my speech. I explained this was because I was ashamed of my intransigence, it seemed so outdated even among our circle of friends. Then he insisted that he had seen the sculptor kiss me during the dancing. All the time I felt so ashamed of the petty quarrel we had fallen into. The air became heavy, our feelings confused. We would say false things, mean things, we didn't know what we were saying, we would dig knives into each other, there was hostility, pain, confusion, blindness. I hated it all. I hated it because it was like a poison, it drowned our uniqueness, what I believed to be the uniqueness of our love, it separated us. I felt shattered, lacerated, wounded. Was this love, this digging of knives into the flesh, cruel phrases, a love that had no faith in love? Poison. Our caresses after that were like life after death. I didn't know if love had grown a new root, or a poison that would hasten its death. I didn't know whether this exposure of the animal awakened the senses, excited desire. Not in me. When he says: "There is a corner of your being into which I have been unable to penetrate," I felt like saying: "The only thing I hide from you is my hatred of your jealousy." And it was his jealousy which drove me away. One evening we had a scene in a restaurant. He became violent. I walked out. I walked in the rain, sobbing, because I feared his jealousy, it would separate us, and I could still hear his desperate words: "There are those who are born to lose, I was born to lose." But I could not tell him it was he who was pushing me away. I sobbed for him, for his pain and frustration. He came running after me. He pulled me into a doorway so I would not get soaked by the rain. He kissed my tears, my wet hair, my mouth. I will never

255

forget these kisses. We went home. We fought. I held my ground. Will I ever find such a passion again? Here in Paris, it seems so light and cheerful and carefree. No madness. No penetration by knives.'

I am profoundly disturbed by the condition of the world, the suffering. I cannot shut my eyes as Henry does.

Gonzalo brings me his conflicts. Should he sign a document prepared by *Paix et Démocratie* exposing capitalist investments in Spain? Signing his name exposes him to assassination. Not signing it makes it the work of a group. I thought attacks should come from a group, because the loss of one man, as a scapegoat, is a loss to the strength of the revolution. Coming from *Paix et Démocratie*, I felt, the attack would worry the exposed ones. They will not know how much documentation, how much proof they have. Will there be more exposures? It gave greater strength to the attack, I felt. Not one person can be disposed of. It will be more effective, unnamed.

I came out of this talk depressed.

I saw Durrell. His book is coming out. Havelock Ellis is interested in both Henry and Durrell. Durrell urges me to publish excerpts of the diary. He says: 'I am altogether an actor, I am all mimetism.' He was born in February, as I was, and very close to my own date.

With the Durrells I relive my discovery of Henry, my conflicts, my acceptances. Durrell is mature, he seems older than Henry. He understands why I protect Henry's work.

Nancy and I hunt for an apartment in Montmartre for herself and Larry.

André Breton came to visit me. I expected he would be poetically and sensitively alert to the atmosphere of my life, to my inarticulate intuitions. He was not. He was intellectual. He talked about ideas, not impressions or sensations. And he told me a story which was the opposite of what I had expected.

He had been talking about the surrealist game of getting together and then engaging in an unplanned action. They will take a train and get off anywhere, a place they do not know, and wait for surprises, things to happen. Or get on a bus, and suddenly decide to stay in a small town, and wait for the unexpected. He tells this with solemnity, more like a King speaking at an audience than a fellow artist talking to other artists. He did not expect comments, only listeners.

Then he said: 'The other day I received a letter from a woman. She wrote a beautiful letter. She commented on my emphasis on "surprise", on coincidences, and said she would like to meet me alone under the Pont Royal one evening at midnight. She would not identify herself in any way.'

I waited for the rest of the story. Breton added: 'I did not go, of course.'

'Why "of course"?' I asked.

'Because I have many enemies, and it could have been a trap.'

When he saw how disappointed I was at his lack of adventurousness, he added: 'I went the second time, though, after she wrote to me. But I was careful to post two loyal friends on the bridge where I could call out to them in case of danger.'

This story, added to his dislike of music, betrayed what I suspected in surrealism, the part of it that is conscious, premeditated and an intellectual technique; it betrayed the man of the laboratory. It was this which prevented me from espousing surrealism, from becoming a totally committed disciple.

As soon as Hélène returned to Paris she became ill again. She said: 'Nothing keeps me here but you. Please come with me to the doctor, he is taking an X-ray. I have a lump in my stomach and I am afraid of cancer.' She added that my understanding of her was all she had. Her illness is the emptiness of her life and I cannot fill it for her. She studied painting with Léger. Léger wanted her to write a book about him in Spanish for South America. She does not want to meet Henry. 'He is all taken up with himself and his work.'

With Henry and the Durrells we talk about sainthood, wholeness, nature, disease, vigorously and marvellously. The universe expands. We reached the certitude that the artist is not *whole*. Only his work is whole. Henry says about himself all I have written about him, that he is *all* there, in the moment,

257

and that it is tragic for human life. He says that whoever reaches an absolute and dies for it, sainthood, or Rimbaud's madness, is right. The artist does not die. Henry touched the bottom of suffering with June, but he did not kill himself. I touched the heights of mystical religious exaltation at fourteen, but I did not become a saint. I plead for nature now, against disease, because the surrealists have encouraged the aggravation of mental disturbances for the sake of the revelations of unknown worlds.

I love the tree in full bloom, not the tree bearing only one branch. I argue in favour of Henry's life, wide, expanded against the life of the cloister and retreat. For there is something beyond giving ourselves to one absolute. Perhaps, I said, wholeness for us is a different thing from the wholeness of the simple man. We may have a core, an absolute which is an equilibrium in space and motion, whereas the unity of a simple life consists of a static choice. No further growth. The artist refuses to die. Perhaps our wholeness is different, vaster, beyond personal wholeness. There is no progress of the personality like a pyramid converging to a point of perfection. Fulfilment is the completion of a circle. All aspects of the self have to be lived out, like the twelve houses of the zodiac. A personality is one who has unrolled the ribbon, unfolded the petals, exposed all the layers. It does not matter where one begins: with instinct or wisdom, with nature or spirit. The fulfilment means the experience of all parts of the self, all the elements, all the planes. It means each cell of the body comes alive, awakened. It is a process of nature, and not of the ideal. One dies when the cells are exhausted, one reaches plenitude when they all function, the dream, desire, instinct, appetite. One awakens the other. It is like contagion. The order does not matter. All the errors are necessary, the stutterings, the blunders, the blindnesses. The end is to cover all the terrain, all the routes. No spaces to skip. Any skipping of a phase only retards the branchlike unfolding. Growth, expansion, plenitude of the potential self. To live only one aspect or one side of the personality is like using only one sense, and the others become atrophied. There is greatness only in fulfilment, in the fullness of awakening. Completion means the symphony. Sublimation means to condemn to immobility certain members of the body for the sake of the monstrous development of others. Like the abnormal sensitivity of the blind, the unusually keen hearing of the mute. It is monstrous. Psychologically, a great personality is a circle touching something at every point. A circle with a core. A process of nature, growth, not the ideal. The ideal is an error. Life is a full circle, widening until it joins the circle motions of the infinite.

First talk alone with Larry. He takes my arm as we walk. He feels that I do not treat him as if he were twenty-six, and that pleases him. I say: 'At times I feel that you are older than Henry. Henry is never aware of the other, only of himself. I can see that you are aware of the other.' Larry had noticed Henry's impersonality, as if detached from all. His relationships are mostly on a false basis. Larry understands this, sees this. Henry exemplifies separateness. He has many areas of insensitiveness, even of hardness. Henry is often not human. Larry could be Henry's son but he has a sensitivity to the other which Henry does not have. Henry says: 'I believe in friendship, not in the friend. People are interchangeable.'

Larry's young, rosy face, but old eyes. He is young in his games, humour, sense of wonder, but old in awareness, as I am. Larry spoke of his own drama. He wants nearness. He feels for the woman, he feels my difficulties. I talk with him and I wonder. Larry understands my acceptance of the artist and my human rebellion against their sacrifice of the human relationships.

Hélène like a windmill, changing her plans every day. I suggest she go and talk to Jung to find out why she cannot find a deep relationship. She is so interesting and beautiful that it is hard to believe she cannot find a love. Too many contraries, cross-currents, rebellions. She cannot give herself. Why?

She says: 'Henry's eyes are so innocent.'

She adds: 'When he bows his head one feels like taking care of him.'

But she does not seek him out. 'I am too selfish. I do not want to serve anyone.'

Larry is fully aware of those moments when Henry becomes unreal, nothing warm or vital there. The artist. Transmutation. The inhuman transposition of life into remembrance. He is not living in the present. He is always remembering.

Larry said: 'I don't want to disappoint you, destroy your idea of me.'

'You can't,' I said. 'I carry an X-ray, as Proust did.'

'Don't get run over, Anaïs.'

The differences of attitudes between Henry and myself are becoming more marked. Differences of character, habits, tastes, friends, way of living, philosophy, books, even attitude towards writing.

I slide so quickly between contrasting atmospheres, I find myself in one day in such different places. One moment I am in a cheap movie house with Henry and his friends, a movie near Alésia, with people who smell bad, and look ugly, where the water closets all have holes in the doors for the '*voyeurs*', another moment I am having tea with friends in the most stylish place, at another I am sitting at the Deux Maggots with André Breton and Henghes. Now I am in my mother's bourgeois apartment, with bric-à-brac from the past, photographs, lace doilies over the armchairs. Later in the office on the Rue de Lille where members of *Paix et Démocratie* are studying a plan to expose the capitalists.

The office is an old apartment overlooking a garden. It makes the room tinted green. It is next to a hotel. And at times, when all is very quiet, and I am addressing envelopes, I can hear what is happening in the hotel rooms through walls or open windows. Once, on a cold day, I heard a man coughing, stirring. He sounded very old. I asked Gonzalo about him. Gonzalo knew him. He said: 'He is not old. He is only forty years old. But he has fought in the Spanish war, and was wounded several times, once in the chest. He has lost all his family. He is all alone, and half crippled.' From then on I felt a connection with this man. His coughing fits hurt me. I could hear the rustle of the newspapers when he lay in bed, reading them. His loneliness. His tragedy. It was like an exhortation to work harder.

*

I will never be able to describe the states of dazzlement, the trances, the ecstasies produced in me by love-making. More than communion, more than any joy in writing, more than the infinite, lies in the unity achieved by passion. It is the only moment when I am at rest, that is the summit, the grace the miracle.

In all people concerned with creation there is an order. In Henry, Durrell, and in me, there is order. In June, Hélène, Gonzalo, the uncreative ones, there is chaos.

Larry says that my concept of a wholeness attained by an equilibrium between duality is not true wholeness. All I do is not break the final cord.

I won't stop living to write. I can only fill the diary.

Larry says that I am more of a chameleon than he is, even after seeing me once in my 'fragile' role, a day when I felt utterly drained, weak, and in need of protection.

These moments of utter loss of strength I never knew to be either physical or emotional. But I do feel helpless. As he had seen me supporting, consoling, arguing, on my strong days, he was stunned by the contrast, said he would put me in a play, a labyrinthian idea he had. I said that if he put me in a play I would probably stop acting in life. The truth is that when I laugh at my transformations, I am at the same time a little tired of them. It seems to me that I traverse a hundred quarters a day, breathe a hundred different airs, am so sensitive to changes, suffer from my dualities and triplicities, ask myself what is it that I can discuss with Larry which I cannot discuss with Henry or Gonzalo.

I am not indifferent to the greater dramas over our heads, but drama is everywhere the same, microcosm or macrocosm, and it is not my destiny to live the drama of Spain, the one of death, war, agony, hunger. It is my destiny to live the drama of feeling and imagination, reality and unreality, a drama underlying the other, a drama without guns, dynamite, without explosions, but it is the same one, it is from this one that the other is born: conflict, cruelty, jealousy, envy. Now in me it all happens in another world, in myself, and myself as an artist who remembers each day more what each day of my life touches in the past. I do not live beyond war, the drama that hastens death, accelerates the end. Perhaps it is a greater agony to live this life in which my awareness makes a thousand revolutions while others make only one, my span may seem smaller and it is really greater because it covers all the obscure routes of the soul and a body seeking truth and never receiving medals for its courage. It is my thousand years of womanhood I am recording, a thousand women. It would be simpler, shorter, swifter not to seek this deepening perspective to my life and lose myself in the simple world drama of war, hunger, death.

From the window of *Paix et Démocratie*, I also see passing the skeletonic figure of Nancy Cunard. Gonzalo tells me that she prefers Negro lovers. She came to the office with a batch of handmade paper on which to print some poems for Spain. The bracelets and necklaces dangled on her drupaceous skin, her over-ripe wrinkled olive skin. I could not imagine her in bed, alive, but only lying like a mummy, all skin and bones. But at least she is to be respected for she has fought for the Negroes, has sought to improve their situation in America, has lived in Harlem and taken up their struggles.

I am puzzling over the meaning of things which do not perplex Gonzalo, I am gnawed by feelings unknown to Henry, troubled by questions neither Rank nor Allendy could answer, writing only in a diary which Henry says should be nailed with a big nail on the wall of his studio and muted forever, and I ask myself is it fear on the part of man, fear of a woman unveiling her own truths? Is there another reason for everyone being against it, one not purely ideological? Larry came today. Larry divided between Henry and me, sharing Henry's hardness, laughter, masculine objective world, and yet better able than Henry to put himself in the place of a woman with a sensitiveness Henry does not have. After the big talk about or against the diary (the night which made me write on the creation of woman) he felt: 'Perhaps Anaïs is right and we are wrong.' Henry never doubts. Larry said: 'Henry achieved the happy-rock feeling for himself but he likes to hack away at others' foundations. As I go home and hack away at Nancy with a little hatchet after respecting you and accepting you for several hours.'

'That is why,' I said, 'friendship in general is such a difficult thing. I feel that Henry undermines my self-confidence, sows nothing but doubts in me. He does not ever give me the feeling that I might be right for myself, as much as he is for himself. He cannot accept my differences, as I accept his. If I hack away at him it is in the diary, never in life. In life I created his faith.'

Larry said: 'Did you ever write down what you said the other day? That was the most marvellous thing I ever heard a woman say. If you didn't put that down I will.'

We had been talking gaily about money matters and I had ended with: 'It is very important that Henry should be permitted to play. Only one of us can play.'

Larry began to look over the volumes I took out of the tin box. But I began to feel uneasy, agitated, and we talked first. His first remark was: 'Why, that is as terrifying as Nijinsky.' We had all been reading Nijinsky's diary.

Larry went away with an armful of volumes after saying: 'You are a strange person, sitting there, surrounded by your black notebooks.'

I feel right about the diary. I will not stop. It is a necessity. But why does Henry attack it? He says I give good justifications for it each time but that he does not believe them.

Nijinsky, writing just before all connections broke with human beings . . .

Larry with his keen eyes, saying: 'I have only smelled the diary writing, just read a page here and there. You have done it, the real female writing. It is a tragic work. You restore tragedy which the world has lost. Go on. Don't stop. I'm sick of hearing about art. What you have done nobody has done. It is amazing. It is new.'

All this warmed me and I asked him: 'Do you think Henry wants it to end for personal reasons?'

'Yes,' said Larry.

When he spoke, and even more deeply than I have noted down, he was afraid again, as he is of his own *Black Book* born out of the deeps. He got up and ended with: 'Just a twenty-six-year-old infant speaking.'

I do not consider him so. He is in terror of this powerful

263

spontaneous creation in him. The healthy English boy, impersonal, witty, with the protective shell of the conventional, startled by the 'monster' in him whom Henry and I treat as an equally mature man. He is unsure of himself, but we are sure of him, both of his genius and his understanding.

He asked me as they all do: 'Please do not write about this or about me in the diary.' I answered, as I always do: 'I won't ...'

The point of Larry's speech was that it answered my question: 'All I would like to hear you say is go on with the diary.' Larry said he could say this wholeheartedly, without hesitation. That the novel did not compare with the diary.

'The diary goes on, but I need faith. This continuous attack on it, as a disease by Rank, as anti-art by Henry, wears me down.'

When I think of suicide I think of it only as a relief and an end to sensibility. That is my disease, my only disease. That is what isolates me, separates me from collective life. I find happiness in the intimacy of friendships, when it is new, but then comes the world in which the friend lives, his other selves appear in relation to others, a different self, smaller, shabbier, poorer, weaker. I see them in the world, and it is not the same person I love in intimacy. Then comes the death of the friendship. I ask myself: Was it a natural death? Or was it a death hastened by my abnormal sensitiveness, my doubts of which is reality, which is the real person, the one revealed to me, or the one acting in the world? Gonzalo goes from me, from his role of amazing storyteller, romantic revolutionist, devoted sacrificed husband, to the Dôme. They drink and knock each other down, fall into the gutter, steal the fishermen's boat and paddle down the Seine and sink it.

DEAR LARRY:

I was thinking of all you said the other day. I have two more volumes for you to read. I hope you will call soon. You were so accurate the other day, so exactly as I imagined you to be. A humorous golden young Jupiter descending abruptly into the infernos of *Tropic of Cancer*, of your own *Black Book*, of Montparnasse, and my diary. Unfortunately there is no going back, you know, and anyway you cannot deceive me, about never having been there before. You have seen it all, and it shows in your eyes. And I have a sort of prophetic hunch that, without any heavy responsibility you might pull me out of my too dark worlds (do not fear this role, one's effect on others is beyond one's power to alter) and perhaps I will be the one to give you the courage to go on, to explode. You can talk to me all you want about the version of *Hamlet* you want to write (and now I understand better it was a prescription for sanity and painlessness you were giving me, for the great classical relief from terror and pain), but what I really understood is what you gave me, whatever that is, I don't want to dissect it but I am grateful for it. There are no solutions, there are displacements. Something in you helped me to displace myself and I breathe better. Thank you. Perhaps the old idea of faith.

Larry and I walked around the Parc de Montsouris. He talked about the diary: 'More terrifying than *Tropic of Cancer*. The collapse of Rank's teachings, incredible. You're like a diamond desiring to be made dust and they all cut away but the diamond is untouched. Henry could have helped you, but you met him too late, when he was burying himself in his work. The diary cannot stop until the quest is over. It is the quest of all of us, only you struggle more. We are all writing about the Womb, but you *are* the *Womb*. They all get caught in your femininity, and you looking so innocent. When everybody thinks you're dead, you're killed, and you lie like a fish at the bottom of the pool, and everybody thinks now you're dead but I can see the fins still moving – almost imperceptibly. Henry could be a real man if he were in life and not a writing machine.'

As we walked, I was laughing with pleasure at the diary being evaluated.

Henry working on *Capricorn*. Writing about sex, blind to all but sex, writing like a maniac about sex.

Suddenly, abruptly, I felt God, as I had felt him in the hospital. I felt this god taking me tenderly in his arms, holding me, putting me to sleep. I felt protected. My nerves were unknotted. I felt peace. I fell asleep. My anxiety was dissolved, and I slept. So the next day when Larry said: 'Someone ought to hold you and put you to sleep,' I remembered the visit from God. I need sleep, I need sleep and rest and peace. I need God.

[OCTOBER, 1937]

The winter came, invading all with grey mists. The city is blackened, smoked, and melancholic. I want to flee. That is it. I want to flee somewhere. Larry says: 'The more you struggle, of course, the less you liberate yourself.' I should have answered: 'But don't you see, if I don't struggle then I want to die. Struggle relieves me, gives me hope. As soon as I lie still I get desperate.'

Moricand's talk spherical. He makes enormous ellipses – catching the Turkish bath in Morocco where the beautiful boy massaged him with such effectiveness that Moricand had to run away from him (his whole face expressing that he did not run away, his whole face bathed in the memory of the pleasure he does not wish to acknowledge). If you press him you will discover that he met the boy again, but you will never know more than that. Yet while Moricand tells about all this, his eyes acknowledge perversity, and one can easily imagine the boy and Moricand together because his pleasure in talking was not that of a spectator but of a participator. Yet nothing said to prove that Moricand was more than a spectator except the sensual mist in his eyes, the mist of the memory of pleasure. He talked like a *frôleur*, a *voyeur*, his talk was full of imprecisions, unreal excitements, unformulated enjoyments, never once crystallizing into a fact. But the quick, knowing

'Ah!' he made at the least indication of an adventure was so expressive that one did not need to continue, one felt that Moricand knew all there was to know or experience. At the same time I felt that it was the expansion, dilation of incidents through his imagination which conveyed the feeling and not the actual bulk of the experiences. Every scene he touched on was immediately inflated, distended, and the implication of mystery, terror, perversity strengthened by the sense of guilt which accompanied them. I thought of the enormous wheels at the Fair carrying little cages travelling spherically, and the illusion of a vast circular voyage. Moricand picked you up on the edge of this wheel, whirled you in space, and deposited you again without for a moment enabling you to stand any closer to the hub of the wheel, to the mechanism or pulse of the wheel, to its axis. Moricand stood at the centre throwing serpentines of iron works in circles, and his face was shadowed by the moving wheel. He took care not to expose himself without this wheel of talk swooping around him carrying people up and around him always at the same distance, breaking the laws of human life which permit people to collide, to feel each other's breath or to pass the same street without meeting, breaking the human laws to establish a kind of fixed stellar system, words used only to obscure his tracks rather than to reveal himself, and to prevent anyone from coming nearer to the hub, himself.

Henry is baffled by what I wrote on the role of woman in creation. I said Marika Norden made herself ridiculous in her *Confessions* because, when she thought she was proving that she was a woman who could not find a male to match her rhythm, she was merely proving that she had no core for anyone to relate to, to match. She was looking for a mate to a centre she did not have in herself.

I have a centre. I never lose sight of those who are on the periphery and those who are at the centre of my affections and friendships. But Henry has no core. Man's impersonal world merely masks the personal.

Henry denies the reality of all this, for him there is no right or wrong, no bad or good, no centre or periphery.

I know it is this constant outward expansion which empties

his work of meaning. It is a gallery, a set of types, a crowd. Then he says: 'We are freaks.' I say: 'We are not freaks. We are exaggerated men and women, we represent others, only heightened. One painter can be a symbol of many painters, as in Proust. Many painters, as in your work, may represent less than one painter.' Henry is not reaching for depth but for quantity. This dehumanizes experience. It is an enlarged world, but empty of feeling, humanity, drama. It leads nowhere. It is thin. Henry's work is flow – sensual dynamism, instinctual dynamism, nature, impulse, appetite. When I first knew him I thought he was creating a work without the dimension of emotion, but that he himself was a man of feeling. I thought feeling in him was inhibited, perverted, ingrown, and masked. Today I am not sure, because he displays both in life, at times utter callousness, at times sensitivity. He is not concerned with insight or understanding.

I want to live from a centre. Henry's expansion is illusory, superficial. He misunderstands me when I talk about a core, he thinks I am talking about ethics, morals, etc. Henry wants to receive a million letters, meet a million people, and I fear that this makes for crowded books but not for depth.

I study the *Fatalité Intérieure* in Hélène. I have watched her reject life, companionship, exchange. I have seen her create opposing currents to all forms of attachments, resist all forms of life, assert her independence, not give herself, and then lament her empty life, wail over her loneliness. She creates her loneliness. She waits to be given. She only likes to enter someone else's ready-made life as she entered mine, to satisfy her appetite without contributing anything to it. She asked Moricand to do her horoscope and then not only refused to pay him for it in any way, when she knows he is starving, but she also alienated him, offended him, questioned all he said, argued with him, complained he was not sufficiently interested in her. She sends for me only to tell me all her troubles, and then when she is well and happy again, she disappears for days to enjoy herself. She talked to me for three hours about the necessity of marrying or not marrying, only to throw the whole question overboard the next day. So I elude her now. All those around me who are accustomed to being tenderly treated, served, protected, pampered, turned away from her demands. And I myself am throwing off the chains of her colourful reign. What she envies, she will not work to attain. Her fate is created by her attitude, the nature of her quest. She never says: 'I want to give myself.' She says: 'I want to be protected. I want this or that. I want a life like yours. I want a brilliant life. I want. I want. I want to enjoy life, to have friends like yours.'

'But Hélène,' I said, 'all this has to be created. It does not just come to one.'

'I want freedom, I want love, I want marriage, I want to travel, I want to be protected, I want to live as I please.'

I glanced over what Henry was writing in *Tropic of Capricorn*, and there it was, the great anonymous, depersonalized world of sex. Instead of investing each woman with a different face, he takes pleasure in reducing all women to a biological aperture. That is not very interesting. His depersonalization is turning into an obsession with sex itself. It is not enough to take a woman to bed, man was given many other forms of expression and relationship. The only personal, individual experience he had was June, because she tormented him, and was thus finally able to distinguish herself from the ocean of women. The way he focuses on sex is an obsession. He is in danger of becoming an Ego in a crowd. (The ego can only perceive a crowd, it cannot perceive an equal.) The crowd is a malleable thing, it can be dominated, dazzled, it's a public, it is faceless. This is the opposite of relationship.

If I could only awaken him to the consciousness of the *other*. One's life as a man is not in relation to the crowd, it is to the friend, the lover, the child.

He says: 'I can have a good time with people who don't mean much to me.' But this is not what nourishes our deepest life.

I need to live in exaltation because otherwise as soon as my life slows down I fall into analysis. Now when I have time I think about Lawrence Durrell, Larry. Larry has an understanding beyond his experience. But I feel that he is fluid. He has more sense of values than Henry, but he too is impersonal. The personal terrifies him.

Beyond a certain point, expansion destroys the personal. What I find in Henry is a vaster world, like an illusion, like art compared with the constrictions of immediate life. But what makes his world so vast is also what destroys his personal relationships. He is acquisitive. He accumulates, he does not concentrate on what he finds, explore it, hold on to it. Is it impossible to have a vaster world, expansion, and keep the intimate and personal? Gonzalo's world is intimate, personal, and he suffers at times from the explorations of others' worlds I engage in, where he cannot follow me, which lies beyond Gonzalo.

Pita and Désirée, militant Republicans, Gonzalo's closest friends when I first met Gonzalo, were slowly estranged by jealousy and envy. Désirée never having succeeded in dominating Gonzalo (perhaps win him) and Pita fascinated by me much to Désirée's insane alarm. They resented the change in Helba and Gonzalo's life, what I was able to do to relieve their poverty. Then came Désirée's envy of Gonzalo's ascension in politics, envy of the printing press which enabled him to be useful to Spain. Pita, turned woman, began to scratch and hiss. He looks feminine. Both were given work at the Spanish Embassy. There they started an insidious gossip campaign, culminating in an open attack: Gonzalo is a fascist spy. He is working for the fascists. He receives money for this, that is why his life has become more comfortable. He was given a printing press by Anaïs Nin, the daughter of an aristocrat. The old Professor Langevin of the Sorbonne, the leader of *Paix et Démocratie*, spoke to Gonzalo, asked questions about me. Gonzalo assured him I was in sympathy with the Republicans and helping him. Fortunately, the professor had intercepted a letter addressed to Gonzalo which said: 'I have spoken to your mother about helping you financially as you begged her to. She refuses to send you money knowing it will be used for revolutionary work, and for a printing press for propaganda for Republican Spain.' Roger Klein had to testify. I offered to declare myself publicly a Republican, to save Gonzalo. We were both incensed at the injustice and irony. I, who have been helping Gonzalo to help the Republicans, being used as an instrument to destroy Gonzalo's career. The consequences were that I was barred from helping at the press, and from even telephoning Gonzalo.

I threw myself into writing. I worked on my portrait of Rank. I wrote the pages on Emily's confessions (*Winter of Artifice*).

I spent an evening with Henry and the Durrells. The evening was devoted to the story of the visit Henry paid to a chiropodist where he had gone to get an advertisement for the *Booster*. Henry was delighting in the humour about corns, dirty feet, etc. Both he and Fred had been there and had their feet done. Henry was hysterical with amusement.

Gonzalo and Henry both spend evenings out with people I could not bear, and both return saying: 'The world gives me nausea, disgusts me. People are foul and dirty.' Gonzalo rages, but returns to them, meets them in bars, spends the night drinking and talking. Gonzalo has a Peruvian friend, Manuel, who is an exhibitionist. He tells me endless stories about Manuel's perversions. He is fond of books, a real *rat de bibliothèque*, and it is there he is inspired to his most daring acts of undressing, in the most solemn and quiet of all places.

When I arrive at the Durrells', I find Fred drunk, Edgar intellectualizing like a machine without breaks, a runaway horse of abstractions, Nancy rebelliously cooking for them all, Larry enduring it all, and I not enduring them, but tired of holding out against drinking, futile talks.

Back to work. Rewriting volume 45 (New York, Rank, Henry). There are in the diary so many flowers like the Japanese paper-flowers, which need to be placed in water to achieve their flowering. So I am putting all the closed buds in water. What a bloom. Emily's full, hilarious confessions. Ten pages on Fez. Pages on Rank's clothes, men's clothes. Pages on the moonstorms. Essay on Rank's philosophy.

I experience the diabolical alchemy so familiar to writers, to man more than to woman. The exaltation spent on awaiting love, on a caress, goes into the pages on Fez. The fire spent on remembering nights of love, the temperature of joy, flowing into a marvellous canto to the streets, a bonfire of words. I sit here alone tonight, detached, in a trance, like the trance of saints, removed from the world, inhabiting and caressing Fez and my mysterious sorrows. I sit on the tip of minarets.

If Anaïs at age eleven could have foreseen Messieurs Paulhan and Grottiesen of the *Nouvelle Revue Française* leaning over the child-diary, marvelling, exclaiming in their beards, and looking at the Anaïs of today with admiration. Henry had come before me with his 'essay' on the diary and his exuberant speeches. Mr Grottiesen said: 'We must study this diary, what it really is, for of course, in Mr Miller's essay there is a lot of Mr Miller, all about the whale, for instance.'

A little man who was sitting there, waiting, got up and interrupted everybody to say: 'I consider it a privilege to have happened by at this moment. I have heard about the diary and was curious to meet you.' Little Anaïs of eleven, sighing to be made a member of the Académie Française.

Gonzalo is disillusioned with politics, the betrayals and retractions. He is foaming at the mouth. His eloquence and fire at certain moments could lead a country into a revolution. But the French are sitting back and Gonzalo is not placed where he can talk to them, he is locked in his office, writing letters, and if he could talk they would not understand his garbled French. Even in Spanish he talks through closed lips.

Idiot Anaïs, you are given a spider web and you want to make a sail out of it and sail a boat. Where were you so intent on going yesterday? All your life is like your quest for a boat. Yes, my running through the Exposition to see again a lovely boat I had caught a glimpse of, a Chinese junk. A boat with a fragile spiderweb sail not made for sailing. I was running through the exhibits, it was Sunday, the crowd was strolling, surprised at my speed. I saw nothing, it was like a fast film speeding by me, the crowd, the buildings, the Arabs I bumped into, as I ran blindly on my quest. A boat! A boat!

The entire mystery of pleasure in a woman's body lies in the intensity of the pulsation just before the orgasm. Sometimes it

is slow, one-two-three, three palpitations which then project a
fiery and icy liqueur through the body. If the palpitation is
feeble, muted, the pleasure is like a gentler wave. The pocket
seed of ecstasy bursts with more or less energy, when it is
richest it touches every portion of the body, vibrating through
every nerve and cell. If the palpitation is intense, the rhythm
and beat of it is slower and the pleasure more lasting. Electric
flesh-arrows, a second wave of pleasure falls over the first, a
third which touches every nerve end, and now the third like
an electric current traversing the body. A rainbow of colour
strikes the eyelids. A foam of music falls over the ears. It is the
gong of the orgasm. There are times when a woman feels her
body but lightly played on. Others when it reaches such a
climax it seems it can never surpass. So many climaxes. Some
caused by tenderness, some by desire, some by a word or an
image seen during the day. There are times when the day
itself demands a climax, days of cumulative sensations and
unexploded feelings. There are days which do not end in a
climax, when the body is asleep or dreaming other dreams.
There are days when the climax is not pleasure but pain,
jealousy, terror, anxiety. And there are days when the climax
takes place in creation, a white climax. Revolution is another
climax. Sainthood another.

I found a new apartment for Helba, overlooking a garden.
A week later she has not yet moved from the damp, black,
smelly cellar room. Meanwhile I am running into debts. With
the Durrells it is all sweet and sane. Henry lives entirely in his
own world. Now and then he breaks down and becomes
aware of others. He weeps for his family. But that afternoon
in his studio, with the Durrells, after he wept over them, he
fell asleep. Nancy and I cooked dinner. When he awakened
he was ready to go on working and writing as before. He is
surrounded by admiring disciples who flatter him and do not
question his opinions. He even cowed Larry with: 'If you
don't understand Picasso there is a limitation in you.'

Larry helps me to keep Henry on an even keel. He has
solidity. He yields, at times, because he loves Henry. 'I don't
want to spoil his enthusiasm. It is worth a thousand francs
thrown away.'

I do not like the *Booster*. It is vulgar and farcical. Strident. Then I feel guilty: 'Perhaps I am too austere.'

At the basis of my life lies fear and doubt, yet I give faith to others. Gonzalo said: 'When I'm despondent I don't like to see you. I hate to spoil the luminous atmosphere around you.' I am alone with my sorrows. My only relief is activity. I see that the press, in Gonzalo's hands, has contributed little to the cause of Spain, in six months, and I could have printed a book on it. I see how Henry's ideas cannot make him sacrifice a whim. So I write. Gonzalo had promised before we bought the press: 'I will print all your work.'

A world composed of a severe father, a Gonzalo forever pursuing danger and destruction, a Henry who is only intermittently human, leaves me in an abyss of solitude. Why must I constantly pursue mirages? Why do I struggle against chaos and not wallow in it as others do?

Hans Reichel's madness. In Henry's studio he monologues: 'No one has ever told me: "I love you." I am full of anguish and anxiety. Everybody is against me. You are hiding the wine. I am sure there is more wine, but you are hiding it. I see you are making fun of me. I can't find peace anywhere. Take me back *chez mes peintures*.' *Chez mes peintures!* As if his paintings were his home, his family, his lover. Reichel clutching at people, physically, violently, so they won't leave him. Always drunk, indifferent to his success, to the money he has made, afraid only that 'the evening will come to an end, and I will be alone again.' Reichel mad. Understanding can no longer bring him back. He no longer believes in anyone.

Henry sees his women more critical, more condemnatory than they really were. He interprets women's silence as a condemnation. He projects his own guilts on women, not men. He expects to be judged by women, not men. Guilt certainly haunts all the men who seem free of it. Henry, Gonzalo, my father. They are not really free of it.

Durrell calls the copies of my diary my black children. They are bound in black. I keep them in an Arabian wedding-chest, violet velvet with gold nails. Lovely to see the coffer open, brimming full. And now this one will go to the vault, to be locked up among other people's jewels and testaments.

Letter to Durrell:

Was in bed all day so I can't go to the Villa Seurat and will have to wait until tomorrow, Tuesday. Will try to pass by your place for tea instead of dinner. Will bring back the Fontanne. Just another pattern, and for the moment, I do not find these fecund. I think patterns and arrangements are only fecund when we get lost, when we vitally need to be re-oriented, but otherwise they are like intellectual chess games, not vital, they kill experience. I feel we should turn to these books only when we are adrift on a sea of instincts or emotions, choking in a drama, suffocating in subjectivity, or in some other acute crisis which has thrown us off course. Wonder what you will think of my essay on Otto Rank for Eliot's magazine *Criterion*. Worked all day. I am glad I kidnapped you last night. When I saw Fred there with you I suddenly remembered all we said once about living horizontally or vertically. And with Fred there it would have been a horizontal evening, and so I took you both away, with a vertical, heraldic devotion.

[NOVEMBER, 1937]

The day began beautifully with Dorothy Norman, of the *American Quarterly*, accepting both 'Birth' story and 'Woman in Creation' essay, and saying she had great admiration for the purity of my work.

The activity Henry has created is extraordinary. He lives in a whirlpool, drawing everyone to him. I am to edit a number of the *Booster* containing women's writing. It is out of a discussion with him and Larry one night that my essay on woman's creation was born. Larry has written a voyage through the womb which is unmatchable. We're re-reading Rank's *Trauma of Birth*.

Gonzalo's activity is increasing because it is a lost cause, and it is his nature to defend what is weak. I feel the Spanish cause is weakening and I fear for him.

Gonzalo admires in me qualities Henry is indifferent to. Gonzalo likes my independence, my struggle to maintain my integrity in spite of my human devotions, my slavery to my affections. Gonzalo admires my rebellions. Henry's destiny is his writing, Gonzalo's the revolution. Henry enlarged my world, made me write, made my life rich and also inhuman. Gonzalo brings me turmoil, danger, blood and death, war and destruction. Henry wants peace and philosophy. Gonzalo wants fervour and explosions. Henry admires a film on China in which is revealed great resignation, passivity, a sense of the eternal annihilating personal sorrow. He was impressed because they do not weep at funerals. This is closer to Henry's attitude. It is his solution to life. Resignation, acceptance, indifference. That is not my nature.

When a desire is blocked most people react with philosophy. But with me a desire defeated is a part of life which is killed.

Visit from David Gascoyne, only twenty-one, a child prodigy. I don't know his poetry, only his reputation. A mystical, poetic boy, but bound like a dead Arab by multiple tight white bandages. He leaves me his diary, full of reticences and evasions.

I remember my first image of the Gonzalo who entered Roger Klein's little room like a giant in a miniature cave – a startling figure – disquieting, dark, fiery, but drunk, dispersed. I aroused him to action. I roused him without knowing the force in him for drama, for rebellion. Is it my fate to inflame revolutionary forces, Henry in literature, Gonzalo in politics?

Denise Clairouin tells me: 'I gave the diaries to Maxwell Perkins, of Scribner. He was interested. Instead of giving them to a reader, he took them home and read them himself. He was thunderstruck. "What a curious, extraordinary woman," he said. He wants you to make an abridged copy. Go to work, Anaïs.'

Because of Henry's description of the whalelike diary, Larry calls me 'the Whale'. And signs himself: 'your ever-admiring limpet.' I had to look up 'limpet' in the dictionary. Then I wrote back: 'Dear Limpet, the whale wants you to know you have the largest, most luxuriously furnished, the most palatial, pearl-covered cabin on the highest desk (outside cabin) with a view of the entire ocean, on the back of the said whale. In fact, this whale, who seems most independent, who to all mariners' eyes seems willing enough to travel alone, would not travel anywhere without the limpet.'

I will never be able to say as Henry said, weeping: 'After all, I am a human being, and as a human being I've done wrong.' Someday I will weep and say: 'After all, I am an artist, and as an artist I've done wrong. I acted humanly.'

Artist. I want to do Jeanne and her brothers better than Cocteau did the *Enfants Terribles*. I want to do June better than Djuna Barnes did *Nightwood*. I want to do Artaud better than Carlo Suarès did the *Procession Enchaînée*.

I love Larry. But I have no warmth for Gascoyne. He leaves me cold in spite of his suffering. He is a prisoner. The sound of rattling chains disturbs me, but I have no desire to break his.

Everything for me divides into warm or cold. Cold people who never act from human spontaneity, but always out of an instinct for self-preservation or acquisition. Warm people who respond to others.

Have gone to work on abridged edition of the diary.

Hélène is changing the curtains of her bedroom. Gonzalo is working for the revolution in Peru, underground. Helba is sitting like an inmate in an asylum doing nothing for hours, or sewing and resewing rags. Henry is writing *Tropic of Capricorn*, and as Larry said: 'a new dimension without emotion.' Henry's creation at times resembles insanity, because it is experience disconnected from feeling – like an anesthetized soul injected with ether. I ask myself: those who get disconnected from a human world of feeling, for whatever reason, who live in a world of their own, wasn't their human core weak to begin with? Where are the deep sources of feeling in my father and in Henry which life succeeded in atrophying? Why is it that I never get cut off from pity, sympathy, participation, in spite of the fact that I am living out my own dream, my interior vision, my fantasies without any interruptions. I dream, I kiss, I have orgasms, I get exalted, I leave the world, I float, I cook, I sew, have nightmares, write in my head, compose, decompose, improvise, invent, I listen to all, I hear all that is said, I feel Spain, I am aware, I am everywhere, I am open to wounds, open to love, I am rooted to my devotions, I *am never separate*, never cut off, never blind, deaf, absent. I hold on to the dream which makes life possible, to the creation which transfigures, to the God who sustains, to the crimes which give life, to the illusions which make the marvellous possible. I hold on to the poetry and the human simplicities. I write about the labyrinth, the womb, Fez, and I carry electric bulbs to Gonzalo's home. Larry is sitting cross-legged on the floor like a soft blond Hindu, with a catlike suppleness and writing with a branding iron.

Old Lantelme, my father's secretary for many years, now retired, comes twice a week to teach me French, saying: '*Elle est vivante, je viens me réchauffé.*' The Joneses arrived from Spain, talking about the terrible suffering of the refugees, but they ate full-course meals with Hemingway, who is taking notes at the front, and when he is not taking notes, he hunts pheasants in abandoned Spanish properties. Jones talks like a somnam-bulist about politics, in a monotonous voice, without anima-tion, in a funeral oration of facts, sound facts he says, which sound as unsound to me as the hysterical statements made at the revolutionary meetings. Lila Ranson calls me up, in her masculine voice. I have only seen her two times, and she calls me darling, 'I must see you, I have left my husband, I am very happy now. I have so much to tell you. When can I see you?'

Gascoyne comes an hour later to see if he can catch his own narcissistic image in the pool of my understanding. The volume of the diary he read enlarged the space of his prison. While he is there I get a call from the secretary of the Countess Lucie to come to dinner.

Henry has been collecting subscriptions to publish the first volume of the diary, and the first one he received was from André Maurois, who added that, however, he did not want all of the fifty-four volumes, his house was too full of books. In between these visits I arranged all the diaries I want to edit in one box so I can plunge into them easily.

I had told Gonzalo that I missed hearing the lonely cough of the Russian captain, friend of Gonzalo's, who had been wounded in Spain, so Gonzalo took me with him when he visited him in his run-down hotel where they do not ask for papers. He was sitting in the waiting room reading the papers. Gonzalo brought him copies of *New Masses*. He once had a room near *Paix et Démocratie* and I would hear him cough, and talk to himself. He looked distinguished and frail, smoking a pipe, and Gonzalo told me he was waiting for the gift of a wheelchair so he could get about by himself. He lost both his legs.

Every time there is talk of Spain there is a tornado in me of emotion and desire to participate. Gonzalo says I would be of no use whatever. And I am thrown back into writing. About my father's games, Helba's packing of her dusty rags and taking a month to move, Carteret luminous and yet appealing to Allendy for help. He says: 'I know Allendy is not a poet but he wants to help me.' He understands my love of Morocco. 'In Morocco one melts into the universal, one loses one's self into others.'

Denise Clairouin: 'Make no changes. It is the document they want.'

I sprinkle leaves of patchouli over the lamp bulbs. I number the pages of the diary and wonder what to leave out. The deserts, the empty spaces.

I don my velvet dress for the Countess Lucie's dinner and sit on her white satin sofa.

Lila Ranson is a writer, plump, forceful. I first met her at a very conventional evening, and she was chafing against conventions. I eluded her because I am tired of breaking others' chains. After several calls from her, her voice so triumphant, I agreed to come and visit her. She ushered me into the bedroom. And there was a replica of June. June with an aureole of angel hair and a voluptuous Viking body. The dusky voice, heavy arms, the fever in the eyes. And they were living the life I never lived with June. She was ill, and she sat up against the flowered cretonne bedhead. Recklessness and adventure in every expression of her face. Lila nestled against her. They talked about their love for each other. They caressed each other. They said: 'You never possess man as you do a woman.'

Lila was clearly the one who would be tormented, jealous. Her friend was clearly the mobile and flowing one. A hardness and passion in her. I had come only for a moment. I stayed all afternoon, fascinated. The wide bed, the purple negligee opening on a sunburnt skin. Lila saying romantic things about 'living together for twenty years'. Her friend contemptuous of these assertions. 'There is no absolute in relationship,' she said. And to me later: 'You look like a girl of sixteen.' The atmosphere unnerved me. I liked sharing the newness of their love, the faith and fire of newness, confidence, that moment when the love seems stronger than anything, the moment before the shocks, the fissures, the irritations, conflicts, the moment before they discovered a world beyond each other which no caresses could solder together.

It was at this moment that I best understood Don Juan: to be always at the beginning, at the first moment of faith and love, never to witness the gradual deterioration, the gradual weakening of the love, the ageing of it, the withering of it. To be always at the first moment, the highest, and to remain there by seeking only beginnings.

Already Lila's friend was sprouting branches that did not stem from the single trunk of their love. She was saying, 'The ideal relationship is between a man and a woman.'

Rebellions of all kinds attract to their activities weaklings who rebel because they cannot master, destroy because they cannot create. I fear that Gonzalo may be part of that lamentable army, those who have always lived negatively. Is it a noble service to the poor, or the hysterical tantrums of firebugs? The firebug being the man who wanted to be a firefighter, but failed. In Helba's and Gonzalo's misery there is no cruelty, but a stubborn self-destruction.

What lantern slides, from the soiled, thumb-worn life of Helba, due to Helba's own inertia, to the white satin salon of Countess Lucie. Lucie sitting on the arm of a white satin armchair, slim, evanescent, eyes dark and selective, critical, aware. Face austerely white, an unexpected austerity because the features, the mouth, are made for sensuality. A white cloud of preoccupation. The fairy tale wears cold wings, she drives an airplane, a car, laughs, talks, but she is lost.

I see Betty Ryan, who is like a delicate Japanese woman, talking about *House of Incest*. She adds: 'When I was a young girl I loved mercury. I carried a little bottle of it. I would pour it in the palm of my hand in school and play with it. I liked how it changed shape, decomposed, separated, took so many forms, yet remained one, magnetically. It was my *fétiche*. I felt an affinity with it. I could go anywhere with it. It was alive and a part of me. With it I could face people, the world.' Her delicacy moved me, her timidity and dreamfulness. Her voice is frail and distant. She did not talk freely to me because she was awed by me. I was the Whale of the black diaries.

Lucie is too much protected by white-gloved butlers, crystals, brocades. But there is darkness in her. Betty Ryan is drugged with the white sleep of reverie, of unreality. She too is so far away and yearning to be awakened. Lucie has had violent shocks but is still dreaming. She wrote a book, which she sent me. In the book a woman dies from the wounds of a man's caprices and his love of his own freedom above all else.

Henry says: 'I want to live a deeper life, I know my defect, I expand too much, I should not, for instance, have done the magazine.' The *Booster* has dispersed his energies.

I did not talk freely to Lucie because of the white fur, the mirrors in which every motion is reflected several times, the butlers nearby, because I no longer have the right dress to wear for my visit to her, because I am sliding into a life without décor, without illusions, without white gloves and aesthetics.

Gonzalo volatizes in cafés.

My father comes to visit me, with flowers in silver paper, and words in silver paper, flowers with wires running through them to uphold them in formal haughtiness, and his words too, pierced with wires, formal and synthetic, all grown in hothouses. 'I am training a Norwegian singer to sing my songs. She wants to sing Spanish songs. She is so cold, I have to inject her with my own warmth.'

'Are you sure,' I said, 'that the notes you are teaching her are the same ones she will sing at her concert?'

I should not really tease him, knowing as I know now that this is the most robust bone in his body.

Hélène decides not to go and live in London. 'I am too attached to you, Anaïs, like a lifeboat to a ship.'

But it is I who am the lifeboat (in size) and she the *Titanic*.

Stock-market news: '*Une timide reprise de la dynamite.*'

Dynamite shares show a slight recovery!

The Henry I first knew was humble and unsure. The Henry of today is self-assured and slightly megalomaniacal. Always talking about China and wisdom, after an evening when he said unwise and brutal things to an English girl.

The Marxists consider Allendy a doubtful left-winger because he published an article on 'Sexuality and Capitalism' in a medical journal. They called it 'exploiting the bourgeois appetites', when Allendy was merely fulfilling his medical function, his doctor's observations. A poet was put in prison for using the name of God in a poem. Gide was ostracized for reporting his true impressions of Russia. I have fought too much for a spiritually honest and free life to pass from one narrow-mindedness to another, from one dogma into another, from one prejudice into another.

Gonzalo says justly: 'You have to look beyond the defects, the discipline. To make a new world demands first of all destruction and severity. The men of today will be sacrificed, the individual will be sacrificed, but for a new order. You have had the strength to expand in site of a bourgeois world, but what of the weak, those who cannot, those who are downtrodden?' This argument always touches me. The weak ones. Those I help every day, trapped in all kinds of miseries.

Gonzalo is sacrificing his Bohemianism. But he finds discipline a conflict. He lives without a clock.

David Gascoyne. Living in a real *sous les toits* room, in an attic, low ceiling and slanting windows. He gave me Pierre-Jean Jouve, a new world, new dreams, a new poison, a new drug. The first to treat the knowledge of psychoanalysis as a poet, to write a novel which is half a poem.

Then to Henry's, Denoël and Steele will publish *Black Spring* in French. Flattering letters. James Cooney, of Woodstock, starts a new magazine [*The Phoenix*], appoints Henry European editor, accepts my 'orchestra' fragment from *Winter of Artifice*, writes of doing all the diaries on his hand press, one by one.

Valentina and Lila come to visit me. Valentina enters like a queen of the amazons, wearing an orchid in which a bird could get lost, an emerald as large as a hazelnut. Lila wears a tailored suit, which she fills out voluptuously. Furs and perfume. Valentina has been coiffed by Antoine. Valentina has been overpowered by Lila's invisible moustache. They took me to hear Suzy Solidor. Cocktails at the Ritz. Not my world. No words to remember. Nothing remains of them when they leave. A *fleur de peau*. *Fleurs de peau*.

I visited Jean Carteret's apartment at the very top of an old apartment house near Clichy. Before I enter he has seen me through a spy-eye in the door, which makes the hallway appear immeasurably long, the person standing in front immeasurably tall and as if standing miles away. I entered an apartment as dark as a dungeon, a black hallway with glow-worm lamps. Jean has to lead me. But his eyes sparkle in a way which reminds me of his own description of an aurora borealis. It passes like a muslin veil in waves, such an immense phenomenon of light and colour that Jean said it seems to stare at you like an *eye*. The eye is the only sense we have which crosses between the finite and the infinite. The aurora borealis is the eye of the world. The eyes of Jean have that quality. They shine nestled between flowing hair and a blond beard. In the gentle way his eyelids fall there is goodness. In the length and softness of his pale eyelashes there is femininity. The nose is pure, the mouth sensual. He is wearing the black wool costume of the Laplanders, a long square blouse like the Russian peasants', but lined with bands of yellow, red and green embroidered in felt.

In his room blood-red predominates. The bedspread, the cushions, and the curtains are dark red. He has covered his windows with Japanese rice-paper pasted on the glass, so that a view of other houses is shut out, so that the eyes are thrown back into the room which is like the cave of Ali Baba, filled with treasures:

Blue painted sleds from Lapland stand upright in the corner, ready to slide heavenward to the planets. Inside of the sled he has placed a small oil-lamp which sheds a blue Arctic light. In his hand he holds a Chinese opium pipe without opium. He does not need opium. He has the gift of reverie. A collection of pipes from all over the world lies scattered. An enormous Chinese gong rings the hours. It once awakened the Tibetan monks, but it came from the flea market. An African pirogue carved out of wood sails on the mantelpiece, with four Africans rowing. Two large ivory-handled knives are nailed to the wall above Jean's bed. Reindeer horns, hung on the walls, support an open book on magic, and a book of erotic tales. Delicate dried coral blooms unexpectedly from the top of a pile of books. The bookshelves are placed high near the ceiling. A sunburst hat from Madagascar hangs from the last shelf. He pulls out a box from under his bed which contains a skeleton found in the Canary Islands. A tree root gathered in Tahiti rivals Brancusi's petrified snakes. Jean is a great wanderer, but he likes to bring back proofs of what he has seen, sand from Mount Athos, liqueurs from Hungary, water from the Black Sea in a bottle, volcanic stones, beaded curtains from Algeria.

We sit on two children's chairs from Greece. Were they carried over not from Greece but from the kingdom of his childhood, from some small provincial town similar to the town of Rimbaud's childhood where he lived so closely bound to his sister? Are Jean and his sister still sitting in these diminutive chairs? Was the child still there, never fully ejected, never outgrown?

His mother forbade him to study the violin, for which he had a passion. He collected instruments which he nailed to the wall. His mother smashed the violin he wanted to play. 'No child of mine will become a good-for-nothing violin player.' The instruments on the wall seem to be playing a silent music which only the buried musician in him can hear. He could not resuscitate this violinist but he became the archaeologist of his own soul. He surrounded himself with eloquent objects. Necklaces intertwined with rosaries. Little bags filled with odorous herbs. He opened more valises, and spilled on the floor erotic post cards from Spain, a Tahitian grass skirt, a pipe carved out of a lobster's toe. He is like a young magician. He likes to disguise himself. He changed his costume several times during the evening.

Spoons, stones, icons, bird feathers, a whip, dried lichen, are not inanimate objects in his hands. They become objects used for Black Masses, conjugations of magic chaos. He wants to possess the whole world in his room. To make up for the lost musician. He probed and pursued the music killed by his mother.

On the wall hangs a huge mushroom-shaped holy water stand. The holy water stand of poisons, I baptized it.

A Turkish rug seems ready for flight, the heavy felt Lapland boots seem ready to wear for hunting in the snow. His lamps are covered with medieval armour hats. A small Chinese scroll lies open on a stand. A pen and inkstand might have belonged to Dostoevsky. Jean offers me incense from India, a cigarette from Germany.

He is possessed with restlessness and wanderlust, forgetfulness, timelessness. He lives in a labyrinth of words, tales, memories. His game is with fetishes. Objects not abstractions. Proofs of his voyages, proofs of all he touched and loved, proofs of his wanderings. Into his rooms he brings back the universe. The violin is muted, he never lays his hands on it, but the music is in him, it floods the place, the harmonies issue from the shell of his misery. He is condemned to wander outside of his violin, yet in every object around him I could place my ear and hear the music his mother was unable to silence.

He talks to me about the conflict of politics. He has the same conflict I have between humanism and dogmas. I am tempted to abandon my individual world to serve a collective world. But Carteret says Marxism is not an expression of our humanism, it is practical, utilitarian, concrete, factual. It is not a selfish, individual life which pulls us away from other systems, collective systems, but another level of life. We live on another level. We have to act on another level. We are not escaping, we are not enjoying an opium life, we are dreaming the dream of life itself, the dream of the growth of man, each man, one by one. Our action is on another level. For these words I was grateful to him. 'This is a realistic epoch, an epoch of concrete details, of economics. We cannot be of use to it.'

Gonzalo says: 'Literature, metaphysics, philosophies, they were never effective without violence. Violence is necessary, inevitable. People cannot free themselves through art or religion. Even to establish religion, violence and revolution were necessary.'

Renata Bugatti came like a storm, with the head of a Roman soldier and the intelligence of a Sphinx. She has such a force that I remember hearing her play the piano at the Salle Pleyel thirteen years ago. I remember the suit she wore, the fierce carriage of her head. I do understand these outsized women. Strange, these women who terrify men are the women who do not intimidate me at all. One can face them in the open. It is exhilarating. They are direct, honest.

I cannot enter the dream of revolution as Gonzalo dreams it, into its essence, its purity. Yet I have such a strong desire that others may live, and to give individually becomes increasingly difficult. Gonzalo attacks this kind of giving because he says it only delays reforms, palliates evils which must be confronted. To give individually means to be submerged, killed and not to achieve a very wide range. One must give collectively.

This is how it is done. You put on a special apparatus resembling that for the deaf (as normally you would not catch the rumble of economic crisis, collective running of factories) and you listen in. Then you talk about *Paix et Démocratie* with lowered eyes, admitting it is an anti-fascist organization and working for Spain. The apparatus registers: a sympathizer to the cause. His eyes warm up. You exchange propaganda. You file his name in the box for *Paix et Démocratie*. Gonzalo is very pleased.

I walked away in the soft rain. A church bell was tolling. This grave gong sounding through the agitated city, a city of nerves, horns, strident sounds. I felt its resonance. What fine receptivity. In this vault in me where I hear only large deep notes, only the marvellous, will I be able to receive the dream of revolution for the good of all? A world of great arches swung over vast spaces – the dreamer learns to span these but I can never forget that the Inquisition tortured human beings who did not believe in Catholicism, and that the revolution will torture and is torturing all those who do not adhere fanatically to it. It is this I cannot accept. Was there ever a pure revolution? A system achieved without human sacrifice?

Renata asked Jean: 'What is your occupation?'
Jean answered: 'My occupation is to learn to walk through all of them in a state of transcendentalism, to live only in the essence, and within the frame of none.' A form of liberty. But

Renata was too primitive to understand this. It was when she used the word cruelty that her long mouth became most expressive. She wanted to be cruel, she understood how one could torture the loved one for the pleasure of consoling him. She talked about herself. She once fell into the hands of the magician described by Thomas Mann. She was under his power for ten days. She wanted to be cured of her fear of the public. He did not succeed in hypnotizing her as he did others but he could make her play against her will. She gave a whole concert under his domination. She believed herself cured of her fear. She left him, and at the next concert the fear returned.

Jean told her that she was always looking for the brother. 'Drama comes into your life periodically.' The writer Colette called out to her loudly in a theatre once: '*Voila le beau garçon de Rome.*'

Appearance of strength, yet filled with fears. 'My greatest fear is identification, of passing into others.' Her father was a celebrated tenor, a gambler, Don Juan. Carteret said: 'You are a mystic.'

I did not see her as he did. She is in a high state of tension, which gives an illusion of power. It seemed to me that I could see in Renata's eyes the demonic little elevator of desire sliding up and down as she contemplated Jean Carteret in his role of visionary. Her gravitation was in danger. I knew and recognized this dizzy fall into a precipice as she contemplated Jean's small and tender ears, the hair on his neck soft as if it had never been cut. His talk creates space, air, rhythms.

Renata was saying: 'In love I always see an adversary. I prefer friendship. All fusion is devouring. I always had the desire to enter a lion's den. Colette had the same wish, she wanted to confront a panther. And the panther threw itself on her and tore her clothes.'

'I love Colette's writing,' I said.

'Why don't you visit her?'

'Because in *Le Journal de Claudine* the girl Colette most hated in school was called Anaïs.'

Work on diary for Perkins. Work for *Paix et Démocratie*. Work for the *Booster*.

*

I no longer believe duality is a weakening element. One can make a strong tool out of it. It all depends on one's flexibility, if one is able to yield to double pressures and move with fluidity between them. It is the rigidity which causes the breaks.

Jean said: 'I believe it is not unfaithfulness which drives the great lovers but that when you are highly sensitized to love, when you vibrate deeply sensually and love passionately, it is like a current in the body which, being perpetual, creates a warm contact with all. I feel so many people physically, amorously, because I am in a state of love, like a mystic, and it is greater than myself, it is immense, this overflow. Just as activity creates activity, energy creates energy, creation creates creation, so passion creates more and more capacity for passion. One's receptivity, capacity, is expanded, and there you have the answer to the amorous expansion of all born lovers. That is why the word fidelity means nothing to me.'

He also talked about his erotic adventures: 'Sometimes I am afraid I am too slow in coming to a climax and tiring out the woman, or too quick and missed giving her pleasure. I am concerned about giving woman pleasure. It is rare when I have known simultaneous pleasure. In one night or two one does not find the right rhythm. I have known so many women and synchronization only a few times. And the woman remains a stranger to me. In me there is always doubt, unsureness, fumbling, failures, or half-fulfilments. And very often to excite myself I have to invent an erotic fantasy, recall an erotic picture I saw, or another woman I desired and could not have.'

Adventures, without the magnetic attraction of love, of stirred emotions, upheavals of feeling which sensitize the body, arouse the nerves, awaken the flesh? The pleasure of love is so much greater than that of adventure. Jean's pleasures seemed pale compared to mine. He said in answer to me: 'You are fortunate to have found eroticism within love, not apart from it as it is with me.'

We talked about schizophrenia, which I see as a lack of contact, a kind of withering of feeling *with* or *for* others. And as I feel too much contact with human beings, the world, I said I must be suffering from the opposite of schizophrenia, empathy, identification with, dispersion into, abandon and loss of self in others. Then why the feeling of loneliness? 'We do touch all things by osmosis, empathy,' said Jean. 'We are in contact with a centre, yet part of us escapes and lives marginally, a part of us in exile, hence the feeling of loneliness. It is that we live in *becoming*, in the future.'

Deep joys in sacrifice, in obtaining Allendy's support for *Paix et Démocratie* rather than his subscription to the diary, in listening to his confidences.

Came home and danced to the radio. Seas of emotion heaving under my feet. I feel a tension which should carry me to the moon.

Hélène is invited by her lover to go to Norway with him. She is renting her apartment. I like her because she can play with experience. Together we could remove any event from its tragic context. It would assume the colour of a dream, a fiction. We told each other vivid and violent happenings as people tell each other their dreams.

Renata Bugatti playing at a concert. Her mask tormented. When I hear her play I hear the man and woman I once heard behind a hotel wall, moaning rhythmically. Renata is seeking to possess the piano, enter the music. It is a *corps à corps*. It is a sexual bout ending in defeat. Her nostrils quiver. Her mouth is designed for cruelty. Her chin is wilful. But it is a defeat. The melody does not rise even when she turns her face upward. It is a substance made heavy by her passion. Her will cannot attain what the man and woman attained behind the hotel wall, a moment of pleasure. Her passion is primitive, blood and guts, and cannot be alchemized into music. The piano she pounds is her own body, with a male violence, and the mask is of the one who never reaches either the orgasm or sainthood. No music rose or passed out of the window. It was too heavy with blood.

This took place at the house of Baron de Rothschild. The vast salon had been turned into a concert hall. We were surrounded by paintings of his ancestors. In front of me, there was a beautiful woman I could only see when she turned her head. She was marred by a dark-brown growth on her chin. I turned my face away. I looked out into the misty green garden. And I saw three full-length mirrors planted there, reflecting the trees, three mirrors in the middle of a dewy garden.

In one day, a kaleidoscope. The lantern slides and I am at the Stuart Gilberts', talking with Denise Clairouin, who asks me: 'And that work on the diary, how is it going?' I answer that it is going well, but I do not confess that I prefer to be writing about the present rather than be condensing the past into six hundred pages for Mr Perkins.

I push myself to visit Helba in her new apartment. It is even more startling to see her, in a clean, airy, lighted new apartment, come out looking like a bedraggled gypsy, wearing one of Gonzalo's shirts, and over this a kimono which she has dyed black and through which the frayed red still shows. On her feet she wears a pair of Gonzalo's big socks filled with cotton wool at the tip, like a rag-picker's Christmas stocking. She is lying in bed reading a book about diseases. The windows are shut, the sun is locked out, she has managed to make this joyous clean white new place almost like the old mildewed cellar where I first saw her. She is busy marking in the book all the diseases she has. 'See,' she tells me, handing me the book, 'I have diseases described on pages 143 and 26, in fact, if I read carefully enough I have all of them. I am copying out a recipe for dandruff.' Her face is yellow and old. My pity is exhausted, I can't respond any more, because all this misery comes out of stubbornness, ignorance and a persistent self-destruction. My doctor gave up taking care of her. 'She does not co-operate, she goes her own way, she pays no attention to what I ask her to do.' I am not eager to stay. It is like visiting a tomb. I am really angry at her will to die, dragging Gonzalo into perpetual anxiety, fear, dirt. It is a rivalry between life and death taking place here, and Helba wins over me each time. When I give her a new apartment, how can she make it look like the old cellar?

I dreamed that my father was conducting an orchestra. There was no one to play the harp. I offered to play it. But the harp was really a spinet with loose notes, one white, one blue, one black. My father said I had only to play the three notes at every silence of the orchestra. It seemed very simple, but when I was about to do it the notes disappeared. I found them later in a box. They were gambler's roulette chips.

Hélène said good-bye with electric-eyed sincerity, tearless. A toy is taken away, one of the dream personages, a large Chirico woman against a blue canvas, half statue, half movie actress, an amazon, but one afraid of burglars and sex maniacs, pouting when she could not get what she wanted. Why are some people like dream personages one cannot become emotionally attached to? Moricand is another. We part at the subway, but I could swear Hélène has never entered a subway train. She merely vanished.

Gonzalo and I were watching candles in his apartment, watching them tremble. I asked him why candles trembled so much and he answered: 'Because they are anxious.'

Jean Carteret understands my life, and I his. 'We deny reality. We seek only the dream.' I see him untrammelled, fluid, free, magical. But he confesses he is only free in spirit. In every other way he is in chains. He is blocked. He cannot be an artist, a lover, a husband, a lecturer, a traveller. He plays at all of them, partially. What I seek is the *Vie Féerique*, when all things happen as in a dream. Not comfort but the smoothness of magical happenings. Not luxury but the stage illusions of beauty. Not security but the drug effects of harmony. Not order but the unreal arrangements of objects as in the dream. Not perfection but the illusion of perfection. Not clock time but the instantaneity of miracles. Not labour but the realization of all wishes. Not service but an immediate answer to all formulated desires. Not peace but the sequence of the dream. Not absence of death but the eternal life of the dream. Not rebellion against change, loss, death, passing of time, but the quest of the eternal in every moment. The transfusion of blood into dreams. The dream includes violence, murder, pain, but no end. In the dream one never touches bottom even after one dies.

[JANUARY, 1938]

I was face to face with my work. There was no more evading it. I began to work and today I am finished with the cuts.

I gave Gonzalo all I had for his rent. It was not quite enough to cover extra charges, but he did not tell me. I was short of money. Gonzalo did not dare face his landlady that day without all of it, and so he slept in an armchair at *Paix et Démocratie.*

Henry projected into space by his writing, away from all of us. Pale. Cold. Henry says: 'I suffer like an animal. I am like an animal. No one can help. No one is strong enough.'

'But Henry,' I said, 'one can get help just by remaining humanly near to others. Strength is a rhythm. Each one of us has his moments of strength when he can rescue others, and his moment of weakness when he needs to be rescued. But you seem unable to stay near anyone.' He is too far, at such moments. Too far to feel. I know what he is doing, and how it surpasses all of us.

I am neurotic, every artist is, but when I feel the earth opening under my feet, I turn to human beings. I lean on them. I seek warmth and love. They save me. I fear Henry's moments of insanity. His equilibrium is tenuous. He has such grandiose ideas of himself and at the same time such doubts. Then a phrase out of Jouve unties the knots in Henry, and he is ready to write again. He is happy.

At least, in pain, or in happiness, I am one who feels the constant rotations and convolutions of earth and of life.

I am sitting at the Café Flore waiting for Gonzalo and he does not come. It is raining. I pick up a newspaper. Once he had said to me: 'I picked up a newspaper and saw on the front page the photo of my best friend, murdered the night before by the fascists.' That is how it could happen. Gonzalo could fail to come to meet me, and that very night ... At the table next to me, a man is mocking the madness of Artaud, who is locked up in Sainte-Anne. He parodies his speech, his fears, his *délire de persécution*. I turn to him and I say: 'It is you who should be locked up and not Artaud.'

But what has happened to Gonzalo? It is nine o'clock. I have not eaten. Gascoyne comes into the café. He is drugged. I hear conversations, superimposed, intellectual, personal, literary, intimate. Gascoyne's Irish friend cannot bring him back with his Irish fancies. A friend of Artaud's stops us: 'There is a man mocking him all over Paris, I want to kill him. Where is he?' One cannot protect anyone. But Henry is never in danger of dying.

Gonzalo had been ill at home, without telephone. At midnight a friend of his came to tell me.

I was so grateful that he was not lying in some gutter with three bullet holes in his body that I entered the Church of Saint-Germain, and though I can no longer believe in prayer I managed to convey gratitude. To what? To whom?

In front of the church door an automobile was burning. The firemen were working at putting out the fire.

My neurosis is utterly different from Henry's, or Artaud's, or Helba's, or Gonzalo's. It is as if by a fluid quality, a facility for identification with others, I became like water and instead of separating from others, as Henry does, I lose myself in others. If people say: 'I hate the tropics, I hate the country, I hate red, or orange or black,' I feel I am the tropics, Louveciennes was the country, red is my colour, this person hates me. Then I get confused. This for me is the labyrinth. Identification, projection. My identification with my father which had to be broken. Myself in June. I see the double, the twins of others. Is it this deep psychological truth I will explore to the limit, and make the base of my Proustian edifice? It is at the basis of my life, analogy, interchange of souls, of identities. Doesn't love mean just that, this growing into the other like plants intertwining their roots, this interchange of soul and feelings. Not an abyss then, but a new world. Not madness but a deep truth. A principle moving us, our inner fatality. We do not act as ourselves. We act. We are possessed. These are the multiple miracles of the personality.

When I was fifteen I wanted to create the black tulip which Alexandre Dumas wrote about. So I invented a formula. I found symbols, I invented signs, a language, and a chemical mixture. I applied it. But I had invented signs without keeping the key or the code to their meaning. I didn't know what elements would produce a black tulip. It remained an esoteric mystery, but for me, the discoverer, too.

Jean Carteret's life is expanded, dilated to the point of abortion. When we meet, the blood rushes to his face, and he falls into a dream. We have lunch together when he is on his way to the Sorbonne. While I waited for him, the waiter said to me: 'The young man who looks like Christ was here earlier looking for you.' Jean reads me what he is writing on horoscopes, or analysis of handwriting, or his conference on Lapland. He is full of curiosity and wonder. He is floating in vast reveries.

Moricand joins us at the Café Flore, he is writing a book called 'The Story of a People who went Mad'. At the bar of the Martiniquaise one gets coffee with rum. It is a smoky place where the phonograph plays dance music constantly. The café is full of pimps, lesbians, Negroes, prize-fighters, homosexuals, prostitutes, jazz musicians. I like the atmosphere. It is dense like a jungle, diffuse, dissolved.

Gonzalo meets two of his friends, the ones he used to go around with constantly. Malkine is stupefied with drugs, his face is haggard, his eyes sunk, his eyelids swollen. Gonzalo is startled by his disintegration. He no longer understands this dying in life, this feeding of the funeral worms long before real death. Malkine is far from his friends. I ask Gonzalo: 'You were drawn to death, to disease, destruction before we met?'

'Yes, I was, but not really. I'm more drawn to life. All that was literary. It was not the real me.'

They talked about Artaud.

Gonzalo is far away from death, he is soaring. He is full of fire and activity.

All these changes are mysterious and beyond me. I change too. Gonzalo has initiated me to his gypsy ways, his timelessness, silences, Bohemian recklessness, his nonchalance. I swing with him into a musical disorder of strewn clothes, spilled cigarette ashes, indolence, into regions of chaos and moonlight. I like it there. It is the light of the moon, of subterranean life. It is wordless. I like the silences of Gonzalo, meditativeness, reverie. It is the most beautiful expression of Gonzalo, the silence of earth itself, the silence of animals.

When he buys shoes they are so heavy, so strong, they seem like the hoofs of the Centaur.

I feel that I am trying to live out Henry's poverty, Helba and Gonzalo's poverty, to come closer to their life. I give so much that I often find myself without a cent. Going to the pawn shop. Thinking: Gonzalo has been here. Henry came out of himself once to play at analysing people, to become me. Moricand and Jean understand this split feeling, this wanting to be others, live other lives, abandon the self. By compassion, by great love, by communion, to reach the *dédoublement* of the mystics. In sorcery this is dispelled by reintegration into the self. We all reintegrate ourselves by creation.

Sullivan writes on Beethoven:

Beethoven had come to realize that his creative energy, which he at one time opposed to his destiny, in reality owed its very life to that destiny. . . To be willing to suffer in order to create is one thing, to realize that one's creation necessitates one's suffering – is to reach a mystical solution to the problem of evil. In these moments of illumination Beethoven had reached that state of consciousness that only the great mystics have ever reached, where there is no more discord. And in reaching it he retained the whole of his experience of life: he denied nothing. So he turned from his personal and solitary adventure . . . this is the last occasion on which Beethoven addresses his fellow men as one of them. Henceforth he voyaged in strange seas of thought, alone. What he had now to express was much more difficult to formulate than anything he had previously expressed. The state of consciousness with which he was concerned contained more and more elusive elements, and came from greater depths. The task of creation necessitated an unequalled degree of absorption and withdrawal. The regions within which Beethoven the composer now worked, were, to an unprecedented degree, withdrawn and sheltered from his outward life. No external storms could influence his work. The music of the last quartets comes from the profoundest depths of the human soul that any artist ever sounded.

Henry seems to be in the world still, but not really. He is suffering from the tremendous travail of the *Capricorn* synthesis. He says that when he looks at his notes he gets all confused as to what happened in reality. It is no longer his personal life. Creation in him is so clearly an art, transmutation. In reality Henry cannot remember dialogue, or exactly what he said, or what was said by others, as I do. He does not remember. And now for his greatest flight, he is liberated of his notes, his realism. He swims in a mutated, synthetized, transformed world. He is driven by a force greater than himself. A while ago he looked ghostly, pale, dazed.

This state, which I understand and admire as an artist, or in other artists, I am unwilling to undergo. I want to stay inside of untransformed human life.

Moricand speaks of continuous or alternating currents, of communion, of adhesion, of resonances. Of the moment when he felt himself going mad he says: 'I was skidding.' In his eyes people have the eyes of animals. 'She had squid eyes.' He speaks of hermaphroditic nights. 'To look at my drawings of perverse children you need dark glasses.' Then he spoke at length about the fact that no matter how violently I live, or where, nothing has yet awakened me from the state of the dream.

Jean, because of his vast, dimensional living, clutches at objects. He has a lust for exploration, change, novelty, a tapeworm of the imagination as Henry has, but he must have objects which *prove where he has been*, a lock of hair from the woman he slept with, objects from other countries. He lives in and for the public. He has to write in cafés, and talk all his interior life away, disperse it all night in talk. He has to be out. He evaporates in endless talk, volatilizes his energy in constant movement. He lives with waste, confusion, and an absence of memory. He seeks the one who is like him, his twin soul.

Gonzalo now says he feels the need of an austere life and devotion to the Spanish cause. I have awakened in him the desire to serve a purpose and to live for others. Why is this, when I thought it was me who wanted to be awakened to a more realistic, more lower-depths life, more Bohemian life than I ever knew with Henry. Was I seeking chaos, mindless living, adventure?

Gonzalo was deeper in life than Henry. He did not belong in the art world. He lived an untransformed, wordless, night-life. And now he takes up the stark, bare, rigid realism of Marx.

We do not touch at all pints. Two people understand each other's dreams, enter each other's dreams as Gonzalo and I did, but then each one manifests the effect of this in para-doxical ways. I wanted to write more, Gonzalo wants action.

Jean keeps *House of Incest* on his desk. He cannot read Eng-lish but finds he can write his dreams for Allendy by placing a page of transparent paper over my own writing. While I am talking to Gonzalo at the Café Flore, Jean sits at a table nearby working on his lecture.

On Beethoven [Sullivan]:

His growing consciousness, that what is called the human life, was withheld from him. This emotional and passionate man was condemned to a fundamental isolation. Personal relations, that should give him a sense of completeness and satisfy his hunger, were impossible. Separation from the world was the entry into a different and more exalted vision.

Gonzalo lives with half of himself in darkness. The op-posite of Henry, who exposes everything, leaves nothing unsaid. Gonzalo does not try to formulate, does not live naked. Was this the life which poor D. H. Lawrence longed for? But he was a writer, cursed with formulation.

Notes on dreams: note fragments of dreams, the edges, the

dark spaces around them. Chirico. Vast deserts. Only a few objects in sight (Tanguy). Mutilations. Variations of colour and tempo. Some musical, some silent. Note recurrent themes and personages like motifs in a symphony. Note moods, anguish or euphoria, diminutive or giant aspect. Timelessness. Awareness comes sometimes before the drama has taken place. Primeval innocence. No recollection.

Walked with Gascoyne along the river. Worked five hours on the diary to the accompaniment of *L'Oiseau de Feu*. Restless. The other night, walking with Moricand and Jean. We passed a shop of wooden objects. I said: 'I have wooden dishes.' Jean said: 'I have wooden spoons from Lapland.' I said: 'I have wooden glasses from the Philippines.' Jean said: 'I have a wooden pitcher from Panama.' I said: 'I have wooden soup bowls from Japan.' Jean said: 'I have a wooden salad bowl from Africa.' We said simultaneously: '*Il faudra se mettre en ménage!*'

If I were rich:

I would send Helba to a sanatorium where she might get well.

I would give Jean a radio-phonograph because he too likes to write to music.

I would give Henry rare Chinese art books he has been hankering for.

I would pension old Lantelme so he would not work any more.

Pension Moricand to be court astrologer.

Sustain all Henry's publications.

Buy a press for myself.

Princess de San Faustino makes portraits of people with a few lines, an egg, a staircase, an arrow, a lightning rod, a ribbon, a serpentine, a knot, a firework, a tower, a circle.* Jean could read her symbols and describe the character of each personage. She asked him to guess mine. He selected one at random for: '*La ligne droite, centre, et les envolées dans l'air, mais fécondantes.*' Kay said: 'Well, this is not Anaïs. I designed this

*She subsequently married Yves Tanguy and painted under the name of Kay Sage. – A. N.

300

one without anyone in mind. It was a portrait of what someone ought to be.' The second time he did guess. He picked
out: '*L'envolée vers l'espace, comme des cheveux d'ange.*' Jean
added: 'If people melted away, this is what would be left of
them on paper.'

Jean is dispersed, lost, confused except in his role of divination about others. Gonzalo looks at these games with the dark
furies of Othello. Gonzalo has buried his drawings, his writings, his reveries, his ecstasies, his gypsy ways, his drunkenness, to serve the revolution. He rages at Jean's fantasies,
Jean's ties with the Psychological Centre.

[MARCH, 1938]

Hitler marched into Austria. Franco is encircling Barcelona, and France, afraid of war, is not coming to its help. Gonzalo came to the houseboat and exploded: 'I will kill myself if I have to live in a fascist world. I'll die in exchange for killing ten fascists.'

When the world becomes monstrous, and commits crimes I cannot prevent, I always react with the assertion that there is a world outside and beyond this one, other worlds, human, creative, to pit against the inhuman and destructive forces. I have learned no other remedy. Gonzalo was ready to kill himself, and Helba, and me, so we would not live in a fascist world. I could not accept his fanaticism and this solution. Suicide?

Why then, does he not go and fight in Spain?

Jean reminds me of my role: 'Your role,' he said, 'is to keep your head above water, to save others from drowning. You must always remain pure, alone, and thus able to guide. You cannot get confused or identified with collective action. Your influence is not in action, but in awareness.'

So I had to struggle to make Gonzalo see that taking a gun and killing us all would not help either Spain or the revolution. His mad outburst left me shaking. All this that is happening is monstrous. But how does one fight such a monster?

I talked Gonzalo out of his impotent, futile rage. No more

drunken despair and will to die. He went back to work at *Paix et Démocratie*.

Jean said: 'Your role is to express what cannot be expressed. You are imprisoned in reality, always, and seeking expansion in transcendent realms.'

First Henry laughed at Moricand's learning, at his *'coïncidences poétiques'*, but then he found his imagery fecundating, the symbolism a new food for him. Moricand wanted disciples. Moricand thinks he found in Henry the brother of Blaise Cenrdars. Henry has found a new way of looking at experience.

Gonzalo cannot create a world as he wants it. I have created individually, personally, a world as I want it which serves as a refuge for others, as an example of creativity. If one does not believe the world can be reformed, one seeks an individually perfect world. The houseboat is now like Noah's Ark. The deluge is politics. An undertow of wholesale treachery, division, collective hysteria, and will to die. They are not dying for an ideal.

By keeping the dream alive one keeps everything alive.

Gonzalo does not understand what I call the spiritual psychological disease of the world, which no revolution can cure, no violence. No change of system. It is this distortion and illness I work at. There is no system that will control man's cruelty.

Before, Gonzalo escaped into drunkenness. Now he needs action, he is in rebellion against reality. He wants reforms and change.

I have created such a powerful dream against death and horror. Gonzalo came from seeing a friend who is dying. 'This place makes me forget everything. It is like a drug. Forgetting is a treachery.'

'This forgetting for a moment is a source of strength. You will go back to your activities with awareness, and not with blind anger.'

He reads César Vallejo's poems with great fervour.

'All I can do, Gonzalo, is balance the destructiveness of the world against creation.'

Albertine, the mousy maid with a gift for silence, gives me breakfast. I work in the studio as long as I can.

When I was a child I took the suffering of the world into myself, suffered with the world, and that did nobody any good. Added suffering to suffering.

The river offers its changing moods. I lose myself, my pain, my anguish at what is happening in the world in the beauty of the river and its shimmering.

Gonzalo talking about his friend, a revolutionary leader in Moscow: 'He's writing me desperate letters about his wife, for me to try and get her out of Barcelona. This is no time to be obsessed with one's wife. He has greater things to do than to worry about saving his wife. . . . They are all too sensitive and too emotional. I wrote back a hard letter. This is no time for softness. That is what is called bourgeois individualism.'

And I see the falsity of this, for it is he who does not leave for Spain because of Helba's helplessness.

Helba knows it too. She came talking about Gonzalo's new hardness. 'It's all talk. It's all because he is so sensitive and emotional. He is trying to pretend to be hard. It is not real. It is all talk. Gonzalo is too soft. Gonzalo was born mistaken [*equivocado*], in error. Born to blunder. He is blind. He is like an animal, or a child. He is not intelligent or philosophical. His friends from the left have given him what they call autocriticism. They told him all this. That he was a romantic, undisciplined. If I talk about the fanaticism of his comrades he calls me a fascist and says he will shoot me with his own hands. He's a little crazy.'

And then, bowing her head, like a woman praying: 'Don't let anything happen to Gonzalo. I would die of sorrow if he were shot.'

Henry, Fred and I went to see Luise Rainer in a film. When we sat at a café afterwards, Henry, who likes her so much, began to talk about her. 'She has wonderful gestures and bearing, such a gracious way of carrying her head, such delicacy. She is very much like you. Her gestures are so light, like wind almost, and she moves so gracefully. You and she have a great deal of affinity. There is at times on her face a deep sadness not called for by the part. A tremendous sadness. That is what you have. It's queer. You are all light and gaiety, but if one catches you unaware, one sees a tragic face. That has so much greater charm, this acquired gaiety, than a gaiety one is born with. It's something you fought for. One feels the luminousness, and at the same time this tragic feeling, a mysterious dual character.'

Henry never understood me as well as at this moment.

Gonzalo lost a friend he loved for twenty years. The poet Vallejo. Gonzalo's friend is dead and he grieves. I went to see Helba at the charity hospital. Came back filled with the horrors I had seen. Sat down and wrote the pages on the dream in the second part of *Winter of Artifice*, the pages on dreams and nightmares. The book is growing.

I playfully discourage Jean from falling in love with me. He already complains, even as a friend, that I am not concentrating on him. 'I want a woman smaller than I am, you love too many people, you have your work, and a crowded life. I am afraid of you. Falling in love with you would be fatal to me.'

The two of us, with our need of great proofs of love, who need to be solidly loved, who fear airiness and fluidity. We can charm each other but we do not trust each other.

I work on *Winter of Artifice*, plunging into part two because I am surrounded by the needs of others, by constant problems, Helba's sickness, never enough money for all of them. Reality traps me every day, heavily, constricts and limits me.

Henry is the only joyous one among us, the 'Happy Rock' he calls himself. He does not care what happens to the rest of the world.

Gonzalo thinks about death. 'And suddenly the heart stops beating.' He tells me how Vallejo never showed his poetry, that he had tons and tons of it all over his room that nobody had ever read. And that he told in one poem, how he would die on All Saints' Day, and then that day came and he did die.

Jean comes and he dramatizes his neurosis, wallows in it. He spends all his energy describing his states of anxiety, the venomous flowers born of distortion. He complacently elaborates, adorns, develops, expands. He confused Allendy in a maze of talks and richness of material, to overwhelm him. He creates this labyrinth so that no one will ever really know him, or cure him, to elude the simple roots of his malady, the simple conflict between instinct and fear of life. He destroys the very loves he courts. He arrests women's primitive response to him, directed at the sensual Jean, out of fear, and then laments he is not loved. He wants to play the young magician and seduce others and then complains no one knows him. He can't write because he aims too high, and can never be simple. How he shatters every spontaneous act with analysis, and exerts a moral tyranny over his desires.

I said: 'Your anxiety is not only doubt of others' love, but doubt of reality. It is a peculiar form of anxiety which requires to be incarnated by the other's love. You are fluid, a dreamer, and all your life is a constant mirage. You need to live through the body of the one you love. You have a gift for making everything elusive, abstract. You have fallen in love with a woman's human love for you. Stop analysing and dissolving what you need. You need the reassurance of being loved steadfastly because you are so easily cut off, you so easily float away into space.' This interested him and he was off again with delectation: 'You see, other people are sewn naturally, loosely, with a space between the stitches to breathe. I am sewn so tightly, with so many stitches overlapping, that I suffocate. I think of not one but a million things at once.'

I said: 'Jean, please stop. The artist in you is enjoying the description of your state of mind, but that is the way you have continued to elude the core of what ails you. You involve, enmesh everyone in your complex involutions. But that is how you elude their resolution. You are creating a neurosis, and have become incapable of a simple act of deliverance. You don't permit the simple diagnosis to take effect. You immediately rush into volatile descriptions, inflations, expansions.'

Women want to bring him down to earth. They are frustrated by his mobility. They feel he escapes from them.

Henry, Jean, and Moricand discussed colours. Henry's favourite colour is yellow, and that is the colour of philosophy. 'Yours,' said Henry, 'is a vanishing colour. You have no determinate colour. You only come out when the atmosphere is propitious.' It is true.

I do understand Jean's anxieties. He sees love as a rainbow, created by the atmosphere, and vanishing. He has no strong earthroots as I have. Every day the life of the instinct, blood and flesh, has to dissipate mirages. Every day the real caress must destroy the ghostly lover.

Henry and I differed radically in our opinion of Pierre-Jean Jouve. I am doing something closer to Pierre-Jean Jouve's novels than any other writer. Am I simply taking a different route from Henry's?

I wrote ten more pages of *Winter of Artifice* today.

Moricand said once while he stood on the gangplank: 'How I would like to know something about your earthly life. Even looking at your horoscope I suspect many things. You're the most real and the most unreal woman I've ever known. Alas, to me you only show your angel side.'

I was lying in bed, in the houseboat. It was four o'clock. A dark cold day. I was working on *Winter of Artifice*, one hundred pages of lyrical sensual stream of consciousness. Henry was satisfied. My life on the boat was a dream. The sun was shining every day, it seemed, many visitors came. Waldo Frank, sighing and pouting, Renata Bugatti, feverish, aggressive, Henghes, Moricand. And then a telegram from Maruca: 'Come and see me immediately. I am divorcing your father.'

Maruca was having breakfast in bed. A changed Maruca. No longer the believing child he had married. A woman with her eyes opened, rebelling, filled with hatred, and talking about how completely he had killed her love.

She wanted me to go immediately to Caux, Switzerland, because my father was threatening to commit suicide. She wanted me to tell him that she would never forgive him, would never live with him again, and for me to force him to plan a new life. She offered him a modest income while he solved his problems.

I went to Caux. I found him dressed in a golf suit, and monologuing. He could not understand what had happened to Maruca. 'She was once so sweet, so submissive.' He was lamenting her hardness. He was worried about missing the Grand Prix for the handsomest automobile at Montreux. He had bought a lottery ticket because now he would be penniless. What Maruca offered him was absolutely inadequate. He was worried about taking one of the maids with him, but which one, because one of them was the only one who knew how to iron his shirts properly, and the other was a good cook. He lamented his fate. And all this lost for a woman he did not even love. But a woman who had been the first to say *no* to him, and this *no* had made him persist, had driven him into a frenzy of pursuit, because he felt if he did not change this *no* into submission, it meant he was growing old, was losing his charm, his power over women.

But this had deeper roots. It is true he had not stayed with Maruca very much during her bout with tuberculosis in Spain (Maruca complained he came to visit her for ten minutes), but I must understand he could never bear illness. He had obtained the best medical care for her. It is true the maid had told Maruca that when she showed my father a nightgown she had embroidered for her mistress, he said: 'I know someone on whom this nightgown would look far more beautiful.'

And now everything was lost. He contemplated the extent of the loss, the house in Paris, the car, the luxury, the glamorous life. He did not contemplate the sorrow of Maruca, who had for so many years deliberately closed her eyes to his behaviour. He almost seemed to have gone out of his way to practice his love affairs as dangerously, as near to the possibility of discovery, as he could. It seemed almost as if he wanted to be discovered, or else had grown so careless, so confident, so thoughtless, that he never expected Maruca to protest. 'And to protest just when I am growing old and ready to settle down, now when I could stay home and give her all my attention.'

I persuaded him to return with me and to see Maruca, to plead with her. Maruca would not see him. He spent the night in my houseboat. I consoled him. He said: 'Throw out all your protégés and take care of your father.'

He opened his luxurious valise, placed his silver hair brush, silver comb, silver bottles on my dressing table. The sight of this exquisite Hermès-fitted valise in the bedroom of the houseboat was so incongruous. And his expression as he surveyed my kingdom. 'This is how you live!' I could not make him see the beauty of the river, of the lights on the river, of the lulling cadences of the boat. He asked me to warm up a bath and then would not take it because the water was not filtered. I had to fetch mineral water. He overlooked the fairy-tale aspect of the houseboat. He bemoaned the loss of luxury, of a wife he had formed to serve him like a slave. 'She was so good at filing my papers, answering my letters, organizing my concerts.' Not a moment of human sorrow for Maruca herself. 'I always thought that if Maruca died I would have you to take care of me. But you would have to change your life, take a decent apartment, and throw out your protégés.'

When the night came, the shadows frightened him, each motion of the houseboat made him uneasy. The creaking of the wood, and the wild garden of designs on the wall from the Indian lamp. My bedroom looked like the bedroom of Hans Christian Andersen tales, with its small wood-trellised windows. I made him as comfortable as I could and went to sleep on the studio couch upstairs.

Had the phantom lover come upon the father asleep to haunt his soul, to defend his daughter from his weight, to defend the houseboat, the poem, the freedom? Who haunted the houseboat that night, protesting against the intrusion of the father, rattling the nightmare to frighten him away? The next day he left for Switzerland to attend to the moving of his belongings. The houseboat sailed on without the father.

When my father came back from Caux I became ambassador between Maruca and my father. I had to carry messages back and forth, lists, objects too delicate to entrust to the moving men, a glass from Venice, a Japanese statuette, a painting. I lived in a maze of petty details, division of property, scenes. I had to mitigate both my father's selfishness and Maruca's anger. I was living their nightmare. Maruca talked to me. It helped her. I tried to tell her my father was selfish and un-conscious of his acts like a child, immature, thoughtless, spoiled, but her answer to this was: 'Yes, children are selfish, but they are also tender and loving, and your father was not even tender with me.'

This childlike woman, who had worshipped her husband as a teacher, god, musician, was now as firmly unyielding as she had been indulgent. She believed nothing he said, not even in his contrition. She even returned to the past to rummage, to add up all the facets of his behaviour, his every word, attitudes, expressions, and decided he had never loved her.

I said all this depended on her definition of love.

But she had accumulated too many reckless remarks, selfish exclamations, thoughtless gestures, the expression on his face when she was ill, when he told his impossible stories, and was utterly convinced he had never loved her at all, by any kind of definition of love. Until now her own love had covered all the fissures, and her own faith healed all the breaks. But this small, secret, gentle life which had nurtured grievances for fifteen years now erupted like a volcano and nothing could stop its devastation. I knew that nothing could stop it, but I tried. I knew the kind of unfaithfulness my father had practiced was not the kind women could forgive, for it did not come from a natural, a primitive, warm-blooded impulse but from a neurotic vanity, obsession, a need of conquest, not a love need, not a real hunger, but a collector's need to prove his power and his charm. What Maruca could not forgive was his idealizing of himself, this self-indulgence covered by hypocrisy. My father was always acting the ideal being. His utter selfishness was disguised. He presented his acts as altruism. He pretended to be teaching, helping, saving women when he was sleeping with them. It was this Maruca could not forgive: the disguise.

'But perhaps he did this to protect you from pain.'

'Oh, not at all. When we were in Caux, not content with having his mistress staying at Caux while we were there, he still wanted me to invite her to be our guest, he even taunted me for not liking her. Let him cry now, I cried for many years. Let him talk about suicide. I know he won't do it. He loves his precious body too much. Let him now measure the strength of my love which made life so soft for him, and let him realize what he destroyed. I feel nothing. He has killed my love so completely that I do not even suffer. I never knew a man who could kill a love so completely.'

I knew she would never waver, but I still tried to appeal to her. I kept saying there were men who always behaved like children, and she and I had accepted the role of young mothers, for thus are so many acts of men transfigured. The woman accepts a maternal role, and then she can forgive anything. The child does not know when he is hurting the mother. A child does not notice weariness, pain. He gives nothing and demands everything. If the mother weeps he will throw his arms around her, then he will go on doing what hurt her before. The child never thinks of the mother except as the all-giving, the all-forgiving, the inexhaustible, eternal love. The child devours the mother.

My father wanted to look at his house for the last time. When we stood in front of it he looked first at the window of his room. 'I will never see that room again. It's incredible. My books are still there, my music, my piano . . . but I . . .' Tears rolled down his cheeks. 'What has happened to Maruca? Such a meek, resigned, patient, angelical woman. A little girl, full of innocence and indulgence. And then this madness . . . I was unconscious of what I did. I didn't know she minded . . .'

It was at this very moment that a mild earthquake was registered in Paris. At the very moment when my father's life was shaken by the earthquake of a woman's revolt, and revenge, when he was losing love, protection, faithfulness, luxury, faith. His whole life disrupted in one instant of feminine revolution. Earth, and the woman, and their sudden explosions. On the insensitive instrument of my father's egoism no sign had been registered of this coming disruption. As he stood there looking at his house for the last time, the bowels of the earth trembled. Maruca was quietly eating her breakfast in bed, while my father's life cracked open and all the lovingly collected treasures fell into an abyss. The earth opened under his perpetually dancing feet, his waltzes of courtship, his contrapuntal love scenes. In one instant it swallowed the colourful ballet of his lies, his pointed-feet evasions, his vaporous escapes, the stage lights and halos with which he surrounded his conquests and his appetites. Everything was destroyed in the tumult. The earth and the woman's anger at his lightness, his audacities, his leaping over reality, his escapes. His house opened and through the fissures fell his rare books, his rare musical scores, his press notices, gifts from his admirers.

One day a Spanish priest turned up at Maruca's house. He had escaped from Spain carrying a statue of the Virgin Mary.

He was a musical priest and had come for shelter. Maruca wanted to please him and took him to dinner at the Bois and asked me to come along. But she had forgotten that it was the day of the races, and the restaurant was full of extraordinary women dressed in the most fantastic fashions. It was the fashion of hair powdered in strange colours, green or gold or blue, and gold and silver cream over the eyelids.

The glittering spectacle all around us was in painful contrast to the talk of the priest. His stories of Spain, agony, hunger, fear, torture, in this setting of utmost frivolity. I begged Maruca to leave. But instead she launched into a full history of her life with my father, with all details, to the great shock of the priest, for what he might have listened to in a dark confession booth he could not face in public, and the violent contrast between history's tragedies, personal tragedies, and the fashion parade was unbearable.

The complaints, lamentations, accusations of the wife were natural enough, he had heard those before, but he had never heard a daughter interpret her father's behaviour so lucidly and openly. 'Respect for the husband,' he murmured, 'respect for the father.'

'And what about respect for the woman,' said Maruca. 'You risked your life to carry away the Virgin Mary on your back, you might have been shot for that, and yet you do not think that man should also have respect for woman?'

I was analysing my father's unawareness. For at moments in Caux he understood he had been monstrously selfish, he understood he had lived out his Don Juanism without caution or delicacy, but the next moment he could not bear to believe this and he launched into excuses, alibis, lies, he put all the blame on Maruca, on the women who tempted him.

He was unconscious of what he had done.

'And if I get sick now,' said my father, 'who will take care of me?'

[SUMMER, 1938]

The last two weeks we lived under the threat of war. Collective anxiety, panic, rebellion, fear. People packing and running away. People faced with the threat of concentration camps, imprisonment, or bombing. Henry stopped revising *Capricorn*. He became ill at the disruption of his individual life. Black days for the world. Crowds awaiting news in front of newspaper buildings. Unrest. Hysteria. This little world I created, out of protectiveness, love, humanity, work, may be destroyed by war, by Hitler.

All of us shattered by tension. We are all packing. Henry leaves for the Dordogne region after giving me instructions about his manuscripts.

One morning I found in my letter box an order from the river police to move out of Paris. All the houseboats had been asked to move out. I had to rent a tugboat to pull my houseboat further up the Seine. What we all feared was that the houseboats were not sturdy enough for any voyage. So I asked Gonzalo to be there, to help me navigate. He was late. The tugboat would not wait. And I had to sail alone. It was raining. I stayed on deck to watch the operations. I remembered my dream, of sailing for twenty years and all my friends standing on the shore asking me where I was going and when would I be back. Here I was in reality sailing past the sections of Paris so familiar to me, past apartment houses where I had lived, and streets I had so often explored. But I was not allowed to meditate on how dreams materialize, for the houseboat was taking in water and I had to man the pump. The tugboat had to slow down, or it would have flooded.

We were out of Paris. We passed under a bridge and reached a factory section. We passed another bridge and reached a boatyard, filled with skeletons of old barges, rusty anchors. A cemetery for boats. They advised me as I passed to continue up to Neuilly. There was room to anchor there. Neuilly! I had circumnavigated only to return to my birthplace. An omen? And my father, too, moved to Neuilly, near where he had lived when I was born.

The apartment Maruca had selected for my father was a comfortable modern place for retired couples. It had a restaurant on the ground floor and maid service. But when my father saw it he had a moment of despair. It had been selected unconsciously by an angry wife placing him in Dante's Inferno, for he was living with old people and he had never recognized his own ageing, he lived in an illusion of perpetual youth, and then his own apartment overlooked a cemetery, which to a Spaniard is a fatal omen.

I visited him faithfully, took walks with him in the same park he took me walking in when I was two or three years old. But I felt almost as Maruca did, detached from him, free of him.

Once I came to see him after seeing Henry off. He was sitting at the piano revising a composition. It was dedicated to the Spanish orphans, but I felt he considered himself one of them. His apartment was meticulously arranged, clinically clean and orderly.

When we took our walk through the Bois he was gently reminiscing about the days when he took my brother and me to play in the same park.

And for the first time, as a consequence of our struggle, he pours out real confidences, utterly sincere. That was what I had sought to obtain because I knew it was the only cure for loneliness. He wept over the lost Maruca, lost to sexual games of no account. 'I cannot even remember their names!' Just a collection of trophies. He now believes that there is a god who has punished him, he who did not believe in God. He expresses remorse and guilt. 'In this very park I took you walking when you were a child. I could have been happy as a father, a husband, a musician, if I had not been obsessed with winning more and more women.' I console him. Now he understands the great strain of constantly playing roles, and he says he wishes he had had this relief from play-acting, this genuine exchange of feelings and thoughts he found with me. 'If only I had found a woman who could have broken through the façade as you did, this is what a true relationship could have been.'

From there I go to visit my mother and Joaquin. They are preparing to go to America. Joaquin has been invited to teach at Middlebury College. He is working on his quintet, and rehearsing for a concert. Mother looks older, sweeter, more easily tired.

From there to old Lantelme, who makes me promise if he dies I will take care of his wife.

Then Helba and I meet for a talk about Gonzalo, who is torn by a great conflict. There is not only the conflict between his nursing of Helba as against political activities, but a deeper one, because his comrades have told him that he is unfit to work at the revolution. He is undisciplined, negligent, and would blunder into his own destruction. He cannot organize, he loses important papers, forgets appointments. His comrades told him he was a romantic revolutionist.

Helba says: 'I lifted him up, I carried him until I became ill. You're the only one who can save him now.'

'But how, Helba? He is tied in knots.'

We were sitting in the Café Flore, and I had to raise my voice so Helba could hear me. A man sitting behind us, on the other side of the potted plants, accused us of disturbing his newspaper-reading. So we had to go out and walk.

Helba said: 'Gonzalo has so damaged his body with excesses that he has weakened his health. One day out in the rain and he is shaking and trembling. If he had gone to Spain he would have been the first one out of the trenches and into a hospital.

'He would also be the one to walk bare-chested and unarmed into the mouth of cannons. He wants to die for some cause, die for an idea, and if we don't encourage him, he will be ashamed later.'

Up early the next day to go to the Villa Seurat to arrange to have it cleaned, to take Henry's typewriter to be oiled, to pick up his mail. He writes desolate letters: 'Everything looks dead and dull. I feel like a ghost.'

Where will he rest to regain his strength? He is worn and nervous.

From there to visit the owners of the small white boat which was tied next to my houseboat, and which I always admired. It was owned by a German painter and he was constantly improving it, rebuilding it, lovingly repainting it. He had asked to see me. Then he told me that he and his wife were Jews and that they were afraid of the turn of events, and wanted to leave for Africa or South America. Would I buy their boat and help them to escape? He did not want to be drafted into the German army, or put in a concentration camp. Their plight moved me deeply, but I am unable to buy the boat. But I found someone who did, and we parted emotionally, like very old friends.

Winter of Artifice lies unfinished. Moricand wants to set me afloat again in the world of dreams and makes me read *Séraphita*, and talks all evening about mythology.

I am living out through others what I cannot live out myself directly: chaos, disorder, tumult, obscure instincts, caprices, fears, fevers, violence. They live it out for me. They destroy what I create. They blunder, they get lost, they fall, they shock me, they hurt themselves, and some part of me is dragged into their destructiveness, and another part of me fights their destructiveness, and another part of me, which is wise, which has passed beyond this, suffers deeply with them, for them, through them. It is my karma, to pass through darkness, confusion, violence and destruction not of my own making, which I have controlled, transmuted, tamed in myself. My deep friendships are like the selves I tried to transcend, the lives I skipped, escaped, by magical ascensions into other realms: philosophy, psychology, art. So the earthy, the demons, the instincts, grasped me in the form of Henry, June, Gonzalo, as if to say you must experience everything, even the Dostoevskian hells, because they cannot be transmuted, they remain all instinct, all nature and chaos.

Tomorrow I place this diary volume in the vault. I must be ready and unburdened for the uprooting to come.

War looms again.

Mobilization.

Women weep openly in the streets. Crowds stand in line at the savings banks to withdraw their meagre savings. There is fear in the air. And Gonzalo thrives on this anguish and feels alive. At last the world and he are synchronized, his personal agonies are matched by the universal one.

Everyone turns to me for help, and I do not have enough for all. I must help Mother and Joaquin to get off to America. I must get Helba to a safe place. The same day I finally get Gonzalo much-needed eyeglasses, he drops and breaks them. I must send money to Henry, give Moricand enough to eat once a day. He begs me to take him to America, as he will starve if I leave him in Paris. Fred asks me to get his typewriter out of the pawnshop.

Gonzalo asks me to teach him organization. I buy him a small loose-leaf notebook and show him how I note down all I have to do, and as soon as it is done I tear the leaf off and throw it away. How light I feel when all the leaves are gone! But this has no appeal for Gonzalo. I said I could not bear the *weight* of things left undone. He admitted they weighed on him.

I am silent when Gonzalo blames everything on the established order because 'capitalism is to blame for everything, even Helba's illness'. I cannot explain to him that there is an individual responsibility and that not all tragedies are pressures from the outside, some come from within us.

Gonzalo tells me: 'I think Hitler is backing down.'

Henry returned.

We all expect a revolution in Germany which would put an end to the war.

Jean says: 'You must permit the work of destiny and not interfere with others' completion of themselves, with their self-punishments or other ways to sainthood or human life.' I have never learned this for others, yet I let no one save me from necessary suffering and error.

*

Moricand came to fetch me one day. Henry had had an accident. It was not very serious, but he had fallen down the ladder leading to the terrace of the studio, he had cut himself against the shattered glass door, had wounds on his back, on the soles of his feet. He could not walk. So all of us were to take turns at running errands, cooking for him, attending to his needs.

Henry needed me, my father needed me, Maruca needed me.

My only pleasure this month was Henry's writing in *Capricorn*. Extremes of sensuality and lyricism, spirituality and the demon. After he wrote the pages on the black star we talked sadly because anciently all literature was symbolical, and everyone understood the symbol, but today we can no longer write in terms of symbol or myth.

Never having lived a truly chaotic, capricious life, I had to imitate it first to gain my freedom. I imitated Henry's erratic whims, Hélène's sudden changes of plans, Gonzalo's irrational behaviour, their unaccountableness, unexpected reactions. So they all lost track of me as I lost track of them. It is really a camouflage. Finally, by imitating this, which I had never been able to do out of considerateness for others (I could not even fail to appear at a café when I promised I would), I began to live genuinely what I tolerated in others. Allowing myself the same freedom they took.

Jean Carteret, who cannot read English, listened to my translation of *Winter of Artifice* and said: 'You walk over water. Others will be afraid. If they follow you they might drown.'

That day on the houseboat talking with my father was like talking to a madman. One moment he was utterly lucid and he would confess he had behaved monstrously, had lived out his Don Juanism obsessionally without protectiveness or delicacy towards Maruca. He recognized his guilt. 'I was like a drugged man, unable to realize what I was doing.' But the next moment he would plunge into self-justification, and he would give a distorted version of what happened. He would put the blame on Maruca, on the other women who pursued and seduced him. He would end by putting himself back on his saint's niche, back on the pedestal, innocent, a victim. He was so possessed by his subjective reality that he did foolish, reckless things which even a stupid man would not have dared. What drove him to take such chances of being discovered, exposed?

[OCTOBER, 1938]

When I look back at the week of the threat of war, when I stopped writing in the diary, I see a cemetery. That the war in reality did not take place does not matter. A great many people died psychically, a great many faiths died. The veil of illusion which makes human life bearable was violently torn.

I saw the precariousness of the individually created world, swept by collective madness.

I saw Henry trembling and groaning, although he was the only one who left Paris and had no one to worry about except himself. Henry in an agony of egoistic concern, raging because peace and security were torn from him by greater, exterior forces. Henry without strength. Cabling right and left for money to sail back to America. Henry a primitive.

I saw Gonzalo ready to sacrifice all individual devotions to war, to death, gloating because the war would make revolution possible. Gonzalo physically courageous, but with a courage for death and not for life. Gonzalo, for whom *Nanankepichu* was merely a warrior's pause between fits of upheavals and a utopian faith in a new world.

Henry's Chinese talk of wisdom had not stood the test of reality. We faced each other like ghosts. Suddenly Villa Seurat looked dilapidated. One noticed the stains on the walls, the fissures, the peeling paint.

Peace was like a cemetery.

Fiction, falsities, fears, prejudices.

How can I believe in any system which incites spying on friends and relatives, which practices cruelty as powerful as the oppressors', how can I believe in anything achieved by bloodshed and torture?

Gonzalo has the necessary blindness to take sides and die for an idea, but I see the inhumanity of all ideas, their falseness. I want to live transcending laws, prejudices, morals. Every system is too narrow for me. I always respected a man of quality when I saw one, a character, a human or creative value. Yet now I became convinced that what was wrong for me might be good for others, to deliver the poor, the slaves, the workers.

Gonzalo convinced me.

The only world I know without walls, injustices, monstrosities, is that of illusion and poetry. For me that is the only liberation. I don't believe man can be changed by outer systems. It has to come from within.

It was the night of peace euphoria. A reprieve. We had escaped a nightmare, a monstrous holocaust, a gigantic tragedy, for a few days.

When I read Gonzalo's books, I see the error and the limitations. But perhaps not for the world. The world is earthy, and needs outward changes, earthy solutions. It cannot liberate itself in space and time. It needs concrete, external changes. It can only deal with outer transformations. Gonzalo does not understand that no economic liberation will free him of his guilt towards Helba, nor me from my inability to cause pain. The weakness and the vices are in us, and therefore they will reappear under any system like Lady Macbeth's bloodstains. Gonzalo and Helba never recognized the weakness in themselves. They blamed society, the doctors.

When I ascend into illusion Gonzalo calls it a negative solution. What irony! How much I have created out of the terror and tragedy of life.

One day, when I returned to the houseboat, I had left on my desk a page from my diary written long ago, but which still seemed to apply today.

This diary is my drug and my vice. This is the moment when I take up the mysterious pipe and indulge in reflections. Instead of writing a book I lie back and I dream and talk to myself. A drug. I turn away from a brutal reality into the refracted. The driving, impelling fever which keeps me tense and wide awake during the day is dissolved in abandon, in improvisations, in contemplation. I must relive my life each day in the dream. The dream is my only life. I see in the echoes and reverberations the transfigurations which alone keep wonder pure. Otherwise all magic is lost, and I awake to touch my prison bars. Otherwise the homeliness, the deformities, the limitations, gnaw into every gesture like rust. This is my diary and my drug. Covering all things with the utter fluidity of smoke, transforming as the night does, all matter must be fused this way through the lens of my vice, or the rust of living will slow down my rhythm to a sob.

Gonzalo read this and wrote the following and left it on my typewriter:

You refuse to put the blame where it belongs, you prefer to draw a veil of fantasy, beauty and forgiveness on an unbearable reality. Anaïs, as human being, is vital and constructive, to care for others have been the words on her escutcheon. But Anaïs the artist flies from the world and seeks the transmutations which might make reality bearable. This paradox between the two Anaïses is caused by the present social system, plutocratic bourgeoisies, exploitive and infamous. I prophetize that one day, there will come a day when Anaïs will see that these prison bars are precisely made of dreams, that she is imprisoned in a prison of dream. And her jailers will keep her there, feeding her on fantasy which will prevent her from turning into a rebel.

Everybody who could had left during the week of panic. The trapped ones, who could not move because they had no money, were glad to see me staying on. Fred, Moricand. Moricand was copying notes on mythology in the Bibliothèque Nationale.

Henry is talking about going to America.

Durrell will publish *Winter of Artifice* in February.

In *House of Incest* I wrote about June: 'She would tolerate no bars of light on open books.' This is true of Gonzalo. He became so embittered, so violent about the books which keep me in a prison of dreams, so convinced that they were prevent-ing me from entering the struggle for a new world, that one day, in exasperation, I said: 'Very well, we'll burn them all.'

Gonzalo took me seriously, and started a bonfire on the quay, where people burned trash from the houseboats. I began by selecting the books I did not care about. But Gonzalo became fanatical, like an Inquisitor. He added to the pile. It seemed like a barbaric ritual, burn the books which taught me to dream. Gonzalo's eyes were burning with a fierce pride. The greatest sacrifice I could offer to his faith: if I stopped dreaming and being merely the nurse to the wounded, I could help to transform the world. His wild faith impressed me. It was like the ritual of San Juan, in Spain. Every year they made a huge bonfire of the contents of their attics, as if to get rid of the past in order to live in the present.

The books burned slowly. The last to be added to the pile were my favourites. There were so many books, and it took so long, that Gonzalo lost patience, and walked away.

When he had gone, it was dark. I rescued the books which had not caught fire. Those were the books of the great un-realists, Strindberg's *Inferno*, Carlo Suarès's *La Procession Enchaînée*, books on surrealism, Rank's *Art and Artist*, Artaud's *L'Art et la Mort*, Pierre-Jean Jouve, Giraudoux!

Jean Carteret is in Lapland, working like a farmer. He lives in a wooden house. When he developed a toothache, the Lap-landers all gathered around him, made him drunk, and pulled the tooth out. He witnessed the throwing of the blessed cross into the frozen river and the Laplanders plunging into icy waters to retrieve it, to gain privileges in heaven.

And I let Gonzalo burn my books, as a symbol of giving up my opium! The individually created world.

Meanwhile the news is tragic again. Gonzalo came the other evening, sick with the horror of having had to expose and judge a traitor. He described the scene. A South American who had worked for the Marxist revolution and then betrayed it. Gonzalo had to question him, break him down, extort his real name and finally confront him with the proofs of his treachery. When the man broke down and sobbed and groaned, this is what he said: 'I thought the revolution was going to take place immediately. I was full of faith. I endured so many days in jail, so much anxiety, the suffering of my family, and all this waiting, my exaltation died . . . I needed money . . .'

Gonzalo's humanity made him feel pity for the man. Condemning him was the hardest thing he had ever had to do. He could not sleep, thinking of him. 'I would rather have been shot in his place.' He vomited, he was physically ill at the realities of politics.

Henry says he has some accounts to settle with America, and that the time has come for this. He has been withdrawing from external life, condemning many of his activities, what I once described as the vice of constant motion. He dreams of Tibet. He says in four years he will retire to Tibet and become a monk.

Henry and I are travelling inversely. I am entering a world of action and violence which Henry abandoned long ago.

Gonzalo condemns my artist's power of staying alive in a cell within a cell within a cell which protects creation from universal destruction, but he never condemned those who take alcohol and drink as inferior forms of escape from reality. He needed drugs to rise into the infinite, above pain. Henry may go towards spiritual worlds, but I am becoming more and more incarnated to live my life fully on earth, as a woman, incarnated by love, in the present. Human life on earth.

Remember it is a dreamer who is travelling in the Métro next to an old woman covered with eczema, who is walking up a muddy hill to a public hospital, who is handing Helba the bedpan, changing the cotton, listening to her detailed recital of the operation. Helba does not try to disguise anything. She exhibits all her pains and sores. Her face is yellow and her hair stringy. Next to her lies a woman of skeletonic thinness, at first I thought she was old, but then I realized she was a young woman, prematurely aged by illness. She was sitting up, and she had made up her face, combed her hair, and tied it with a ribbon. Helba told me she was a prostitute, and that she was dying of syphilis. I looked at her with an admiration I did not have for Helba. To meet death, this young woman powdered and painted her face, wore a ribbon, and I admired her effort to confront reality with a touching effort at defeating its ugliness.

How long will I hold the secret drug which does not destroy me, which permits me to hold on to the ecstasies, to turn away from Helba, who makes everything uglier?

I felt it coming while I walked. It always happened when I looked at the monstrous aspects of life. It was a strange emotion, like drunkenness. It caught me in the middle of the street like a tremendous wave, and right then and there a numbness passed through my veins, the numbness of the marvellous. I knew it by the current power of it, the manner in which it seemed to lift my body, the air which seemed to pass under my feet, I knew it by the force of it, its delicacy, by its effect on my eyesight, a kind of blindness, blurredness. The street became suddenly illuminated. An uncapturable mood passing, which I could not retain or fix forever. A vision, a state, a sleep, which the next moment would be lost. It was as if I had learned to fly over the street, and was permitted to do so for a number of hours, and then, without cause, the obstacles I had transcended suddenly crystallized again and arrested me. Collision. With this drunkenness which made every object, every colour, every voice, every passer-by, every incident, every caress extraordinary, marvellous, there was also a fear, a fear that it would not be sustained or continuous. It was a state of grace, only I could not discover what made me fall away from it. Perhaps if this state continued, this state of joy, this joy which enveloped the body and raised me into musical spheres, this joy would make me breathless and ultimately kill me, from excess of pleasure.

The danger lies in flying low, in awakening. There are days I feel the descent, from a sphere where motion and flow are never interrupted, to one where gestures are broken.

Here everyone seems to be living behind prison bars. The air is charged with dust. People aspire to reach the planets, when the world about them becomes intolerable, but it is an unnecessary voyage. There is a certain way of breathing, of walking, of seeing, which transports the being into space. In this space the same spectacle of the street exists, but it undergoes a transformation. The outer aspect, the sores, the cancers, miseries, poisons appear on the crust only. And what dazzles the eye and blinds one to them is the extraordinary brilliance of the games *people are playing in space,* beyond themselves. *Le jeu intérieur. They were able to play because they believed the cruelty and horror were intermittent, would pass.* They did not see any impasse. In the infinite there is no impasse.

There are various forms and states of ecstasy. Some are musical, one is possessed by sound, as if one lived inside of a vast bell. There are white ecstasies caused by beautiful objects, paintings. There is ecstasy achieved by immobility, others born of excess of feeling.

I know the secret. I have retained the sense of wonder of the child. I cannot wake up. When I cook I do not expect to get burned. I am surprised when I am burned. When I go out I do not expect rain. I dress gaily and I am caught unaware by the rain.

We say it was God's punishment when lightning struck the Edison monument, which attempted an eternal flame. What do we say when a train is wrecked which was full of monks returning from a pious visit to Our Lady of Lourdes of the Miracles?

There is a whorehouse for the blind, and the prostitutes are blind too. Must write a story about that.

There are limitations to Durrell's understanding of my work. He believes in objectivity, which anyone who has gone deeply into study of motivations cannot possibly believe in. He believes in respecting forms already established for the novel. I believe in a form which is constantly mutating.

Moricand says he identifies me with the myth of Arethusa. Arethusa, unable to reach for an impossible fulfilment in love, turned into a fountain, nourished others with her tears. This made me laugh. A rather ridiculous personage, Anaïs, as ridiculous as Don Quixote. Moricand says the fountain is the diary.

Jean writes from Lapland:

The reindeer is not absolutely silent, but he won't eat anything touched by man's hand. The Laplander must wear gloves. Later we're pushing on behind the fjords of the Arctic Ocean, to Utsjoki. We may meet wolves, there are a lot of them and they love reindeer and men when they get hungry. Having no revolver I will have to push them away as the postman does, by throwing behind the sled lighted matchboxes.

[JANUARY, 1939]

At midnight on New Year's Eve the most terrific sadness at the state of the world.

A mute blank pain.

I find a little door open, tiny, on the infinite. I will write another book, about the houseboat. Helba in her rags, sewing, taking buttons out of a box marked OVARIAN SUPPOSITORIES. Albertine, the mousy maid, and her abortion in the little cabin. The foetus I had to throw away into the river. Her valise with a child's reader in it. My father's shipwreck. Postman afraid to walk up the *passerelle* to the houseboat. On the quays the man with the wooden leg stamping on a fallen five-franc piece someone else wanted to pick up. High tide. So many stories to write. Only in creation can one fashion a world without failures, death, war.

Proofreading *Capricorn* with Henry. Transported by the writing in it.

Henry writes: 'I must either go home immediately and write a book or begin an absolutely new life. As I cannot begin an absolutely new life it will have to be a book.'

A book which will begin: 'I am behind the bar of a prison. I am a prisoner. Always looking at a free life I wanted and could not have.'

But of course, I had the dream, this blessed drug which is given to all prisoners of distinction. Only dreams did not calm my hunger because my dreams did not lead me away from life but towards it, always guiding me towards realization, so that I always collided with a wall: I wanted to live out my dream. It was not enough to be illuminated. I always awakened to the presence of the barred window. I had a gift for freeing others and not myself, because I took on the responsibility of setting them free.

Because of the million webs of protection I threw out, so that Henry could write, Gonzalo could propagandize, Helba could fight for health, send money to her mother, so that Joaquin could give his concerts, Gonzalo get eyeglasses for his failing eyesight, Henry go to London, Lantelme not worry about what will happen to his wife, Moricand eat, for all these reasons I am trapped as no one was ever trapped. I cannot escape from my vulnerability and my compassion. I made a prison out of devotions, fraternities, indebtedness, loyalties. Henry did not free me. Gonzalo awaits the revolution as a solution to everything.

What is this prison? The difference, the violent contrast between what I dream, wish, and the reality which diminishes, shrinks, interrupts, shrivels all things.

E. Graham Howe:

So as we wait for the impossible, it is not surprising we sometimes feel that life is not worth living. . . . The law of reality keeps us balanced and holds our omnipotence in check. We have a ladder ascending into Heaven and another descending into Hell, and the one which is ascending into Heaven is tangential on the plus side of this ascending scale. If we keep the rhythm of life we have our ups and downs as travellers do. But if we want all the ups and none of the downs, we prefer to go up the ladder to Heaven, where there is to be no frustration or resistance and no experience of the negative at all. In this way many people succeed in living a life which is almost entirely one of fantasy. But if they do, the price they pay on the balance is that they are excluded from a life of reality. No matter how they may seek to avoid it, Hell will be pursuing them all the time, if they must have their Heaven of As You Like It. . . . The expression which is known as depression can be more clearly understood as coming to those who are not willing to be depressed, i.e.: to fall down according to the falling rhythm, or to let go when the time has come to lose. Depression is characteristically associated with over-conscientiousness, and so it is particularly liable to befall virtuous people. This is because they feel it is their moral duty to hang on to all good things, fixing them forever against the moving law of time. . . . Fantasy I would define as imagination used as a means of flight from reality . . . as distinct from the make-believe of the creative imagination (which is towards life). The make-believe of fantasy is away from it.

Gonzalo said: 'The Indian is not a mystic. The Indian is a pantheist. The earth is his mother. He has only one word for both. When an Indian dies they put real food in his tomb, and they keep feeding him. At night, in the immense solitude of the mountains I used to come upon one of their cemeteries. And there they were, by the light of torches, eating a banquet right over the tombs, and practising orgies to share these real pleasures with the dead. When bodies are not placed in coffins a combustion takes place, small explosions of blue flames. The sulphur burns. These small lights seen at night, weird and frightening, like witchcraft, led the Indians to believe it is the soul departing from the body.'

We are all in deep despair over the tragic fate of Spain. Barcelona about to fall into the hands of the fascists. Persecution of the left-wingers in France. Gonzalo wondering where he will go.

My father is selling his furniture and his marvellous collection of books on music to go back to Cuba, to the refuge of his cousin's home, the place he had tried to escape from for thirty years. Back to his starting point.

Meanwhile Joaquin is giving a concert in Havana before sailing for America.

Thorvald is all alone in Bogotá, separated from his wife and children.

Meanwhile I am metamorphosed into a sponge, absorbing all the tears of the world, accumulating sorrows, unable to erase anything. An ocean of sensations, enough to quench the thirst of several human beings.

In the houseboat story there will be a phantom lover, dreamed, not seen, who comes every night out of the river with a noise of chains and splash of waves, when the candles are lit and the incense burning, and who is gone when she awakens.

In 1938, in the diary, I wrote about mirrors and metamorphoses, and found similar descriptions in the Tibetan *Book of the Dead*. In this book they are called 'bardo' states, leading to rebirth, second birth, but the atmosphere, images, visions, hallucinations are the same. Also affinities with my labyrinth story:* 'When I was eleven years old I walked into the labyrinth of the diary,' etc., in which I annihilated sense of time and reappear at the end of the labyrinth the same little girl.

All this exists then, metaphysically, whereas the attacks on my writing dealing with my subjectivity, and writing things which could not have meaning for anyone, from Durrell, Henry, made me feel at times that I had carried my fantasy so far that it was inexplicable to others. Today I recognize their metaphysical authenticity. Writing like *House of Incest*, and all the fantasies for which I will not be loved, contain the purest essence of my meaning. It comes from the distillation of my experience, and are descriptions of states which the Tibetans understood.

I have been humanly the least lonely of women, live surrounded by family, friends, all those I love, but there is a world into which I go alone, a Tibetan desert.

I may be sitting in a café listening to the music, drinking coffee. The lights are vivid, the music violent. I am keenly aware of everything, from the stains on the table to the face of the man sitting farthest from my table, aware of what the waiters are discussing. I feel my body alive and warm inside of my fur coat. I am wearing a hood with a fur edge. I feel at moments I am an actress. I am a Polish countess, a Hungarian singer, an Eskimo bride, all out of novels. The men always believe in my disguises. They believe. They never step behind the stage to say: 'You are lying. You were lying when you sewed the hood on your coat. You are not what you seem to be.' If I answer: 'What am I?' it only precipitates my departure. As soon as someone denies my existence, appearance,

*See *Under a Glass Bell*. – Ed.

and I am exposed as a disguised being, as a spy from another world, this other world opens its luminous jaws and engulfs me. I am here only while someone believes in me, while some human being swears to my presence and loves me.

Someone could spy on me and detect my non-human origin. I wash too easily, too lightly. I do not wear out my clothes, I cook too lightly and too quickly. I leave no disorder behind me, no tumultuous traces of living. My bed is not wildly disturbed, disarranged.

When I am ejected from the ordinary world I must not lament. I must enter very boldly into my world, with the feelings I have, eyes open, alone. It is not a world in which one is humanly married, bound. Marriages happen on earth.

Strange things are happening. When I discovered the Tibetan world, the states of being so familiar to me, I thought perhaps I died long ago and I'm on my way to something else, maybe a rebirth, a state of vision.

Henry meanwhile is obsessed with Balzac's *Séraphita*.

When men talked at the café about being sad after sex, I asked them why I did not feel this sadness after sex. It was Henry who answered me: 'Perhaps because for you it is not everything. People for whom it is the only means of connection are sad at the fleetingness of this union.' It is true that for me it is only one kind of union, or expression of union, but there are others.

Another time Gonzalo joined me at the café and talked to me about the friends who died in Spain, about the treachery of the anarchists in Barcelona, about one of his friends who got his face slashed in a café, about Helba who has an abscess in her womb. 'The whole room smells.'

Another day I sat in the café with Henry, correcting proofs of *Winter of Artifice*. There was a thick fog outside. Henry is in love with *Séraphita*. He carries the book around and places it on the café table.

As we proofread *Winter of Artifice*, in spite of its bad technique and defects we see new meaning in it.

Gonzalo has flashes of intuition, as June had. But then the blindness returns. He lives in another world.

When Helba gets very ill, he comes to me like a child, lost and baffled. I decide on a plan of action. We walk to the doctor. I wait in a café. In the café later he looks at my hands. 'They look transparent. My god, Anaïs, are *you* all right?' I can't add to his anxieties. I cannot tell him Dr Jacobson is not pleased with my persistent anaemia. He is going to have my lungs examined. On the way home I thought: 'Perhaps I will die.' And just then a funeral procession passed me. Perhaps I am ready to die. I cannot live in the barbarism of war. Gonzalo weeps over the loss of his friends who died in Spain. Helba's death does not seem important now. A useless life. But Gonzalo's mother was fragile, was dying for many years, just like Helba. She is still alive at eighty. I do not believe in Helba's near-death.

Gonzalo's life is in the streets, vagabonding. It is dispersed in talk. He is always starting a great motion which appears like a giant project and turns out to be the revolutions of great energy. He starts with a force which seems capable of turning the world upside down and ends in a café throwing dice with the beggars of the Rue de Beaune. He needs independence like a wild horse, he cannot harness himself even to Marxism, which he believes in.

Henry wrote about June: 'I thought I had found a female Vesuvius.' He was as deceived about June as I was about Gonzalo. I thought Gonzalo's volcanic nature would bring a new kind of freedom. I thought with the fire and faith in him he would burn all the chains, start a new world. But he is bound like an animal.

Strange that, like Henry, I was always awaiting the one who would represent evil, and lead me into dark experiences, a life like Richard Burton's. Because this part of me was always submerged by the need to protect or care for others. June could have done it. Gonzalo and June were really alike. But what happens is that two people create a new alchemy. They interact upon each other and what takes place is not the leadership of one over the other, but the consequence of this interaction. There was no great evil in either Gonzalo or June, just great adventurousness, but both change in relation to me. It is like the children born of a couple, who are exactly like neither one, but something else again.

Even for love of Spain or Marxism, Gonzalo cannot give up staying up all night and sleeping all morning. An apéritif can make him keep Helba waiting two or three hours for her food when she is ill.

There are people who cannot change from the inner to the outer, who must be pushed from the outside. They are the ones who need revolutions. There are those who can rise above life, transform it, free themselves, and for these the revolution is not necessary. I can see how necessary it is for those who cannot escape into creation, create an illusory world, those who cannot dream or create an individually perfect world.

Gonzalo said: 'Way up in the mountains of Peru, a mountain twice as high as Mont Blanc, there is a lake set deep inside of a bower of black volcanic rocks. An immensely deep lake in the middle of eternal snows. The Indians go there to see the mirages. What I saw in the lake was a tropical scene, richly tropical, with coloured birds, lush vegetation, flowers. The Indians call these mirages Fata Morgana. You should take that as a pen name for your diary.'

'So you think all of my world is illusory, like Don Quixote's,' I said, 'yet why do you come and rest in it when the world outside becomes monstrously horrible? Are you resting on a mirage?'

Gonzalo has not led me out of my world into a better one. I thought my father would lead me into a vaster world of experience, but he could not do it because he was bound in guilt, and this guilt took the form of idealizing his actions, and camouflaging them. Henry was never a leader, he was always letting things happen. Somehow or other, the man who could take me out of my own world never crossed my path, or if he did he disguised himself in my presence.

When I helped Henry with his own proofreading I was amazed by his pages on June in *Capricorn*. No longer June and Henry but something born of Henry's imagination. Henry describes himself as a puppet sitting on June's knees. And while he writes of her power, at the same time he crucifies her. It is frightening, his ruthless vision exposing a woman as nature, as a mirror, as a soulless void.

*

When Larry made a vivid description of Anna Wickham, her enormous body, moustache, hair in her nose, heavy paw-like hands, her heavy voice, I said: 'She must have hair in her womb too, like a sea urchin.' This set Larry laughing and gave birth to the 'Paper Womb' printed in the *Booster*, December 1938, later known as 'The Labyrinth'.

Larry put it: 'My god, Anaïs, you're always opening new trap doors. Trap doors on the infinite.'

[FEBRUARY, 1939]

My father was giving his thousandth concert in Paris. I was sitting in the front row. While he was playing, in the middle of a composition, he suddenly let his arms fall to his sides, sat absolutely still, and then fell over, his head hitting the keyboard. For the public it was a stroke, but for me it was an overwhelming, crushing realization of his solitude, anguish, the death of a life he loved. I rushed to the reception room. They had laid him on a bench, and a doctor was attending him. They had opened his shirt at the neck. He was unconscious. The doctor said: 'It is not the heart.' I took him to his apartment in Neuilly in a car some admirer offered. He regained consciousness. Several friends were there. He lay on the bed. When his glasses are off he opens the vague eyes of the very nearsighted. He did not seem to recognize anyone. But he pressed my hand. I felt a heartrending pity, terrifying, but passive. I could not weep for my father, for all links with him were broken, but for a man, any man, who was losing a world, who had been the darling of women and of fate for so many years. White hair. Elegance. Loneliness. All the women around him, tonight too, four or five, fluttering, sighing, exclaiming, worshipping him, all of them around him but not near enough. I did not want to go too near to him, although someone cried out impatiently: 'Make room for his daughter.'

It is his daughter. They seemed to want to keep me out as if I were another rival for his affection. I could not come any nearer, one cannot come any nearer to my father than his adoring circle around him now. He barred the way with his masks and his self-love. His self-worship isolated him. I could not console him. This was one of his deaths. He died because he could not yet envisage another life. With the end of protection, luxury, of love affairs, of his marriage, his life ended. There was something broken. His ghost was going to Cuba, for him that was a kind of exile, a country without culture, without music, without all the richness of Paris. He died at his thousandth concert in Paris, of the burden of regrets, of memory, of a life so rich and glamorous and brilliant which was coming to an end. I did not hurt him. I never said to him, as Maruca said: 'My love is dead.' I fulfilled my belief in illusion which gives life. I gave understanding and compassion. But I did not give him my life as I once did as a child, when his departure killed some part of my being. I did not let him cling to me. Very gently and quietly I made him understand he could not expect a total love from me, I let him see the difference between our two lives. I offered to share with him the simplicity of my life on the houseboat. He knew I had many ties, bonds, and loved ones to protect. But what he demands always is one's total life, slavery. That night, in his room, pity crushed me but no guilt. He was fulfilling his destiny. The punishment was great. For him Cuba meant exile from all he had loved. But he had sought only his own pleasure, and made no sacrifices for anyone. It was a kind of death, on that stage, alone with his piano, and today he was weeping over himself, and I was weeping over him.

The houseboat so far away from Paris, so isolated, became a dangerous place. I no longer had the protection of the hoboes sleeping under the bridge. I had to give it up. I took an apartment on the Rue Cassini, next door to the building where Balzac wrote *Séraphita*. I have one big room and an alcove for the bed. The bathroom and kitchen are combined, the bathroom being an afterthought. So I can watch my cooking while I am taking a bath. It has one large long window, placed at such a height that I can see the heads of passers-by. Just the heads passing by. I am again near to all my friends, within walking distance of cafés, bookshops, etc.

Henry is going through a mystic stage, he looks fragile, luminous almost. He sees few people, goes rarely to cafés, prefers meditation, reading, returns to his studio filled with ideas, plans, is writing about *Séraphita*, about his past and June as a great crucifixion. He gives me full due for what I am, and says, talking about the great liberation he feels, 'Of course, for this you had to be crucified,' and by this makes my sacrifices a joy. He wrote a whole small book by hand for my birthday, he fixes up his notes, he paints beautiful water colours, listens to music, is content with his explorations. We can talk laughingly about his 'errors'. I had opposed the *Booster*, the letter about Alf, the Gold pamphlet, the letters from the messenger boys, all because they took so much of his energy, they were mere jokes, and they cost all the money which could have been applied to a book. He had to give them away, and very few people liked them. I felt they were mere practical jokes. All of these are now piled up in his closet, wasted. He admitted I was right, laughing too, yes, he knew, he confessed they were childish, and then he added: 'But I would do it all over again.'

Now he wants to print *Séraphita*, involve Durrell in a loss of money and give the world something it cannot assimilate, just at this moment *Séraphita* is a tribute to the past. However, he has dropped the *Booster*, which was bleeding all of us.

When proofreading *Winter of Artifice* he picked out the phrase: 'The poet is the one who calls death an *aurora borealis*,' which was a phrase I dreamed. Or: 'Sparked the great birds of divinity, the eternal moments.'

Gonzalo is drinking all night. I waited in the café and he did not come. I went for a walk, passed by the Coupole, and saw him at the bar where the women never go, standing among friends, in a state of beatitude, completely drunk.

My father came to see me. I lit all the small lamps and perfumed the place. He thought this might be our last talk together because he had planned to leave on a certain ship to Cuba.

The date of departure was not fixed. There was much confusion. He had reduced his belongings to thirteen cases of books and music. We talked gently about other things. I had no forebodings. But when he left me, he fainted in the courtyard, and a stranger helped him home. I never knew this till he wrote me later. 'I knew it was the last time I would see you.'

Gonzalo was in a desperate state because he had been subjected to another seance of autocriticism practised by the Marxists. They had told him all of his virtues and faults, scolded him for drinking, disorder and weakness, but with kindness. They had praised his capacities too, all the gifts he wasted by chaos. They had told him he had a great gift for fraternizing with workmen, for talking to them, for convincing them.

Helba was in the hospital again. I cooked special things and took them to her. Once I cooked a chicken. When Gonzalo and I went to visit her she took delight in pulling it out from under her pillow and saying: 'See, I am so ill I could not eat.' It had been there a week. I said: 'Why didn't you give it to someone who could eat it, you are surrounded by hungry people.' The need of a stage prop to dramatize her lack of appetite was stronger than the need to help or give.

Gonzalo aspires to order and asks me to impose on him. I tried to explain it could not be imposed by others. It had to come from him.

In three years Gonzalo has changed. But he has no will. He is easily discouraged, easily influenced, easily thrown off his course, easily depressed and distracted, unbalanced too. He says himself: 'I'm crazy. I'm a Russian. Only Dostoevsky would have understood me.' Or: 'I would prefer to be given a machine gun. That's what I'm good for, just to shoot off a machine gun.' He hates to read or write. He prefers to talk. The Jesuits tried to discipline him in school and they failed. All I can do is keep him from destroying himself. He serves no one and no cause well. Spain, Marxism, his wife, his friends only get spasmodic devotion. He sticks to nothing, finishes nothing.

I reached a point of such physical weakness I had to be

given a transfusion. I felt I was carrying the burden of Gonzalo's terrible moods, Helba's operation.

When he drinks Gonzalo never talks about the present, about Montparnasse, his present life. He reverts always to the beautiful early years.

He has talked all night with Antonin Artaud, with Breton, with Tristan Tzara, with Paul Lafargue, Picasso, Miró, but of this he tells me nothing.

While he talks a friend is waiting for Gonzalo's help at the Peruvian Embassy, Helba is waiting for him at the hospital, and on other days I am waiting with food for Helba spoiling on the fire, and meanwhile Gonzalo may be looking at books on the bookstalls or throwing dice over a counter to gamble for an apéritif, and when I finally do see him he says: 'I'm tired out.' The day has fallen apart, he is discouraged, he is defeated by his own abortions. He wants to fight in Spain. He wants to go to Russia. He wants to see China. He wants to change the world. But it is night, he's tired, he will take another drink, eat a banana, and begin talking about his childhood. About the condors, the bread trees, the tree of the shadow that kills. 'My father once gave me a little Negro boy for a servant, who had been born the same day as I had. A little Negro from the jungle. We were inseparable. But he died from the bitter cold up on Lake Titicaca.'

Gonzalo wants to write about Artaud, who is in the insane asylum, he wants to tell all he knows about Artaud, born of working with him on his play. But this intimate knowledge will die with him because of his laziness. He never wrote about his beloved friend Vallejo, the Peruvian poet. He never wrote what he wanted to write about *House of Incest*, and how it breathed, he said, like the mouth in Cocteau's film, the mouth in the palm of the hand. His day is a cemetary of negations. All this weighs heavily on me because I love creation so much. Now and then he can do a printing job, always too late, and then he has to work all night. All would be well if he accepted this. But it gives him despair. As soon as he wakes up he starts weaving a web which will choke him, as if he were a human spider who had woven a web to catch itself rather than its food. His terrific vitality at this construction exceeds my power to cut him free. We start our days inversely: he to break a glass, spill the wine, burn the table, drink the alcohol which will dissolve him, talk away his plans, drop the line he has set for the press, forget to telephone. And I to dominate every detail, to leap over obstacles, to reach my aim, to write my several pages a day, to fulfil all my obligations. All that I create, a page of writing, or an elated mood, or a solution to a problem, if I bring them to him he carefully, skilfully tears apart. If by extreme adroitness, swiftness, I manage to prepare the food for Helba, he is sure to destroy its effectiveness by arriving so late that visitors' hours are over, Helba complains bitterly, and the whole day is wasted. At other times his tangles cause me such pity that I wonder why I have engaged in this struggle against destruction. I don't know whether this stumbling, helpless, blind giant child is a curse put upon me for my desire for freedom and supreme lightness, liberation, desire to master life. Avalanches fell upon my attempts to turn destruction into creation. But why do I engage in this game? I feel unequal to the struggle, yet I feel if I abandon it, Helba and Gonzalo will drown.

At times I think I am Henry describing June and I am writing my own *Capricorn*. But Henry was blind while it happened while I am not blind.

My father was preparing to sail for Cuba. I thought I had reached detachment and that I would not feel the separation. Now I know I will never see him again. It hurt me deeply, even when I say I no longer love him. Perhaps I was weeping over his own pain too. He did not want to see me. Could not bear the pain. That afternoon he had come had hurt him so deeply.

A few days before he left, when I was trying not to think of him at all, when I was trying to remember that I had not pitied him at all during the disruption of his marriage, not helped or protected him, nor tried to keep him from going to Cuba, that I had been silent, evasive, and neutral, keeping control of myself not to utter the last murderous words: *My love for you is dead*, suddenly I pictured him vividly, first when he fainted at the piano during his concert, then when he was lying down on the bench in the reception room, his collar open, and at the remembrance of his slender, elegant effigy, unconscious, such a burning pity filled me that I almost cried out: *My god, I love him*. Love what? Someone whose every word and act displease you, is an antithesis of your beliefs, whose every aspiration you cannot share, whose mask is false, whose habits, manias, idiosyncrasies are distasteful, superficial, vain – and then this figure lies on a couch, this body empty of its consciousness, silent, lies with eyes closed, the supreme comedian's act, this simulation of death, which was to reveal to me the treachery of love that believes itself dead but which is only suppressed, denied, and which resuscitates as soon as the loved one dies, this love with a thousand lives, which you believe buried, and is buried beneath a hundred layers of scar tissue, old wounds nothing but scars, and let the cause of it die, as he seemed to have died, a preface to his final death, and this love is there, wild and strong. It was hibernating. My father lay like an effigy, like those statues they place over the tombs of famous people in Spain, and my love which had died a thousand times, and been buried, was reawakened, intact. Why? The slender figure does not speak, laugh, carry on its performance, it lies still, exposing the fineness of its contours, the essence which every act and reality denied, this escapes still from the tomb of a dead love, and is alive in me. Does love ever die, I ask, and will die asking. For years I buried it, I buried it in a novel which will appear while he is sailing away, I buried it when I let him decide to go to Cuba, I buried it by not acting as the refuge, the mother number III. Over and over again I buried it. I buried it under other loves. I looked at him without illusion. Yet when he left, the night before he sailed, I wept over him, and awakened in the morning thinking of him. I never know death or indifference. Time kills nothing in me, even though I tried to deliver myself of all possessions through art.

Les Parents Terribles of Cocteau contains the truth which is beyond good and evil, this monstrous mixture of love and hatred, this incredible paradox of nobility and baseness. Marvellous theme, the nakedness. The aunt, the truthful one, never deceived by her own acts of sacrifice and revenge. Never any falseness. I live by this kind of lucidity now. I

342

cannot bear self-deception. But Helba, Gonzalo, Henry, cannot bear the truth.

Helba and Gonzalo live in a false Catholic world of false nobilities, false sacrifices, false interpretations. If I confront them with a true mirror of their acts, they cannot bear it. They prefer their illusions about themselves and me. I live in a clarity which places me very near to Cocteau's play, which revolted everyone else. A transparent world.

I have unmasked myself, but now I suffer from others' self-idealization.

'Quels monstres!' said the people as they walked out of Cocteau's film. But it is not the people who are monsters. It is that the face of truth is monstrous because we are not accustomed to it. We are always covering it up, veiling it. We are not used to its true features.

What fascinates me are the nuances of each day, the subtle changes of character and its relativity. I want to be the writer who best described relativity, dualities, ambivalences, ambiguities.

I have learned to play Gonzalo's and Helba's Catholic games. It consists in mixing, muddying, aborting, exaggerating out of guilt and love of suffering. They thrive on pain and catastrophe. Every now and then when their absence of vision and power torment me, I revenge myself by descending into their own realm and playing their game as they do. In other words, I make a mess of my own life and pretend things are happening which my intelligence would not allow.

I tell Gonzalo I may have to go to America, and then they contemplate their helplessness. They believe me. They both show anxiety. Then I go to visit Helba again. In her presence I feel pity and kindness again. She looks childish and innocent. But I know her will and her self-centredness. I know that there is a certain delight in her, for the day I leave she will be alone with Gonzalo again. Helpless again. By this time my game has given me enough pleasure and I see Gonzalo and Helba as children again. Perhaps I am not as wise as all that. Perhaps within me there is a sick Helba in need of protection, a wild Gonzalo in need of emotion. And perhaps that is why I love them and Helba is right to believe I will not desert them.

I was watching Helba's face. Around the soft lines of her mouth there was goodness. She has no jealousies. She is purified by illness. She is passionless. She is more generous. Yet when she asked me: 'Are you really going to America?' she lowered her head, raised her eyes as if she were looking over the rim of eyeglasses, and in this look I saw a canny, tricky Helba, the one who knows so well how to exploit her disease, dramatize her sufferings. The shrewd suspicious Helba looking for a fissure in my story. 'Fill my hot-water bag,' she asked, and gave strict orders as to how she wanted it done.

Through love it is I who fall into traps, yet when I was a girl I did not like to play the fairy princess but the dark, evil, crafty queen. Through love I am enslaved, as I am enslaved by the helplessness of Helba and Gonzalo, but another side of me seeks ruses by which I could escape. In this case my escape to America was a mere fantasy.

[SPRING, 1939]

Refugees from Spain began to slip into Paris. The laws were rigid: if one sheltered or fed them there would be a punishment of jail and a fine. These were the fighters, the wounded, the sick. Everybody was afraid to help them. William Hayter hid them in his studio. Gonzalo and I scoured Paris for empty rooms or apartments. Carteret was still in the south of France, so I got his key from a friend and Gonzalo took to his place two Spanish gypsies who had been noted for their courage. Through the war they had been utterly fearless. But now they found themselves in a place which aroused all of their gypsy superstitious fears: skeletons under the bed, knives on the wall, books on magic, incense burners, Tarot cards. They fled from there in terror. And we had to keep on finding places. I was busy cooking gallons of soup, which had to be brought in small containers to Hayter's studio. Gonzalo asked me to hide the printing press in my cellar. I spent hours at the Cuban Consulate, trying to find out who was in sympathy with the refugees and who would give them passports to Cuba. I established contact between Gonzalo and the Consulate. Everyone was sheltering at least one refugee. Some were terribly ill with dysentery, old wounds. A friend of mine drove some to the country. It was a tragic month.

*

The more Gonzalo and I spend time and energy taking care of refugees, the more exaggerated Helba's scenes become. Every now and then Gonzalo begins to perceive that she is exaggerating, but then only for a moment, and he returns to his blindness. Last night she had an 'attack'. Gonzalo said it was a kind of convulsion. I had to nurse her while he went to get the doctor. Finally it was discovered that she had drunk a glass of petrol because the Indians think it is good for stomachache. She was taken to the hospital. She survived. She will survive all of us. But Gonzalo is always convinced she is about to die. As he believes Helba is a victim of outer forces, he will never be able to put his finger on the source of the evil, Helba's own evil soul who wishes to rule others by theatricals. I cannot show Gonzalo how much of her troubles are brought on by herself. Gonzalo is a romantic, and it is all the more touching when I know he was born on the side of the strong, the powerful. Gonzalo, the big one, was born in power. He remembers exerting his authority. The director of the Jesuit school was staying at their home. Gonzalo was about seventeen. An Indian was sent to fetch the mail. He did not return. He got drunk. He came back to the hacienda twelve hours late. Gonzalo was incensed. He had the Indian stripped and flogged. The director heard the Indian's cries and came out of his room. When he saw what was happening he called Gonzalo: 'You've been six years with us and yet you can act so savagely. One must rule but with humanity. You must act like a Christian.' Gonzalo evolved from a feudal system to the ideas of Marxism. And Helba, as the stricken Job, deaf and crazy, born in poverty and ignorance, stands for the figure of a Christian martyr.

Henry is taking his Chinese reincarnation seriously. He asks me to get him some ginger, which he eats while making faces. But it's Chinese and he must get to like it. He writes small books by hand, like my diaries, for Emil, Durrell, Edgar and me. Each one has a theme, and he illustrates them with water colours. They are delightful, personal, enchanting. A delicate Chinese Henry working these jewels of friendship with playful spirit. Durrell's is a riotous fantasy on words and rare expressions. Mine is about writing. His article on *Séraphita* is appearing in *The Modern Mystic*. He finds similarities between Balzac and himself. Identifies with Balzac.

The next day his peace collapses. He is in despair at the slowness of response from the world, he rages under the passivity of Kahane, rejections from French publishers, the taboo on his books in America. He is not getting his due materially.

To escape from a monstrous reality I began to work on the houseboat story.

Pain and fatigue disappeared.

Henry finished his essay on Balzac. Edgar said to him: 'You used to be all for the earth, and now you're all for heaven.'

Henry took me to see the house of Balzac on the Rue Raynouard, Passy. A sort of country house in the middle of the city. The front of it gives on a busy street, but the back opens on a hill which inclines towards the Seine. And it is there we saw the trap door, the stairs leading to the hillside through which it is said his mistresses escaped from angry husbands and he himself escaped from creditors. It was secret, mysterious, peaceful. It is a museum, guarded by a pale and ghostly woman who speaks in a whisper. There is Balzac's portrait, a big one, showing the butcher's neck and the extra-ordinary visionary eyes. The manuscripts and books are kept in locked bookcases with glass doors. We were allowed to look at some of the first editions. One was a book of engravings of *Les Femmes de Balzac*. We looked at the portrait of Séraphita and Henry swore it resembled me. Henry wanted to give the museum a copy of his essay on Balzac. When we were looking at photographs and documents in a glass case, Henry said: 'Do you suppose one day people will be bending over our manuscripts and photographs too?'

He gave me a book on Zen Buddhism.

Henry is going through a kind of agony of his ego. He is trying to kill the selfish man in himself, the ego. He wavers between wisdom, understanding, and sudden attacks of aggressivity and dictatorship. He loves to recall all his insolences, his tauntings, and could murder those who oppose him. The war calls out his fear, self-preservation. The spiritual man is struggling against the instinctive man. I can see the conflict, for he expresses both simultaneously. He is angry one moment, and the next he talks like Buddha.

We went to see the masks and dance costumes of Java and Sumatra and he looked at all of them with delicate attentiveness.

He observed that I do not break with people by explosions, but by silent evasions. I glide off.

Talking about war he said: 'I feel like an animal that doesn't want to be caught in a trap.'

[SUMMER, 1939]

I wrote the story of Albertine, the maid on the houseboat. It is an exact portrait.*

In August we all went travelling. Henry went to Greece to stay with the Durrells, I went to Saint-Tropez with Helba and Gonzalo.

Saint-Tropez was a paradise, with its many deserted beaches fringed with pine-tree forests. A Tahitian life, all day in bathing suits, cooking under the trees, just behind the beach. The limpid waters by day, the cafés so lively at night, all along the port, music, dancing. Having breakfast in the café in the morning I could see all the yachts being washed and polished for the day. A beautiful, lively place. Heat, languor, great thirst, long bicycle rides. The bloom and softness, the vivid colours of beach clothes. The girls riding bare-breasted on the back of open cars. There was an intensity about the pleasure, as if we all knew it would be the last of the beautiful summers.

Dancing in the port cafés at night, or sometimes joining the village dances on a street corner, with the village band, dancing with the postman and the carpenter and the bicycle-repairman. Gonzalo moving in and out of the bamboo bushes like a real Indian, hair wild, sure-footed, eyes shining like an animal's, Gonzalo climbing trees, cooking over a wood fire, remembering his childhood in nature. He seemed to find his youth

*See 'The Mouse' in *Under a Glass Bell*. – Ed.

again, his innocence, his wholeness. He and Helba lived in a small cottage in the hills, and I nearer to the port in a rented room.

Winter of Artifice arrived, all in blue. It was a hot day. I was dressed in my Spanish cotton dress and wore a red flower in my hair. I sat in the café and friends gathered around to look at the book.

In one of the nightclubs they would put out all the lights and announce: 'This is the *quart d'heure* of passion. You may kiss but you must not be caught at it.' The lights would suddenly go on again, and many were caught. Fifteen minutes of passion!

Jean Carteret arrived and slept in a tent on the beach. We would meet for breakfast at the port, at Sénèquier, where the *croissants* melted in the mouth. Jean talked about his adventures in Lapland and showed me photographs. Gonzalo and Helba never got up before one o'clock.

At the beach Gonzalo read me a description of the Exhibition of Agriculture in Moscow. Jean Carteret talked about astrology, while Gonzalo snorted fire in protest against such absurd mystical beliefs.

Hundreds of bicycles speeding up and down the hills. The lifeguard invited us to have a *bouillabaisse* at the beach, cooked by himself in a giant iron cauldron, if we would catch the fish he needed. We did, and we sat around the fire that evening inhaling fumes of saffron and garlic, singing while the *bouillabaisse* boiled.

Once while we swam, the water vibrated with a frightening sound. The cannons were rehearsing. Airplanes began to practice, flying above us.

Then Gonzalo discovered a place where the patron made absinthe, and he started to drink it secretly and it made him wild and insane. The gaiety of Saint-Tropez and the infernal life of Helba and Gonzalo were in violent contrast. Gonzalo no longer came in time to enjoy the sun and the beach. Helba became ill and Gonzalo stayed indoors with her. At the same time he was angry when I left for the beach without them. I did not know he was drinking and could not understand his madness. He became so impossible that I threatened to leave. I packed my belongings and went to the bus station. I missed the bus. I came back and found Gonzalo sitting in front of my locked door looking so dejected and crushed that we ended by laughing, and he confessed to his absinthe binges, absinthe the drink which made the French poets insane.

A few more days of joy, of eating sweet and juicy fruit at the beach, of dancing, of sitting around campfires at night, of sitting at the port cafés and watching the Dufy spectacles of sailboats and joyous people passing.

And then

WAR.

Mobilization. The sorrow of women.

All the yachts vanished overnight, and all the visitors. I returned in a train filled with soldiers.

[SEPTEMBER, 1939]

Gonzalo and Helba safe in Saint-Tropez. Henry safe in Athens. I am sending money orders right and left, going from one post office to another (one is not allowed to send big sums) with my handbag hanging from a strap across my shoulder. Monday war was not certain, but anguish was in the air like a poisonous fog. The calm too, the calm before catastrophe. Yesterday in the street I saw the headlines: WARSAW BOMBED. Now it means war. We can no longer hope for a revolution in Germany which would put an end to the war.

One cannot read the signs on restaurants and movies or cafés. Rain. People colliding in the darkness. The punishment. Selfishness grown too big. The personal and historical problems insoluble because of selfishness. The world problems insoluble because of selfishness. Duality and schizophrenia everywhere. The death instinct stronger than the life instinct. Panic. A million people turned criminal because of their weakness, capable only of hatred. A million people knowing only hatred, envy and fear. War was certain. A war of horror and blackness. The drama for years enclosed within human beings, now enacted wholesale, open nightmares, secret obsessions with power, cruelty, corruption. So much corruption can only end in bloodshed. I see all this as I walk the streets, and I do not feel a part of the crime, but I will have to share in the punishment. At six o'clock I had a feeling there would be no war. I wrote to Henry. Nothing is known. We are not told anything. Poland invaded and the world waiting for England and France to declare war, a real war. Waiting and piling sandbags against the windows. Art treasures crated and hidden in cellars.

Perhaps we will never have a war, nothing but this poisonous fog of fear and suspense, a continuous nightmare.

First air-raid signal. Danger. Darkness. A war is going on which people doubt will become a real war. It may be a mock war to satisfy those who clamoured for it. We are being deceived, and what is happening is a mystery. Scant news.

War declared.

Nothing left but to share humanly in the error, and the suffering of the world.

Henry's war-letters.

My only concern is whether I will be cut off. Even now if I wanted to cable [James] Laughlin I doubt if I could rely on him. There are others there who might really do something for me, I am sure of it. Such as William Carlos Williams, Dorothy Norman, Paul Rosenfeld, Huntington Cairns, Mencken, Dos Passos, certainly Faulkner, Ben Hecht, Ben Abramson, Gotham Book Mart, etc. I can think of dozens, but how to reach them quickly and effectively I don't know. The best thing would be for me to croak, then they would all cash in handsomely. I am wondering if you took my things from the safe at the Obelisk Press office. To leave them in Paris seems really risky. The notes and manuscripts I left there are worth thousands of dollars, a fortune to someone if I should die tomorrow. Remember that I carry about with me a will and testament leaving everything to you . . . If you do go to America and if it is at all possible, I hope you take my manuscripts and my books with you.

Gonzalo's letter full of anxiety about my safety.

New money blockades worry me for my orphans. Gonzalo struggling to return to Paris, working at grape-picking. His letters are human. I spend my days juggling through laws and difficulties to send money to Henry, Gonzalo, Moricand.

The police know me. Soon I will have exhausted all my trickeries. I begin to pack boxes in the cellar. This volume will portray the end of our personal lives.

Moricand came to say good-bye. He has signed up with the Légion Étrangère. He had to lie about his age. 'What else can I do? I am starving.' We have a farewell dinner at the Brasserie Lipp, with Jean Carteret and other friends of his. He carries tied to his belt the aluminium cup and plate, knife and fork of the Légionnaire. He bequeaths me his fragile eighteenth-century cologne bottle, crystal with encrusted specks of gold. He repeats that I must live by a cosmic rhythm, not a personal rhythm. I weep because I can no longer save anyone. You cannot save people, you can only love them. You can't transform them, you can only console them.

Paris at night. I step out of the restaurant into darkness. It is a sensual experience. I recognize no one. I stumble. I hear the voice of a man I am sure I could have loved, but he vanishes. Mysterious blue and green night-lights here and there.

Moricand talked about his childhood as if he were parting from it. 'I used to enjoy smelling camphor and eating ginger at the same time.'

I am amazed that all of us begin each day anew automatically as before, knowing we might die tomorrow. I dress simply. I powder my face. I paint my eyelashes. Meanwhile the radio announces tragedy, horror, suffering. It is engulfing us. No more anaesthetic. I wear a magenta coat and black skirt, leather moccasin shoes, a leather Arabian bag slung over my shoulder. I read the newspapers. I listen to the radio.

When I cannot bear the horror any more I read *Fille de Mamouri* by Etsu Inagaki Sujimoto. I realized the great power of form, and my own struggle against it. This explains my love of Jeanne because she was a poet, my following her into her own world and bruising myself against her formal life, so contrary to my own essence and unwillingness to play games. This formality irritated me in Moricand. But it broke down when he read *Winter of Artifice*. His letter then became a cry of human sorrow at having feared 'life in the raw', missed human life because of his squeamishness, over-delicacy. But as he confessed his unnaturalness, his precautions against experience, I also became aware of the nobility in these dying forms. The armature of the aristocrat, something which sustains him through everything, becomes courage. So I wrote him a beautiful farewell letter, telling him all that I had admired in him, his sense of poetry and aesthetics, his pride, his wit and grace. Poetry in his case became a form of heroism. His sense of ritual, ceremoniousness. He was really an Oriental brutalized by Western life.

I detested formality but loved form. A nuance. I understood when Gonzalo told me how infinitely more civilized the Inca was than the European. He was delicate, noble in behaviour, he had irony, a sense of ritual and dignity even in his amusements, even at orgies. I could never part with my own form, even when drinking. Yet I felt that it alienated me from others and wished for vulgarity. Henry mistook this style for pride. For him such a bearing could only be artificial, not natural. He was completely mystified by the behaviour of Moricand. He would have found the same stylization in a Japanese peasant, a Spanish peasant, or an Indian.

I love naturalness, but I wanted it beautiful too. Some races are naturally poetic. The poetic sense of the Japanese seems to be based on a rigid form which has become a prison for their feelings. Etsu knew it well. To arrive at sincerity, for example, becomes difficult if you have a cult of hospitality. I received in Louveciennes people whose behaviour I despised and yet I would not show it while they were in my house. It was enough that I knew how I felt, that was my sincerity.

The death of houses, how they seem to collapse as soon as we leave them, as soon as we prepare ourselves to leave them. I remember the house in Richmond Hill did not show any decrepitude until our life in it came to an end, when we left for Europe. Then as if we had sucked the living glow out of it, suddenly it appeared decrepit and shabby. So with Louveciennes when I returned from America a different woman, when Louveciennes ceased to be the centre of my life and I spent more time in Paris. In one day it grew old, like a deserted lover, old and empty. It withered. I was amazed to see its defects, its mouldiness. Or was it my vision if it which altered? So with Villa Seurat when Henry left it during the first war-alert. It suddenly lost its glow. It began to break down.

The rain and the wind came through a broken windowpane. The hotwater heater was worn out. The paint on the walls suddenly appeared soiled. The need of repairs appeared hopeless. Because life had withdrawn from it. Anguish about war dispersed us. Tragedy seeped into the houses, from outside. It could not be shut out any longer. Villa Seurat and other places once so illumined with life began to die under my eyes. Houses turn to corpses overnight when we cease to live and love in them.

Paris no longer has any rich life of its own, it is strewn with memories already. One speaks in the past tense.

It was through Gonzalo that I began to perceive and touch the world of the future. Observing the crumbling of a beautiful individual world I created, I can now hope in a collective one.

Gonzalo returned from Saint-Tropez full of hope and confidence. The war would assure the triumph of Marxism. Events were proving him right.

Henry escaped to Greece, which is consistent with his philosophy. Gonzalo's Peruvian Consulate offers to pay for his trip back to Peru.

What sad days. Human sorrow everywhere. Unlike Henry, who can leave a sinking ship without a backward glance, I feel a strong link with France, a deep empathy. Henry turned his back on it, without regrets. I worry over France's tragic fate. Moricand is taking long training hikes with the Foreign Legion. I have to nurse my concierge through a breakdown because her son is drafted and she is a war-widow, so she is sure her son will die too.

Then Moricand suddenly reappears! In training he collapsed, and then they realized his true age and dismissed him! So more dinners of consolation at the Brasserie Lipp.

I seek the luminous points, the living moments. I study Marx so I may not feel this cataclysm, this convulsion, as death but a revolution, an evolution. I seek to understand if there is to be a better future.

Henry's way is not my way. He thinks he has reached an Eastern detachment. But he may have reached a crystallization of the ego. The ego's life as supreme law. Moricand was shocked by his letters. Detachment, objectivity, descriptions of delectable meals, new friends, new pleasures. 'My belly is full. My wallet is full. The world is right.'

In war you only lose your life once, in life you die so many times.

I am one of the few who can say today: 'I have loved each day as if the loved one were to die. As if I were to die tomorrow.' I have loved and lived to the full. All my friends, when we sit in cafés, or walk the dark streets, have regrets for what they have not done, not loved, not given. These last few days it is as if they wanted to catch up with all they had not dared to do. I hear cries of regrets for the days they did not live, enjoy, taste to the brim. I was never careless, inattentive, thoughtless, indifferent, absent, or asleep.

Some are rushing into love affairs. Good-byes become entanglements, parting from the life they knew becomes a wild last-moment marriage to it. Friendships become violent, and manifested. One exchanges gifts, promises, words of appreciation. One tells the other how much he meant, counted, adds up qualities, praise, because it may be the last.

Moricand's testamentary dinners. We eat in crowded cafés, seeking lights and noise. He introduced me to Werner Lenneman, who acted in *Metropolis*. He was the German Jewish star who by staying so long in water during the filming, lost his voice and ruined his career. He had been merely surviving in Paris. He told how trapped he felt, how he felt the same anxiety he had during the making of the film when the waters rushed around him and the city was to be flooded. He felt trapped, because he would end in a concentration camp. He was a distant relative of Thomas Mann's. With so many burdens I could not help him. But he assured me that all he needed was money for a ticket to Switzerland and there he would be safe. That seemed such a small thing to ask for, and so I promised to get the money. I sold my camera to Man Ray, and pawned my father's coat-of-arms ring, and another ring, and brought the money to the café the next evening.

Gonzalo is planning to go to Peru and claim his inheritance which is due to him, and work for Marxism, and as soon as he announced this to Helba she fell ill with a lung abscess. She returned from Saint-Tropez well, she was eating in restaurants, she went shopping. She was fixing up her rags for travelling with zest. She was to leave for New York with me and await Gonzalo who would join her after Peru. That same day she got ill. It was pleurisy. That night in their chaotic studio, tending the stove for Helba, reading by candlelight, eating food I had brought from my place, listening to Helba's laments, heating linament every twenty minutes. I had such a feeling of despair that I wept. Gonzalo was at a meeting.

I want to understand the new world. I do want to evolve and change with it. I am beginning to understand it. Why was I so slow? I am nimble and quick-witted, yet I cannot accept ideas intellectually, as ideas. I have to drink them, eat them, live them, they have to become flesh, to become a human drama. For me to understand Marxism with the head means nothing, I must really feel it, live it, believe it.

How strange that Russia, all chaos, mystery, mysticism, hysteria, exaltation, should be the first to accept dialectic materialism. I think of the madness of Dostoevsky, religious fanaticism, and the instinctive life of Russia.

I believe more in Gonzalo than Henry, because Henry has lost contact with human life. At the end of the *History of the Russian Revolution*:

In the mythology of the ancient Greeks there was a celebrated hero Antaeus, who, the legend goes, was the son of Poseidon, god of the seas, and Gaea, goddess of the earth. Antaeus was very much attached to the mother who had given birth to him, suckled and reared him. There was not a hero whom this Antaeus did not vanquish. He was regarded as an invincible hero. Wherein lay his strength? It lay in the fact that every time he was hard pressed in a fight with an adversary he would touch the earth, the mother who had given birth to him and suckled him, and that gave him new strength. Yet he had a vulnerable spot – the danger of being detached from the earth in some way or other. His enemies were aware of his weakness, and watched for him. One day an enemy appeared who took advantage of this vulnerable spot and vanquished Antaeus. This was Hercules. How did Hercules vanquish Antaeus? He lifted him from the earth, kept him suspended in the air, prevented him from touching the earth and throttled him. I think that the Bolsheviks remind me of the hero of the Greek mythology. They, like Antaeus, are strong because they maintain connection with their mother, the masses, who gave birth to them,

suckled them, and reared them. And as long as they maintain connection with their mother, with the people, they have a chance of
remaining invincible.

Poetry and mysticism led to separation from vital human
drama. Duality led me into impasses. Paradox between *House
of Incest* and *Winter of Artifice*, between my diary and creation
of fiction. When Gonzalo talks about interaction, interrela-
tion, I understand. I see flow and movement. Wherever I see
life and growth I follow. All I know is that I am in contact
with vital elements. I am not cut off, or lost. I am not sharing
with Moricand talk of age, death, the past, the end. Not hiding
or escaping. It does not frighten me to have to revise all my
values again.

Moricand joined the Légion Étrangère because he wanted to
die in style and elegance, because he loved me and could not
have me, because I was overburdened and could only help him
in small ways, because he died long ago, long before I knew
him, because for him it is the end of a world, of his world of
elegance, grace, noble attitudes, romanticism, the end of
subtlety and delicacy, because he wasted his love on an empty
dusty little whore, because he was always terrified of life and
never lived to the hilt, because he missed all its vital currents,
because in astrology he only found the reflection of his own
fatalism and self-destruction, because he could only see demons everywhere, because he really desired young boys and
never had them except by caressing them in his erotic drawings, because he had known only two great friendships, with
Blaise Cendrars and Max Jacob, and every other friendship
was a mere echo of these, because he, like the analysts, was
condemned to comment on dramas which he could never
enter and play a part in, because he was a sage, and a timorous
jeune fille in life, because he was tired of his own involved and
oblique language, his labyrinthian excuses and apologies, his
long evasions, his hopeless craving for luxury, his struggle to
keep until the end his white starched collar, because his knowledge of the secrets of the stars was his only possession, because this was the end of the Neptunian age.

Now he offered his services to the ambulance section. We
did not know when he would leave. Moved by a presentiment
I spent the day looking through his letters and horoscopes

and wrote the story of Moricand because I was losing him.*

When I listen to Gonzalo, read René Maublanc's *Synthèse*, I realize that my own Christian remedies were ineffectual, my individual charity powerless except in a small radius, and my individual sacrifices useful only to a few. I know that I brought nothing to the great suffering of the world except palliatives, the drug of poetry, the individual loves which change nothing in the great currents of cruelty.

Unwittingly, I turned a Bohemian and a bum into a man who is fulfilling his first ambition, his youthful desire to save the Indians of Peru from oppression and near-slavery.

Jean hurt his foot, and limped down five stairs to call me to bring food. I cooked a stew. There was a friend of his there, and we decided to say I had made the stew out of dried reindeer meat, the kind they leave for months on the roof of their shacks, to freeze and dry for use all year. As the friend lost his appetite at the idea, we finally confessed it was plain French stew!

The morning of the air raid foolish Anaïs rushes to Helba, thinking she would be hysterical, and forgot she was deaf and never heard it!

The second air raid brought out the anti-aircraft guns. A shell from them fell into my courtyard and through an automobile top parked there.

Jean comments on Moricand trying to join the Légion Étrangère (Moricand had told us about his clothes falling apart, his shoes disintegrating in the snow, they were given no uniforms, no shoes, there was snow on the ground, they walked for hours): 'He went on purpose to expiate not having lived, all his evasions, escapes, puerilities, *Mièvreries*. It was an act of courage.'

Last night I sat in Gonzalo's studio to keep him company while Helba slept upstairs in the balcony room. We sat around a square table, with a bulb hanging from a wire covered with blue paper (according to war regulations). Helba complained now and then in her sleep. Gonzalo poured coal into the

*See 'The Mohican', in *Under a Glass Bell*. – Ed.

360

stove. The rest of the studio lay in darkness, haunted by open trunks, Helba's theatrical costumes and rags. Gonzalo talked about the future world. In this blue light, with Helba complaining, the linament heating over the stove, the hot water for her tea boiling, Gonzalo's face so black, his suit so worn, I felt I was back in Dostoevsky's revolutionary days.

But this was not nihilism, it was a touching revelation of Gonzalo's faith. A re-created world. And I asked myself if the artist who creates a world of beauty to sustain and transcend and transmute suffering is wiser than those who believe a revolution will remove the causes of suffering. The question remains unanswered. Was art, like religion, a mere palliative, a drug, an opium? Some of the artists I knew were destroyed by the same poverty which destroys the people. Artaud is insane in Sainte-Anne.

Henry escaped. He writes from Grand Hotel, Athens:

I had a taste of the sun, the light, the pure air. I needed that. In fact, I can't get enough of it. I am like a man who has been starved for a long time. And I seem to be cured of city life. I like the country now, the isolation, the absence of excitement, even books. I practically do not read at all. I haven't read a newspaper since I left Paris. Passing the kiosks I see the headlines, quite enough for me. I don't care about the details. Add to this I find Greece a wonderful place. Just the bare landscape, and this absolutely miraculous light and colour in which everything is bathed. France now seems like a closed book to me.

Everything we do now seems like a wake. Dinner at Rosalie's, once so full of gaiety, now empty. Most of the foreign artists have been sent home by their embassies. Overnight, it seemed as if one would never see again perfumed women, tea rooms, Opéra crowds, the Paris of serenity and rare rose gardens, of tender gardeners, well-swept streets, gentleness of manner.

It changed aspect, as if all the handsome and young people had been drained away, leaving only cripples, beggars and old people, leaving only a grey city of men and women without magic, or was it that it left only those we were not in love with?

We were given gas masks. Lights in the buses like the pale night-lights in hospitals. You cannot count your change. I saw the outline of military gear against the moonlight. Farewells every night. Taxis travelling slowly as in a deep fog.

When you live closely to individual dramas you marvel that we do not have a continuous war, knowing what nightmares human beings conceal, what secret obsessions and hidden cruelties.

I felt I had not shared in the hatreds, angers, and love of destruction, but that I would share in the punishment. But I knew the origin of war, which was in each of us, and I knew that our concept of a hero was outdated, that the modern hero was the one who would master his own neurosis so that it would not become universal, who would struggle with his myths, who would know that he himself created them, who would enter the labyrinth and fight the monster. This monster who sleeps at the bottom of his own brain.

The wars we carried within us were projected outside. The world was waiting for France and England to declare war. A general war. I had seen all the private wars, between lovers, husband and wife, brothers, children and parents. I had seen the secret love of destruction now mobilized. And now all of us were waiting, and piling sandbags against our windows, and crating statues, and burying paintings in the cellars.

Destiny was taken out of our hands. But it was the same madness, the same personal fears that were let loose upon the world. While waiting for the ultimate war, which would engulf all of us, I tried to understand all that happened. While waiting for the magnified irrationality, I had alrady suffered from all the personal irrationalities around me.

You give your faith, your love, your body to someone, year after year, and within this human being lies a self who does not know you, does not understand and is driven by motives even he cannot decipher. In one instant, all that was created between you, every word said in trust, every caress, every link as clear to you as a piece of architecture, an architecture born of feeling, of mutual work, of memories, is swept away by some inner distortion, a twisted vision, a misinterpretation, a myth, a childhood being relived. And this was the madness we were about to enter on a grandoise scale. For war is madness.

*

Paris at night. I stepped out of a café, a restaurant, into darkness. I recognized no one. The person I was going to say good-bye to vanished into darkness. What a profound, total isolation. But then, as I lost my intimate contacts, I entered into contact with the world. A world of gentleness was gone. A world of collective suffering was beginning. I had the illusion that when one loves, just as when we create human children, we create a permanent image of love like an iron statue by a sculptor. I was horrified to discover that the image the other person carried within him bore no resemblance to one's own, or that it could be annihilated by another love, or by a misunderstanding, or a distortion, or a failure of memory. This gave me a foretaste of death. We were not enshrined in the other's heart, and the one we loved was often immured, alone, separate from us. The war destroyed our illusion of strong, unshatterable intimate world of personal loves.

All my actions were concerned with preserving our small world from death.

At the first air raid, I would not hide. I wanted to encounter war and see its burning face. It is at such moments that one becomes fully aware of life, its preciousness.

Before the war, I asserted through art the eternal against the temporal, I set up individual creativity against the decomposition of our historical world.

I had severed my connection with it, but now nothing was left but to recognize my connection with it and to participate humanely in the error. Henry simply refuses to share sorrows. But I knew I could not separate myself from the world's death, even though I was not one of those who brought it about. I had to make clear the relation of our individual dramas to the larger one, and our responsibility. I was never one with the world, yet I was to be destroyed with it. I always lived seeing beyond it. I was not in harmony with its explosions and collapse. I had, as an artist, another rhythm, another death, another renewal. That was it. I was not at one with the world, I was seeking to create one by other rules. And therefore, how could I die in tune with it? I could only die in my own time, by my own evolutions. I did not belong to any epoch, for I had made my home in man's most active cells, the cells of his dreams. Through love, compassion, desire, you get entangled and confused. But the artist is not there to be at one with the world, he is there to transform it. He cannot belong to it, for then he would not achieve his task, which is to change. The struggle against destruction which I lived out in my intimate relationships had to be transposed and become of use to the whole world.

Foreigners were asked to leave, not to become a burden to France. My husband was ordered back to the United States. It was time to leave for New York. Alone I might have chosen to stay and share the war with France. I was not glad to escape tragedy. There was little time to weep, to say good-bye, no time for regrets, just time enough to pack.

Because Helba and Gonzalo needed winter coats for New York I could not afford the price of excess baggage on the plane for the diaries. I had to leave half of them in the bank vault. I took with me only the recent ones in two briefcases. Few clothes. Left books, trunks, household goods, pictures, in storage in Louveciennes.

We all knew we were parting from a pattern of life we would never see again, from friends we might never see again.

I knew it was the end of our romantic life.

INDEX

365

On the following pages are other recent paperbacks
published by Quartet Books.
If you would like a complete catalogue of
Quartet's publications please
write to us at 27 Goodge Street, London W1P 1FD

THE JOURNALS OF ANAÏS NIN VOL I 1931–1934

'The unpublished diary of Anaïs Nin has long been a legend of the literary world' – *Edmund Wilson*.

'Will take its place beside the revelations of St Augustine, Petronius, Abelard, Rousseau and Proust' – *Henry Miller*.

'A writer of real force in contemporary literature' – *Lawrence Durrell*.

Autobiography 75p

Also available as Quartet Paperbacks are
   The Journals of Anaïs Nin
   Volume 3:   1939–1944   £1.00
   Volume 4:   1944–1947   £1.00

PROTEST

J. P. Donleavy, Allen Ginsberg, Norman Mailer, Colin Wilson, Jack Kerouac, Kingsley Amis, John Wain and others.

One of the most significant developments in post-war literature, on both sides of the Atlantic, was the meteoric rise of the realistic school of writing as practised by the authors in this book. Stripping away all pretension and hypocrisy, they wrote of truth, celebrating man as he is, and in the process brought to bear a powerful social criticism. They were the true spokesmen for their age. This is an important source book for all students of modern literature.

Edited by Gene Feldman and Max Gartenberg.

Fiction 60p

CAIN'S BOOK

Alexander Trocchi

The darkly brilliant bestselling novel about the twilight world of the junkie.

'An immensely enjoyable book, with all the ego-maniac vitality of the early Henry Miller' – John Pearson, *Sunday Times*.

'It is different from other books, it is true, it has art, it is brave' – Norman Mailer.

'It has a black, icy brilliance . . . a journey to the end of the night by a man who has explored the deepest pot-hole of the human spirit' – Kenneth Allsop, *Daily Mail*.

Fiction 50p

THE ENGLISH ASSASSIN

Michael Moorcock

The third novel in the Jerry Cornelius tetralogy: in which Cornelius rises from the deep to witness the destruction of the world – and to poop the biggest party ever thrown west of London's Ladbroke Grove.

'The best of the Cornelius novels this far' – *Oxford Mail*.

'A master story-teller unwinds a tale which Tennyson would have turned into immortal verse' – *New Statesman*.

'Zany, grotesque, fantastical, Gothick, outrageous' – *London Evening News*.

Fiction 45p

George Mackay Brown
with drawings by Sylvia Wishart

George Mackay Brown is one of Scotland's most gifted poets and short story writers, whose work is universally acclaimed. He lives in Stromness, where he has always lived. *An Orkney Tapestry* is his testimonial to his native land, a celebration of the roots of a community which mixes history, legend, drama and folklore into a rich and varied tapestry.

'George Mackay Brown is a portent. No one else writes like this or has this feeling for language ... His is an inate talent: as true as that of Yeats' – Jo Grimond, *Spectator*.

Literature/Travel 50p